Aristocracy and the Modern Imagination

Aristocracy

and the Modern Imagination

Charles A. Riley II

UNIVERSITY PRESS OF NEW ENGLAND

Hanover and London

University Press of New England, Hanover, NH 03755

Printed in the United States of America
5 4 3 2 1

LIBRARY OF CONGRESS CATALOGING-IN-PUBLICATION DATA

Riley, Charles A.
Aristocracy and the modern imagination / Charles A. Riley II.
p. cm.
ISBN 1-58465-151-2 (alk. paper)
1. Arts, European—19th century. 2. Arts, European—20th century.
3. Modernism (Art)—Europe. 4. Artists—Europe—Psychology.
5. Aristocracy (Social class)—Europe. I. Title.
NX542 .R55 2001
700'.9'034—dc21 2001005371

For LIU KE MING

There is a sense of fullness in the room and work goes on much better when someone dear is by the while.
—Bertrand Russell, *The Amberley Papers*

When we took our bicycles down the winding path along the ancient evergreens of the Confucius family mansion, you taught me how to say "descendant" in Chinese: *hou dai.* Your mother and I joked that you were the Empress Cixi's *houdai.* We enjoyed being held in the elegiac contemplation of the home of China's last and finest aristocratic family and traced the footsteps of my great-grandfather along those same byways of old Qufu. Your nobility is rooted in that defiant grip you maintain on integrity, intellect, and beauty. These essays are my tribute to a true aristocrat of the mind.

Contents

Preface / ix

Introduction
High and Low
1

CHAPTER 1
Genius over Genes
The Circle of George Sand, Eugène Delacroix, Franz Liszt, and Frédéric Chopin
32

CHAPTER 2
Painters of Privilege
Pierre Puvis de Chavannes, Edgar Degas, and Henri de Toulouse-Lautrec
65

CHAPTER 3
A Knight at the Opera
Hugo von Hofmannsthal and Richard Strauss
91

CHAPTER 4
Members of the Club
Algernon Charles Swinburne and Frederick, Lord Leighton
124

CHAPTER 5
Peer Review
Bertrand Russell and Ludwig Wittgenstein
154

CHAPTER 6
The Irish Ascendant
William Butler Yeats and Francis Bacon
187

CHAPTER 7
King of the Cats
Balthus
202

Epilogue
The Masked Ball
222

Notes / 227
Bibliography / 239
Index / 244

Preface

Art can take root and bloom in an astonishingly broad range of conditions. I have eagerly climbed the creaking stairs of many scruffy loft buildings to reach studios before the sun sets and the neighborhood becomes deserted. Students of literature and philosophy can recite the litany of classics written by starving artists in prison or freezing garrets. We marvel at how hardy the creative spirit can be. Yet there are other ways for artists to set out. Many enter their art careers as diligent craftsmen, content to earn a living at what fascinates them (Piet Mondrian is but one example). Then there are those who begin life not just with wealth and station but with the aesthetic or intellectual advantages these circumstances bring. What difference would an aristocratic upbringing make, I wondered, in the formation of the artist? An even more intriguing set of problems arises in a consideration of how an aristocrat's identity might affect his or her becoming a Modern artist. What do you do if you are both the earl of Bedford, scion of one of England's most prominent families, and also Bertrand Russell, among the most radical and controversial philosophers of the Modern age? We are so accustomed to the idea that all the traditional patterns of thought and behavior must be laid aside in order to be thoroughly Modern. Yet there are traditions, rites, and traits (self-assurance, a historical worldview, an innate sense of quality) that persist, to the benefit of Modern art and thought.

Let me make it clear from the outset that I am not an aristocrat but have known both artists and aristocrats well enough to understand the affinity. It was my privilege to be raised intellectually on the assumption that the aura of the work of art was a genuine, celebrated, even necessary condition of its beauty. That thought has long been under ideological siege, particularly within the arena of Contemporary art, in which I have been involved in various capacities since graduate school. These brief essays begin with the premise that artists (chosen by personal preference rather than for the purpose of being historically comprehensive) themselves might be invested with an aura that, as Walter Benjamin posited with reference to the object, can be linked with distance and authenticity.

The pejorative for this is elitism. Manet once asserted that art is a circle—you are either in or out. So is the aristocracy. The royal houses of Europe upon which these titles are built are so closely intertwined that there are many inevitable connections—Hugo von Hofmannsthal and Ludwig Wittgenstein were blood relations. Hofmannsthal's greatest essay was in the epistolary form, addressed to the Viscount Francis Bacon, distant progenitor of the painter Francis Bacon. Lord Leighton knew the Countess de Castiglione socially. Some connections are more appropriate to the artistic context. Eugène Delacroix taught Pierre Puvis de Chavannes, and Balthus kept a studio on the Rue Furstenberg within sight of Delacroix's former studio, viewing Delacroix as a presiding spirit of the district. Issues of genealogy and succession were part of the day-to-day fabric of their lives.

Much of the passion in this book comes from firsthand experiences of people and places associated with the figures under consideration. One blissful summer at the Scottish country house of my mother's cousin, Margaret Harvie-Anderson, MP—a picture of whom, taken on the day of her induction into the House of Lords as Baroness Skrimshire of Quarter, bedecked in red velvet and ermine, is a family heirloom—was spent playing Chopin on the ivory-keyed piano, under a plaster frieze by Robert Adam, in a drawing room not far from the one where Chopin himself serenaded Jane Stirling, whose descendants were friendly neighbors of my cousin. The gracious rhythms of country house living may be a distant memory, but they have not faded. That summer I drove from Scotland to London in the bewitching presence of Margaret Stonborough, Dame Margaret's Parliamentary assistant and the grand-niece of Ludwig Wittgenstein (her grandmother's portrait by Gustav Klimt would have been known by Hofmannsthal). Twice in my life I have spent glorious weeks in the library of the Schloss Leopoldskron, during the Salzburg Seminar (thanks to the University Press of New England), in the gorgeous paneled room where Hofmannsthal joined Max Reinhardt to concoct their play *Jederman*. Another summer was spent in the hills above Lausanne, where Balthus maintained his courtly residence, and then I found myself profiling him in the aftermath of his stroke for the disability-related magazine I created. The college where I have taught tormented Russell with its narrow-mindedness, and I have found the miserable atmosphere of hypocrisy to persist.

Throughout the time I was writing this book, I was outside the cozy confines of academe and frequently dependent on the kindness of such dear friends as my mentor, Patrick Cullen, who spent many an afternoon guiding me as we tended our roses. It is also my pleasure to thank Lisa Hahn, Dr. Marc Wilk, Brian Bernstein, Esq., Susan E. Goodman, Byron Holinshead, and Peter and Barb Peck. I often wrote in between editorial passes at the magazine, and I must credit my wonderful colleagues for all their hard work and patience, including Fran Ahders, Fred A. Eno, Jane S. Van Ingen, Melani Guinn, Patrick Beaumont, and Stephanie Campagnano. I imposed too often for interlibrary loans upon Bev Christiansen and Jane Minerva of the Cutchogue Free Library and drew upon my old seminar notes from splendid teachers, including George Ridenour, David Bromwich, Jonathan Arac, and Daniel T. O'Hara.

Two editors knocked heads over this manuscript—one of them the author; the other, Phyllis Deutsch, without question the most brilliant, assiduous, and genuine editorial mind with whom I have ever had the good fortune to collaborate in my twenty-one years of book and magazine publishing. Over an unforgettable lunch we excitedly hit upon the idea of the book, and stage-by-stage from that shared origin she has made invaluable contributions to the content, approach, and style, never blinking when thorny conceptual problems cropped up and interjecting her own fascinating insights, as a professional historian, where they were needed most. I owe her an immense debt of gratitude. My favorite theme in this book is the notion that artists and aristocrats are walking anachronisms. So too are editors who care about the integrity and quality of a scholarly text as much as Phyllis Deutsch does. It is also my honor to have had the assistance of Mike Burton and Marilyn Houston.

Many others have helped make this book possible, through their comments and suggestions, shared insights, and tender concern. I gather what I can from the studios, galleries, auction houses, museums, conservatories, and rehearsal and concert halls. Among the artists whose conversations I treasure, I am particularly grateful to Mark Milloff, David Hockney, Brice Marden, Mark di Suvero, Peter Halley, Lawrence Carroll, Mark Innerst, Nancy Haynes, Walter Abish, Tan Dun, Robert Wilson, Bettina Witteveen, Charlie Clough, Stephen Mumford, Michele Basora, Byron Janis, Chuck Close, Willard Boepple, Lucas Reiner, Barbara Ernst Prey, Robert Burke, and Tracy Heneberger. Many prominent figures in the arts also have supported my work, including Asher Edelman, Joel and Sherrie Mallin, Warner H. Kramarsky, David Collins, Jennifer Vohrbach, Richard Milazzo, Carol Greene, Christopher Burge, Michael Findlay, Susan Dunne, Robert Pincus-Witten, Michael Hache, Akim Monet, Michael Kelley, Cecile Panzieri, Arthur Danto, Tricia Collins, Kazuhito Yoshi, Seward and Joyce Johnson, Bruce Krajewski, Peter Simpson, Ashton Hawkins, Omar S. Pound, and Francesca Rosenberg.

For their magnanimity and swift assistance in providing the color illustrations, many previously unpublished, allow me to thank Andrew Ferren and Diana Cross of the Metropolitan Museum of Art in New York, Jennifer Doyle of Christie's Images, Inc., Chris Ketcham of The Phillips

Collection, Amy Lipton of the Tony Shafrazi Gallery, Kim Mitchell and Mary Lou Strohlendorf of the Museum of Modern Art in New York, Laura Wyss of the Michigan Opera Theatre/Detroit Opera House, and Carrie Hamilton of the Jan Krugier Gallery, New York

Among those who have supported my work I would like to thank Debbie Ayres of the Aspen Music Festival, Ann and Leonard Kent, Tom and Maxine Hunter, the friends organizations of the Art Institute of Chicaco, the Los Angeles County Museum, the Speed Museum, the Cincinnati Art Museum, Mrs. Elizabeth Sanders, Mr. and Mrs. Lawrence Kyte, Cincinnati Museum, the Princeton Library in New York, the Orlando Museum, Opera North, the Hopkins Center and Hood Museum, Virginia Lemoyne and Juliet Waite of Art Focus/Art Au Point, Barbara and Jerry Schauffler of the Friends of the Oakland Museum, Debbie and Bill Richards, Heywood and Bea Alexander, the Randolph Colloquy, and Kay Sato of Hutton House.

My family stands by me no matter what byway I pursue, and to my mother, my artful sister Robin, my medical mind Diane, and my kind cousin, Stephen Horne, I am eternally grateful. The book is dedicated to my loving wife, Liu Ke Ming, who knows all of what went into it and what it means.

Cutchogue, New York
August 2001

Aristocracy and the Modern Imagination

Introduction

HIGH AND LOW

To hit a moving target in an age known for speed is a risky proposition, and the definition of Modern in the twenty-first century is nothing if not mobile. A canon that thirty years ago might have seemed in danger of closure is now, thanks to assiduous academic and curatorial repair, flung open for debate, tinkering, and overhauling. The textbook checklist of what constitutes the Modern—an extended historical moment characterized by individualism, contingency, democracy, self-consciousness regarding the process of creation and the autonomy of the work, skepticism about ideology and politics, iconoclasm and fragmentation that questioned and escaped from traditional forms, spiritual and psychological anxiety, resistance to the past, and in the case of abstraction, lack of interest in the present—was already loosening and becoming more heterogeneous under the pressure of Marxism, feminism, cultural studies, and postcolonial theory. Further weakening of the restrictive roster is understandable as curiosity broadens our aesthetic horizons.

The aim of this study is to expand current ways of looking at the Modern canon to include figures who have been overlooked or undervalued and to appraise the role of what may seem to some a completely antithetical element in a movement supposedly based on revolution and the overthrowing of the old order: the aristocracy. Reaching back as far as the magnificent circle of George Sand, Eugène Delacroix, Frédéric Chopin, and Franz Liszt and moving ahead to the strange case of Balthus, who died in 2001 at age 92, these essays push the chronology and criteria of standard accounts of Modern thought. In our Postmodern era, many critics and theorists would find the ("Romantic") circle of Sand too early for this category and Balthus too late, and the figural or formal qualities of their work would put off others. However, these essays do not attempt to promote the idea that the artists and writers they examine are Modernists. The aim is to reveal the Modern qualities of their lives and work. As we shall see, Modernism and Modern are not the same.

This study examines how artists born and raised in the European aristocracy brought their heritage to bear on the page, stage, or canvas. It includes men and women self-identified as upper-crust who made use of the patronage systems of the aristocracy and the educational background available to them to create art that was revolutionary in its time and continues to challenge us in the ways that Modern art must, by provocatively posing the question of its relation to the past and its vitality in the future. It argues that this group of artists, aristocrats not only in their heritage and breeding but in their personal manner and the roles they played, introduced important, if as yet unexamined, elements into Modern art based on their consciousness of rank.

The moment for this revaluation is evidently upon us. To start the new millennium, the Museum of Modern Art in New York took the bold move of temporarily rehanging its permanent collection to reflect an astonishingly different view of the canon from its previous, abstraction-oriented one. One of the easiest and most delightful ways to grasp the history of Modern visual arts has always been a stroll through MOMA (its comfortably maternal nickname), arranged until now to highlight abstraction's revolutionary interruption of the painterly and sculptural traditions. It made Cubism, Surrealism, Abstract Expressionism, and Minimalism the dominant quartet of schools in its account of the lineage of twentieth-century art. From the heroic breakthroughs in perception of Cézanne, Picasso, and Braque through the muscular painterly techniques of Pollock and de Kooning or the systematic and severe theories of Kandinsky, Mondrian, and Donald Judd, the story of Modern art was fashioned by critics and academics (never to be embraced unqualifiedly by the artists or wholeheartedly by the public). It also obeyed a strict chronology so that, by charter, when paintings by van Gogh, Gauguin, or Seurat became too old, they were traded or shipped off to other museums because they were no longer sufficiently Modern. Four years ago the museum's dynamic director, Kirk Varnedoe, penned a lively volume that cleverly took its title, *A Fine Disregard*, from the bending of the rules of soccer that led, through "a fine disregard for the rules," to the creative breakthrough that gave the world rugby. While Varnedoe's accent is upon the intentional infraction that rebelliously yielded a glorious and violent new sport, let's not overlook where the anecdote is set: on those playing fields of Eton where the aristocracy (including Shelley, Swinburne, Churchill, and others) learned those rules well enough to understand why a creative breach of them—what Picasso once called the "criminal interruption"—might be considered "fine."

Today's MOMA is a far different place. The curators of the revisionist rehanging have dramatically altered the story propounded by the museum's curators from the 1960s, under the stewardship of director Alfred Barr, through the Varnedoe era. From the moment the doors were reopened in late 1999, even a cursory survey indicated that the return of the figure and a renewed interest in such stalwart genres as portrait, still life, and landscape had made their way back into the vocabulary of the institution. The accompanying catalog, by the critic Robert Storr, verifies this impression. From its title, *Modern Art Despite Modernism*, to the emphasis its final pages lay upon such traditional values as the necessary virtues of draftsmanship, it offers a refreshing rethinking of the role of the tradition. Storr identifies a cadre of artists—Bonnard, Balthus, Bacon, Derain, Vlaminck, Leger, De Chirico—whose figurative and Classical paintings compose a rigorous alternative to the old Picasso, Braque, Kandinsky, Matisse, and Mondrian contingent that had dominated the walls. As Storr carefully explains, ideally setting up a premise of this study, "While it is fair to say that much art made in the twentieth century is intentionally anti-modernist, one cannot say that it is antimodern. No art made in modern times is antimodern, even when it strives, as a great deal does, to flee backward in time by either resuscitating archaic styles, depicting lost worlds, or evoking primordial states of mind in which the clocks have stopped."[1] How poignant that image of the stopped clocks will seem when we reach the moment onstage when Hugo von Hofmannsthal's noble heroine, the Marschallin in *Der Rosenkavalier*, confesses that at night she sometimes roams her palace attempting to freeze time by halting the action of the clocks.

While Storr and his team rehung MOMA, other New York institutions were dealing with an aesthetic, economic, and public relations crisis brought on by the controversy surrounding the British avant-garde *Sensation* exhibition at the Brooklyn Museum. Uptown at the Metropolitan Museum of Art, the response of the director was stern and unequivocal. He happens to be an aristocrat. Phillipe de Montebello is the scion of one of Europe's great families and certainly one of the most suave figures in the world of art. He is, in this regard, the successor to Lord Kenneth Clark at the National Gallery in London, another aristocrat who had decided views upon the importance of linking Modern art to a tradition. De Montebello's silken-toned Acoustiguide tours are irresistible to many Met visitors, and his high-minded management of the museum has made him one of the most powerful people in the business. So it was all the more dramatic when, in the midst of the turmoil surrounding the *Sensation* exhibition, with the mayor's office threatening to padlock the Brooklyn Museum in part over an image of the Virgin Mary by Chris Ofili that used elephant dung as well as paint, de Montebello broke ranks with other museum directors and the art world in general and sided with Mayor Rudolph Giuliani in his condemnation of the exhibition. The language of de Montebello's stern words on the subject was interesting in light of the traditional bent of this study. In a letter to the opinion page of the *New York Times*, he essentially called the art junk, unworthy of a museum setting. Subsequent interviews not only on the issue but on Contemporary art in general—one reporter bluntly asked if he hated it—gave de Montebello the opportunity to elaborate on his view of Modern art as taking its place within an evolutionary framework. The fact that an aristocrat took the firmest stand against the most cutting-edge, avant-garde test case since the Mapplethorpe exhibition was thrown out of Cincinnati by the courts is at least an amusing anecdote for consideration in this examination of the aristocracy and the avant-garde.

For one thing, this raises the issue of power and how it is exercised both in the art world and in the wider world. It is no secret that the nobility has steadily lost political power as the significance of "landed gentry" has declined and political or economic change has overtaken them. The thesis of this study is not the simplistic notion that there has been a quid pro quo movement of this influence into the arts. The purpose here is to trace the artistic path of certain powerful individuals who, by genius as much as by genes, wielded their influence in the domain of culture rather than politics.

Historically, the elimination in 1999 of the six hundred hereditary peers in the House of Lords was foretold in the early eighteenth century, when the landed gentry began to lose sway to what became known as the bagatelle nobility and now by the life peers (remember, distinction in the arts lands you a title). In France, by the early eighteenth century, only 10 percent of the nobility could claim aristocratic lineage going back at least 150 years, and the *noblesse d'épée* (hereditary) was superseded by the growth of the *noblesse de robe* (those appointed by the court), the *gens de robe* becoming an educated class of mandarins who, in the salons that had begun a century earlier, began to dominate the artistic taste of the time as they did the political and economic scene. The hotels of the Marais, where *bienséance* held sway, placed a premium upon conversation, the art of improvisation, and even ambivalence—"an interface between arcane gossip and public deliberation," in the words of historian Bernhard Giesen.[2] The transition of the *lumières* from royalists to *parlements*, the paradigmatic *querelles entre les anciens et les modernes*, heralded the end of an era for the aristocracy of the land. This study accepts a broader range of claims to aristocratic rank than the *pur sang* requirements of *Burke's Peerage* and other handbooks of nobility, mainly in the interest of showing what the effect of a noble upbringing has had upon a particularly fascinating group of artists and thinkers. From close relations of the king (Sand and Lautrec) to titles of far later vintage (Hofmannsthal, Leighton, and Wittgenstein) and even earnest impostors (Balthus), this study runs the gamut of degrees of aristocracy.

Within the dazzling quartet of Sand, Delacroix, Liszt, and Chopin—only the first of whom was landed gentry and an aristocrat in the purest sense—each artist cut a dashing figure in salon-style gatherings. Balthus brought a vivacious breath of fresh air to the French Academy in Rome during his tenure as director. Francis Bacon stood most of the London art world to champagne and was a player in the casinos of Monte Carlo. Swinburne's conversation bewitched Henry Adams, who attempted to capture it in a riveting scene from *The Education* that includes a cameo appearance by Bertrand Russell's father, Lord John Russell. Hofmannsthal and theater impresario Max Reinhardt held court at Reinhardt's elaborate palace outside Salzburg, the Schloss Leopoldskron. Although Degas was a curmudgeon, he was the focal point of salons in Paris, where Mary Cassatt and others revered him. Life was a movable feast for Toulouse-Lautrec, whether in the bordellos of Paris or its drawing rooms, until his mother had him committed to a lunatic asylum to halt the ravages of alcoholism.

Even as these artistic representatives of the great houses of Europe were scaling the peaks of their disciplines, the political and social power of the royal houses was fading. That historical pattern adds an elegiac element to much of the art they produced and at the same time offered an opportunity for change and liberation. The novelist Hermann Broch, whose study of Hofmannsthal is the most incisive to date, offers this touching description of the "abstract" state of the emperor of Austria in the twilight of the Habsburg era: "Immense was the shell of solitude in which he lived his uncannily bureaucratic, abstractly punctual official life, no matter whether in the Vienna castle or in the simple Biedermeier villa at Ischl where annual hunting vacations took him, always in abstract exactness, always in solitude, always in dignity. Wilhelm I was called the first soldier of his empire, Edward VII was the first gentleman of Europe, Franz Joseph I was the abstract monarch par excellence."[3]

We are so accustomed to the Horatio Alger stories of Picasso, Soutine, Jackson Pollock in his blue jeans and T-shirt, like the great blues musicians who emerged from dire poverty to charm royalty, that it seems odd to think of an artist whose life was spent surrounded by exquisite examples of the paintings or music that would shape his or her future. Yet this background of privilege can place the tradition at the fingertips of a creator in ways that make it possible for an intimate and deep knowledge of the past to grow. It also means that, once grasped, the tradition can be transcended, moved past and left behind. Perhaps the most stunning example in this study is Swinburne, whose mastery of prosody from Greek lyrics and tragedies, as well as Restoration drama and the Romantics, was firmer than that of the Oxford dons who were his teachers. That should come as no surprise to those who know that, either at home in the elegant country house that is the family seat of the earls of Ashburnham or at Eton, he was known for spending his childhood days in wonderful libraries with a massive folio opened in front of him, absorbing the classics from the time he could read. As an undergraduate he sat at the elbow of Benjamin Jowett and corrected the translations from Greek classics, with the rather rude occasional pointer, "Another howler there, Master." This offered him a secure foundation for innovations in prosody that led in the direction of Modern poetics. He knew as well as any critic where he was original and where he was derivative.

The childhood of Hofmannsthal was marked by weekly evenings at the opera and theater, where the future librettist was in turn fascinated by the rich pageant onstage and the dark, empty imperial box, sign of an aristocratic era in decline. Where the operas of Strauss and Hofmannsthal build upon Classical models—either *Ariadne auf Naxos* and Molière or *Rosenkavalier* and Mozart suffice as examples—the deep familiarity with the originals affords a sure sense of the line of demarcation between traditional and Modern. Russell as a young boy was given the gold pocket watch of his grandfather, twice prime minister of England, to remind him of his family's expectations, and the young Wittgenstein listened to Brahms playing one of the many pianos in his family's Viennese mansion and was expected to join in the brilliant dinner-table conversation that followed the recitals.

One result of this "grooming," if you will, is the tendency among these artists to become virtuosi. Perhaps it was because they were so young and fortunate when they were first exposed to the arts or because they grew up in a culture of display and even excess that we have accounts of the dazzling performances of Swinburne when reciting, of Liszt and Chopin in the concert hall, or the fluid ease with which their friend George Sand would write her way through a complex novel, juggling the lives of a dozen characters and interjecting long meditative passages on society or politics. This *sprezzatura* is achieved only with confidence, and it seems fair to wonder if one of the reasons these artists were able to carry off their grand designs in such style was not, at least in part, the sense of security and poise their titles imparted.

The artists and thinkers gathered in these pages are eccentric to the familiar group portrait of Moderns. In some cases, too, they represent the tradition against which the better-known Modernists rebelled or, as in the case of Balthus and to a certain degree Hofmannsthal, created their art in the spirit of rejection of what they saw around them. Where Picasso usually stands, Francis Bacon and Balthus take their places. Swinburne and Hofmannsthal are not nearly as well known as Eliot and Pound; Liszt and Chopin may not be considered as monumental as Brahms or as cutting-edge as Schoenberg and (another aristocrat) Anton von Webern; but the longer the study of Modern aesthetics goes on, the broader its parameters become—"minor" or heretofore forgotten figures play more prominent roles. In fact, many of those under consideration here—Swinburne is the quintessential example—were far more important in their time than historians have acknowledged, and consequently they had far greater influence on the earliest stages of Modern thought than has been admitted. The measure of this is their impact upon the thinking of those contemporary figures, usually of the emerging generation, who are given credit for the breakthroughs commonly viewed as central to the rise of Modernism. Appropriately enough, within the context of a study of aristocracy, this becomes a matter of succession. The day that Swinburne's obituary appeared in the *Times*, William Butler Yeats remarked to his sister, "Now I'm king of the cats." That is scarcely today's view of Swinburne, whose reputation has slid in association with the archaic and flaccid diction of the Victorians.

Connections of this kind are valuable, because long before there was talk of Modernism as a movement, the paintings, operas, poems, and philosophy that have come to be called Modern were being conceived under the influence of the figures considered here. That is how the term *avant-garde* becomes indispensable, allowing for a reappraisal of the importance of artists, composers, and thinkers who are generally thought of as belonging to other movements. Chopin and Liszt, for example, are generally relegated to the category of Romantics; Frederick, Lord Leighton, to the even more problematic (because it was retrospective) school of the Pre-Raphaelites. According to either chronological or stylistic reasons they do not support the conventional argument for what makes music, literature, or art Modern. It is simply too convenient to echo Virginia Woolf's "on or about 1910 the world changed," because, for one thing, the date is too late. For another, at a time when we look at Cycladic figures and comment upon how Modern they look, having had Giacometti and Brancusi teach us to see in this way, the shifting view of the origins of the Modern is too elusive to pin down in terms of one watershed year, figure, or work. Establishing a chronology is problematic in another way.

Conceding that the aristocracy has become a splendid and permanent anachronism anyway, the premise is that artists are also anachronistic, existing outside their own time either by virtue of being prophetically ahead of it or (the Pre-Raphaelites and Balthus are prime examples) belonging in spirit to a Golden Age that never actually existed. Whether artists in fact or aristocrats in fiction, one shared characteristic of all is that defiance of time that the curator Robert Storr found to be one of the paradoxes of "deliberately anachronistic art." He uses Francis Bacon and Balthus as prime examples of what he calls a "baroque anti-avant-garde" style of the Modern.

What matters in the case of the artists under consideration here is that each opened avenues that in their time were so daringly unfamiliar and original that they were considered avant-garde. Considering the personalities involved, most of them self-assured by dint of their upbringing, this fearless assumption of a leadership role is not surprising. One of the strongest voices in the specialized study of the avant-garde was Renato Poggioli, who numbers among the many types of refusal (remember that the Salon des Refusés was the dynamic center of Modernism in painting), the refusal of the *profanum vulgus*, a certain hostility to the common idiom. Poggioli's avant-garde becomes an elite:

> The attitude that flaunts its enemy's insult is often the fruit of an aristocratic disposition. The motive involved is always that which leads a king to found the Order of the Garter or to choose *honni soit qui mal y pense* as a motto. Although we have often mentioned the plebeian boheme, a tough-guy tendency, a demagogic nature and nearly anarchistic leanings, here we can—and ought to—say, without fear of repetition or contradiction, that the avant-garde spirit is eminently aristocratic. Bontompelli recognized this truth, though he based his judgment more on aesthetic than on psychological reasons: "The avant-garde is by nature solitary and aristocratic; it loves the initiated and the ivory tower." On the basis of such a tendency we ought to establish a similarity, identity even, between contemporary avant-gardism and positions such as those taken by Flaubert or Baudelaire: positions, in the first case, characterized by a universal antipathy for the bourgeois spirit and opinions rescued in the second case, by a hatred for "la bétise au front de taureau." Furthermore, these same attitudes were to be carried to their extreme consequences by the direct heirs and disciples of Flaubert and Baudelaire, the decadents.[4]

Poggioli's thrust makes the avant-garde a minority culture, what today would be called marginal. Surprisingly, given the drift toward finding heroes from the lower classes on the part of most historians, he describes the avant-garde in terms of the upper: "As against classical art, which flowered in an aristocratic climate, romantic art and avant-garde art are aristocracies subsisting and surviving in the democratic, or at least demagogic, era."[5] Poggioli was not alone in associating the avant-garde with aristocracy. Peter Burger's response to him, also titled *The Theory of the Avant-Garde*, stresses the "autonomy aesthetic" in functional terms as "a social realm that is set apart from the means-end rationality of daily bourgeois existence."[6] Historically, much of the work under consideration here was made when *l'art pour l'art* were still fighting words. Poggioli describes thinking that is critically based and power-hungry, if not potent: "At the moment it has shed all that is alien to it, art necessarily becomes problematic for itself. As institution and content coincide, social ineffectuality stands revealed as the essence of art in bourgeois society, and this provokes the self-criticism of art. It is to the credit of the historical avant-garde movement that they supplied this self-criticism."[7]

In a famous passage on the origins of poetry that stands to Modernism as Wordsworth and Coleridge's preface to the *Lyrical Ballads* does to Romanticism, Wallace Stevens meditated upon the dynamic of the avant-garde and particularly upon that difficult question of how to sustain its revolutionary ardor. Stevens was a wealthy businessman and latter-day dandy who, like his acquaintance, the composer Charles Ives, as well as later American poetic voices such as Robert Lowell and James Merrill, had the luxuries of time and education to be a force in the American avant-garde. Stevens called poetry "a cemetery of nobilities" in an essay that echoes both Mallarmé and Eliot in their theories of poetry as language that has been raised to purity. While the conclusion of this passage is often quoted, the manner in which Stevens sets up his definition is directly related to the province of this study:

> It is hard to think of a thing more out of time than nobility. Looked at plainly it seems false and dead and ugly. To look at it at all makes us realize sharply that in our present, in the presence of our reality, the past looks false and is, therefore, dead and is, therefore, ugly; and we turn away from it as from something repulsive and particularly from the characteristic that it has a way of assuming: something that was noble in its day, grandeur that was, the rhetorical once. But as a wave is a force and not the water of which it is composed, which is never the same, so nobility is a force and not the manifestations of which it is composed, which are never the same. Possibly the description of it as a force will do more than anything else I can have said about it to reconcile you to it. It is not an artifice that the mind has added to human nature. It is a violence from within that protects us from a violence from without. It is the imagination pressing back against the prison

of reality. It seems, in the last analysis, to have something to do with our self-preservation, and that, no doubt is why the expression of it, the sound of its words, help us to live our lives.[8]

This well-known passage, one of the most enduring and memorable definitions by a poet of what he does, is poignantly written in an almost confessional mode. For Stevens, poetry was in part an act of coping with the drudgery and pressures of running a major insurance company and coming home to the demands of a neurasthenic but beautiful wife (immortalized as the figure of Mercury on the dime). One thinks too of Eliot, another upper-middle-class American poet, who left his desk at the bank each day to return to a difficult and beautiful wife, the aristocratic Vivienne Haigh-Wood, who resurfaces in this study by virtue of her affair with Bertrand Russell. Stevens's use of "violence" invokes a familiar tenet of Modernism, particularly after World War I, namely, that the chaos of a shattered world order would be reflected in the prismatic disruptions of Cubism, the raw fragmentation of Eliot's poetry, or Schoenberg's chamber opera *Pierrot Lunaire*, to name just three examples. The art under consideration in this study, while not entirely free of the rage and disorder of this strain of Modernism, is for the most part inclined to a more lyrical, more Classical, more coolly contemplative exploration of the whole rather than the fragment. It also subscribes to genres—opera, drawing-room plays, full-length portraiture, and the long narrative poem—that are closer to the tradition than the iconoclastic, form-questioning works usually considered to be the core of the Modernist canon.

When Poggioli observes that the ideal disposition for an avant-garde artist is that of the aristocrat, he is emphasizing the fearlessness that originality necessitates. These aristocrats were unafraid of being leaders, arbiters of taste, or advocates of other artists in their time in examples of noblesse oblige that set them apart. Sand saw to it that many of the most promising writers of fiction of her time were published, through the pull she exerted with publishers afraid of losing a best-seller if they alienated her. Without the championship of Liszt as conductor and performer, it is fair to say that the cult of Wagner would never have taken root, depriving musical Modernism of what the esteemed critic and vocal expert Will Crutchfield calls a "futuristic" voice. The importance of the new sound was not lost on Liszt at a time when Wagner was scarcely understood by even the most advanced of musicians. Delacroix had the power and the courage to make and break reputations in the Parisian literary and artistic worlds. Swinburne was the most strident and feared literary and art critic of his time (much like Ruskin, who championed Turner), an intrepid advocate of works by poets and painters outside the canon, including the

Pre-Raphaelites, William Blake and Walt Whitman (whom he linked in one prescient study) as well as the Marquis de Sade.

Hofmannsthal had a direct line to the opera intendants not only of Vienna but across Europe. Russell ruled the cloistral politics of Cambridge and drew upon a deep balance of familial favors in London's corridors of power. He had the clout to make sure one of the most important philosophical books of the century, the *Tractatus Logico-Philosophicus* of Wittgenstein, would be published, under his foreword. Between them, Degas and Lautrec wielded an almost scandalous degree of power in the gallery world, with back-to-back and often simultaneous exhibitions of their works in many media, and Puvis de Chavannes took up where Delacroix had left off as the painter of choice for public commissions. Although a modest man who had to lie low by necessity during the Nazi occupation, in part due to his title, Webern was the most effective guardian of the torch of his master, Arnold Schoenberg, honoring him with concerts and publications in addition to his own musical acts of homage in his work. Balthus was André Malraux's right-hand man in the French ministry of culture. As important artists, some might say, they had the right and the duty to throw their weight around in the art circles of their time. Yet these heavy hitters did so with a difference. Because of their upbringing, they knew how the mantle of leadership is worn.

The identities of the artists and thinkers under consideration in this study have been shaped at least in part, by being aristocrats as well as artists. To what extent their work is also formed according to this dual identity is often a more difficult matter to demonstrate. The most touching example of this is offered by the novel *The Leopard* by Giuseppe di Lampedusa, a real-life nobleman pondering the meaning of being the last of his line in an age in which the role of aristocracy is so changed. This is not the sole example of a royal subject of a cutting-edge work of art by any means. Two of the most engaging literary calls to the Modern were J. K. Huysman's novel *A Rebours* and Villiers de Lisle Adam's play *Axel*, which had such a powerful impact upon Yeats when he saw it in Paris in 1924. Set in a Gothic castle in the Black Forest that is hung with ancestral portraits of German chatelaines and barons, its spirit is articulated by the principal character, Count Axel of Auersperg, of whom one servant remarks, "To me his eyes do not seem to belong to a man of this century."[9] Itself the work of a nobleman, first produced under noble patronage, the play is the subject of further discussion in the essay on Hugo von Hofmannsthal, where we examine the question of whether the validity of an aristocratic character drawn by another aristocrat is greater than one created by a commoner. Des Esseintes, the fictive aristocratic hero of *A Rebours*, is the ultimate aesthete, whose jewel-encrusted turtle set on a vividly colored Oriental carpet is among the most unforgettable gestures of decadence in the history of Modernism. With *A Rebours*, *Axel*, and Hofmannsthal's *Tower*, the Symbolist movement received its baptism in prose and drama, establishing a taste for the lyric poetry of Baudelaire and Mallarmé, the paintings of Moreau and Puvis (beloved of des Esseintes), and the music of Poulenc and Satie. The literary characters who epitomize the changes of the era—the shifts of moral and aesthetic codes that created Modernism—include D. H. Lawrence's Lady Chatterley as well as the nobles skewered in *Women in Love* (Russell, among them, was nearly driven to suicide by the betrayal of his friendship), and Lord Henry Wotton of Oscar Wilde's *Picture of Dorian Gray*, not to mention Wilde's own Bosie, young Lord Alfred Douglas, who sometimes seems more like a fictional character than a real person. So do Vladimir Nabokov, Isaak Dinesen (the Baroness Blixen), who wrote *Out of Africa*, and Horace Walpole, Earl of Orford.

In our time, editors and publishers know that royals are hot commodities, from the House of Windsor to historical voices of wisdom. Japanese readers, driven by a longing for a guide to traditional values, have bought millions of copies of a new translation (by a nun) of the courtly *Tale of Genji* by Lady Murasaki Shikibu, called the world's first novel and written by a lady-in-waiting at the imperial court in Heian Japan (794–1185). The entire cast of T. S. Eliot's play *The Cocktail Party* consists of English aristocrats who rather too strongly resemble Russell's London set. A running joke through Jorge Luis Borges's influential story, "Pierre Menard, Author of the Quixote," is the constant flattery of the Countess de Bagnoregio and the Baroness de Bacourt, latter-day incarnations of Madame de Sevigny, whose patronage the narrator is at pains to acknowledge and whose amateur "literary feats" (including the 'golden pages' of another personal portrait of Menard) he extols. Like a character out of Borges or Garcia Márquez, the filmmaker Luis Buñuel, director of *The Discreet Charm of the Bourgeoisie* (1972), was the son of an elegant provincial grandee, Don Leonardo Buñuel, from Calanda in northern Spain. David Thomson, a film critic for the *New York Times*, observed that he was "like a visitor from another world."[10] Nor was Buñuel the only aristocratic filmmaker, as Von Sternberg and Von Stroheim (more a would-be nobleman than an actual one) demonstrate.

Proust's *A la Recherche* is so imbued with his infatuation with the aristocracy that it seems apt to draw an analogy from the novel for the type of art under consideration here. After all, the tenor of Proust's evenings was set by the blandishments of dear friends who happened to be counts and princesses, from the Comte Robert de Montesquiou, the most famous of his noble supporters and in himself a singular figure in the history of Modernism (thanks to portraits by Whistler, Giovanni Boldini, and the Prince Troubezkoy), to a circle that included the de Noialles (art patrons about whom more is to be said in connection with Balthus), the Fitz-Joneses, the Count and Countess Potocka (whose forebears play a vital role in the life of Chopin), the princesses de Brancovan and de Chinnay and the Comte Boni de Castellane. Proust's lovingly rendered aristocrats, including the magnificent Baron de Charlus, are drawn from life, as are those of Hofmannsthal, Delacroix, Degas, and, less affectionately, Balthus. It has been the fashion to read *A la Recherche* with particular attention to the perspective of Monsieur Swann. An antihero built along the lines of Joyce's Leopold Bloom—and in this connection, too, the Jewish background of the character is significant, as it will be in our consideration of Balthus, Hofmannsthal, and Wittgenstein—his perspective reflects the conventional expectations of Modernism as set forth in Baudelaire's seminal essay "The Painter of Everyday Life," the ironic heroism of Richard Strauss's "Domestic Symphony," or the exalted peasants of van Gogh's portraits.[11]

The emphasis is upon the artistic qualities inherent in the bourgeois man's life. For schematic purposes, let's call this Swann's Way (with the cautionary note that in the novel this path does not exactly lead through slums and potato fields but sticks to high-society neighborhoods and the salon scene, where art and music are the expected fare). The Guermantes Way, the course this study elects, is that of the aristocracy. Think of it as the other route to Modern thought, via artists and works that hew to tradition and continuity, the very basis of any nobility and the antidote to the usual Modernist rhetoric of iconoclasm and revolution. There is no question which is the more scenic route. Swann's Way leads past the severe districts of Cubism and Minimalism, the arid rigor of Positivism in philosophy as well as in the magnificent ruins of Eliot's *Waste Land*, the raw sociological and political fare of Benjamin Britten's *Peter Grimes*, England's angry young men and their kitchen sink dramas or Arthur Miller's bleak *Death of a Salesman*, and the jagged fragments of Pound's *Cantos* or Schoenberg's chamber music. On the other hand, the lush landscape of the Guermantes Way offers enticing views of the formal gardens of Hofmannsthal's opera libretti with rich orchestral scores by Richard Strauss, the wilder shores of Swinburne's sea poems, and the overgrown drama of paintings by Delacroix and Bacon, as well as the finesse of Webern and Chopin. Parallel most of the way, the two paths are not in the end mutually exclusive. After all, Proust joins his in the marriage of the bourgeois Swann's daughter Gilberte and Robert de Saint-Loup, one of the noble Guermantes.

Most definitions of the Modern still rely heavily upon that old dichotomy between high and low (art and popular culture) that was the eponymous subject of a divisive and not altogether convincing exhibition at the Museum of Modern Art in New York in 1992. Recent critics have stressed the "marginal" status of both subject matter and authors, which plays conveniently to the interests of political correctness in cases where these are drawn from the proletariat or "underprivileged" minorities. The tribal artifacts and motifs that were source materials for Picasso, Giacometti, and Stravinsky; the folk songs and tales meticulously collected by Yeats, Dvořák, and others; the reverence for the art and writing of people with mental or developmental disabilities among the followers of Dubuffet and Art Brut (not to mention the more recent work of Robert Wilson, based on the poetry of an autistic man) are all "low" weapons wielded by artists intent upon beating back the hegemony of the bourgeoisie. By the time this theory reached Andy Warhol and his soup cans or later Postmodern invocations of the mass media, especially rubbish like animation on the Web, the predilection toward the "low" had become clear. That view of art as a class struggle has always left out a group that has its disdain for the bourgeoisie no less genuine than that of the bohemians: the aristocrats. By privileging this group of artists and their work, the "high" end of Modern art is brought back into focus. Some recent histories offer variations on the theme, including the important new study by T. J. Clark, *Farewell to an Idea: Episodes from a History of Modernism*. With each renewed attempt at writing the history of this ongoing movement, fresh opportunities open themselves to reevaluate the meaning of the term. For T. J. Clark, the discontinuity with earlier generations is still key:

> "Modernity" means contingency. It points to a social order which has turned from the worship of ancestors and past authorities to the pursuit of a projected future—of goods, pleasures, freedoms, forms of control over nature, or infinities of information. This process goes along with a great emptying and sanitizing of the imagination. Without ancestor-worship, meaning is in short supply—"meaning" here meaning agreed-on and instituted forms of value and understanding, implicit orders, stories and images in which a culture crystallizes its sense of the struggle with the realm of necessity and the reality of pain and death.[12]

By raising the issue of meaning in the context of intergenerational conflict, Clark leaves the door ajar for a view of modernity in terms of the tradition. He posits a secular climate in which art is specialized and abstract; and as in so many similar studies, the transition into Modernism is conceived in terms of abstraction. In the present study the hardy strain of figural painting will challenge that assumption. Clark outlines a political and economic argument that suggests that the good old capitalist confidence in the sign and the system is shaken. Modernism is a rattling of the old order, just as Romanticism had been: "Exiting from positivism—casting aside the possibility of art's going back to the moment at which sensation becomes sign—is in practice exiting from the hope of art's inhabiting a public, fully translatable world. And that—more than positivism or materialism per se—had been the utopian motor of Modernism from Courbet and Monet to Seurat and even van Gogh."[13] The same "utopian motor" is sensed here in the work of Russell, Hofmannsthal, Puvis, and Webern, although not to the exclusion of a public mode (it was Russell, after all, who wrote the best-selling history of philosophy to make the arcane more accessible to a broad audience). In Clark's eyes, this specialization leads to blurred identities, particularly with regard to the play of rebels and conservatives in such central careers as Cézanne's, as well as that of the more populist Puvis.

Clark turns to Freud and the theory of dreams to venture a definition that conveniently (for us) steers the argument in the direction of art that is both timeless and public in its scope: "Here is one definition of modernism, then: it is the art of 'the time that is not yet ripe'—always pulled to and fro between private (defensive) and public (expository). Always dreaming of the public life."[14] In the footsteps of such critics as Herbert Read, Clement Greenberg, and Michael Fried, Clark describes how Modernism found its subject matter in itself. He writes, "Not just that modern artists often turned away from the detail of the world in order to revel in the work of art's 'essential guidelines,' but that the turning away was very often associated with a class attitude or style not unlike Duke William's, or, at least, an attempt to mimic that style—its coldness, brightness, lordliness and nonchalance. Its 'balance, largeness, precision, enlightenment, contempt for nature in all its particularity.' Its pessimism, its strength."[15] Remarkably, this leads Clark to the example of Jackson Pollock, whose "largeness and lordliness" (after Clement Greenberg's critique) conjured an "atmosphere of courtly device." Clark concludes, "He was, need I say it, a petty-bourgeois artist of a tragically undiluted type—one of those pure products of America (of Riverside County, California) we like to believe will go crazy strictly on their own terms. It is hard to think of him playing the aristocrat for long."[16]

Even as he debunks the Greenbergian valorization of Pollock, Clark raises the long neglected values of enchantment and charm in art, those courtly features that play right into the hands of a study in which beauty, luxury, and elegance as critical terms are resurgent. Returning to Pollock at the very end of his massive study, he adds, "Abstract Expressionism, I want to say, is the style of a certain petty bourgeoisie's aspiration to aristocracy, to a totalizing cultural power. It is the art of that moment when the petty bourgeoisie thinks it can speak (and its masters allow it to speak) the aristocrat's claim to individuality. Vulgarity is the form of that aspiration. Or we could say: Abstract Expressionism is the form of the petty bourgeoisie's aspiration to aristocracy, at that fateful moment when the bourgeoisie itself no longer so aspires; then the petty bourgeois has to stand in for a hidden—nay, vanished—bourgeois elite."[17] The parallel with the dandy, the subject of the epilogue to this volume, is fascinating, and so is the implicit assumption that art that is not vulgar would be genuinely aristocratic.

When Clark veers from the fundamentalism of previous criticism, he finds himself in unexpected territory, bumping into aspects of art that are softer and more tradition-minded, no longer needing to remain "scabrous or otherwise low." He avers: "An art of high negativity—books about nothing, paintings done with consciousness deliberately on hold—is not necessarily anarchical, scabrous, or otherwise low. On the contrary, it has often come out of courtly surroundings. Dukes have gone in for it, on horseback, as part of their general 'contempt for nature in all its particularity.' Negative is stylish."[18] The *via negativa* of Modern literature, an inevitability in any history of this nature, comes stylishly into play in this study in the essay on Swinburne and his relation to Flaubert and Mallarmé, followed by a consideration of its impact upon Wittgenstein. If anything, the poetic element in the paintings of Balthus or the operas of Hofmannsthal and the idealism of many of the artists under consideration here constitute a holding position against the negative onslaught of Modernism. There is an innocence and high-mindedness about many of these artists that refuses to concede to the bleak negativity of Eliot's *Waste Land*, the *Negative Dialectics* of T. W. Adorno, or the black monochrome paintings of Robert Rauschenberg.

By starting with the identity of the artist, this study counters another truism, that of the Modern work of art as inward-looking, self-reflective, and self-sufficient. This assumption was the darling of the New Critics in the 1950s, for whom the literary "verbal icon" waited to be deciphered. Painting and sculpture that took as its target the idea of representation subverted the importance of the subject matter to highlight the importance of facture. Clearly, the rise of abstraction in the visual arts, of literature about language (most of which is based on Wittgenstein's philosophy), and the theoretically rigorous movements in music and architecture were all tailor-made for a critical approach that concentrates upon the work, not the maker. This study focuses upon the importance of the artist's identity and background in the development of the work and the progress of modernity, with one eye lifted toward the possibility that what the artists knew or felt as nobility might qualify them for leading roles in the campaign to advance the avant-garde. This is our cue for focusing on creators and works that are just as contemptuous as any of bourgeois shortcomings—George Sand or Hugo von Hofmannsthal on the topic are scathing—but arrive from a social and aesthetic point of view that begins "on high." Rather than emphasizing the private scope of the poem or canvas, it traces the public drama of poets such as Byron and Swinburne, whose work was shouted in unison by undergraduates marching around the quadrangles of Oxford; murals by Puvis de Chavannes and Delacroix; posters by Toulouse-Lautrec; massive concerts played or organized by Liszt; public lectures and political rallies that starred Russell; the high-profile political exploits and literary profligacy of Sand; or the shift from lyric poetry and prose to the public drama by Hofmannsthal, whose pageant-play *Everyman* annually transforms the city of Salzburg into a stage. The scale and mode of the art was public, and the matter was often nationalism (as in the case of Yeats, Delacroix, and Hofmannsthal).

The critical chorus embraced impersonality at a time when the art and poetry lent itself most readily to a denial of the warm and breathing being who stood behind it. In the 1970s in particular, one went from the laboratory-white gallery in which a cube of polished steel (thinking here of the Minimalist work of Robert Morris, Donald Judd, or even Carl Andre) or square canvas of pure white or leaden gray paint (Robert Ryman, Ellsworth Kelly, early Brice Marden) to a building, perhaps by Mies or Philip Johnson, that evinces a Platonic indifference to human scale or form in its perfection—hungry geometries—and then to listen to compositions by John Cage, Phillip Glass, Pierre Boulez, Iannis Xenakis, and those who, in their enthusiasm for mathematical or other ideals, ignore the "human" appetites for harmony and melody. With abstraction and Minimalism in the ascendancy, the impersonal held sway in both art and criticism until quite recently. Lost in this orthodoxy of the artwork as object ("Presentness is grace," rhapsodized Michael Fried in one of the great paeans to Minimalism) was the interest in who the artist was and how his or her life affected the work and the progress of the career. In this study the notion of art as a career assumes particular importance. When "Henry" announced to the Toulouse-Lautrec family, one of the most distinguished in France, that he intended to live in Paris rather than in one of the ancestral castles and pursue art as his profession, the thankfully brief crisis that ensued was nearly as unpleasant as the dramatics attending the realization, earlier in his childhood, that he had a permanent disability. An uncle lit a fire in the courtyard and burned the paintings the artist kept in storage in the family castle. The problem, for his father mainly, was that the image of the family was at stake and that a career in the arts was "unsuitable" as well as unprecedented.

Readers may recall the pompous tone in which Christopher Plummer, playing the baron in *The Sound of Music*, flatly stated that "the Von Trapp family does not sing in public." The same indignation was heard in the households of most of the characters in this book. Bertrand Russell was plainly destined to become prime minister and a powerful member of the still potent House of Lords, just as his father, Lord John Russell, had been, not a maths don; and Wittgenstein's siblings were aghast when young Ludwig parted with his share of the family's immense fortune and his claims to a title, to retire into very modest digs on the fringe of the Cambridge University campus to teach with Russell. The Wittgensteins even feared he was insane. Swinburne's very proper parents agonized over his rise to literary (and other) notoriety in the artsy world of London and the wild stories they heard about the company he kept in Chelsea, eventually enlisting the help of a prim gentleman named Theodore Watts-Dunton to take him out of circulation and essentially baby-sit him in suburban Putney. It would be an exaggeration to say that Francis Bacon's extremely class-conscious father could not handle the young artist's choice of painting as a career; well before that decision was made, the proud heir of the first Viscount Francis Bacon, philosopher and favorite of Elizabeth, had been thrown out of the vast country house when he was discovered before a mirror wearing women's underwear. The only artist considered here who went into the arts with his parents' blessing was Hugo von Hofmannsthal, groomed to be a man of letters by his family.

At the basis of this decision is the difference between private and public lives and the way in which that defines the artist and the celebrity. We did not need the funeral of Princess Diana to teach us that aristocrats, even in the 1990s, lead high-profile lives. The slew of magazines and media outlets that thrive on the misdeeds of the House of Windsor, to name but one unfortunate example of royals hounded by the press, are proof enough that, as in the days when they commanded what one would call power, political and economic, the aristocracy is still a matter of public example and scruple. Anyone who has attended a village fête or charity ball with royals can attest to the public expectations held out to them. They are by no means left to lead a quiet existence as private citizens. Even the last Chinese emperor, Pu Yi, could not hide during his waning years as a zoo attendant in Beijing. His memoirs became an international hit when Bernardo Bertolucci made a feature film about him.

There is another type of celebrity who receives very much the same sort of treatment in society. As with royalty, the artist is the one the eyes follow at the party, making the host and hostess nervous and setting trends in fashion and décor. As with the disenfranchised aristocrats, the artists draw attention more from their presence than from any conventional power. Neither aristocrat nor artist sends troops to fight, balances budgets, lays off thousands of workers, or acquires billion-dollar companies, yet they turn heads. The figures under consideration here were, in many cases, powerful in their time, as measured not merely by the simplistic yardstick of their monetary success in the marketplace or concert halls but by using the subtler index of influence and the degree to which their works changed the intellectual, aesthetic, and even popular tastes. Is it because they were brought up to be actors on the public stage or simply because their work was so powerful that Liszt, Sand, Delacroix, Bacon, Hofmannsthal, Russell, Swinburne, Degas, Lautrec, Leighton, and the others had such a profound effect upon so many? Even their choice of media reflects a propensity to cast the net wide and draw in more than just the elite, private audience.

Notably, Hofmannsthal gave up a promising start in poetry that began at the tender age of seventeen and a guaranteed role as one of the leading lights of Viennese café society for the prospect of reaching a broader audience from the dramatic and operatic stages. In a similar vein, Delacroix used his position as a lion of the salons of Paris to score a series of major mural commissions in churches and government edifices, including the palace of the Louvre, making him, à la Rubens, one of the most ubiquitous artists of Paris even to this day. Lautrec turned his academy-trained hand to the creation of big, splashy posters for favorites of the nightclub scene, clearing the way for a long line of artists, through our own time—thanks to the generous cooperation of advertising agencies and clients such as Absolut and Philip Morris—to produce massive campaign visuals or create works (Warhol, Gilbert and George, Nam June Paik) on a scale that far exceeds the relatively private expanse of the framed canvas that hangs on the hall wall. Francis Bacon's massive, gold-framed portraits made him one of the first artists of our era to achieve the kind of celebrity status, particularly in London and Paris, generally reserved for movie stars and politicos—reveling in the crowds of thousands who would push their way through his openings or crash the banquets afterward. That kind of mass excitement recalls as well the hysteria that often attended a concert performance by Liszt, one of the first virtuosi, along with Paganini, to elevate the star power of his predecessors (Mozart and Beethoven among them) into a matrix for composition that had the powerful import of, say, a big splashy Delacroix mural. Russell took his hereditary knack for inciting a crowd to help advance such causes as woman's suffrage and the antinuclear campaign, becoming one of the world's best-known philosophers. Lord Leighton's painting *Flaming June* was among the most often reproduced, ubiquitous images of Victorian England, an icon of the mass media created by a baron who simultaneously attempted to keep the Royal Academy pure and elitist but wanted to educate the masses in art history along the lines of Ruskin.

This type of broadband effect leads to different territory, again, from the hermetic, abstract art of the Cubists, Minimalists, Pantonalist composers, and others who appealed so strongly to critics who prefer the cracking of a private code (precisely what one might expect of the aristocrats, actually). Beyond the public scale and loquacity of these works, there are other, more technical differences between the "noble" Moderns and the better-known variety. One of these is a stronger relationship to the tradition. Ever since Modernism breathed its first heady gulps of the oxygen of "the new," the necessity of rejecting the past has been a rallying cry. "Make it new," insisted Pound. Robert Hughes titled his lively account of Modern art's rise *The Shock of the New*. Covering much the same ground—the breaking of old forms, the severing of outworn ties, the repudiation of the traditional canon—has led to critics writing of "Music Discomposed" and the various anti-idealisms of twentieth-century philosophy. The literal translation of these ruptures in art itself brought the iconoclastic philosophy of pragmatism; the prismatic shattering of bottles, faces, violins, guitars, and other forms in Cubism (and later, the cutting up of real violins in the work of Arman, the crushing of cars by John Chamberlain, the cracking of panes of glass by Marcel Duchamp or the tearing and cutting of Kurt Schwitters's Merz collage, the slashing of the canvas by Lucio Fontana); the rapid-fire sequences of citations in Eliot's *Waste Land* and Pound's *Cantos*; and the staccato musical languages of interruption of Schoenberg and Stravinsky. Even the house itself is interrupted in the "inside-out" architecture of Mies van der Rohe, Phillip Johnson, and Rem Koolhaas, and particularly in the wild discontinuities of Frank Gehry's buildings.

In our time we are a good deal more accustomed to finding beauty in fragments and the artfully destroyed, having had a century of this work to enjoy—we know we should admire the collage of Schwitters, the tougher kaleidoscopes of Braque and Picasso at the peak of their powers in 1914. It is important to recall what a revolution was caused by the initial wave of "anti" gestures that gave birth to Modernism, which is the moment at which we are taking up this story, concentrating on the figures, such as Sand and Swinburne, Lautrec and Hofmannsthal, Russell and Wittgenstein, who were among the first to be considered Modern. Medium by medium, the traditional forms and conventions came under attack, from narrative and prosody in literature to the figure in painting and melody and harmonies based on thirds and fifths in music. Thanks to the rapid succession of world wars and the lowering threat of mass destruction from nuclear weapons, a perpetual state of crisis, skepticism, and paranoia enhanced the feeling that the artist in tune with the times was simultaneously "creator and destroyer." By bringing to the foreground this group of noble Modern masters and examining works such as the poems of Swinburne or the plays of Hofmannsthal, the portraits of Balthus and Leighton or the later compositions of Liszt, many of which have fallen into neglect, we enjoy an opportunity to visit a forgotten wing of the Modernist palace, filled with undervalued works by artists who exerted a far more potent influence upon the course of aesthetic development than history records.

As it turns out, in our time the prevailing trends in art take us back to their examples. The recent rediscovery of the figure in contemporary painting—thanks in part to powerful exhibitions of not only Bacon but Lucien Freud and Eric Fischl, as well as of the sculptor Magdalena Abakanowicz—has attracted an astonishing number of students to life classes at conservative bastions such as the New York Academy and Boston University, making the study of Bacon and Leighton in particular, as well as Balthus, look timely. There is probably no better preparation for the contemporary operas of John Harbison (whose *Great Gatsby* made its debut at the Metropolitan Opera House in 2000), John Corigliano, or Thomas Ades than the study of the Marschallin in Strauss and Hofmannsthal's far more elegant opera, *Der Rosenkavalier*. The standard opening gambit of a dissertation or book of literary theory using Postmodernism is a "slippage" of meaning in literary language—the example of Swinburne's poetry "without a center" (to borrow Eliot's main objection) comes to mind. The crisis of language described in Hofmannsthal's epistolary essay that uses the voice of a fictive noble character addressing the Viscount Francis Bacon, "The Letter of Lord Chandos," is even closer to the mark, and it is dated 1901.

Perhaps more than any other group of artists we could gather, these figures recognized the need to challenge the past in order to be Modern and to be original. This is the Oedipal conflict writ large. It feeds directly into the realm of genealogy, one of the most fertile and controversial areas of Postmodern thought, traced from Nietzsche through Michel Foucault, Gilles Deleuze, and Felix Guattari, not to mention the family romance that is the basis of Harold Bloom's work. The importance of the hereditary line in a discussion of these sons and daughters of Europe's great families is perhaps obvious, but the variety of ways in which it is addressed in their works and lives adds subtlety and substance to what in many other critical contexts is mere metaphor. Lautrec, Bacon, Russell, Sand, and many of the artists in this study were torn by the question of inheriting a title and its impact upon their identities as artists. They were justifiably concerned about the way in which their artistic colleagues would perceive them. While the most rapid growth among Web sites continues to be the viral explosion of family tree search engines, the close scrutiny of these often intertwined figures from the upper classes seems, again, a remarkably appropriate topic for today. The discovery in April 2000, at a biotech firm called Oxford Ancestors, of the connection between genes and genealogy by proving a link between surnames and unique sections of DNA, offers scientific support to the notion that the inheritance of a name brings with it certain inevitable characteristics. As Professor Bryan Sykes, who published the study in the *American Journal of Human Genetics* in April 2000, told the BBC, "It puts every family on a par with the aristocracy, in being able to trace ourselves back to an original founder."

Aristocracy and genealogy are forces capable of producing art of great power. Much of the art under consideration draws its strength from solid grounding in the past. From the fierce figural paintings of Bacon to the verse tragedies of Swinburne and from the Mozartean operas of Hofmannsthal to the string quartets of Webern, these artists turned to genres at the very core of the tradition, even to the point of being considered conservative. It could be argued that the circumstances of their upbringing had a great deal to do with this. At the vast country estates of his father and grandmother, Bacon looked up at the tall formal portraits and sporting pictures that would eventually be translated into his overscale, indistinct portraits and snarling wild dogs. Hofmannsthal was at the opera nightly with his parents, glancing over wistfully at the empty red velvet seats in the imperial box. Chopin and Liszt grew up on the vast estates of Eastern European nobility, where the greatest composers of an earlier age, Haydn, Mozart and Beethoven, premiered their compositions. Degas's father, Auguste de Gas, was an intimate friend of Marcille and La Caze, renowned collectors of Old Master paintings, who shared their enthusiasm for fifteenth- and sixteenth-century Italian painting with the young artist. Degas's first portraits, including one of the family of the Baron Bellelli that is today a highlight of the Musée d'Orsay, are saturated with echoes of these Old Master works.

That high road of the studious artist who is respectful of the tradition but willing to break through to modernity is one element of this study. Another is the darker byway of decadence, which is important not simply vis-à-vis the rather notorious debaucheries of Bacon, Balthus, and Swinburne (who was a main target of Max Nordau's notorious examination of *Degeneration* in 1895), but with respect as well to the overall subject of what factors precipitated the aristocracy's decline in power. Russell was even barred from teaching at City College in New York for his views on sexuality. Any biographical study of a group of artists is bound to wander into questions of an alternative morality, but decadence was a historical force in the advent of Modernism. Storr views it as the result of dashed hopes and expectations:

> Art that aches for a glorious yesteryear but markedly fails to achieve the excellence it emulates is commonly called decadent. Modern culture has long been haunted by the prospect of its own disintegration. The pervasiveness of an organic view of civilization's growth and deterioration has been buttressed by the tale of Rome's rise and fall, its grandeur and corruption. . . . Making a virtue of what they considered an inevitability, numerous artists thus enthusiastically embraced the epithet "decadent" and cultivated personae to suit the role of the enervated, dissipated, or debauched aesthete at the end of his tether and at the end of the line historically. Dandies of this sort were self-made mandarins, and their personal style was simultaneously a pastiche and a parody of highborn manners and taste. The masquerade's piquancy derives form this doubling of impersonation and send-up, longing and clowning, qualities underscored by the bourgeois or petty bourgeois origins of many dandies.[19]

Most dandies were self-appointed aristocrats and in the case of the Decadents, descended from a wild line of rakes that included real aristocrats—specifically Lord Byron, the Marquis de Sade, and, less renowned but at least as interesting when it came to the particulars of his thoroughly depraved life, William Beckford, author of *Vathek*, one of Swinburne's favorite books. In recent years no aristocratic forebear has been as trendy or stylish as Sade, as is evident from the immense popularity of "the divine Marquis" in Structuralism and Deconstruction, particularly in the writings of Roland Barthes, Georges Bataille, Michel Foucault, and Jacques Derrrida, as well as a peculiar spate of recent books and biographies and one idiotic feature movie, called *Quills*, within the past two years. In a newspaper article about the sudden rage over Sade, biographer Neil Schaeffer, comparing him to Norman Mailer no less, takes the low road: "He explored the bottom line of human nature, the worst imaginable; he is modern because any writer who explores the depth of human nature is modern." The editor of Schaeffer's life of Sade, George Andreou, told the same *New York Times* reporter that Sade's contemporary appeal lies in his "ability to recreate himself, kind of Madonna-like." Lower and lower, the echelons keep dropping. According to Francine du Plessix Gray, author of *At Home with the Marquis de Sade*, published the same year by the trade house Simon and Schuster, "He had manic energy, which is not unlike Jackson Pollock, and the raw, animal release of energy—Titian, Beethoven—is very much the center of the greatest art. That doesn't mean it necessarily creates great art or did in his case; he taught me the importance of energy." One of the final comments in the article came from Princeton historian Robert Darnton, who noted that a culture that is now less uptight about sex is fertile ground for a new appreciation of Sade: "Sade fits in; he's very modern, no longer avant-garde, has lost his punch so to speak; he's no longer in the 'Hell' section of the libraries." Many of the same arguments could be made on behalf of Byron or, as we shall see, Balthus, Swinburne, and Liszt, whose erotically charged works ignited revolutionary change in the arts. When it comes to bolstering the argument for the modernity of these figures, it helps to resort to the scandalously sexual character of their works. As with Byron, Beckford, and Sade—one could also cite the earl of Rochester in this regard—the licentious quality of their fantasies and real lives, free of the constraints suffered by their social inferiors, helps make them feel more post-Freudian from the standpoint of their ability to shock.

Jean Baudrillard, in the introduction to his novel *Seduction*, puts his finger on the appeal of eighteenth-century nobility for twentieth-century writers by wistfully noting that, in the eighteenth century, seduction was still a viable basis for their art: "It was, with valor and honor, a central preoccupation of the aristocratic spheres."[20] The unlikely success of a film version of Laclos's *Liaisons Dangereuses*, like the equally improbable hit public television series *Brideshead Revisited*, based upon Evelyn Waugh's depiction of a young aristocrat whose homosexuality offered the irresistible spice of the forbidden, upon which ratings rise, attest to the permanent fascination with the decadent dimension of the aristocracy. On a higher level, two recent artistic successes, both eccentric and sexually risqué, suggest that this formula is still potent. Thomas Ades is the rising young star of English composers, in many ways the new Benjamin Britten, whose controversial two-act chamber opera *Powder Her Face* made its debut at the 1995 Cheltenham International Festival when he was only 24, followed by extremely successful runs, with the composer conducting, at the Aspen Festival and the Brooklyn Academy of Music. Its main character is identified in the libretto by Philip Hensher only as the Duchess, a latter-day version of the fading grandeur of Hofmannsthal's Marschallin but based on the racy, real-life scandal of the duke and duchess of Argyll, whose very public divorce in the 1950s gave the media the sort of juicy material that the House of Windsor has provided since. No one who has seen the opera, which in many ways is a brutal and cynical portrayal of the duchess, is likely to forget its fourth scene, set in a hotel room in the 1950s, in which the Duchess summons room service and, having told the young servant to "forget who I am, forget who you are," proceeds to reward his efforts with fellatio, lasting well over thirty bars in the score and concluding with the scenic directions "absolute stillness" followed by "clears her throat."[21] Many in the audience chose to leave the theater—after the scene was over, of course. At glamorous Aspen it was the talk of the town all summer.

It would take another book entirely to recount the full story of aristocratic patronage and influence in the history of Modern art. From the ever-present Comte de Montesquiou in the Paris of the 1860s to Wagner's mad King Ludwig, through the high-profile role of Prince Charles in the critical conversation regarding contemporary architecture, the role of the royals in the arts is far more important than most realize. While aristocratic patronage is not what it once was—the Rockefellers have supplanted the Borgias, and Catherine the Great ceded that ground to Charles Saatchi—there are a number of fascinating examples of noble efforts on behalf of the avant-garde. One institution in particular—the Guggenheim Museum—has, since its inception in 1949, represented a path-breaking attempt on the behalf of European aristocratic connoisseurs to promote cutting-edge art in the United States. The original name was the Museum for Non-Objective Art, and the core of its ideology, as well as its holdings, was Kandinsky. It reflected the excitement caused by his slim book, *Concerning the Spiritual in Art*, which gripped the thinking of contemporary American artists and critics. The guiding spirit behind the project was an Austrian baroness, Hilla von Rebay, who led Solomon Guggenheim by the nose, essentially to ensure that a killer building by Frank Lloyd Wright and a premium group of paintings by Kandinsky, Mondrian, Malevich, and the Suprematists could be brought together in the service of art that was outré. The baroness's story has been told in full in a recent biography.[22]

In what may be a fascinating coincidence or an extension of the tradition of the baroness's legacy, the Guggenheim in our time has been saved again by another member of a great European family. During the Contemporary art market's boom in the 1970s and 1980s no figure was more mysterious and welcome than the Count Giuseppe Panza di Biumo. Wherever a gallery took a chance on a Minimalist or sparely Conceptual installation, the hopes were high that the count would stop by and buy. Reports of his auction appearances or afternoon visits to the more experimental galleries and alternative spaces of SoHo and the East Village of New York exceeded real sightings by far, and few dealers and artists actually know what he looks like to this day. He shunned openings and the scene on Saturdays when the art world turns out for gallery-hopping, opting to slip in and out of deserted shows on weekday afternoons, leaving a buzz of excitement or puzzled looks on the faces of hopeful gallery assistants. "Was that him?" one asked me one day—it was—and this writer, an arts journalist for the leading gossip rag in the trade at the time yet sworn to secrecy, was unsuccessfully besieged for his phone number and address for weeks afterward (he was holed up in the Mark Hotel on Park Avenue). The excitement of the dealers was well founded. The count was spending millions (of dollars, not lire) on cutting-edge art, buying at a crazy pace supposedly to fill his seventeenth-century palace in Tuscany, where old stone walls were bathed in the fluorescent light of Dan Flavin sculptures, and huge, brutal Richard Serra steel plates protruded from the boxwood in the ancestral gardens. Sixty years after the Baroness Rebay inaugurated the museum, the Guggenheim announced it was acquiring by gift and purchase a substantial chunk of the Panza collection, valued at $100 million. In one stroke the Guggenheim had leapt to the forefront of museums in their holdings of Minimalism. One Manhattan dealer, understandably concerned to maintain his anonymity yet familiar from the inside on the way the count secured many of his most important works, divulged that he is not really the count but the younger brother of the true count and proud to display the title.

The Contemporary art scene has other noble habitués. Among the most colorful is the couple nicknamed TNT—the Prince and Princess Thurn und Taxis, whose collection of "blue chip" artists in various castles in Switzerland represents one way in which they lend their support. Another association is more direct. Princess Gloria, whose exquisite features and golden hair turn heads at museum events, has been the subject and inspiration for numerous works of art. One is a high-toned portrait by Francesco Clemente, famously commissioned for $160,000 and featured in the fatuous Styles section of the *New York Times* in November 1999 in the context of the newly fashionable portraiture and its relationship to the works of John Singer Sargent or Ingres. Greater works celebrate the princess, notably a rapturous portrait made by Robert Mapplethorpe in 1987, not long before his death. While it sounds like a typically Warholian effort to pander to celebrity and wealth, the work is among the artist's most powerful in the genre.

As in so many Mapplethorpe images of strength, lighting and composition are its mainstays. The subject's eyes are tightly shut (as in the great portraits Mapplethorpe made of Ken Moody). Her head is slightly tilted to her right and her only adornment is a necklace of large pearls that collect and reflect the head-on blast of light with which her head and shoulders are dusted to a whiteness that shocks against the black velvet backdrop Mapplethorpe used. The work is an example of Mapplethorpe's unadulterated classicism, an homage to the purity of the Greek sculpture he also photographed in the same manner (as in *Hermes* or *Apollo* of 1988). These are shots taken up close yet leaving the subjects divinely distant, the soft hollow of their blank eyes and sealed lips a model of aristocratic restraint. The light that floods the figure of Princess Gloria penetrates more than it highlights, much as it pours through the translucent outer edge of the marble sculpture. This severe contrast of white light and pure shadow invokes the chiaroscuro of Caravaggio, who incised his outlines to heighten the sharpness of the image. When the princess sat for the portrait, Mapplethorpe was already the most notorious of many contemporary "bad boys" of the avant-garde, and certainly no courtier. He belonged to the club of Jean-Michel Basquiat, Keith Haring, and Christopher Wilmarth. The great paradox of the work is the timeless elegance and purity with which he seals her beauty, a species of classical portraiture taking on a noble subject that might have been offered to the court of her great-great-grandmother. Set this work beside one of the aristocratic portraits made by Ingres, master of the sharp line and formal homage, and the proximity of spirit and even of technique would be immediately apparent. It has its echo in the haunting yet austere portrait of the Countess de Noialles by Balthus, to be considered later in this study.

In so many of the arts the royal traditions of patronage and the thematic involvement of aristocracy as the material of great drama had their impact upon Modernism. What would dance be today without the quintessentially aristocratic contribution of the "white" Russian émigrés acting together with the court of today's Prince Rainer to create the Ballets Russes de Monte Carlo, in which Nijinsky and Stravinsky would advance their reconception of the danseur noble and classicism in an intellectual as well as artistic climate that was ready for them, leaving behind the awful "dancing collective farm" (as Stravinsky sneeringly called it in a 1939 lecture at Harvard) that seized Shostakovich and the chilling grip of Stalin's art that had to be "national in form and content." It was Shostakovich, after all, who took a queen and made her a peasant in his retelling of Shakespeare, *Lady Macbeth of Mtensk*. As a recent exhibition at Hartford's Athenaeum has shown, the central figure in the Ballets Russes, Serge Diaghilev, was a young aristocrat brought up to revere the arts and the preservation of his own imperial culture. At the turn of the century, this was a tragic enterprise. A diary entry written in April 1905, after Diaghilev had traveled in Russia, expresses his fear that a "time of reckoning" is at hand:

> Remote estates boarded up, palaces terrifying in their dead splendor are strangely inhabited by the nice, mediocre people of today, unable to endure the gravity of past regalia. Here it is not people who are dying but a way of

> life. And that is when I became quite convinced that we are living in a terrible moment of crisis: we are destined to die so that a new culture can be resurrected, a culture that will take from us the relics of our weary wisdom. This is what history tells us, and this is what aesthetics confirms. And now, plunged into the depths of artistic images and thereby invulnerable to reproaches of extreme artistic radicalism, I can say boldly and with conviction that whosoever is certain that we are witnessing a great historical moment of reckoning and ending in the name of a new, unknown culture is not mistaken—a culture that has arisen through us, but will sweep us aside. And hence, with neither fear nor doubt, I raise my glass to the ruined walls of the beautiful palaces, as I do to the new behests of the new aesthetics. And all that I, an incorrigible sensualist, can wish for is that the impending struggle not abuse the aesthetics of life and that death be as beautiful and as radiant as the Resurrection![23]

As the great music historian Richard Taruskin has shown, both Stravinsky and Bartók, while drawing their thematic material in part from ethnomusicological research into folk tunes and dancers, were forging a new "objective" synthesis of the Classical style and the powerful Modern currents in the arts. The result was a sophisticated, international idiom that most importantly defies time as well as locality. Taruskin singles out the Stravinsky concerto for piano and winds as a milestone and a particularly strong influence on Bartók: "Stravinsky's concerto was the bellwether of this uprooted composer's 'objective' or 'Neo-Classical' manner. It spoke (or tried to speak) neither Russian nor any other particular dialect, but rather a musical Esperanto, its vocabulary laced with references to Bach, the perceived fountainhead of 'universal' or 'timeless' values."[24] About the same piece, Bartók commented, "Truly, one gets caught up in this miraculously beautiful sounding machine music, music of pulsating rhythm—no tears, no emotion." Stravinsky was doubly an artistic aristocrat, combining hereditary links to both the arts and nobility: his father was the leading bass baritone of the Imperial Opera in St. Petersburg, a friend of Count Tolstoy. Another important creator who emerged from the White Russian circle was George Balanchine, who re-created the danseur noble for the twentieth century, its embodiment becoming Peter Martins at New York City Ballet, now its artistic director. Les Ballets de Monte Carlo, the successor to Diaghilev's company, is the domain of Princess Caroline. She has just hired Jean-Christophe Maillot, whose professed loyalty to tradition was shown in his recent production of *Romeo and Juliet*, to Prokofiev's score: "My aim is to take this classical world—its codes, its aesthetic, its dancers—and find a new approach. The alternative to classical dance is not automatically modern dance.

There are other propositions which are more subtle and, for one, more interesting."[25]

As in dance, so too in design have aristocratic tastes been a major factor in the shaping of Modern style. According to Deborah L. Silverman, in her history of Art Nouveau, the aristocratic brothers Edmund and Jules de Goncourt, descendants of Old Regime nobility on their mother's side, were largely responsible for a rococo revival in Paris, particularly when they completed their home and showcase in Auteuil in 1869: "At once the place of work and rest for the brothers, the house was conceived as a sealed fortress where the Goncourts could live completely surrounded by vestiges of a lost aristocratic culture."[26] Tracing the development of the *style moderne* in décor through the 1890s, she points to the role of aristocratic patrimony and the *ralliement* of Catholic and republican aristocrats from 1839 in the arts. Private spaces, such as the de Goncourt home as an extreme example, were modeled after the chambers of Louis XV and Alexander III. She also manages to tie the dangerous flowers of Art Nouveau to the contemporary birth of psychology. As she writes, "If the ideals of the *ralliement* and organic solidarity were constrained by the fractious necessities of real politics, they would blossom more freely in the noncontingent realm of art. In the craft movement, the political architects of the *ralliement* and solidarism would participate in a social form that lay behind their realignment efforts—the solidified ranks of one elite. Politicians and cultural officials would converge in promoting the artistic equivalents of aristocratic affirmation and bourgeois solidarism, an apotheosis of republicanism in transformation."[27]

With the decline of Europe's monarchy, the rise of America's power economically and in the arts indicates a shift that would be worth yet another book, examining the role of an American aristocracy, based on wealth, that produced some of the great early Modern works, including those by Mary Cassatt, William and Henry James, John Singer Sargent, Henry Adams, and, extending this to our own time, Robert Lowell and James Merrill (scion of the investment banking house). Between Eliot and Pound, Pollock and de Kooning, Charles Ives and Wallace Stevens, the emigration of Schoenberg and Einstein, the Americanization of Modernism (*pace* the Parisians) began in the 1940s to reflect the fast pace and vigor of New York. A superb start in this direction has been made by Lawrence Rainey in *Institutions of Modernism: Literary Elites and Public Culture*, his book on patronage and the American "aristocracy of sensibility" that supported such rising talents as Pound and Joyce.[28] The shift to America was foretold in Adams's prophetic substitution of the Dynamo for the Virgin, his theory of acceleration and with it "destruction, multiplicity." Understandably, this buried the visibility of the European nobility, replacing it with a cultural elite of wealth (although it should be noted that Europe and Asia had their own examples—the great composer Francis Poulenc, for example, was the son of the founder of the giant pharmaceutical firm Rhone Poulenc, and Yoko Ono's prosperous and noble father attended school with the emperor of Japan).

Abstract Expressionism signaled the triumph of American art over European. The critic Cleanth Brooks, in his seminal study *Modern Poetry and the Tradition*, declared the victory of American Modernism over the "lifeless conventions of Victorians": "The history of modern American poetry as written by the Untermeyers and Monroes tends to take something of the following form: The modern American poet has rid himself of clichés, worn-out literary materials, and the other stereotypes of Victorianism. Having sloughed off these dead conventions, he has proceeded (with the critics' hearty approval) to write of American scenes, American things, and the American people."[29] The more Modernism became an American phenomenon, the further from its creative center the aristocratic class seemed to drift. The history of this process began to efface its origins, which is why there is today a need to recollect the contributions made to Modern art by the figures in this study. As Broch wrote vis-à-vis the Vienna of Hofmannsthal's era,

> Wherever there is an upper class—and if the nobility officiated as the upper class anywhere it was in Vienna—it will be acknowledged as the bearer of culture, not only did it always possess members—even in Vienna—who took such a task seriously, such as Count Wilczek and Count Lanckoronsky (to whom Hofmannsthal dedicated the "Speech in the House of an Art Collector"), but the artists themselves who fit into such traditional realms are not automatically to be called snobbish. . . . The artist's claim to nobility, founded on the strength of self-transcendence, this was the mission of assimilation, and Hofmannsthal would have been the last to think it might be fulfilled through social relations with the aristocracy. For there is no accomplishment with which one can buy one's way into a class: one must be born even into the proletariat for class membership to guarantee a social place within the total population. And, inversely, whoever chooses the artist's freedom is excluded from the class into which he was born and becomes subject to the kind of ancient proscription that is reserved for the "free man," which is what the Germans call an executioner.[30]

This is an odd note on which to end. The decline of the political and economic power of the nobility in the period when modernity took hold brought with it a loss of authority and also pressure to assert an identity, to claim a role in the new order. The urgency of this predicament, like the crisis mentality at the root of so many Modern movements, stemmed from a typical aristocratic concern. What happens when the line of descent is broken? Once a dynasty ends, it is nearly impossible to effect a restoration. The guarantee of an aristocratic order's meaning is its continuity. Whether by making art in the grand manner of the tradition or, paradoxically, adding their own innovations and power to the avant-garde and sustaining the "tradition of the new," these great artists who were aristocrats found a way to stem the erosion of their authority through works that had permanent resonance in the advance of Modern art and thought.

I

Genius over Genes

THE CIRCLE OF GEORGE SAND, EUGÈNE DELACROIX, FRANZ LISZT, AND FRÉDÉRIC CHOPIN

Accustomed as we are to the central courtyard of the Louvre being filled with long lines of bored tourists inching their way toward I. M. Pei's glass pyramid, imagine a quieter and more intriguing scene in 1848. It is just after noon, and bright sunshine fills a corner of what is today known as the Richelieu wing. A uniformed attendant snaps out a billowing white cloth and drapes it over a small round table as another sets out glasses, wine, and silver for a luncheon. The minister of propaganda of the Eleventh Provisional Government will hold a tête-à-tête with his most trusted counsel. Moments later, arching their backs to shake off the effects of the feverishly paced morning at their desks inside, Alphonse de Lamartine and George Sand emerge from the massive, ornate doorways at each end of the courtyard to share lunch, sunshine, and fresh air. To the accompaniment of the cooing of pigeons, they spend their brief (occasionally extended) break talking of the poetry of Robert Browning, their favorite Latin prose stylists, a recent painting by Delacroix that alludes to a Rubens canvas inside, a new play by Sand's protégé, Alfred de Vigny, at the Comédie Française. Too soon the time arrives for them to resume their work on the tense task of holding together a deeply divided interim government.

For all its brevity, the moment has its undying significance. It draws together the arts and politics, history and the avant-garde, man and woman, the empire and the republic, in one vibrant meeting of the minds. Here is a glimpse of the republic of philosopher-kings worthy of Plato, when the daughter of one of the most distinguished Bourbon families, alongside Zola and Flaubert one of the leading novelists and critics of the day, occupies a seat of power in a government headed by another, if lesser, aristocrat, capable of holding his own in an informed discussion of the notoriously difficult avant-garde poetry of Browning or the equally daunting work of Delacroix—the leading artists in the corridors of power, holding office and incorporating their political ideas into their art. Sand wielded authority in a way that anticipates the role played in our time by Václav Havel in Czechoslovakia, Carlos Fuentes, Mario Vargas Llosa in Peru, or that nearly assumed by the conductor Kurt Masur in East Germany. When she became minister, Sand had been one of the most closely read correspondents for *Le Figaro*, a behind-the-scenes instigator who was eventually persuaded to step onstage. She was born to lead. Her family history is filled with many stories that are chapters of the nation's history, and public service is part of the code of honor. On the other hand, in what we call the private sector, she was born to write, to be a leader of the avant-garde and a thinker on the aesthetic issues of the moment, an arbiter of taste and a literary voice of such originality that, along with Flaubert, she ushered in Modernism in French fiction. Such duality epitomizes the involved leadership that this study celebrates.

This was a time and place when four of the world's greatest artists gathered daily in deed, in thought, and in love. Florence in the age of Raphael, Elizabethan London, and Paris during the 1840s basked in the excitement of an excess of talent. In a typical day the early-rising Eugène Delacroix would begin setting out his palette with the morning light flowing through the skylight of his studio at the rue Notre Dame de Lorette (later, the Rue Furstenberg and now more closely identified with the artist because it is the site of a museum dedicated to him). He might be partway through an intricate passage laden with rich colors when his servant announces a visit from Sand, her head and hand still aching from writing until four in the morning under the spell of the strong coffee she habitually brewed from eleven the night before into the wee hours (when her children were asleep and the reams of fiction flowed with enviable ease). In another hour or so, not far from Madame Sand's apartments, Franz Liszt completes his morning prayers and braves the ugly temper of the Countess Marie D'Agoult, whose many children are making too much noise for him to play or compose. It will not be for at least two hours, usually after one in the afternoon, that he will be able to take his carriage across town to the beautiful rooms of his dear friend Frédéric Chopin. At the moment, Chopin, having returned from the salon of the Countess Delfina Potocka or some other grande dame at four in the morning, is still sleeping.

Liszt will be among the first people, after his Polish servant, that Chopin sees that day. The two take turns at the big, specially tuned Pleyel piano, or they play duets, with Chopin taking the bass part, trying out passages from each other's most recent compositions, discussing harmony or gossiping about Sand or Delacroix, either one of whom is likely to stop in at any moment. By evening, all four friends are united at one salon or another, where Sand will hold forth on politics and the latest popular novel, Delacroix will be asked his opinion of an addition to the art collection, and Liszt and Chopin will be prevailed upon to play. Their improvisations will enchant the nobility of Europe until well past midnight, offering glimpses of music's future in wild passages that never make it to the printed page—at which point Chopin and Delacroix will cab it home together, talking of Mozart, while Sand and Liszt drift their separate ways with a word of encouragement for projects in progress.

Many of those works would take as their subject matter the memorable phrases, images, and expressions that were the daily priceless gifts of these artists to one another. For example, Delacroix's painting *Lelia Mourning over Stenio's Body* (1839) is based on a scene in Sand's novel *Stenio*. It depicts a former courtesan who retired to a convent (as Sand did, at the behest of her family) after becoming disenchanted with her wayward lover, the poet Stenio. The dramatic high point of the novel, depicted by Delacroix, is the moment when Lelia sees the recovered corpse of Stenio, who, after seducing her sister, has drowned himself. It is one of Delacroix's dark, brooding works, small in scale and dramatic in its Caravaggesque balance between the morose shadow and the white of Lelia's habit and Stenio's shirt. Sand, in turn, fed the endless maw of her writing (seventy novels in all, volumes of autobiography) with the offhand comments and artistic exploits of her three friends.[1] For their part, Liszt and Chopin (well before their breakup and the serialization of *Lucrezia Horiani* in *Le Courier Français* in August 1847) took comfort and inspiration in the company of Sand and Delacroix—in Chopin's case, relying upon her in part as a nursemaid. The source materials stemmed from the work of their friends, but the specifics of this influence are more easily lost in the abstraction of music. Friendship as lively and close as this depends upon shared views and experiences. In the case of these illustrious figures, the adhesive by which they were bonded seems an equal mixture of art and aristocracy. Without doubt, the former takes precedence in the formation of their identities both severally and as a group, but the mutual attunement is unquestionably based upon their respect for one another as equals on a social level as well.

Too bad they weren't. Sand had by far the bluest blood, directly related as she was to both the Bourbon kings and the most distinguished family of Berry. Liszt's parents, both of whom died when he was quite young, were far less grand, but he was brought up in the belief that he was a minor aristocrat and certainly maintained this fantasy by association or liaison, particularly through his long-term relationship with the Countess d'Agoult, directly followed by the Princess Sayn-Wittgenstein. With both Chopin and Liszt we enter the nebulous world of Polish and Hungarian titles, to which both exercised their claim, though in truth, under remarkably similar circumstances, the fathers of both were closer to royal retainers than royalty itself. Delacroix was the least aristocratic by the criterion of genealogy but reputedly the illegitimate son of Talleyrand, to whom he bore a strong resemblance and, his detractors sniped, also to whom he owed many of his earliest state commissions. In person, the dandies Chopin and Delacroix would strike twentieth-century observers as the most noble of the four in bearing and mien, whereas the rough-and-ready, democratic Sand would be far more difficult to pinpoint as a noblewoman, except on those occasions when she brought her upbringing and school training to bear on impressing someone who needed a reminder that she was a direct descendant of the Marechal de Saxe. On one such occasion, dressed fashionably in the colors of the Polish court rather than in the man's suit with cigar she famously sported most of the time, she captivated the fancy of Chopin for the first time.

This was a gang of four that wielded practical power in the art world of their time, able with a biting comment or gentle push to sink or elevate some young talent aspiring to the stage they shared or relegate an enemy to the chilly cellar of conformity and obscurity. Sand exercised tremendous influence upon the main publishing houses of Paris, partly by virtue of her own popularity. As a best-selling author she could terrorize her editors into taking on the work of younger writers, such as her lover (before Chopin), the aristocratic Alfred de Musset. Paris was publishing's French-language center and also a small world. By throwing her weight around, Sand could see to it that a work would be accepted, and then promote it as a reviewer and often-quoted salon guest whose opinion not only found its way into print on the hot-blooded literary gossip pages but circulated with astonishing rapidity through word of mouth. She was a cross between the elitist Tina Brown and the mass-market Oprah Winfrey. Given her penchant for thin, elegant cigars, had she lived in our time, one can easily imagine her gracing the cover of *Cigar Aficionado* magazine or, given her political smarts, *George*.

Sand was anything but sentimental, and it is precisely the Modernist edge that makes Sand and her circle of avant-garde cohorts so interesting today. Along with her championship of the cynical, penetrating fiction of Musset, her friends also held the gate open to avant-garde art and music.

Without Liszt's tireless support, it is safe to say, the ascent of Wagner would have been halted in its earliest phase. Many in the art world of Paris at the time knew the benefits of Delacroix's teaching and championship. His efforts on behalf of Corot, whose silvery harmonies now seem so much more staid than the wild essays in bright tones of his proponent, offer one example of how the all-important state purchases for museums could be guided by the advocacy of a well-placed and opinionated artist. Between their teaching and performance practice, Liszt and Chopin shaped the next generation of pianists and their literature.

Sand, Delacroix, Chopin, and Liszt were among the jeunesse dorée of the era, keenly aware of the waning of their families' power over political history and at the same time the waxing of their own ability to alter the course of art history. But Paris in their day was not lacking in leadership in the arts. It was a magnet for significant figures, and the gang of four was often joined in their adventures by Victor Hugo, Honoré de Balzac, Dumas (*père et fils*), St. Beuve, Stendhal, Madame de Staël, the aristocratic Goncourt brothers, Lamartine, Heinrich Heine, Hector Berlioz, Robert Schumann, Felix Mendelssohn, Vincenzo Bellini, Gioacchino Rossini, and a bevy of aristocratic patrons, as well as others, such as the Rothschilds, who aspired to aristocratic status. At the center of all this was Sand. Prolific on the page and tireless in conversation, she had an opinion about everything and frequently incorporated her polemics into her fiction. Balzac would arrive at her apartment with bags of groceries to cook up a storm and talk long into the night about literature and writing. Others stayed until morning, including, in the spring of 1833, the younger, aristocratic Musset, whose literary success came at a tender age, partly through her support. As with Chopin, he was eight years younger than Sand. Her novel *Elle et Lui* is a thinly disguised account of the course of their love. They created a scandal by living together at her place, where he drew as she wrote. Another lover was the playwright Alfred de Vigny, also an aristocrat, who then pursued Marie Dorval, later reputed to be another lesbian lover of Sand.

As her romantic inclinations suggest, for all her advocacy of the rights of the *demos* and her Romantic inclination to side with the wisdom of the peasants of Berry, Sand was a patrician through and through. She was of the ancien régime, too, though when Napoleon III made himself emperor in 1851, as hypocritical as it may seem, she supported him for the simple reason that he had been a personal friend for decades.[2] This emblem of the raw strength of Modern feminism drew her distinguished lineage from her father and her resourcefulness from her Parisian mother. Her mother was both a pathetic and somewhat comic figure in her story. Having married into one of France's foremost families, she, in turn, suspected the fortune-hunting motives of the Baron Casimir Dudevant when he courted and married her daughter Aurore (George Sand's real name). Her suspicions were unfounded as he had not only a title (not quite so exalted) but a vast inheritance, and his Gascon estate may have been nominally bigger than her own. The reason for maternal caution? Though she came from a lower-middle-class background, she was aware that few families in France could claim such an impressive line. Sand's great-great-grandfather was Augustus II, king of Poland and the (illegitimate) next of kin to Charles X and Louis XVIII. He was descended from the Marechal de Saxe, France's most splendid military hero of the eighteenth century, immortalized in the histories of Carlyle and others.

The most colorful guide to this majestic family oak is Sand herself. In *The Story of My Life*, Sand gathers letters, military citations, and excerpts from her own work interlaced with her opinionated accounts of her life and times, into a five-hundred-page encomium to her forebears. It is racy and readable and makes fascinating side-by-side reading with Bertrand Russell's distinctly similar project about his family, *The Amberley Papers*. As with Russell's loving but not uncritical genealogy, she blends humor with history, humility with honor. It is clear from her own account why Sand, as writer and in person, was at ease in every situation and in all conversations, whether with high or low: "The blood of kings was mixed in my veins with that of the poor and lonely," she writes, not without a certain pride.[3] This becomes the point of departure for a foresighted philosophical meditation on the plural nature of her ancestry. A point of resentment, even anger, in the autobiography as in the novels (particularly *Mauprat*) is the centrality of patrimony to patrician lineage. Would this have been different had her mother been the bearer of the aristocratic genes? At least we can conclude that her keen awareness of the peaks and valleys of her own family background, as well as personal experience, blessed her with a gift for creating characters representing all the strata of European society:

> What constitutes each one of us is the result of a mixture, or a parity, of bloodlines, and the continuation, ever modified, of a succession of types that are likened to one another, so I have always concluded that the principle of natural heredity, which pertains to body and soul, was grounds for a sufficiently important bond between each one of us and of our ancestors. . . . For we all have ancestors, high and low, plebeian and patrician; ancestors signifies *patres*, that is to say, a succession of fathers, for the word is not used in the singular. It is amusing that the nobility has appropriated this word to its own advantage, as though the artisan and peasant are presumed not to have any lineage, as though one could not bear the sacred title of

father without having a coat of arms, as if legitimate forefathers would indeed be found more commonly in one class than another.[4]

As a preface to a full hundred pages on the exploits of the Marechal de Saxe, her most famous forebear, there is a splendid ambiguity in this passage. Its bitter tone with regard to the proprietary insolence of the aristocracy is matched by a reverence for the significance of lineage so pious that it is clear that Sand's sense of who she was had to have been molded by it. She converts this ethically into an uncharacteristically stiff (and, given her own marital track record, somewhat ironic) panegyric to what some now call "family values." She laments the way the nobility "hoards for the benefit of a class of rich and powerful people the sacredness of family, a principle which must be dear to all mankind."[5] As she continues, the intellectual and political history of France unfolds in personal terms, a story that her family influenced deeply and directly. She recounts it using the lens of one central notion: "Just now a truth has come to me, which is that the idolatrous cult of family is false and dangerous, but that respect and solidarity in the family are necessary. . . . The philosophers of the eighteenth century upset the cult of nobility, the Revolution overthrew it, but the religious ideal of the family disappeared in this destruction, and the people who had suffered from hereditary oppression, the people who laughed at blazons, got used to regarding themselves solely as the sons of their works. In this the people were mistaken, for they have their ancestors just as kings do. Each family has its nobility, its glory, its titles—work, courage, virtue or intelligence."[6]

Down from the pulpit of these exhortations to domestic virtue, Sand's autobiography strikes a chord when she moves from the distant exploits of the marechal to the intimacy of her account of her grandmother Aurore, known as "La Konigsmarch," for whom she was named. Although the Sand legend has dwelled on the hard-riding, cigar-smoking, and sexually predatory figure of the novelist in man's clothing, it is fascinating to read this adoring portrait of Aurore von Konigsmarch, who made an indelible impression upon Sand with her talent at the harpsichord, accompanying herself singing works by Pergolesi and others, though the instrument was usually out of tune and one of her hands was paralyzed with arthritis. Her encomium to her grandmother, friend of Voltaire and Buffon, portrays a lady who knew Rousseau well enough to call him "the sublime bear" and recounts a comical story from family lore of how he stole from the family orchard. Sand clearly emulated her character and degree of accomplishment: "She had that large manner, that unadorned simplicity, that purity of taste and distinguished pronunciation, that no one has any more, that no longer exist today."[7] Two comparisons come to mind: Delacroix, in a passage from his *Journal* (to be examined below), extolling the "elegance" of the good old days, and Russell in his autobiography, also admitting how completely enamored he was of his noble maternal grandmother. In nostalgic moments like this, the artist tips his or her hand, revealing an abiding faith in the grace of an admired style. It happens to be the mode of the genuine aristocrat from a bygone era.

Later in her autobiography, Sand snipes at the hopeless efforts of actors and the nouveau riche to acquire "that large manner" and bridles against her own predicament in being sent to a convent school where other countesses and baronesses in training were taught manners. It would have been rather like the Swiss prep schools for wayward billionaires' daughters in our own time, except that Sand received a first-rate education, particularly in the arts. Precisely because she knew from delightful afternoons at the decrepit harpsichord of her grandmother what noble manners were, she can smell an imposter a mile away: "Conventional manners were an item of such great importance in the lives of members of the old high society that today's actors mimic them only with much difficulty, despite their studies. I have met some of these old, graceful beings, and I can only say that, regardless of their male and female admirers, I have seen nothing more ridiculous or less pleasing. . . . Gracefulness, as conceived before the Revolution—acquired grace, in other words—was the torture of my early years."[8] It takes an expert, who lives in that world, to tell the fake. As in the case of Hofmannsthal, who shaded his characters with his intimate knowledge of what is good form among aristocrats and in that way gave them a three-dimensionality that many caricatures of the nobility lack in twentieth-century drama, one of the strengths of Sand as novelist was the authenticity of her characterization and the sure powers of observation that made the details in her encounters so right. Because she knew the nobility firsthand, she got them right on the page. Although Sand maintained later in life that the convent years were among her favorite ("I was happier in the convent than anywhere else for there, as no one really knew the details of anyone else's past, no one could speak to anyone else about what would probably become of them"),[9] she complained of the silliness of rigorous training in differences among greetings—for example, of a princess, a duchess, a marquise, a countess, a vicomtesse, a baroness, or the wife of a judge. On the other hand, her ten-by-six-foot cell had a splendid view of Paris and a Louis XV gold harp, and the chapel altar boasted a Titian. No wonder she kissed the convent wall as she left.

At the outset of the memoir she takes aim at the gossips and critics who portray her as the spoiled child of a rich noble family, pointing out that, had they done their homework, they would have been aware of the illegitimate children on her father's side and the struggle with poverty on her mother's: "I especially suspect my foreign biographers of an aristocratic bias, for they have all bestowed on me (those who ought to have been better informed) an illustrious origin while ignoring a very visible stain on my blazon."[10] In the eyes of critic Germaine Bree, the pattern of Sand's life was set in her teens, when she shuttled as mediator between the patrician, solid, and artistic example of her grandmother and her unstable, unsophisticated but streetwise mother, for whom she became a guardian and support.[11] Attracted to younger men all her life (the magic number seems to have been eight, as both Musset and Chopin were eight years her junior), she would often find herself trapped as the supporting central pillar in intergenerational family groups, notably with Chopin and her two problem-plagued children.

Well before she became a famous novelist, Sand temporarily left the family estate at Nohant to make her way in Paris on her own. For those accustomed to thinking of Sand in terms of the blazing literary star she became, the means she contrived to earn income will come as a surprise. She began painting decorative wooden boxes. At first she went to Paris only to pick up new materials and sell the finished wares. She began visiting the museums during these business trips. This artisan, painting every day and trained in music both at school and by her grandmother, began to feel the tug of a vocation. It is no wonder she could become the intimate friend and respected colleague of Delacroix, Chopin, and Liszt. She knew the fundamentals of their métiers, such as the mixing of paint, the tuning of an instrument, the copying of masterworks of the past they revered. From the troubling contradictions of her dual existence as commoner and courtier, a path of clarity and fulfillment opened. From this point on, an identity of honor and distinction was hers for the choosing, to be earned by hard work and backed by talent. She would be an artist. Her memory of the visits to the paintings of Titian, Tintoretto, and Rubens clearly shows how this change came about:

> I began to be singularly moved. I would contemplate, I would submit, I would be transported into a new world. At night I would see parading before me all those great faces which, at the hand of the masters, took on the seal of spiritual authority. It is in beautiful painting that one senses what life is, as in a splendid summation of the shape and expression of beings and things too often obscured or blurred by the movement of reality and by the judgement of one who contemplates them. . . . The universe was revealed to me. I saw into the present and the past at the same time. I was becoming a classicist and a romantic, simultaneously, with no knowledge of what that feud signified. The world of truth surged forth through all my own fantasies and all the ignorance of my own viewing.[12]

The rapturous language of the conversion experience, along with her protestations of innocence commingled with omniscience, brings Sand closer to us than in most of her fiction. From this point on, princes and barons defer to artists, whether painters, musicians, or writers (these distinctions seemed to trouble Delacroix, Liszt, and Chopin more, judging from their letters and journals). Genius triumphs over genes in the shaping of her career and her brilliant alliances. The proof, of course, is in the fiction. The voice of Sand was as intimidating as her productivity. The following passage from her last novel, *Marianne*, was much beloved of Flaubert. It presents the reverie of the character Pierre, the countryman. There are echoes here of Milton's Satan, for whom "the mind is its own place." The reverence with which that character was held by Byron and others who helped shape the Romanticism of Sand and her circle should make the allusion seem quite natural:

> "What I must guard against is daydreaming," he said to himself. "Lost in my own imagination I evaporate like mist in the sun. When I manage to express my delight in things, I am happy. So why should the same not apply to suffering, if I were to try and express it today? For I am indeed suffering, the devil knows why. And I could continue to do so for a very long time to come without ever discovering the reason why. Out of the clouds! Consciousness emerge! Let us see things for what they are! If I can formulate something then it must exist. If it turns out to be nothing, it will disappear!" Musing thus, Pierre sharpened his pencil, opened his notebook and, sitting on the grass in the shade of the willows and the alder, wrote as follows: . . .[13]

The next chapter opens with a writing sample, Pierre's spontaneous and eventually abortive attempt to capture sensation in its immediacy. Like the letters between Flaubert and Sand, the focus is on the act of writing and its difficulties as well as the slippery nature of language. As with much of this rapidly paced novel, with its short chapters and brief encounters, furtive glances of love and longer meditations on desire, the reflexive mode predominates, and that is precisely why it has such a Modern feel. In this brief meditation, Pierre is leading himself toward catharsis. The process will be part thinking, part writing. It is wonderful and ironic that at this point in her life Sand, for whom the writing of fiction (not letters, by the way) was seemingly effortless, was engaged in an important correspondence with Flaubert, for whom it was, famously, torturous. For Chopin at the piano and Sand at the writing desk, the transfer of thought to art was so rapid, seamless, and fluent that a passage like this, however refined in an editing process or touched up later by scholarly editors, closes the gap between writer and reader. They were the two masters of the impromptu performance.

Sand's gimlet eye for the nuances of class distinction is one of the strengths of *Horace*, a novel that has the wit of a painting by Manet brought to life. It is a tale of the demimonde told through the eyes of an aristocrat who is training to be a doctor and passes the time closely observing, not always dispassionately, the nineteen-year-old Horace, based closely on Sand's former lover and coauthor, Jules Sandeau. The early fiction they wrote together, with Sand shouldering the main burden of the writing, led to her adapting his name for her pseudonym. The fictional Horace has learned all he knows about love through the novels of Hugo, Jules Janin, and other Romantics. At least he's well read. Part of the impossibility of his situation is due to pretense, for Horace subscribes to the aristocratic tastes of the time and is in fact a bit ahead of the fashion. He prefigures the dandies of the next generation. They were known as *les incroyables*—self-styled imitations of aristocratic trendsetters. Baudelaire and Villiers de L'isle Adam were literary copies of the fashionable and highly public nobility of the generation before. Sand's character is all the more Modern for being the first in a close series of stepping-stones to an archetypal role of today's art scene. The progression is laid out in Susan Sontag's seminal essay, "Notes on 'Camp,'" in which she writes, "Detachment is the prerogative of an elite; and as the dandy is the nineteenth century's surrogate for the aristocrat in matters of culture, so Camp is the modern dandyism. Camp is the answer to the problem: how to be a dandy in the age of mass culture."[14] Just to turn this back to Sand, there is no question that her early inklings of what an "age of mass culture" might be like are written into her work and certainly are part of the fabric of her high-profile life, a figure at whom tourists from England and the United States would gawk and write home about as well as the strategist behind the interim government's publicity machine. She would have found camp completely understandable and could have made a superb novel on the theme.

One of the preoccupations of Sand's biting portrait of her former lover Sandeau in *Horace* is his insistence on being seen on the town with Marthe, his beautiful but reluctant *grisette*, and part of his downfall is his ridiculous addiction to haute couture, as his tailor's bills are a major factor in his financial ruin. Sand sacrifices him as a sympathetic character in part as a critique of false pretensions to aristocracy, which betray the artificer who tries too hard to imitate the outward trappings of nobility without the support of breeding, education, valor, or a sense of honor. He wounds others and himself, and in his ignorance as well as selfishness he misses the surest way to redemption. In what is recognizable as her own impassioned voice, Sand reveals her view of the novelist's dual function as progressive and protector of the best the past has to offer: "Without our even realizing it, literature performs its miracles. It revives the poetry of former days; and, putting to rest in the past all that had been for intellectuals of the past the object of just criticism, it brings to us, like a forgotten perfume, the unrecognized riches of a taste that is no longer open to discussion, since it no longer reigns arbitrarily. Art, although it poses as egotistical ('art for art's sake'), creates progressive philosophy without realizing it. It makes its peace with the mistakes and shortcomings of the past, to preserve, as in a museum, the monuments of its conquest."[15] Sand, along with her circle, is customarily classified as a Romantic writer, yet this passage takes on one of the seminal ideas of the aesthetics of the next century and, rather than conservatively refuting it, raises the stakes a notch by looking ahead to another Modern principle, the selective use of the past. While Sand's life has long been a convenient nineteenth-century example of the proto-feminist, her work also merits consideration for its aesthetic prescience.

Among those who listened in the evenings as Sand read the manuscript of *Horace*, nodding in approval as he recognized the real people being skewered under fictive guises, was Eugène Delacroix. As with Sand, although on a far less exalted scale, the story of Delacroix's life follows a parabolic course through cycles of prosperity, belt-tightening, and self-made success. He was born into elegance and prosperity, living his happy early childhood years in the splendor of various diplomatic residences offered by the government to his father, Charles (1741–1805), who was ambassador plenipotentiary to the Netherlands, then minister of foreign affairs, and eventually prefect of Marseilles, Bouches-du-Rhone, and the Gironde. Living in grand style thanks to the perks of high office, the prefect also accumulated vast real estate holdings, specifically the better part of the forest of Boixe near Angoulême.

Then, as so often happens in families whose fortunes swing with the winds of historic change, it all came tumbling down. His father died in November 1805, when Eugène was seven, but the real calamity struck nine years later when his mother died (she was the daughter of Jean-François Oeben, the renowned *maître-ébéniste* and cabinetmaker to Louis XV and the marquise de Pompadour). It was then disclosed that the father's land and investments, supposedly worth 800,000 francs, were mortgaged to the hilt and undermined by the pilfering of his attorney, Jean Pierre Louis Bouders. The estate was left with a debt of 175,000 francs. Hounded by creditors, his mother had been living on a modest pension as well as the annuity from her license to a tobacco shop, unable to pay down the debt. Delacroix became part of his elder sister Henriette's household, and although her husband Raymond de Verninac, a diplomat and former ambassador to Turkey, was generous, Delacroix was penniless as he started his career as a student in the studio of Pierre-Narcisse Guerin at the Ecole des Beaux-Arts. Henriette and her brother Charles-Henry overcame the effects of this early tribulation. Charles-Henry rose to the rank of general and became a baron de l'Empire. Another brother, Henri, was killed at the battle of Friedland in 1807.

Once on his own, Delacroix turned both aspects of his childhood—its polish and gentility as well as the cunning and grit learned from hardship—to full advantage. On the one hand, after a bitter taste of financial ruin he was driven by the fear of its recurrence to work hard and cultivate a successful career by whatever means lay at hand. On the other, he had been fortunate enough to grow up in a milieu that prepared him to hold his own gracefully in society, and he parlayed these skills and his exalted connections to attain, as did Chopin and Liszt, a station beyond that entitled him by his birth. Indeed, all four of these great figures stood outside conventional class and national distinctions, which is why their artistic identity as a group became so important to them. In each other's society they were assured acceptance, and the public role of artist raised them significantly from their origins.

They happened to live in a period when the transfer of power from the hands of the aristocrats—whose claim to power was land, from which displaced figures such as Liszt and Chopin, as well as Delacroix through bankruptcy, were cut off—was swinging them toward other qualifications for leadership. From politics and even social domination, they moved into cultural and intellectual roles, using the publicity they commanded to build a platform for their views. When it came to the ideas their art conveyed, we're right back to the theme of nobility through the ages, beginning with public service and nationhood. Chopin in his polonaises, Liszt in his Hungarian dances and ecstatic tone poems on themes of power, Sand in *Marianne* (the very emblem of France), and Delacroix, of course, in his mural commissions as well as the iconic *Liberty Leading the People* were all involved in the promotion of the culture toward which they felt deep responsibility and a special tie. They join Hofmannsthal, who celebrated the glories of imperial Austria, in this regard, as well as Yeats in his devotion to Young Ireland. While Modern art is customarily viewed as a turning away from this kind of rhetoric, inward to private visions, there is and will always be a public arena for art; and certainly Sand and her circle ushered in the Modern approach to national themes in an age when the innocence of propaganda was wrecked.

The Delacroix family's reputation in diplomatic circles was already sufficient to bring him a number of Bonapartist patrons, but, like Chopin and Sand, he could play both sides of the Legitimist coin. Whispers of the connection to Talleyrand counted for much. Later in life he would be unfailingly generous to emerging artists whose work met his standards, but at the start of his career he relied upon the network through which state acquisitions were determined. A dear friend, Adolphe Thiers, became minister of the interior in 1832, guaranteeing access to the circles of power involved in public commissions. Then Frédéric Villot, another friend, became curator of paintings at the Louvre. The private support of the nobility also helped. Delacroix's early supporters included the duc de Moray, Napoleon III's half brother, who commissioned him on more than one occasion at a time when his major paintings brought him between 30,000 and 35,000 francs. He was also a favorite of the duc d'Orleans, who bought *The Murder of the Bishop of Liège* and *The Jewish Wedding in Morocco*. The duchesse de Berry, a close associate of Sand, bought *King Jean at the Battle of Poitiers* (although she and the artist never did agree upon a fair price), and the duc de Fitz-James bought *Milton and His Daughters* straight from the Salon of 1827–28. Through Chopin, Delacroix gained the patronage of Count Tyszkiewicz and Count Grzymala.

Every up-and-coming artist and critic ought to be required to read Delacroix's rich, opinionated journals, not just for inspiration but for historical insight and guidance in the responsibilities and joys of being an artist. In addition to being piercing analyses, they are full of accounts of amusing encounters with the aristocracy, mostly elevated by thoughtful commentary on a painting he had seen in a palace or a piece of music he had heard at a salon. On 9 April 1856, Delacroix recorded an idea that occurred to him at the salon of Countess D'Houssonville, immortalized in a painting, now at the Frick Collection in New York, by his rival Ingres. After listening to Gounod and Mozart as sung by Pauline Viardot, his friend Bertin commented that the music was beyond the popular taste. Delacroix took exception:

> In periods like ours the public develops a love for details because modern works of art make people accustomed to look for subtleties everywhere. And contrary to what Bertin says, if you wish to please public taste, this is not the moment to paint on broad sweeping lines; this should be reserved for those infinitely rare minds who rise above the level of public demand, and still draw their nourishment from beauty as it was understood in the great periods of art; in short, for those who still love beauty, that is to say, simplicity. Yet we need pictures painted on broad sweeping lines. Works of art have this quality in primitive periods. The root of my idea is the need to belong to one's own period.[16]

The circle of Sand endlessly debated this question of the relative standing of their own age and its artists vis-à-vis the greats of the past. The phrase *enfant du siècle*, after all, is Musset's, and in a certain specific sense each of them corresponds to it. When Delacroix underscores "the need to belong to one's own period," he anticipates Rimbaud's injunction, "It is necessary to be absolutely Modern." It would seem to contradict implicitly the anachronistic or retrospective inclination of many of the artists considered in this study, most notably Puvis, Leighton, Balthus, and Hofmannsthal, who fashioned their aesthetic according to their valorization of past masters. But it is not the final word in Delacroix's journals on the subject. On the one hand, rejecting the stuffy academicism and low-brow sentimentalism of their time was a launching point for becoming Modern, in that it compelled them to find an original and powerful art that upheld their ideals. On the other hand, Delacroix in particular deplored the decline of art since the sixteenth century and, along with Flaubert, was adamant in his belief that the bourgeoisie were leading France down a path to philistinism. As wildly different from the hyper-English Pre-Raphaelites as Delacroix seems (on canvas his free-flowing style is certainly at odds with their tightness), his reading of art history can be strikingly similar. It also resembles the siege mentality one sees in Hofmannsthal and Balthus, that is taken for an elitist view. One wonders whether Delacroix and Chopin, who revered eighteenth-century music in particular and, like Stravinsky, was closely connected in sensibility to both Mozart and the Baroque, ever argued this point. Consensus on one issue was easier: All four in the Sand circle shared a sense of being on a mission that left them with an agonizing dilemma: How does one aim high, even to the dream of perfection, in a time of decay?

A buzzword in this vital discussion was "elegance." An aesthetic criterion not often invoked in our time, "elegance" (like Russell's "luxury") is naturally germane to aristocracy and art. Reflecting on the opera *The Secret Marriage* by Cimarosa,[17] Delacroix wrote that it was "not a higher state of perfection, but perfection itself. No other musician has this symmetry, this expressiveness and sense of the appropriate, this gaiety and tenderness and, above all, this all-pervading leaven that enhances the other qualities—incomparable elegance; elegance in expressing tender sentiments, elegance in humor, elegance in the gentle pathos that characterizes the opera."[18] Despite all the clichés about the messy Romantic tempest within which Delacroix was supposed to have lived, it is vital to understand that for him, as for his three dear friends, the recognition of genuine taste, of this essential elegance, was foremost, even to the point where Delacroix wore it like a mask to conceal inner anger. It is in their art and in their lives, down to the fastidious taste in haute couture of

Chopin and Delacroix and the elaborate, not to say palatial, households maintained by Liszt. They detected this refinement in others, or its lack, and carried it into their own work and lives because they had been brought up within its embrace.

It was also part of the motivation, along with the economic incentives involved in being seen in the right salons by prospective patrons, for participating in the social scene. Many of the most valuable aesthetic insights in the *Journal*, penned after long nights in the salons, involve taste, style, and manner and their relationship to elegance. In one almost comic entry, dated 20 February 1852, we are invited to conjure the image of the bored Delacroix turning his back on the glitterati to concentrate on a painting by Dürer: "The same mob of stupid people, worse music and bad pictures on the walls—except one, a nude man by Albrecht Dürer which held my attention the whole evening. This unexpected discovery, and Delsarte's singing at Bertin's the night before, made me reflect that there is a great deal to be said for going into society, exhausting though it is and futile though it may appear at the time."[19]

They could be snobs, too, and class consciousness is an element in the *Journal*. The tone is all in this account of a visit from the already popular Millet on 16 April 1853:

> They brought Millet to my studio this morning. He spoke of Michelangelo and the Bible which, he says, is almost the only book he reads. This explains the rather pretentious look of his peasants. Moreover, he is a peasant himself and boasts of it. He belongs to that constellation or crew of bearded artists who made the revolution of 1848 or encouraged it, thinking, apparently, that it would bring equality of talent as well as equality of wealth. But Millet himself seems to me to be above this level, and the small number of rather similar paintings by him which I have seen show a deep, if pretentious, feeling struggling to reveal itself through an execution that is either dry or confused."[20]

The barbed comments reveal Delacroix weighing Millet's talent and behavior in a balance that is kept honest by his admiration, however reserved, for the work. Delacroix's evenhanded treatment of other artists and friends is a notable aspect of the *Journal*, which occasionally reads like the infamous *Diaries* of Andy Warhol that deflated so many reputations upon their publication in 1989. Even Sand is not immune: "These writers are all alike. Even poor Aurore shares the same faults among her other valuable qualities. Neither of them works, but not because they are ideal. They do not know how to work, that is to say, they cannot prune, condense, summarize, and pull their work into shape. The need to write for so much a line will be fatal to stronger talents than theirs. They accumulate capital from the volumes they pile up; it is impossible to make masterpieces."[21] There is a great deal of merit in this observation, however nasty it may seem under the circumstances (Delacroix and Sand were very close at the time). It also leads right to the edge of a theoretical cliff that this study skirts continually, the way in which materialism assails the ideals of the traditional aristocracy. Awkwardly, we'll be back to this later in these pages in a consideration of Degas, who changed his name and started to sell his pastels because suddenly he had to; with Leighton, whose townhouse was an emblem of his career success; with Bacon, who played the art market like a violin; with Russell, whose books were best-sellers; and with Balthus, who at his death had a painting on his easel that he reportedly hoped to sell for over $4 million.

The traditional aristocratic amateur whose love of intellectual pursuits and the arts is unblemished by the need for compensation is only one scenario. The lucky few, like Swinburne and Hofmannsthal, whose family wealth enabled them to forget about the problem of money entirely, are far and away the exception rather than the rule. Taking this momentarily to another time and place, let's glance at a recent observation by a critic whose work in this area is perhaps the most authoritative of our time. Within the context of a study of intellectual and artistic life in Ireland, the Marxist critic Terry Eagleton writes, "Nineteenth-century Ireland is a striking illustration of Karl Marx's dictum that those who dominate the means of material production will also tend to control the means of intellectual production."[22] Sand, Delacroix, and the others mentioned here were successful or wealthy enough to do just that in their time, and one aspect of their modernity is the way in which they wrestled with and redefined the aristocratic view of capitalism and art. Delacroix's comment on Sand is, in fact, hypocritical, given the fantastic success he enjoyed as a public artist. Elsewhere he is even less loyal: "I am fond of her, but I must say that I don't think her work will last. She has no taste."[23]

Delacroix appears far more benevolent and art historically astute in his encounters with Corot. According to his journals, Delacroix visited Corot's studio, already an admirer, in 1847; and the next year, not by coincidence, the work that ended up in the collection of the Musée de Douanier was probably seen on that day. *Le Bain de Berger* was bought out of the Salon of that year, where Corot was awarded the second-class medal. Delacroix also sent Constant Dutilleux to see Corot's work. The wealthy fellow painter from Arras bought one of Corot's pastoral works and became a significant collector and champion, bringing to Corot a devoted circle of artists and collectors (including the painter and photographer Charles Desavary; the collector Adelbert Cuvelier; the painter

Alfred Robaut, author of the catalog of Corot's paintings; and collector Leandre Grandguillaume). The nobility followed. Corot's first aristocratic patron was the duc d'Orleans, who bought two works from the Salon of 1839 for 1,000 francs each.

The duke was also an avid collector of Delacroix (as well as Paul Delaroche and Alexandre Decamp, under the tutelage of the artist Ary Scheffer) and a powerful influence upon the Musée de Metz, which added a Corot to its collection in 1840, and the Musée Calvet in Avignon, which purchased *Site d'Italie* in 1841. In 1848 it became an annual rite for the state to purchase one of his works. Corot's view of Delacroix was brief and picturesque: "He is an eagle; I am a lark" (C'est un aigle et je ne suis qu'une alouette). Of Corot, Delacroix wrote in the *Journal*: "He told me to go a bit ahead of myself, abandoning myself to whatever might come; this is how he works most of the time. He does not accept that one can create beauty by taking infinite pains. Titian, Raphael, Rubens, etc. all painted easily. . . . Notwithstanding the facility, there is still work that is indispensable. Corot delves deeply into a subject; ideas come to him, and he adds while working; it's the right approach."[24]

The emphasis on the improvisatory method, as well as his facility, is not surprising given the fleet company of musical and literary improvisers (Liszt, Chopin, and Sand) with whom Delacroix was running. It is particularly revealing to set the comment about "ideas come to him, and he adds while working" beside the additive enchantment not only of Delacroix himself but particularly of Liszt and the fluvial Sand (who, in the interest of full disclosure, was paid by the word). This is the habit, also, of others in this study, notably the expansive Swinburne, Puvis, and the prolific Russell. It is a leap to infer that there is something inherently aristocratic about this kind of creative process, but in an age when the short lyric poem, brief orchestral or chamber work, and tight interplay between the drawing and the painting prevails, it is notable that so many of these supremely educated, confident creators would produce long or large-scale works from a creative or studio process that flowed and added on with such regularity and ease, so little reflective restraint or destructive backtracking and editing. The economy of diction that, in part thanks to Minimalism, is ascribed to what we consider Modernism, is sacrificed to a different set of aesthetic values that privilege fluidity and scope.

The cardinal compliment paid by Delacroix to Corot is the opening sentence of the journal entry: "Corot est un veritable artiste." In the world of Delacroix and his friends, this was the ticket of admission. Having enjoyed what he had seen in the Salon, Delacroix went to the studio ("Il faut voire un peintre chez lui pour avoir une idée de son merite," a sentiment more art experts of our day ought to share). Beyond the verbal accounts of the mutual influence and admiration, there is compelling visual testimony in the quotation by Corot of Delacroix's *Les Femmes d'Algier dans leur appartement* (painted in 1834 and bought from the Salon by Louis-Philippe, to be displayed at the Musée Luxembourg as well as the Exposition Universelle in 1855 and Delacroix's posthumous retrospective in 1864) in his own *Jeune Algerienne couchée sur la Gazon*, begun in 1871 and completed two years later. While some historians have used photographs and radiographs to indicate that Corot has posed his central figure too differently to represent a direct borrowing from Delacroix, the divided color, splendid red robe, and leopard skin on which the model reposes all attest to a close study of and homage to the earlier work. Like Pound's poetic tribute to Swinburne, to be considered later, or the Mozartean invocations of Hofmannsthal and Strauss, this type of close allusion, parallel both in style and content, is the ultimate homage.

By the time Delacroix had been chosen by Baron Haussmann to serve for ten years on the omnipotent Municipal Council, his life had, enviably, become a continual round of high-minded encounters with great art and its makers. A typical journal entry records an evening of chamber music and fine paintings. He endearingly enjoys a charmed existence:

> What a life I am leading. Such were my thoughts as I listened to the exquisite music and especially to the Mozart where everything breathes the peace of a well-ordered age. At my time of life, the turmoil of violent passions no longer disturbs the delicious sensations that works of art give me. I don't know what it means to have to deal with official papers and cope with boring tasks, as most men do. Instead of thinking about business, I think only of Rubens or Mozart; my chief concern for a whole week is the memory of an aria, or of a picture. I go to my work as other men hurry to their mistress and when I stop, I take with me into the solitude of my home, or abroad when I go in search of distractions, a delightful memory that bears no relation to the lover's uneasy pleasure.[25]

Delacroix's lofty attainments in paint are in many cases spontaneous responses to the stimuli of impassioned encounters with art and artists, not only the distinguished company he kept but, as critics of his work have pointed out, fruitful dialogue with the paintings of Rubens (another example of the statesman-artist) as well as, less frequently mentioned, Titian and Rembrandt. He defied the curé's orders and painted on Sundays at the church of St. Sulpice in order to have the organ and choral music as his direct sustenance. His literary sources were just as exalted, led by the poetry of Byron, which found its most adroit interpreter ever in Delacroix. From 1813, when he painted *The Giaour, a Fragment of a Turkish*

Tale, through other treatments of that poem and *The Bride of Abydos* (1824), to the extravagant and magnificent and, in its day, controversial *Death of Sardanapalus* (1828), which brought official censure to its youthful creator, Delacroix, particularly in his early work, was clearly attuned to Byron's dramatic sense and vigor; and he was determined to bring it alive without the deadening effects of academic ideas, either literary or scholarly. The oddities of spatial effect in *The Death of Sardanapalus*, set on a stage so steeply raked that the figures seem to tumble from the king's vast bed down toward the viewer in a cascade of Michelangesque bodies and colors, is among the unquestionably Modern elements of the work, which had a profound effect upon van Gogh's tilting floors in the interiors he created at Aix. Delacroix was reading Byron while working on his revolutionary *Massacre at Chios* in May 1824, enraptured by the tales of Byron's death the month before at Missolonghi. The circle of Sand had an extraordinary knack for moving from one art to another, but Delacroix and Chopin in particular were capable of moving from text to paint or sound in a seamless, fresh way that sacrificed none of the originality that is usually the price paid for taking another work as a starting point.

Pulling Delacroix into the orbit of Modernism against the gravitational effects of Romanticism is easier once we turn from the history paintings to the studies from nature. Among the most infamous Delacroix images are the fierce beasts locked in mortal combat: lions and leopards dashed onto the canvas with wild flourishes of the brush. Like the angry animals of Francis Bacon's works—the Nazi guard dogs, sullen baboons, and toothy monsters—Delacroix's bestiary tends toward the predatory. The uncertain outcome of encounters between lions and people in his pictures has been viewed by some as part of the artistic strategy of building suspense as well as "a metaphor for Delacroix's acute concern over the precariousness of civilization, his fear that the law of the jungle might prevail over humanity's fragile defense against barbarism."[26] They convey many of the same anxieties that Bacon's rough beasts induce, and it certainly bears remembering that Delacroix created many of these works after being an eyewitness to the carnage in the streets of his beloved Paris during the short-lived revolution of 1848, just as Bacon was assigned the

"idealizations" of the second and third versions, through which he "corrects" the problems of the earliest impression to bring the work closer to the "ideal." As Delacroix put it in a revealing passage from his journal, with specific reference to the "overdetailed execution" of Rubens and the act of painting from a model:

> The execution is applied to a theme that has been realized in imagination; therefore the superabundance of details that slip in as a result of imperfect memory cannot destroy the far more interesting simplicity that was present in the first exposition of the idea. And as we have already seen in the case of Rubens, the frankness of the execution more than compensates for the disadvantage caused by the superabundance of details. If therefore you can introduce into a composition of this kind a passage that has been carefully painted from the model, and can do this without creating utter discord, you will have accomplished the greatest feat of all, that of harmonizing what seems irreconcilable. You will have introduced reality into a dream, and united two different arts.[27]

As Shelley in his "Defense of Poetry" walks the reader through the act of composition, so Delacroix, in 1853, reveals the secrets of his studio practice, which turn out to be close to the spontaneity and experimental spirit of gestural abstraction in the twentieth century. That means either that Delacroix was well ahead of his time—he was—or that all painting shares certain common procedures. As with the Impressionists, who fed upon the precedent set by Delacroix, particularly when it came to color, the closer relationship between palette and canvas as trying-out areas for color combination was already a step in the direction of abstraction. This has been acknowledged by artists we do not hesitate in branding Modern. An unrealized but obsessive project for Cézanne was the "Apotheosis of Delacroix" about which he wrote to Bernard as late as 1904: "Le talent de Redon me plait beaucoup, et je suis de coeur avec lui pour sentir et admirer Delacroix. Je ne sais si ma precaire santé me permettra de réaliser jamais mon rêve de faire son apothéose."[28]

The historical apotheosis of Delacroix was a movement in painting to-art historians to be tremendously important contributions to the development of Modernism. Flower pictures? Of all the tired genres, overrun by amateurs and trampled by the sheer quantity of academic copying, adding tier after tier of nearly identical canvases in the Louvre as well as in museums in Amsterdam, London, Vienna, and elsewhere, it seems the least likely medium for a breakthrough in painting. Yet Delacroix took to the format passionately for experimentation in color and the relationship between figure and ground, two principal compositional issues of early Modernism. When one thinks of the key moments in the careers of masters such as Picasso, Matisse, and Mondrian, they too pivoted upon floral still life painting. Because Delacroix was thoroughly rooted in academic training, there are deliberate references in these paintings to the genre works of Jean-Baptiste Monnoyer, Jan Davidz. De Heem, and Jan van Huysum. Delacroix felt he was creating "a pure classic" and breaking new ground. It is significant that he never sold or gave away any of the flower paintings created in 1848–49, two of which made their debut at the Salon of 1849. They were found in his studio after his death.

The flower paintings were a tribute to the passion for gardening he shared with George Sand and another aristocratic friend (and possibly lover), Josephine de Forget, with whom he "prowled around rose bushes" at his country house at Plombières. Real roses were but the premise, however. The further into the series Delacroix moved, the more painterly and innovative it became, and some scholars speculate that he had in mind a decorative scheme integrating at least three of the canvases—an idea also pursued by van Gogh when he created several brilliantly colored canvases of sunflowers to decorate his house in Arles for the arrival of Gauguin. In poor reproductions or from a distance in museums, the paintings seem conventional and staged, a cross between the Old Masters mentioned above and Delacroix's pallid eighteenth-century predecessors such as Boucher and Fragonard. Close up, they explode in intense colors, such as the loud—and louder still—reds against bright whites of *A Basket of Flowers Overturned in a Park*, surrounded by the dark greens of the background (Delacroix was a keen student of the shadows of Poussin). Aside from playing complementaries against one another (red and green), few combinations of color can be so volatile as a saturated red and a brilliant, undivided white, which is precisely what Delacroix had the sheer guts to place dead center in the painting.

The flower paintings had immediate impact. Even though they were by Delacroix, a Salon perennial and fixture on the art scene, their brazen energy inspired the critics in a way that only a brash newcomer usually does. As Gautier wrote, "This is, quite simply, an orgy of color, a feast for the eyes. What is praiseworthy in these two canvases, aside from the excellence of the color, is the stylistic treatment of the flowers, which are usually treated in a totally botanical fashion, without any regard for their bearing poise, physiognomy, or character. Each flower has its own particular mode of expression, be it gay, sad, silent, noisy, brash, modest, demure, lascivious, open or closed, mild, fierce, unsettling or soothing. They also display specific attitudes, their own special brands of coquettishness or haughtiness—none of which is conveyed by common flower painters concerned with trifles."[29] Even an art historian in 1999, eyes undimmed by all the chromatic fireworks that have burst upon art since Delacroix (the Fauves, glowing clouds of pure pigment from Mark Rothko, the neon of Peter Halley) can scarcely contain his excitement: "Bravura works, they reveal Delacroix's deep-seated ambition to revitalize the genre by means of a kind of realism in which stylistic convention and decoration would serve the contemplation of nature—and not the reverse."[30]

The epitome of bravura is Franz Liszt. A dear friend to Delacroix, his equivalent in sound, Liszt as Modern has his champions in two eminent scholar-pianists, both of them so stodgy of mien that it is difficult to associate them with an avant-garde phenomenon like Liszt. One is Charles Rosen, who places Liszt at the cusp between Romanticism and Modernism. The other, who goes further, is the eminent Alfred Brendel, whose Beethoven sonata series at Carnegie Hall celebrates the rite of canonic interpretation of the Classical piano repertoire. Since the 1970s, Brendel has brilliantly used programming, one of the most formidable weapons in his intellectual arsenal (which includes some of the most inspiring writing to come from a musician since Dietrich Fischer-Dieskau), to make the point that Liszt is not just a proto-Modern or prophet but a Modernist in full. He has juxtaposed, for instance, the Beethoven sonata op. 111 with the six *Klavierstücke* (short pieces for piano) of Arnold Schoenberg and a generous selection of Liszt études and short works. The program underscores Brendel's view of Liszt as an early pantonal composer, not only (in Brendel's words) "the first to depart from the salon"[31] but, as Brendel's predecessor Busoni noted, "the model for all musical fountains that have flowed ever since" (punning on Liszt's "Jeux d'eau à la Villa d'Este"). In Brendel's scholarly eyes, "Almost independently of Wagner's *Tristan* chromaticism, Liszt ushers in the music of the twentieth century."[32]

This is not a casual claim, especially considering the source. The literature that passes through Brendel's fingers guides him to judgments based on the hand, not simply on the reading of scores, the experience of listening, or theory. It proceeds from how Liszt is played to a secure sense of where in history he stands. Brendel's favorite Liszt is, not surprisingly, the most serious, abstract, and eccentric. None of the light party pieces for him. This means the B minor sonata leads the way along with the "Weinen, klagen" variations on Bach and late works, such as the "Mosongi Mihaly" and the études. Brendel bases his approach on fidelity to Liszt's scores, much as one abides by the Beethoven sonatas note by note, rather than attempting to add his own formidable array of effects to the performance in a "Lisztification"[33] of the work, as happens when a "performer pretending to be another Liszt" overdoes it. On today's concert scene, Lisztification is something that happens to many pieces by other composers as well, a shattering of the codes of intentionality that protect composers' stylistic legacies. Brendel advocates scrupulous attention to Liszt's own clarified, later versions of the pieces. The outcome of this measured, text-driven approach is hardly dry, of course. As written, Liszt's works are full of the pyrotechnics and dramatic shifts in key and tempo for which his legendary Mephistophelean image, built upon thorough acquaintance with the example of Paganini, is notorious.

Beyond overcoming the technical barriers Liszt built into the work, through a mastery of technique that unites performer and composer, the next problem posed is that of adhering to the program. Brendel is renowned for following the historical precedent of Liszt's own playing. It sounds ludicrous, given the disparity between the donnish Brendel quietly settling down to play and accounts of the flamboyant Liszt whipping the crowd into a frenzy, but there are other reminiscences of Liszt that must be given their due. According to Borodin, Liszt was an exciting performer (his reputation preceded him—all those tales of swooning women) but also, and this is not so widely known, a careful one. As Borodin wrote in a memoir about the sobriety of Liszt's playing, "His tempi are moderate; he does not push them or become hotheaded."

If this conservatism seems pale against the received image of Liszt the wild smasher of pianos (contemporary accounts, particularly from horrified English critics, deplored his destruction of two keyboards in a single evening), it does gibe with another vital element in the understanding of Liszt's "grosse Stil" (grand style): his nobility. Again, it is Brendel who offers an insight: "I consider it a principal task of the Liszt player to cultivate such scruples and distil the essence of Liszt's nobility."[34]

Arriving conveniently enough, for a study that proposes him as an emblem of power, in the year of both a comet and a continent-convulsing war—1811—Liszt was to the manor born in almost exactly the same way Chopin was. He spent his earliest years on a great estate to which he would not accede as heir. Esterhazy is a magic name in music history, a place where, most famously, Haydn was resident composer, regaling his patrons with weekly symphonies and string quartets. Liszt's father, Adam, was a steward to the patron of Hummel and Cherubini and was a Magyar of noble descent, according to the composer's best biographer,

Sir Sacheverell Sitwell, who knows genealogy and European aristocratic bloodlines from the inside, as a baronet. Adam married an Austrian who had a bishop among her ancestors, rather a salient detail given Liszt's late tendency toward asceticism and his aspiration to be composer laureate of the Vatican (a highly ironic goal in the face of his prodigious erotic experience and the fact that at the time he was living outside marriage with the Princess Sayn-Wittgenstein in Rome). A prodigy, young Liszt was taken to Beethoven in Vienna and anointed as a fellow artist by a kiss. The polyglot, immensely talented young man lived not only during a time of political chaos (the revolution of 1830, plunging his own Hungary into turmoil) but of artistic iconoclasm as well. At age twenty, he fell in with a radical group of composers and soloists that included Berlioz, Paganini, and of course Chopin, who was a year older. They reinvented the composer as performer, adding a fiercely unattainable character to the familiar legacy of Bach, Beethoven, and Mozart. As Lawrence Kramer explains in his enormously influential and powerful book, *Music as Cultural Practice*,

> When it comes to music, we find impossible objects at their most familiar in the form of bravura pieces. The "transcendental" aspect of Romantic virtuosity, the satanic mystique of Paganini and the daemonic/erotic aura of Liszt, derived in part from the sense that these musicians were driven to create works of superhuman difficulty—objects impossible to anyone but them. This makes the identification of the composer/performer as a charismatic, all but indescribable presence essential to the expressive situation. The esthetics of bravura reduces music to sound production. What the audience sees is a theatrical icon of the inspired musician; what it hears is a highly charged extension of the performer's touch, breath, rhythm: the body electric, in Walt Whitman's phrase."[35]

From the start, Liszt showed his genius for role playing, including that of the aristocrat, the scandalous celebrity, and the possessed virtuoso. His youth was spent under the spell of Lord Byron's poetry. He was prepared masterfully for the technical demands of the stage by his teachers, Czerny and Salieri. Liszt was a critical composer at first, making transcriptions and fantasies based on original works by Berlioz, Wagner, Glinka, Gounod, Saint-Saëns, Cui, Dargomijsky, Bach and Beethoven, of course, and Schubert. The list is peculiar because it is so diverse, as though there was not a voice that Liszt could not recapture at the keyboard. Later pieces took works of art by Raphael and Michelangelo, poems by Dante, Petrarch, Byron, and Hugo, or moments along the *Années de pelerinage* for their inspiration. His viable beginning as a Modern can be traced to the first of the *Transcendental Etudes* in 1834, composed in a sequence of twelve that followed the key sequence C major, A minor, F major, D minor, B-flat major, and G minor, dedicated to his master Czerny. Contemporaries began to feel the stirrings of a music of the future, as they had in listening to Wagner, whom Liszt championed. Baudelaire, in *Mon coeur mis à nu*, relished the contradictory nature of Liszt's wild side: "To glorify the worship of images (my great, my only, my primitive passion). To glorify vagabondage and what one might call Bohemianism, the cult of multiplied sensation, expressing itself through music. Refer here to Liszt." His modernity was felt by fellow composers, mainly through its recklessness. In 1911, upon the centenary of Liszt's birth, Bartók praised the "formal confusion" of the Hungarian rhapsodies, and Moscheles wrote of the "chaotic beauties" in his music. He gave the mother tongue to Bartók and to later Hungarians such as Gyorgy Ligeti and Gyorgy Kurtag, who then took it in the direction of Webern. The golden period of his composition, the Weimar years (1848 through 1861), was marked by a strange and unprecedented loosening of mood and the discovery of what might polemically be called the "anti-sonata" in more flexible musical forms that miraculously maintained their unity. Today, with pantonality behind us, it is far easier to pinpoint the ways in which Liszt shaped musical Modernism, as Rosen does so well:

> The attempt of the early nineteenth century to substitute third or mediant relationships for the classical dominant amounted to a frontal attack on the principles of tonality, and it eventually contributed to the ruin of triadic tonality. Musical style is moving from the dissonant passing notes of classical tonality towards the dissonant "passing phrases" (to use Bernard Shaw's excellent term about Strauss's music) of the early twentieth century. Renouncing the force of tonal opposition may eventually have weakened the tonal language, but it did not weaken the music, which in fact had gained a new source of power. . . . The strictly defined hierarchy of diatonic relationships was traded for a new conception of the chromatic continuum, in which a dazzling variety of harmonies could blend with one another in a kaleidoscopic exchange of energy. Many of these later piano works are experimental, foreshadowing the music of Debussy and the atonal composers of the early twentieth century. They cannot have had much influence on these developments, however, since they were essentially private and little known, and the importance of Liszt to history cannot be explained by an appeal to his late style. In any case, even the best of the late works are less impressive than the music of Debussy and Schoenberg to which they appear to point.[36]

Without contradicting as eminent a historian as Rosen, who, like Brendel, has the benefit of performing the works as well as analyzing the scores, there is an aspect of Liszt that deserves further mention. His power as thinker is overshadowed by accounts of his powers as performer. Kramer invokes the *Faust* symphony as a demonstration of the "privileged position of the spectator" and the eroticized "hegemony of the gaze."[37] Considering Liszt's view of his own social position, as well as the company he kept (from the Countess Marie d'Agoult to the Princess Sayn-Wittgenstein, just to mention the amorous side), this view from on high is biographically important. Others maintained this image of Liszt as well. The Grand-Duke Karl Alexander of Saxe-Weimar once said to Busoni, "Liszt was what a prince ought to be." As Kramer continues, "For the gaze is the privileged act through which power and pleasure are harmonized."[38] That potent combination of power and pleasure, in a way that is different from Bach, Beethoven, and other massed music—partly because it emanates from the soloist—is the vein of Modern gold that Liszt discovered.

Nor was he alone in pushing the limits of the virtuoso. The impossible desires of Chopin were completely in tune with Liszt's own and the terrifying violence as well, because in part, Chopin and Liszt had traveled such similar paths. As one Polish biographer of Chopin notes, "Like many classless people standing astride different artistic and social circles, he was fascinated by the rich and exalted, at the same time preferring the company of the simplest and most humble."[39] The sentence might refer as easily to Liszt as to Chopin. His father left Warsaw with Count Pac to become a tutor in the noble household of the Countess Laczynska, a cousin and godchild of the even more noble Countess Ludwicka Skarbek, where Chopin's mother, a "poor relation" and cousin of the clan, was living. She was a talented pianist with a fine voice for singing. Like Sand's, Chopin's was a dual nature that knew both gentility and the rough necessity of self-reliance. Arriving in Paris for the first time in September 1831, he carried his own bags from the stagecoach to an inn, an image completely at odds with the pampered prince of later stardom when he and Liszt set the precedent for what is today called "glam rock" style. The play of high and low in his music, as with Liszt and later composers such as Dvořák and Bartók, brings together folk tunes and dances of the countryside and the elegant, complex patina he applied to them as a latter-day incarnation of the court composer delighting a slew of aristocratic patrons.

One of the paradoxes of Chopin's career is the difficulty of reconciling his deprecatory remarks about public performance (he played only thirty public concerts in his thirty-year career, seven of them as a prodigy in Poland) with the broad popularity he and his published works enjoyed. At home in the salon or palace, he was sickened by negative reviews and referred to the paying audience as "people I don't know." He complained to Liszt, "I am not at all fit for giving concerts, the crowd intimidates me,

I feel paralyzed by its curious look and the unknown faces make me dumb."[40] Those few concerts were staged (and often canceled) for maximum effect, in part because of their rarity, with high ticket prices and never an empty seat when, in Paris (most famously, at the Salle Pleyel), London, or Vienna, Chopin actually deigned to play for the public. Berlioz sniffed, "He comes down from the clouds once a year and allows himself to be heard in Pleyel's salons, and only then the public and the artists can admire his magnificent talent." In his preference for the private and socially superior or equal audience ("For me today this is the most necessary thing because good taste seems to come from there; you, at once, have a greater talent if they have heard you at the English or the Austrian embassy; you play better right away if Princess Vaudemont protects you")[41] he stands apart from many of the figures in this study who were far more comfortable with a mass audience and courted the spotlight. Through the examples of his friends, however, and of Paganini, with whom he was fascinated (having seen him as a boy in Poland and having attended all his concerts in Paris), Chopin was familiar with how the role of Beethovenian cult figure was to be played before the masses, giving it his own "reluctant noble" accent.

Chopin's patrons were the aristocrats whose names grace the dedicatory pages of his published works and whose daughters or wives made up more than half the roster of his students: Prince de la Moskowa; Baroness Charlotte de Rothschild; Comte de Perthuis, whose wife Emilie was Chopin's pupil and who gave him his Sèvres dinner service and the vases inscribed "Louis-Philippe, Roi de Français"; Count Wodzinski; the Orsetti family; Prince Adam Czartoryinski, who heard him as a child at the Blue Palace (the Radziwill mansion); Archduke Konstanty; Empress Maria Feodorova, who chose him to play for royal visitors as a child, earning him a diamond ring from the czar; the Stirling family in Scotland; the duchess of Gainsborough; Lord Falmouth; Queen Victoria, for whom he played when she was twenty-nine, Princess Cristian di Belgiojoso-Trivalziao, and others. Chopin was particularly at ease with the exiled Polish aristocrats in Paris, such as the Czartoryinskis, Radziwills, and Potockas. Playing politics and hedging his alliances, he could also be

day yet worried over the idea that being a professional musician would doom him to the social status of a tradesman. Later in life Chopin would compose his own twenty-four preludes in all major and minor key signatures after the example of the *Well-Tempered Clavier*, which has forty-eight preludes and fugues. Entering a noble house through the front door, as an invited guest, was of vital importance to Chopin. While a student at the Warsaw Conservatory, under the tutelage of a follower of John Field, whose nocturnes were a strong influence, Chopin was invited to the estate of Prince Radziwill, where he accompanied the regent, a cellist, in selections from Gounod's *Faust* as well as in a polonaise of his own. Chopin was completely happy: "I could have stayed there until I was thrown out."[42]

His talent was his ticket, but his manner made him more than the diversion for a brief interlude at a social event. As one biographer adroitly notes, "While this guaranteed Chopin social standing, it also introduced into his life an element which was to endure—a slight aura of amateurishness which assured him an exceptional reputation in some circles, and unwarranted contempt in others. Even when he became a professional musician, people found it hard to think of him as one."[43] The capitalistic monster was wont to rear its ugly head on occasion, and Chopin's constant battles with Haslinger, his publisher, are testimony that he was not an utter naïf. The legacy and impression was, however, more genteel. From his own time to ours, the music of Chopin has been the darling of amateurs, although in an era when the piano in the parlor is far more rare than it was even fifty years ago, there are fewer who know the pleasure of learning Chopin with their fingers rather than in a concert hall or via stereo.

Chopin's musical diet, beginning with the counterpoint lessons of his Silesian German tutor, Jozef Elsner, included a steady stream of concerts in Warsaw by opera stars such as Angelica Catalani and Henrietta Sonntag. He attended all eleven of the concerts given by Paganini in Warsaw and recitals by pianist Johann Nepomuk Hummel, choral works by Handel, and in Berlin and Vienna, where he went to study, operas by Meyerbeer and Rossini. In his early days in Paris he was at the opera nearly

the rooting of Modern aesthetics was as the muse and nurse of Chopin and untiring champion of Delacroix and Liszt. Her written record of the extraordinary times they shared repeatedly privileges talent over bloodlines, which is just as well for Chopin as Sand outranked him by a considerable margin in the genealogical department.[45] After circling one another warily in the salons of Paris, they met on 24 October 1836, at the Hôtel de France, where she was staying, as were Liszt and the Countess Marie d'Agoult. Sand was on the rebound from a divorce and a rapid-fire series of love affairs, and all that biographers can produce about their first encounter was that Chopin played for her and the assembled company. She began to pursue him amorously, with the help of Chopin's dear friend Count Wojciech Grzymala, a forty-four-year-old bon vivant who a year later made it possible for the two of them to see each other almost nightly.

Chopin's first two appearances in her autobiography are anonymous, and the later one strikes the theme of Chopin's ethereal tendency to reside on a higher plane: "There is another soul—no less beautiful and pure in its essence, no less sickly and troubled in this world—that reappears with a similar tranquility in my conversations with the dead, and on my expectation of that better world where we must all meet again in a brighter and holier light than that on earth."[46] If one adheres to the widely held belief that the most daring of Chopin's innovations are lost to history, having been improvised after midnight in the salons and never transcribed—like the finest moments of jazz from the wee hours in New Orleans clubs, which, legend tells, live in the memory of those who were lucky enough to be there—then Sand was the one person who was in the best position to understand Chopin's significance. She heard him in those late-night flights of sheer inspiration and invention. She listened, as well, by daylight the morning after as he sorted through the same ideas in search of their written incarnation. As she recalled, "For eight years, his piano, initiating me daily into the secrets of its master's inspiration or meditation, revealed to me the raptures, perplexities, victories or torments of his genius."[47]

While Chopin is unquestionably a far greater presence in the history of musical Modernism than Swinburne is within the literary canon, there is a tie between them that is difficult to ignore in light of the direction taken by poetry and music even in our own time. Both men were fluid exponents of pure sound, able by virtue of their prodigious technical gifts and surplus of inspiration, to scale dizzying heights of lyric rhapsody. Their legacies converge in the sense that Swinburne was the most musical of poets of the age, inspired as Chopin was by revolutionary themes and ballad forms, just as Chopin was the most poetic of composers, particularly in his ballads. As Chopin was, in the opinion of at least one esteemed expert, "the greatest master of counterpoint since Mozart,"[48] Swinburne was the archprosodist, the first since Alexander Pope and Ben Jonson to import correctly the complexities of Greek and Latin verse forms into English. This has been the basis for their lasting influence upon generations of later artists for whom technique and lyricism must be fitted tightly together (James Merrill and John Ashbery in poetry or Claude Debussy, Elliott Carter, and Roger Sessions in music). In his brilliant examination of Chopin's romanticism and originality, Rosen stresses the relationship between Chopin's program-less narratives and the never-ending melodies of Bellini.

As with Liszt, the secret to Chopin's power and his Modernism is not simply the liberties he takes with classically established key relationships. It is the new priority of sound and sound alone. This is the endgame of the virtuoso, an extension of sheer pianism, much like Swinburne's nearly abstract echolalia, that strange chanting that can be set beside Joyce's *Finnegans Wake* for its abstract qualities. As Rosen observes: "He is ruthless, capable of asking the pianist to try for the unrealizable in delicacy as well as violence. The unrealizable in Chopin, however, is always perfectly imaginable as sound. His structures are rarely beautiful or interesting in themselves on paper, as are those of Bach or Mozart (to name his favorite composers): they are conceived for their effect, even if the intended public was a small and very private one in some cases."[49] Even this aspect of the similarity between Chopin and Swinburne, creators of art that "works on the nerves of the listener," as Rosen deems it, makes sense in light of the neurasthenic nature of the creators themselves. The pressure against the frontiers of form and material—namely, sound—is created by a willingness to experiment that is the hallmark of all that we consider Modern.

Rosen identifies counterpoint as the core of Chopin's modernity, pointing to the example of the preludes: "In passages where the texture and harmony appear most radical and most ambiguous, Chopin's counterpoint (which, as he remarked to Delacroix, was the 'logic' of music) is the controlling agent."[50] The violence and unexpected turns of a Chopin work, its weird side, are also what makes it Modern, echoing Schlegel's "chaotic is the character of the Modern." As Rosen points out, both Chopin and Liszt broke the age-old relation of tonic to dominant as the foundation of Western triadic tonality: "The attempt of the early nineteenth century to substitute third or mediant relationships for the classical dominant amounted to a frontal attack on the principles of tonality, and it eventually contributed to the ruin of triadic mentality."[51]

As with Liszt, Chopin's foresight as a musical thinker was eclipsed by the drama of his life and his reputation as a virtuoso. Rosen writes, "It is difficult to appreciate today how radical was the synthesis embodied in Chopin's études. The major technical problems in these pieces are most often ones of touch and balance: they increase the strengths and suppleness of the hand, but they also develop the performer's ear. Chopin's coloristic invention is at its highest in the études, and nowhere is it more evident that this coloristic imagination is fundamentally contrapuntal in nature—or, rather, that the counterpoint is fundamentally coloristic, the interweaving of different lines of texture."[52] As concert pianists such as Byron Janis, who nearly had to leave the stage due to the effects of psoriatic arthritis, and Gary Graffman, who did briefly retire, there is pain associated with the demands of these pieces by Liszt and Chopin. Comparing them, Rosen notes, "Chopin's sadism is usually more subtle than that of his contemporaries and in most of his works actual pain is associated with emotional violence."[53]

The double life of Chopin as effete nobleman and raging avant-gardist is found not only in the music but through glimpses left in his correspondence. He echoes his dear friend Delacroix in this passage: "All the dinners, evenings, concerts, dances that I have had up to my ears bore me . . . in a salon, I pretend to be calm, but returning home, I thunder at the piano."[54] The explosively emotive side of his compositions was felt by the privileged few who did hear him play. After Chopin's concert of February 1848, the marquis de Custine told him: "You have gained in suffering and poetry; the melancholy of your compositions penetrates still deeper into the heart; one feels alone with you in the midst of a crowd; you have turned a public into a circle of friends; you are equal to your own genius, that says it all."

Like Leighton and the revival of interest in early Florentine painting, Chopin was fascinated by the Baroque revival of his day, particularly the rediscovery of Bach. Later in his career, however, the transparency of Bach's structures gave way more and more to chromaticism and the direct translation of thought into the language of sound. Szulc has written that Chopin's music was "the expression of thought by sounds; the manifestation of our sentiments by sounds; the art of expressing thoughts by sounds; the expressing of our perceptions by sounds."[55] This is the immediacy so often associated with the breakthroughs of abstract art, particularly the tight relationship of painting to drawing. Anyone familiar with the rhythmic, aching tenderness of a Cy Twombly painting—part brushwork, part handwriting—will feel as well the sense of a thin membrane between impulse and performance in the rubato (in its time, called the *temps derobé*) of Chopin's *Nocturnes*. As Rosen writes, "Technical display in Chopin, after the early works, is transmuted into tone color or dramatic gesture—we may say, to accept the prejudices of Chopin's own generation, that it has been ennobled. This is the source of much of the poetry in Chopin's music: it comes from the transformation of the vulgar into something aristocratic. Its power depends in part on our unconscious sense of how commonplace the material originally was before it reappears with an aura of iridescent sonority."[56] Given T. J. Clark's views of the transformation of vulgarity into nobility in Abstract Expressionism, cited above, and the general sensitivity to high and low in aesthetics today, there is something uncannily proleptic about Chopin's achievement.

It is a cliché and a cheap expediency to conclude an essay on Chopin with the often-repeated lament—and here the obligatory bow to Keats as well—that a life cut short tragically might well have produced so much more, arguably progressing that much further into Modernism, had he lived longer. Chopin, so closely identified with and even bound to the piano as a compositional tool, was unlikely to have burst onto the next level of chromaticism that came with the timbral innovations of orchestration in France, Russia, and Vienna. Aside from its lack of originality, as an ending this thought overlooks the degree to which Sand's circle fulfilled one another's expectations and cleared the way for Modern innovations that were all but spelled out in their works. The elegance demanded by Delacroix is answered in Chopin's ethereal writing for piano, while Chopin's idealistic musings on the spontaneous movement between thought and the artistic medium are embodied in Delacroix's canvases. The heroism and sheer power Sand calls for in her criticism and fiction is amply supplied by the figure of Liszt onstage and his thundering octaves on the page, while his yearning for a frank artistic realization of conflicting passions is more than satisfied by the often veering, always fluid, and mercurial expression of her thoughts and passions in prose that hurries to keep pace with her mind. They made themselves and each other Modern in the daily exchange of what mattered to them most: art and its making, the age and its progress.

2

Painters of Privilege

PIERRE PUVIS DE CHAVANNES, EDGAR DEGAS, AND HENRI DE TOULOUSE-LAUTREC

Three closely watched personalities of the Parisian art scene from the 1860s to the end of the century—Pierre Puvis de Chavannes, Edgar Degas, and Henri de Toulouse-Lautrec—today appear to compose a strange and disparate trio. The relative obscurity of Puvis (if the Boston Public Library murals were by either of the other two, there would be tour buses pulled up outside every day), the popular "sweetness" of Degas as museum box-office draw, and the sexually charged nastiness of Lautrec are current valuations at variance not only with one another but with the full historical truth as well. In their time they were tightly linked by their approaches to painting and by their prosperous, noble family backgrounds. The connections extend to historical intersections of some importance, including allusions to Puvis in two important early paintings of Degas and an infamous parody by Lautrec and his friends that hung in his studio from his student days. Arranging the three according to degrees of either modernity or nobility yields an amusing inverse ladder by which the most aristocratic by far, Lautrec, was also the most advanced in terms of Modern subject matter and style; the least distinguished by birth (though immensely proud of the "de" in his signature), Puvis was so conservative in his aesthetic theory that, like the Pre-Raphaelites and Balthus, who admired him, he rejected the present and advocated a return to archaic values in the arts, painting scenes of timeless, mainly mythological symbolism. Between them stands Degas, who changed his name from De Gas to distance himself from an exalted if financially troubled clan. His career embraced both the firmly rooted imitation of the Old Masters and the loose, brushy vitality of the Impressionists. There is more to his modernity. Where Puvis signed a petition to reverse a court decision granting photography the status of an artwork in terms of the copyright protections of the day, Degas embraced the new instrument in experiments that shaped his later paintings. As with Delacroix (with whom Puvis studied briefly), both Puvis and Lautrec were major players in the evolution of public art: Puvis in his huge-scale commissions for the Paris Opera as well as the Boston Public Library and other public buildings and Lautrec in his wildly popular posters (torn from walls by collectors almost before the glue had dried) and the outsized canvases mounted on the booth of the dancer La Goulue at La Foire du Trone in 1895. There is nothing inherently Modern about murals. From the caves of Lascaux and the villas of Pompeii to the mosaics of Byzantium, the frescoes of Florence and the great Baroque ceilings of the seventeenth and eighteenth centuries, the medium has a long and distinguished history, particularly in a sacred context. Where Puvis and Lautrec broke fresh ground was in the rapid secularization of both the content and the occasion for public art, as we will see in greater detail with respect to the complex and unusual commission Puvis executed to celebrate the commercial success of the port of Marseilles and the even more ad hoc and notorious advertising gigs that Lautrec enjoyed courtesy of the vaudeville stars who were his friends and patrons.

If there is one quality that unites them, aside from the fortunate circumstances of their birth and their now indisputable roles in the rapidly unfolding progression from the chromatically rich Delacroix to the even more daring painterly world of the Impressionists, the Nabis, and the school of Pont-Aven, it is a certain chilly reserve in their attitude toward the subjects of their portraits. These are three artists who (like Giacometti, to choose a tougher artist closer to our own time), were poets of the space between the artist or observer and the subject. This Yeatsian "cold eye" has a twin significance in this study. It is both Modern in its projection of the individual's alienation and ever-alert irony and aristocratic in its hauteur. Even the high moral tone of Leighton's allegories cannot compete with the punishing isolation of Lautrec's portrait of *The Englishman at the Moulin Rouge*, a character assassination in paint that takes the spontaneity of Manet and the incisive observation of Daumier, strips the comic relief and leaves an analytic victim so exposed that the entire vacuous life of this wastrel is opened for all to see.

Puvis was, in his starry-eyed idealism, perhaps the least ironic of all Modern artists. He was similar to Leighton in this regard, beyond which both of them espoused Classicism and Medievalism as sources for their retrospective movements. The idyllic yearning for a Golden Age was the opposite of the cruelly sardonic Lautrec or the notorious curmudgeon Degas (nicknamed "the Old Bear" by Mary Cassatt and her circle). As with Hofmannsthal's operatic characters, the erect, often faceless figures of a Puvis painting reflect a more impersonal attitude. Could it be possible that this elegant artist would prove an apostle of that cold, airless approach to the figure that Warhol, Katz, and others have adopted in our time? Those statuesque silhouettes of Puvis were acknowledged as a powerful influence on latecomers, including Seurat, Gauguin, and the school of Pont-Aven, who also introduced dreamy and static players, faceless as well, in their color-drenched landscapes. The connection is not coincidental, as the painters of Pont-Aven were more than conversant with the eccentric but powerful idiom of Puvis. One of the most often quoted axioms of twentieth-century abstract art is the famous sentence that opens Maurice Denis's "Definition of Neo-Traditionism," which, as Puvis scholar Aimee Brown Price points out, was written directly following his appreciative viewing of Puvis's *Poor Fisherman*. It reads: "Remember that a painting—before being a warhorse, a nude woman, or some anecdote—is essentially a planar surface covered with colors organized in a certain order."[1] Brown links the flatness of Puvis with the aesthetic of abstraction and vividly shows the connection, as well, between this powerful painting, to be considered later in this chapter, and the figures by the shore of Picasso's Blue Period paintings.

Puvis's contemporary reputation made him, like Mallarmé and Moreau, an allusive presence in the collection of J. K. Huysman's fictional Count Des Esseintes. The major works, including a huge *Childhood of St. Genevieve* in the Pantheon, were studied and meticulously copied by aspiring artists at the academies, becoming the target of parodies by students who naturally took aim at the immensely powerful and popular figure. His importance to the rise of Modern art, convincingly seen in the recent exhibition at the Van Gogh Museum in Amsterdam that brought together works by Van Gogh, Gauguin, Seurat, Picasso, Matisse, Prendergast, and Puvis, is partly spelled out in T. J. Clark's *Farewell to an Idea*:

> Sometimes in an epoch of transition, when contrary notions of art—almost contrary notions of the category—are in contention, a single artist emerges above the fray. Everyone lays claim to him or her, for extraordinarily different reasons. He or she comes to stand for the possibility of art continuing its vital contact with its past, but also for the violence that has to be done to that past if it is to be made usable; he or she is a left-over, a simpleton, dreaming of the Golden Age in the midst of the Third Republic's vulgarity; and yet also a sophisticate, an Alexandrian, playing with his or her belatedness. The art that results from this is above all productive of interpretations,

> and imitations of a brilliant (forced) kind. The more forced, the more productive. Feed on this artist's naivete, seems to be the watchword, celebrate this artist's bleeding white of his or her "sources," and painting may still be able to declare its endgame a new start. In 1891 the artist was Puvis de Chavannes. He was as dear to Seurat and Signac as to the Minister of Public Instruction. The symbolists worshipped him, the neos worshiped him, he was given the best walls of the Republic to cover. His name was a catch-all simile for everything grand and improbable that art could nudge into life.[2]

Puvis in his time was also a legendary reactionary. He was among the foremost petitioners in a court case that determined whether photographs might be protected as works of art under copyright laws. Today the question would seem strikingly familiar to students of intellectual property. Puvis was dead set *against* the definition of a photograph as a work of art, signing a petition (along with Ingres, Isabey, and other established artists of the most conservative stripe) asking the court to revoke its decision to grant that status. The 1861–62 case, incidentally, involved pirated photos of aristocrats, namely, Lord Palmerston and Count Cavour, made by the commercial studio of Mayer and Pierson.[3] By comparison with Degas and Lautrec, who both embraced the camera as an amusement and a tool, Puvis saw it as a threat and denigration of the admirable practice of image making by hand.

The conservatism of Puvis also extended to his disdain for Impressionism, that riotous, exuberant style sweeping Paris at just the time when he was soaring to the height of his popularity. It seemed as though the looser the brushwork and more lush the colors of the Impressionists became, the tighter and paler Puvis would paint. The epitome of this was the stately clarity of *The Sacred Grove*, his most important painting of 1884. Its delicately delineated composition and ghostly tones could not be further in technique, effect, and spirit from the perpetual motion of the vibrating colors and rushing strokes of the exactly contemporary, vivid canvases of Monet and Renoir.

Every movement in art has its absentees, those who prefer to ply their own course in defiance of reigning critical and artistic trends. During the heyday of geometric, color-field painting in New York in the late 1960s and 1970s, when the laying down of a straight edge of masking tape supplanted the laying in of a figure, there were nonbelievers still working on *écorché* and life drawing, although in art schools these classes were suddenly undersubscribed. Puvis was a holdout in just this respect, although it must be pointed out that Degas shared his passion for history painting (particularly from 1854 through 1865, when, heavily influenced by Puvis, he completed his own *Semiramis Building Babylon* and *Scene of War in the Middle Ages*), as did Manet, although it was Manet who famously observed that being dubbed a history painter was "the most wounding insult that can be made to an artist."[4] Puvis, who, like Degas, had been encouraged by his prosperous and conservative father to train in a profession before deciding on art as a career, came to Paris to study engineering. His first decorative paintings were done at the family estates in Brouchy, as well as in Lyons. Most of his early murals were created for these mansions, including his brother's in Brouchy, which he decorated at the family's invitation in 1854–55. The subject of one panel in the dining room is the return of the prodigal son, an ironic enough choice for a young artist coming back from Paris where he was supposed to have studied engineering. As Puvis commented, "It was some nerve on my part, and the family must have had quite some trepidation. Think of it, a completely new beautiful dining room! Evidently, if one were to redo it, it would be better, I believe; but however, for my debut in decorative art, it's fine. In any case, I found my road to Damascus."[5]

Minor nobility on both the maternal and paternal sides with, however, major wealth, especially from land holdings, gave Puvis a comfortable head start. It was his largesse as much as his title that separated him from the crowd of art students in Paris, much as Gustave Caillebotte's and Frédéric Bazille's wealth consigned them to a certain role among the early Impressionists. In 1856 he was introduced to the Princess Marie Cantacuzene, who became his wife and sat for a number of evocative, lyrical portraits in the early years. His career breakthrough and rapid rise to eminence began with the Salon of 1861, when his twinned paintings *Bellum* and *Concordia* were acquired by the state and installed at the museum in Amiens. By mid-decade, the sheer acreage of his decorative commissions became the measure of his power, as he completed murals for public buildings in Amiens, Lyons, and Marseilles and in Paris for the Panthéon and the new Sorbonne. This minor nobleman, like Frederick, Lord Leighton, rose eagerly and rapidly through the ranks of state recognition as conferred by the Legion d'Honneur, becoming a *chevalier* in 1864, an *officier* in 1877, and a commander in 1889.

The popularity and official laurels eventually bestowed upon Puvis were ironic, given the confusion that his earliest works created. Like his near contemporaries Moreau and Redon, who never attained the same level of success, Puvis used materials and themes that were outside the mainstream. At first, his style baffled the critics, who, confronted by tonalities and surfaces that were radically different from anything being produced in the studios of Paris at the time, did not even think they were oil on canvas. Observers wondered if Puvis used encaustic or tempera or some other strange medium (for his matte surfaces, to imitate fresco, he did mix wax with his paint in a medium known as *peinture à la cire*, a favorite of Delacroix as well). He was also an enigma to viewers attempting to read the vaguely referential narratives and mysterious iconography of the pictures. His elusive subject matter suggested at the same time imprecise evocations of Pre-Socratic Greek conversations with overtones of current French idealism. This eccentricity, which later historians have attributed to the bizarre spiritualism of the early Symbolists (parallel with the way that certain literary scholars overdo the Rosicrucian beliefs of Yeats), set Puvis apart from his contemporaries. Both subject and medium, then, contributed to the odd appearance of his paintings. Blissfully oblivious to the raised eyebrows of critics and the snide disdain of younger avant-gardists, Puvis aimed high, literally and figuratively, with his painting, striving to create major works when the casual essay, fast and deliberately tentative and incomplete, was becoming the order of the day. The very notion of a twenty-minute scramble to evoke the shifting effects of sunset at the end of a humid summer day on the Epte, by which Monet practically uses the canvas to display the paint piled and twirled on his palette, is diametrically opposite to the flat, patient surface of a painting in which an indefinite time of the day is slowed and held for an eternity. Puvis may well have called one of his canvases *Summer*—the calendar page is never flipped in this permanent twilight he created. The exalted strangeness of Puvis was captured by Gautier in one of the best early appreciations of his work in a review of the Salon of 1861:

> His spirit moves in the highest spheres of art and his ambition exceeds his talent. The very aspect of his two large compositions, *Bellum* and *Concordia*, catches the eye. Are these cartoons? Tapestries? Or are they rather frescoes removed by some mysterious means from an unknown Fontainebleau, these immense canvases surrounded by a frame of flowers and symbols like the paintings in the Farnesina. What means was used to paint them? Tempera, wax, oil? It is hard to tell. The tone scale is so odd, outside the usual color scale; they are the neutral tones or the skillfully deadened ones of mural painting which clothe buildings without introducing harsh reality and give an impression of objects more than they represent them. Puvis de Chavannes—let us emphasize this point at a time when so many palaces and monuments are being completed, awaiting their covering of frescoes—is not a picture painter. He wants not the easel but a scaffold and large wall spaces to cover. This is his dream and he has proved that he can achieve it. In an era of prose and realism, this young artist is naturally heroic, epic, and monumental though a strange outcropping of genius. He seems to have seen no contemporary painting and to have come directly from the studio of Primaticcio or Il Rosso.[6]

Gautier, a poet renowned for his dedication to lyric style in an era dominated by the example of Flaubert as quintessential Modern stylist, picks up on one subtle aspect of the puzzle of Puvis that has a direct bearing upon others in this study. He feels that the painter presented an epic or poetic sensibility at a time when prose was on the rise. Indeed a new era of prose was dawning, first in the visual world (Manet was its herald) and in the "musical prose" of Brahms as analyzed by Schoenberg. In literature, aside from Flaubert's virtuosity, Baudelaire and Mallarmé turned from sonnets to prose poems. In English letters, a few decades later, the revolution led by Ezra Pound would have as a rallying cry, "Poetry ought to be at least as well written as prose." The mixing of journalism, design, printmaking, and popular song writing with artistic careers served to extend this infiltration of prose. Certain figures in this study, notably Swinburne and Puvis, are categorically opposed to this trend. They represent the persistence of poetry through its transformation at the hands of technically inventive and "well-versed" artists, of whom Puvis and Swinburne are prime examples.

Puvis as Pre-Renoirite is, most importantly, "not a picture painter" but dually a remnant of the great age of the fresco and a prophet of the all-encompassing, walk-in work of art as exemplified in our time by Matisse's chapel at Vence, Rothko's chapel at Houston, and similar wraparound installations of paintings by Cy Twombly. Huge in scale, ambitious in aim and strikingly spiritual, all these projects share that yearning for majesty that only an acknowledged masterpiece can supply. While the economics of the commission structure and the massive studio Puvis kept might make an interesting study, just as the horrifying saga of greed and broken promises has made the Rothko estate fodder for art journalists for years, the major mural projects of Puvis seem to transcend mere art commerce by serving more public ends and, like Rothko's work, aspiring to transcendental effects. Understanding the composition, colors, and style of Puvis requires the contextual knowledge of the buildings in which they were sited, since, to take but one example, Puvis keyed his palette to the stone surrounding the painting. One of the great difficulties posed by seeing his paintings against white walls in a museum is the loss of this historical and contextual information.

Modern life was completely beside the point for Puvis. As perfect an example as any of the anachronistic stance of the artist (even Balthus, so like Puvis in his treatment groupings, dresses his subjects in roughly the garb of the time in which they were painted, whereas Puvis prefers the Greek peplos), Puvis went to the opposite extreme from the journalistic attention to the details of the moment that so enchanted Manet, Monet, and the later Degas, as celebrated in Baudelaire's great essay, "The Painter of Modern Life." Even Puvis's *Poor Fisherman* (1881), one of the "warmest" and most affecting of his dramatic works, places the figures in a strangely calm, unknown inlet of an indeterminate sea of milky green, upon the horizon of which floats that signature Puvis landscape motif—the long, low distant range of hills. It rises slowly and undramatically from the level sea, and like a solid cello note underlying a passage in a trio by Brahms, it stretches evenly to the right edge of the canvas. Even the color is uniform, a lilac-tinged gray blue nearly identical with the tone of the far hills in other works by Puvis. The shadow-like contours of the cape and peninsulas defining the bright, still expanse of water are early signs of the stylized landscapes of Gauguin, Denis, and the Pont-Aven school of landscape. The bearded fisherman, his eyes dark and downcast, shoulders slumped and hands folded over one another either in prayer or unworkmanlike idleness, has a saintly rectitude in his tiny, empty boat, particularly against the taller, leaning mast that logically ought to be the perpendicular element in the composition. The crisp outlines of his arms and angular face are typical of the anatomy of Puvis, whose figures barely surpass silhouettes in musculature and draping. Behind his boat, on a flower-carpeted bank, an infant sprawls asleep on a bright red blanket, and a dark-haired, androgynous young woman clutches wildflowers tightly in both hands, eyes also fixed on the ground and away from the fisherman, her father. Puvis explained: "It isn't a woman, but a young girl at an awkward age. The mother is dead and the little one is there to watch over her brother; she picks flowers with her little monkey hand, feverishly, mechanically. The child who, in this strange flowerbed, didn't do as much would be unnatural. I have a horror of illustrating novels in oils, my only excuse is that I borrowed this vision of misery only from myself."[7]

Picasso, painting his tragic Blue Period family tableaux two decades later, would have been thinking of this renowned painting, hanging not far from his studio in the Musée du Luxembourg, where it had been installed in 1887 after its acquisition by the state. An admiring critic called it the "ultimate emblem of poverty (synthèse de la miserere)." The physical and emotional separation of the figures in this powerful family scene, their lack of interaction, raises an inescapable sense of distance and isolation, a significant trait not just in the work of Puvis but in that of Degas, Lautrec, and later, Balthus, as well as in the dramas of Hofmannsthal and Beckett. Pushing this perhaps too far, it is also observed in the philosophical inquiries into the near impossibility of shared experiences by Wittgenstein and the solitude of the elderly, forgotten Swinburne in his deafness. Insofar as there is a kind of defiance or self-involvement spelled out by this stance, it may seem harsh, if accurate, to point out that this very quality is part of the aristocratic makeup of the artists. In a more sympathetic vein, let's remember that this was a period in which the authority of the nobility was in question, and aristocrats who were artists might particularly be said to suffer from a siege mentality from occupying a no-man's-land between their families and society. The work took Puvis several years to complete, in a period of depression after completing his first Paris murals, the Saint Genevieve cycle at the Pantheon. Scholars have shown that it was indebted in part to the work of Jean-François Millet, whom Puvis had met and admired. Now in the Musée d'Orsay, when it was initially bought for the national collections, Puvis was dismayed ("I didn't judge it a museum painting").[8] He himself called it "a painting of conscience" that was meant to show the "invisible" poor in their hardship.[9]

As with so many of the figures in the paintings of Puvis, each character in *The Poor Fisherman* appears to dwell in a world of his or her own, oblivious to others in the scene and to the gaze of the painter and observer. In the far more crowded masterwork, *L'Eté* (*Summer*), at least forty figures are depicted. Not one makes eye contact with another; even, most extraordinarily, two mothers cradling infants glance away. A man on the viewer's right appears to wave to someone across the way, but following the direction of the gesture to see an acknowledgment—a natural enough device, used traditionally in holding together groupings like this in a large composition—there is no receipt or return of the signal. In the distance, a furtive echo of the wave cast in the same direction is offered by a tiny figure dabbed in ochre against the paler gold of a wheat field; perhaps the far figure wields a scythe, but he is too tiny to read clearly. Each of the distant groupings echoes a foreground ensemble, fully realized standing or reclining figures that look ahead to those of Matisse and Kandinsky, squiggles of pure color that deftly become credible depictions of people. Most tantalizing of all is the only figure that might be considered central, a half-clothed woman with a child clinging to her hip, whose outstretched right hand at first seems extended to a woman seated at the base of a birch tree, also reaching upward and just barely missing contact with the woman's right hand. Then you realize the gap is even

The sum of this isolation of figure from figure and of all the characters in the drama from the viewer, whose regard none returns, is a distancing effect. Elsewhere in this study we have encountered this chilly gesture—from the solitary figures behind glass in Bacon's portraits to the withdrawal of Hofmannsthal's cool-headed counts and countesses from the romantic entanglements of the other characters in the drama flaring around them. In the case of Puvis it is fascinating to put this together with an essential technical fact: Most of his work was created to be seen from relatively far away, as murals or on ceilings. Gérôme, who despised the paintings of Puvis, put his finger on the problem with this snide observation about the murals: "They are not bad from a distance . . . from a great distance, but they do not bear analysis."[11]

Puvis assumed Delacroix's role as the man of the hour when it came to public commissions, but he played that part in a manner utterly different from his one-time master. The divergence accounts in many ways for the modernity of Puvis, our link between the abstract creations of Frank Stella and Sol LeWitt, the two most prominent muralists of today, and the generation of Rubens. Certain constants come with the territory. Like Delacroix, Tiepolo, and others working in the genre, Puvis created under the constraints of traditional mural and ceiling techniques and resorted to many of the same strategies. This offers at least one excuse for the flatness and clean delineation of the figures. It physically invests them with a remoteness that their averted eyes and aloof postures reinforce: Puvis's characters both were and acted distant. In this regard they echoed their creator.

At the height of his career, Puvis had become an immensely powerful figure on the Parisian art scene, known for his extreme devotion to craft as well as to the ideals of art. Visitors to the studio at the Place Pigalle, including the printmakers who translated his paintings into editions, had better arrive early in the morning as he was wont to clear them out by nine to start again on the latest of many commissions. Eventually, he transferred his base of operations to a vast hangar he designed (drawing on his engineering background) in Neuilly. It was brightly lit by end-to-end skylights and equipped with scaffolding and tools that allowed

means, so different from the painterly luxuriance, even excesses, of Delacroix and the Impressionists, make the style of Puvis instantly recognizable. As Puvis wrote, anticipating the purified language of Wittgenstein, Mallarmé, and the Symbolist poets as well as the clean look of Minimalism, "I have dreamt of a more and more sober, more and more simple art. I have condensed, amalgamated, compressed . . . I have tried to say as much as possible in a few words." This ascetic quality is found as well in the meditative emptiness of that vast studio in Neuilly, with just a few movable tables and a rolling ladder occupying its airy space, so vastly different from the cluttered, salon-style showplaces (including Puvis's own) in Paris that it seems far closer to the huge, light-filled studios of painters today, in particular of the rural retreats of Robert Mangold, Ellsworth Kelly, and Jasper Johns.

The stately procession in the friezelike Sorbonne murals appealed to those troubled by vulgarity and speed, not only of cultural change but of life at the time. Naturally, it was the artists who took first notice. Degas praised the "slow, majestic figures" and delivered the ultimate artistic compliment by directly quoting from *Bellum* in his similarly anachronistic *Scene de guerre au Moyen Age*, shown at the Salon of 1865. Other admirers, many of prominence, were similarly attracted. It is perhaps easy to see why Puvis would appeal to government leaders looking for safe public art—he was no Diego Rivera, likely to toss an incendiary passage into a courthouse mural. His appeal to the utopian mentality was instant. As T. J. Clark writes in a recent account of Modernism that accords far greater importance to Puvis than do most, "Reactionary agrarians like Count Melchior de Vogue, for example, dreamed in front of the great mural called *Summer*, which Puvis showed first in 1891, and were confident that the painting could point a way forward beyond the class struggle. 'This work is great, because it speaks from on high to the crowd, as did artists' creations in days gone by.' "[13]

With all this looking backward to an age of Classicism and timeless values, it remains to be seen how Puvis fits into a chronicle of Modern art. Clark makes Puvis a pivotal figure in the transition from Romanticism; and certainly the individuality of Puvis's vision, his ability to put his own stamp on what is usually the most impersonal of painting (decorative commissions for public buildings), is one way in which he asserted a Modern sensibility. Another indication is the path that certain paintings by Puvis took after the end of Impressionism. Darlings of the most advanced connoisseurs, including Degas himself, they often ended up in the hands of collectors of Modern paintings, appearing next to works by Matisse and Picasso in their homes.

One such avant-garde acquirer was the American financier Duncan

Phillips, whose tastes ran the gamut from Puvis to Mark Rothko and Francis Bacon. Two strong paintings by Puvis were in his possession and are mainstays of the museum in Washington, D.C., that Phillips's heirs maintain: *Messilia, Greek Colony* and *Marseilles, Gateway to the Orient*. In 1941, Phillips used them as the centerpieces of an exhibition titled *The Function of Color in Painting*. The fourth gallery of the show was subtitled "The Function of Color in Descriptive Suggestion." It put together the two paintings of Puvis with Constable's busy brushwork in *On the Stour*; Turner's *Slave Ship*, now at the Museum of Fine Arts in Boston; a Degas interior (*Women Combing Their Hair*, 1875–76); and a small gouache on paper by Max Weber, entitled *Conversation*. The flecks of white and masses of blue and green in the Constable, with the bright white of the Turner and the very lightly painted whites and blues of the Puvis, composed a magnificent harmony of subtle colorism in landscape. The range of hues in the room was by no means vast, remaining on the cool side of the spectrum, but the didactic point about Puvis and his art of suggestion was gracefully made. As with the paintings of Bonnard and Matisse that are among the highlights of the Phillips Collection, as well as those by the Americans Edward Glackens and Maurice Prendergast, the faceless figures and blurred focus emotionally are found in the study for the Marseilles mural. It was commissioned in 1862, during the city's giddy rise to prosperity, for the new Palais Longchamps built by Henri Esperandreux. Like the sort of lengthy peroration in the House of Lords in praise of a Docklands project that was a staple of Edwardian Parliaments, cloaked in Classical allusions to the extent that the engineering marvels were only alluded to, the painting offers a paean to worldly prosperity through only the most ethereal, Golden Age imagery. No smokestacks belching black clouds—just those typically languid puffs of gray he always floated in a blue sky.

Surprisingly, the Puvis paintings hold their own in Phillips's High Modernist collection, fitting right in with the painterly abstract works of the 1940s and 1950s, much as the works by Matisse do. Phillips wrote more than the checks, and in his commentary on *Marseilles* he touches upon the quality of experimentation that characterized Puvis:

> The classicist, too, knows his moments of self-questioning. Perhaps he indulges wayward or willful impulse, enjoys evocative suggestion as a change from the pursuit of clean statement, and sensuous colors a holiday when for a while he has nothing more to say with incisive or too calmly measured line. In such a mood perhaps Puvis de Chavannes delighted in the subjects for those murals at Marseilles, subjects which permitted him a romantic play of imagination, especially in the preliminary sketches which were done

entirely by his own hand and which in no way committed him to irrevocable compositional decisions. For the brief time when these sketches were on his easel, he was a searcher for he knew not what, a taster of rare flavors of commingled color, a gleaner after time and its personal memories.

One of the sincere young admirers of the anti-Impressionist Puvis was an artist today considered one of the big names of Impressionism: Degas. As several early allegorical works show, including *Semiramis Building Babylon* (1861) and *Young Spartans* (1860–62, reworked until 1880), the very style of Puvis, as well as his compositional sense, were echoed in the apprentice work of Degas. There were curious parallels between their lives, too. Degas was a reluctant nobleman, pushing himself hard to make it in the Parisian art world. When the esteemed art historian John Rewald published an essay in 1946 on Degas and his early career, the opening page bore the coat of arms of the De Gas family, and the most important plate was a meticulous, calligraphic rendering of the artist's genealogical tree. Rewald viewed the alliance between the distinguished Orleans family of the banker Auguste-Hyacinthe de Gas of Orleans with Marie-Celestine Musson of New Orleans, Louisiana, as a prophetic link between the old and new worlds. Another of the Musson daughters, Eugénie, married the duc de Rochefort.

The De Gas family of New Orleans rode the volatile boom-and-bust cycles of the cotton markets, and Edgar's career (much like that of Delacroix) was shaped by dramatic changes in family fortunes. As Rewald points out in a footnote, an elaborate family genealogy purchased in 1869 and tracing the family to a fourteenth-century family of landowners in the Lower Languedoc, its nobility supposedly confirmed in 1670 at the diocese of Uzes, turned out to be a fake. The ennoblement of the De Gas family actually occurred much later and was subsequently enhanced by marriages into older and more famous aristocratic families. This privileged heritage, a point of pride for his parents, vied with mythology in giving Degas the subject matter for his earliest paintings. The American and French sides of the family held a reunion in 1863 and traveled to Italy on holiday, where "a family tradition has it that Edgar Degas, who was then already thirty and had devoted more than ten years to painting, although he had not yet exhibited at the Salon, either in Naples or Florence, drew a portrait of his aunt the Duchesse de Rochefort."[14]

One particular period of Degas's career that has recently become the focus of critical attention is the American sojourn. The New Orleans branch of this sophisticated family welcomed the young painter and his brother René in 1872, just after the proclamation of the Republic. He stayed until early 1873, returning to France just before the death of his father in February in Naples and the opening of the Impressionists' first group exhibition in April. The De Gas family fortune had been almost completely dissipated, and a downturn in the price of cotton made it impossible for the reliable New Orleans branch of the family to make good on their debts. Edgar de Gas, as he was known at least through 1870 according to the Salon catalogs, changed his name to Degas at the time when his family's plight reached its nadir and began to consign works to the dealer Durand-Ruel. Art was no longer a gentleman's pastime. He switched medium to pastel, an easier sell, and swallowed his pride to trouble the wealthy painter Gustave Caillebotte for support in creating a publication devoted to the graphic arts that earlier he would have asked his family to underwrite.

While there is little biographical evidence to suggest that Degas took his nobility as seriously as he did his identity as artist, he knew the ignominy and pain of a great family's decline. Into one early masterpiece, painted over the course of nearly a decade with the hearty encouragement of his father, he poured a vast amount of what he had learned about the fate of the aristocracy in the contemporary world. The four figures in *The Belleli Family* (1858–67) were intimately known to Degas—they were his Aunt Laure and her family—and meticulously drawn or painted by him over and again in preparatory studies for the large work. He preferred to call it a tableau rather than a portrait because of its richer, more complex texture in terms of both narrative and composition. Baron Gennano Belleli is shown in profile, awkwardly, with his back and the back of his armchair to the painter, his eye downcast. A few steps away, centered, his two daughters wear frilly white cotton smocks over black dresses. One figure stares at the painter, all concentration and noble politesse—that is Giovanna, in life and art a perfect example of aristocratic decorum. Her sister Giulia, at the painting's center, is impatient. She has one foot on the floor and another tucked under her and gazes longingly into the far corner of the room. The most enigmatic figure in the work seems straight out of a painting by Holbein. She is Degas's Aunt Laure, lost in thought, bolt upright in black silk, with one hand casually draped over the shoulder of Giovanna, and the other—the detail is slightly troubling—pressing its fingers to the small marquetry table beside her, as though for support. Her gaze follows her daughter's across the room, completely oblivious to the line of sight of her husband and angled away from the regard of the painter. Although she was neither tall nor beautiful, her erect bearing and calm air make her the most arresting figure in the work. As critic Jean Sutherland Boggs comments, "She represents the supreme ideal of balance."[15]

Nobody in the picture is smiling. For a twenty-first-century audience guessing at the source of the unhappiness, it would be difficult to blame the surroundings. The Old Master drawing on the wall with its gilt frame, the decorative objects on the mantel, and the elegant furniture all connote comfort and elegance. What could be so tragically wrong? It reminds me of the skeptical response of mainland Chinese theatergoers in 1984 when Arthur Miller took *Death of a Salesman* to Beijing. They could not imagine why the members of a family that owned a refrigerator, a car, and a house all their own could consider themselves to be failures. It takes a smattering of inside knowledge to feel the humiliation in the scene. The irony lies in just that well-appointed interior and the circumstances of the fashionably attired family members posing for their portrait. The morose figure of Baron Belleli and his, in actuality, rather high-strung and sickly wife are embarrassed to be—temporarily, of course—living in rented rooms in Florence while in exile until their political fortunes improve with Unification in 1860. Aunt Laure was accustomed to the magnificent Palazzo Pignatelli in Naples, which had been acquired by her father. The baron, his eyes partly on a collection of papers on the table near him, is detached and troubled. Degas has perfectly caught the mood of these landed gentry in detention, disenfranchised and frankly worried about their future. Moreover, he achieved this by combining techniques and painterly approaches from the Renaissance and from his own time in a fascinating way, so that the painting is not just a historical record of a moment of transition in family and European history but also the embodiment of a transition in art history. As the viewer scans this work from left to right, the technical and conceptual aspect of the painting changes from an early Renaissance handling of portraiture in the faces of the mother and one daughter to an early-nineteenth-century approach to the central figure and finally becomes more Modern as it moves right, offering intimations of the Impressionist to come in the figure of the father and the reflection in the mirror, a passage the presages not just later Degas but the marvels of Bonnard and Picasso who succeeded him decades later.

The traditional side of the Belleli painting is open to dissection according to a few known influences. Degas was often in Italy during this period, when studying, looking, and absorbing was as important as painting. As with Ingres, Corot, and Puvis, in whose footsteps he followed, he discovered little to hold his interest among those examples of contemporary painting that were to be found, driving him to become saturated with the close observation and copying of Old Masters. The Belleli tableau bears traces of his fascination with Holbein and Bronzino, particularly in the rendering of Aunt Laure, but the main documented influence is Van Dyck, as is shown in his comments and letters of the time. Specifically, the year that Degas began the Belleli painting he had done a number of copies and studies of Van Dyck's portrait of Paolo Adorno in Genoa. As Degas wrote about the Van Dyck, "Artists no longer paint such a woman with such a subtle and distinguished hand. Was this the result of van Dyck's love for the countess Brignole? Or, indeed, do I find the work charming even though there was no such feeling. Her head in its grace and delicacy is life itself."[16] The young artist's fascination with the Van Dyck resonates in the image of Aunt Laure. Art historian Henri Loyrette also speculates, incisively, that Degas may have had in mind Henri Daumier's *Man of Property* (1837), another timely image of a nobleman in straitened circumstances, dramatically set in a comfortable interior and strikingly similar in the way it poses the figures.[17]

However early, this is Degas, and the deployment of color as well as the technical bravura of the painting are breathtaking. Full light suffuses the ice-white aprons and pale faces of the mother and daughters, while the father and a large ormolu clock on the mantel become enmeshed in shadows. A slightly green tinge in the blue wallpaper and in the Oriental carpet under their feet holds the work together harmonically, and the accents of gold in the frames of a drawing and a mirror, as well as in the candlesticks and other ornaments, are strong but subtle. The cleverest, most understated touch of all is the imitation of the Old Master red chalk drawing on the wall, framed in gold. It is an invention masquerading as a vaguely recognizable drawing in the family collection. In fact it is a portrait of Laure's father, Degas's stern and dignified grandfather, quietly inserted into the scene as a period piece. The manifold significances of the fake Old Master drawing include both personal and art historical statements. Recall the fake, vintage title purchased by the family. What better way to distance oneself from a stately grandfather than to render him in a style and simulated medium of several generations earlier? And can you imagine a more self-possessed young artist than one who slips a convincing representation of an Old Master drawing into a painting influenced by Van Dyck yet incorporating as well elements of the new art? The allusion functions at least both ways, as homage and as irony, to help Degas launch a career that rests its feet on a firm Classical foundation and casts its eye on the horizon. In 1918, after the artist's death, the painting was acquired for the national collections with the assistance of the comte and comtesse de Fels, who persuaded the artist's brother, René De Gas, to allow the sale to occur. It is now in the Musée d'Orsay.

The Belleli tableau hangs by the quintessential Impressionist paintings and pastels for which Degas is best known. Their modernity stems from a number of devices. A favorite of art historians is more sociological in nature than art historical. They extol Degas's penchant for undramatically depicting the common man or woman, such as milliners, store clerks, girls in the corps de ballet, and their sad-faced violinists. There are other Modern touches, though, including technical devices that are very much a part of the repertory of painters today. Degas was a master of dramatic cropping, introducing ideas along this line that have shaped the photography of the twentieth century. He also created a revolutionary new way of addressing the artist's point of view in such works as the pastels and paintings that depict dancers or the musicians in the orchestra pit from an elevated position, as though drawn from a box seat. Finally, Degas, in the Belleli portrait and in later works, found a way to pack a great deal of emotion (the indignation of those aristocrats in exile!) into paintings that are coolly, almost dispassionately rendered. As Rewald observes,

> Degas held with Delacroix that nature was a dictionary in which one finds only words, the elements that make phrases and stories. Realism meant to him not so much the faithful representation of an individual model or object, but the ability to perceive and to render some typical aspects of his time. Beyond the individual, he knew how to discover social, professional, or human types. But in exploring these exclusively for their pictorial possibilities, he escaped the danger of creating merely historical documents. . . . Degas's "intuition for the contemporary," his desire to achieve that line which would "precisely render life" had led him to search almost systematically for new angles and aspects.[18]

This returns the focus to the artist, who he was and what he felt. Even as a young man, Degas made a profound impression upon others, in part by his hauteur. "No one was quite sure what would become of him, but his manners, his cultivation, the urbanity of his conversation, the already well-known fierceness of his remarks, the intransigence of his positions, and a charm mixed with brusquesness made him a figure who was both feared and respected."[19] Degas was a notorious curmudgeon, and the unflattering depiction of his "dancers like little monkeys," as he called them, is but one example of how his general hardness found its way into the painting. In this way he was similar in temperament to Lautrec (as well as Bacon, Balthus, and strangely enough, Warhol). The least attrac-

and Lautrec showed that same bitter, brutal irascibility. In both cases it fomented when a childhood of privilege was interrupted by disappointment and sudden hardship (the same thing happened to Bacon). With their lives of ease and beauty interrupted, both Degas and Lautrec turned from the suitable occupations of their class to the profession of art. They also discovered a truth of Modern aesthetics: A picture does not have to be pretty or of a pretty subject to be art. The delicate pastel tones of Degas that find their way into best-selling calendars are seductive enough to distract viewers from the plainness of the ballerinas in costume. In the paintings, pastels, and voluminous graphic work of Lautrec, this loss of innocence manifests itself in a sharpening of profiles, a deliberate accentuation of the gauche or even the ugly.

Another Modern tendency shared by Puvis, Degas, and Lautrec was that powerful sense of what T. J. Clark calls contingency. As we have read, Duncan Phillips detected "self-questioning" in Puvis; as for Degas and Lautrec, they made the process of their revisions so much a part of their art that many of their works are palimpsests of pentimenti and multiple attempts to solve the same compositional problems. One common characteristic of many of their works, related to this notion of contingency, is how lightly they are painted or the pastel is applied, to the point where the underlying canvas or paper figures prominently in the chromatic makeup of the work. How often does Degas simply add a strip of paper to augment the scale of a pastel or drawing and supplement what many in his time would consider a finished and integral whole with a band of color or added detail? Late in his career, particularly, Lautrec was wont to rework lithogaphic stones until they took on the near-abstract appearance of a Bacon painting, as in the case of his *Chien et Perroquet*.

One of the most astute recent writers on Lautrec is the poet John Ashbery, who keys in on these hesitations and attempts to explain them biographically. Ashbery feels that for Lautrec "uncertainties as to what he felt about his subjects" as well as "stuffiness" that robs the interiors of air and space are directly attributable to the artist's background. "Would Lautrec have been a different, and greater, painter if the accident which caused his physical deformity had not forced him away from the culti-

intended to amuse or shock on the spur of the moment, yet they somehow managed to pierce conventional wisdom about the making of art in ways that yielded originality. Through these breakthroughs, Lautrec's technique and subject matter forced their way into Modern aesthetics.

On the basis of his family background alone, the idea of Henri Marie Raymond de Toulouse-Lautrec-Montfa as a high priest of the Modern was highly unlikely. His first name honors his paternal ancestor Henri V, Comte de Chambord and the legitimate if exiled heir to the French throne. The other references are to the city (Toulouse), town (Lautrec), and parish (Montfa) where the family seat was located. No artist in this book is as distinguished in his lineage as Lautrec, first son of a comte. But for a conspiracy among his family members to deprive him of his inheritance because of his disability and what they perceived to be his mental instability, he would have been heir to a minor empire of family estates, including the Hôtel du Bosc in Albi, assorted hunting lodges, Paris townhouses, and chateaux. This family saga, like Sand's, was permanently grafted to the history of France and makes for even more colorful reading. His grandmothers were sisters and his mother, Adele, had married her first cousin Alphonse as part of a ploy to keep the vast estates in one family. Alphonse was a graduate of Saint-Cyr, a second lieutenant in the Lancers and a horseman and hunter. Like the stern paternal absences that deflected Bacon and Swinburne into their careers, the scorn of Lautrec's father drove him into art. He was also a complete mama's boy. "J'ai deux vies," he said to a friend, contrasting the rambunctious life of the art crowd with the formal strictness of his mother's high tea. Time and again he tapped Adele for support, mainly financial. As his most reliable biographer writes, "His letters to her are full of relatives and chateaux, inheritances and sporting events, horses, wines and carriages. . . . Adele's over-decorated salons were full of knick-knacks and sombre Louis XV furniture, with family arms engraved on the silver, and formed a startling contrast to Lautrec's bohemian quarters, just a few minutes' walk away."[21]

The family was horrifyingly manipulative, and the lengths to which they were willing to go to preserve their land holdings and reputation are but one indication of the challenge Lautrec faced as an artist who elected to live in and represent the demimonde. The intermarriage that set him up genetically for his disability was the product of this paranoia, a way to keep the wealth in the family. The main estate of Le Bosc was overshadowed by ill fortune. When phylloxera began destroying vines, his grandmother sold Le Bosc to his aunt, keeping it out of the hands of Henry, as he preferred to be called (in English, the language he frequently used for his correspondence). It was not just his disability that convinced the family that he should be kept out of the loop (he never knew of the disposition of the property until years after) but his choice of career. At eighteen he had gone to Paris to study art. The machinations continued, as his father sold other property that should have been his, symbolically rejecting him. Lautrec was technically in line to inherit the title and the property. As a child, kidding around, he signed an early notebook "Monsieur le Vicomte," a temporary honorific he could use until he assumed his full peerage. His family had other ideas. His father encouraged him to use a nom de plume to sign his art. When his father became a virtual agoraphobic, living in a tower on his brother's estate, Lautrec's uncle committed the ultimate act of familial rejection of an artistic career and held a Savanarola-style auto-da-fé in the estate courtyard, right under the window of Lautrec's father. The eight large paintings burned with the trimmings of the grapevines, which would now be worth hundreds of millions of dollars on the auction market, had been left at Le Bosc. They were committed to the bonfire "to protect the honor of the family name."[22] As his uncle declared, "This rubbish will no longer dishonor my house."

To his credit, Lautrec was oblivious to his family's despicable behavior because he was living it up in Paris at the time and studying hard under the aegis of some of Paris's best painters. As his biographer, Julia Frey, notes,

> Henry's independence, possibly strengthened by his sense of entitlement as an aristocrat from a family with a tradition of eccentricity, kept him quite free as an artist. He welcomed classical training to acquire the skills he needed, and his work quickly began to show an expertise in perspective and draughtsmanship; but his need to establish his own sense of independent identity, both from his family and from his training, kept him from feeling philosophically bound to observe the limits of classical taste, and he was intrigued, rather than annoyed, by accidental effects of light and movement. In his later work he would repeatedly focus, for example, on the bizarre distortions of this models' faces made by stage footlights.[23]

He was also enjoying himself, in a style that has become part of the Lautrec mystique, ridiculously portrayed in movies as well as played up in historical accounts of the period. Some of his partners in crime were either noblemen or affected the demeanor of aristocrats. Lautrec and Puvis were not the only aristocrats on the scene. Degas, although of an older generation, was a presence, and Lautrec worshipped his pastels, taking friends on pilgrimages to see paintings and other works owned by friends who were collectors.

A fellow student of painting, Sir William Thomas Warrener, was to be immortalized by Lautrec as *The Englishman at the Moulin Rouge*, about which more below. Comte Antoine de la Rochefoucauld was a dilettante, painter, and arts patron whose work was often on view and who was associated with the Salon de la Rose and Croix at Durand Ruel in 1892, curated by Sar Merodach Josephein Peladin, a poet, journalist, and freelance curator. They were part of the mystical fringe, proto-New Age aristocrats interested in medievalism and Rosicrucianism. Baron Dujardin, Anquetin's friend, shared the Montmartre night life. A dandy with a lace-trimmed handkerchief and monocle who once fought a duel, he loved art and literary theory. Along with Paul Verlaine and Adolphe Moreas, Dujardin became an important leader of the Symbolist movement, supporting the publication of *La Revue independente* and *La Revue Wagnerienne*. A cheerleader as Lautrec made the rounds of the brothels and nightclubs, he bought many of the larger variations on Degas brothel scenes.

Lautrec played the art market like a master, using every connection he had as well as one of the oldest tricks in the books, the parlaying into sales of celebrity connections, including his friendship with the rising stars of the Moulin Rouge. Some biographers have been puzzled by his motivation for hustling so hard. Degas sold his art to recoup family losses. Lautrec sold for other, less obvious reasons. "Henry, although his annual allowance kept him from serious material want, was profoundly concerned with selling his work. He accepted any commission he received and asked the highest prices the market would bear. To him, selling his work was not so much income—although he was always short of money—as a form of recognition and further evidence to his family that he was a serious provisional artist. His family responded with ambivalence, embarrassed by his style, by his subjects, by the tone of the magazines in which he published and by his unaristocratic commercialism."[24]

He achieved overnight fame, à la Byron, at age twenty-six with a poster for the Moulin Rouge of La Goulue, her bottom scandalously highlighted. In terms of high and low, Lautrec had no fear of the nether echelons, one of the reasons that art historians have no qualms about including him among the Moderns. Even his literary tastes, linked by admirers with Nietzsche, Balzac, and other high-toned authors, in actuality ran more to sappy plays by Eugène Scribe and the cheap novels of the day. He was downright Warholian in terms of his attunement to popular culture. This accords well with his blossoming into fame as a magazine, poster, and print artist, reaching the largest possible public by eagerly appealing to a socially broad cross-section. Even as he painted one of his greatest works, *The Englishman at the Moulin Rouge*, a portrait of Warrener (an aristocrat slumming in Paris in the 1880s who studied at the Académie Julian), Lautrec had in mind the print that would be made from the painting. It is one of the artist's most engaging and at the same time unforgiving portraits, playing upon Warrener's aristocratic bearing yet lacing it with an undignified lasciviousness. As with the dramas of Hofmannsthal, it draws on the nostalgia and sadness of the last waltz of the nobility in an era when they were becoming more and more peripheral, but it invests this theme, romantic in Hofmannsthal, with an edge that is more Modern. No one is going to feel too sorry for Warrener, who is clearly ripe for the comeuppance his dissipated life has coming to him. In a weird transformation, he becomes a veritable silhouette in the later print version.

Lautrec's monetary success as an artist arose from an unusual segment of the art market that was remarkably like the most commercial aspect of today's gallery scene, where dealers readily divide between low-pressure, quiet havens for recondite or cutting-edge work and the bigger, more businesslike organizations (now including auction houses) that exist to sell, sell, sell. Lautrec was firmly in the latter camp, churning an endless series of paintings exhibitions into rolling waves of further action through the multiples and using all the press he would draw as a celebrity and nobleman to amplify his market value even further. Despite his good name and commitment to salesmanship, Lautrec was turned away from the fashionable Cercle Volney and the Salon, the conservative art world that his family would have known. He was, however, accepted in Montmartre. "Here at the center of the privileged world of well-to-do bohemianism in belle-époque Paris, in this odd mixture of elegance, beauty and snobbishness, of intentional marginality, Jewish intellectualism, internationalism and high living, Henry at last found a meeting of his two worlds, and he felt very much at home."[25] Among the friends who made him most at home were Thadée and Misia Natanson, whose circle of artists and intellectuals could better appreciate Lautrec than could the stiff upper classes from which he had voluntarily emerged. Only a rank amateur would think that art is an easy life, fit for lazy types who want only to play all day in the studio. Not only is it hard work to sustain a life in art economically, but motivation is a constant problem. Different personalities have different ways to stoke their appetites for long, solitary studio sessions, and in Lautrec's case, not unlike Warhol's, the prospect of action and recognition from the marketplace was clearly a primary source of inspiration. It does not take a degree in psychiatry to sort out why Lautrec would so highly value the approval of the art scene through its patronage, having been first ignored and then excoriated by his family for pursuing his vocation.

Where and how Lautrec showed his work is part of his modernity. In the case of both Lautrec and Puvis de Chavannes, the strangeness not only of their style and subject matter but even of their art itself kept them apart from more conventional artists. In 1893, La Libre Esthetique in

Paris and the William Morris–led crafts movement in England meant that artists turned to decorative media such as glass (Paul Albert Besnard), wood panels (including Gauguin), and screens (Emile Bernard). Beyond new media, there was the movement into what in our time is called "alternative spaces," the cabarets artistiques and ad hoc exhibition locales that Lautrec used in order to be almost constantly on view. There are two ways in which this is ahead of its time. He found a means of reaching a far broader audience than his academy-trained classmates had. Second, his choices of medium, subject matter, scale, and styles were liberated by this extramural, extracurricular adventurousness.

Lautrec could be as harsh on the reigning masters of painting as he was on the upper classes of society. As a student, he made a particularly savage parody of Puvis's *Le Bois sacre cher aux arts aux muses* (*The Sacred Grove, Beloved of the Arts and the Muses*). It was a large painting, bigger even than the epic original, which measured 69 by 152 inches. Lautrec was assisted by a team of painters from his teacher Cormon's atelier although Lautrec was the only one with enough courage to sign it. The parody counters the original and its creator element by element. Puvis is committed to the pure and timeless. The irreverent students introduced a clock reading five minutes after nine. Where Puvis's anonymous denizens of the Golden Age seem completely ethereal, Lautrec invades the scene with a group of nineteenth-century intruders, men who were of the moment, including Anquetin and his friend Edouard Dujardin, a writer, as well as Maurice Barrès, a journalist, politician, and writer. The lowest blow is struck by the inclusion of Lautrec, shown from behind relieving himself as the others pass by. Biographers have suggested that the gesture of protest was prompted by the fact that Lautrec was impatient with the allegories that Cormon had him do, and no artist was more readily identified with the mode than Puvis.[26]

There is a whole stream of Contemporary art that is thematically linked by urination, from Marcel Duchamp's notorious *Fountain* through the Oxidation paintings on copper of Andy Warhol to the inflamatory *Piss Christ* of Andres Serrano. The disrespect shown by the act itself invokes the desire to shock that is a hallmark of so much Modernism. Fortunately, this type of crude gesture is not the only link between Lautrec and the art of our time. Critics have associated Lautrec and early abstraction—either pointing to the priority he gives to the shape of a glove in his posters of cabaret singers or recounting the anecdote about Thadée Natanson, claiming that Henry had rescued a spoiled proof of three red dots, two large and one smaller, upon which Thadée had bestowed a big gold frame.[27] There are shades here of Adolph Gottlieb and the Abstract Expressionists, just as the swirling curves and even furniture of *Chien et perroquet*, a lithograph done on 8 February 1899 and drawn directly on the stone, look very like a Bacon drawing.

In his day, as brilliant and wildly original as these early moments of abstraction were in the eyes of some admirers, for nonbelievers they were sure indications of the dissolution of the artist's mind. His family in particular were convinced that alcoholism had overtaken his talent. Lautrec's celebrity and genealogy caught up with him in real life. In 1899 he was committed to an asylum by his mother. The papers had a field day with the nobleman gone crazy. Edmond Lepelletier wrote in *L'Echo de Paris* on 28 March:

> The fruit of such genealogical trees is generally shriveled and eaten away by a worm at its heart. . . . The last descendant of a worn-out lineage, the painter of Montmartre looked like a caricature of his forefathers, puny stunted deformed. His virgin palette and his unused brush, like a shield that was seldom dented and a sword that remained too often idle in its scabbard, proved only too well that all he had inherited from his ancient blood was a fondness for pleasure and a distaste for that proletarian virtue, hard work. Either through weakness or hubris he continued to flaunt the glorious name of his ancestors. He did not have the modesty to adopt a plebian pseudonym. Unfortunately Toulouse-Lautrec did not conduct himself like one of the great men of his line.[28]

History has, of course, recorded a far different verdict. Where Lautrec succeeds, Ashbery suggests, is in "ennobling the commonplace."[29] In such paintings as his *Moulin de la Galette*, one of several paintings on the theme (Renoir and Picasso also accomplished theirs) he carved out his own technical and conceptual territory. When they did not submit to gimmickry, his innovations pushed art ahead in various technical ways, particularly with regard to printmaking. Lautrec prided himself upon being au courant—his passion for American-style cocktails, which he mixed personally at a corner bar at some of his openings, is one memorable example—and certainly his ability to have show after show is testimony to a self-imposed pressure to keep up with the acceleration of the time, the psychology of which can be related to the fin-de-siècle mentality. The epitome of Decadence, sharp as in our day Warhol would be, Lautrec moved in the immediate present with an eye toward the future, a powerful antidote to the romance with the past of Puvis.

Wherever the art historical debate over the true course of Modernism leads, few would deny the centrality of Picasso; and when it comes to selecting the canonical Picasso, no matter what ideology prevails, it would be almost unthinkable to overlook the great tragic paintings of the Blue and Rose Periods. Now icons of the tradition and stylistically so often identified with Picasso that even the most callow first-time visitors to museums can scarcely misattribute them, the great Blue Period masterpieces of 1902 through 1907 seem to stand alone. However, a salient biographical detail or two and a keen eye for the resemblance between the way two artists work might suggest a path from one to the other that in no way belittles the originality or accomplishment of Picasso while suddenly placing the earlier artist in a more Modern light.

Before skipping to the obvious narrative link, try testing your eye. At the National Gallery in Washington, Picasso and Lautrec hang side by side. The sure line, sharp features, and commixture of sadness and irony in their paintings are shockingly similar. A sheaf of connections and coincidences between their paths, which never actually crossed, shows why Picasso was saturated with the influence of Lautrec at an early stage of his development. In Barcelona in the crucial year 1898 he came under the aegis of a small group of painters and intellectuals at a taverna called El Quatre Gats (Catalan slang for "the secret gang"), headed by Miquel Utrillo and his mistress Suzanne Valadon. They taught him the basics of international Modernism, not just in art but in terms of the ideas of Wagner, Nietzsche, and Wilde. Valladon, a former circus acrobat who became an artist's model after a fall from the trapeze, fired his imagination with heady tales of the studio sessions in which she had worked with Puvis, Degas, and Lautrec. Picasso's painting took on many of the stylistic characteristics of Lautrec; and when he went to Paris about a year later, his subject matter and the circles in which he moved—thanks in part to Utrillo, who was there to open doors for him—intersected with Lautrec's world at more than one point. In addition to drawing from Puvis's ceiling at the Panthéon, he drew a portrait of Jane Avril, Lautrec's most famous subject, and visited the extraordinary women's prison of Saint-Lazare, run by nuns, where Lautrec found free models (Picasso's masterpiece *The Laundress* is based on a drawing he did there).

Picasso painted his own version of *Le Moulin de la Galette*, after Renoir and Lautrec, which coincidentally was bought by a patron of Lautrec from Toulouse, Arthur Huc, publisher of *La Dépêche de Toulouse*. Now at the Guggenheim Museum in New York, it was the first Picasso in a French collection. The young Spaniard's first dealer in Paris was Berthe Weill, who had established her business by selling Daumier and Lautrec prints. She showed Picasso at her gallery, at 25 rue Victor–Masse, a few steps from the home of Degas, who couldn't stand her mainly because she was Jewish. His next dealer, Ambrose Vollard, commissioned, for a one-man show in June 1901, the first catalog essay on Picasso's work. It was written by Gustave Coquiot, who also happens to have been the author of the first monograph on Lautrec. Of course, his essay compared Picasso with Lautrec, as well as with Degas, although he called their influence a "passing phase" in the young newcomer's development.

At this point, with the remarkable blossoming of Picaso's Blue Period, the more familiar story of twentieth-century art takes over. It has always been a challenge to imagine what direction Picasso's legendary gaze had traveled in. If Modernism is a valorization and originality the prize, it would be difficult to absolutely judge who has priority in any of these respects. We have come from gazing upward at the ceilings of Delacroix and Puvis to staring down with Degas and Lautrec at the denizens of the demimonde. The strangeness of the angle and the freshness of the view are what unite these great Modernists in one vein of creative superiority.

3

A Knight at the Opera

HUGO VON HOFMANNSTHAL AND RICHARD STRAUSS

Unless your taste in opera runs to twentieth-century Baroque—not a contradiction in terms when elaborate productions of *The Rake's Progress*, *Der Rosenkavalier*, and *The Ghosts of Versailles* remain among the most popular recent offerings at major houses—or you frequent used-book stores with deep drama collections, you are unlikely to have run into much by Hugo von Hofmannsthal lately. The perfect embodiment of the princely Viennese aesthete, he was in his day the librettist for the greatest of Richard Strauss's operas, the star of literary Vienna, a dramatist both popular and substantive, and a prose stylist far too admirable to have slid into such obscurity. He was also the prophet, thanks to a wrenching and now forgotten essay, of the Postmodern sensibility, particularly the crisis of language precipitated when words are dislocated from their referential function due to what Jean Piaget called the "arbitrary nature of the sign."

Raised in a grand household in imperial Vienna, as was his distant relative Ludwig Wittgenstein, to be the family's courtly intellectual, Hofmannsthal fulfilled his sophisticated parents' expectations by carving out a strange yet important role in Modern theater history.[1] His work tensely unites Neo-Classicism (in a manner reminiscent of Swinburne, whose poetry he extravagantly admired in published essays, as well as of Stravinsky and Balthus) with the savageries of Expressionism and Freudian psychology. The latter should be no surprise, as Hofmannsthal came of age in Vienna during that glorious age of the arts dominated by Egon Schiele and Gustav Klimt. The main character of each Hofmannsthal opera was a woman, whereas the plays took men as their leads; and if one were to choose an image for the cover of an edition of his libretti, a Klimt of a woman with a look of longing on her face would be perfect. The cover of a volume of the plays might be one of Francis Bacon's anguished portraits of a man in a business suit.

The psychoanalytic depths of Hofmannsthal's characterization reflect ideas that were in the air in Vienna and found a receptive intelligence in a young man who might strike some as outwardly too upper-crust and conservative to give them much credence. According to translator and editor Michael Hamburger, however, Hofmannsthal's library included first editions of both Josef Breuer's *Studies in Hysteria* (1895) and Freud's *Interpretation of Dreams* (1900).[2] This helps account for the raw Oedipal quality of *The Tower* (*Die Turn*), a play in the tradition of Symbolist dramas such as *Axel* by Villiers de l'Isle Adam and *Pelleas et Mélisande* by Maurice Maeterlinck. It is not performed often, especially in translation. Major opera houses are far more likely to produce attractive stagings of *Der Rosenkavalier* (1911) or the charming and quite funny gloss upon Molière's *Bourgeois gentilhomme*, a period piece serving as a gilt frame around the one-act opera *Ariadne auf Naxos* (1912). The soul-searching, if less elegant, first collaboration of Hofmannsthal and Strauss, *Elektra* (1909), like *The Tower,* carries the argument for the modernity of Hofmannsthal well into the dark, destructive territory plumbed by contemporaries such as Schiele, Klimt, and rival playwright Arthur Schnitzler. The unfettered emotions released in *The Tower* are surprising, because they seem to emanate from a youthful Romantic, some young Werther, an image that could not be further from the outward aspect of Hofmannsthal. Prim and courtly in person, he played his nobility (bagatelle, unfortunately) to the hilt, even to the point of quietly resenting the awkward gulf between his social status and that of Strauss.

However, there was a limit at which Hofmannsthal preferred to turn and seek again the radiance of a beloved period in Austrian cultural history—that chandelier-lit era of Maria Theresa—and in the end it was the *burgerlich* but more intrepid Strauss who ventured further into Modernism by pursuing musical ideas of daring originality to their extremes. Although he bears the same name as the renowned Johann Strauss and his three musical sons, Richard Strauss was not part of that Austrian musical dynasty at all. He did pay homage to the Waltz King in one of the best-known passages of *Der Rosenkavalier*, an exquisite, perfectly "Straussian" waltz. Yet Richard Strauss was a German and, according to a recent biography, thoroughly middle class in his taste and upbringing; although it must be pointed out that not only was he the son of an orchestral player at the opera, but he married an opera singer. He was born and raised in Munich, the son of Franz Strauss, the first-desk horn player of the

Munich Opera orchestra (beloved of all horn players still for reducing the unplayable horn call in Wagner's *Siegfried* to the shape that is used today). His mother was from the brewing family of Pschorr, and although not fabulously wealthy, the family was comfortably off. Strauss's father carefully oversaw the boy's musical education, and he graduated from the University of Munich in 1882. One of the few unflattering observations often repeated about Strauss was that he was a little too fond of making money, particularly as an internationally renowned and sought-after conductor (a protégé of von Bülow who took his master's place as principal conductor of both the Meiningen and Berlin Philharmonic orchestras). His avarice could lead to embarrassing gigs such as a concert he led and was paid quite handsomely for in a Manhattan department store, or it could end in such innovative projects as the first full-length film of an opera, an unevenly performed *Rosenkavalier* that Strauss conducted on camera in 1912. Strauss's wife, the soprano Pauline de Ahna, was a vigorous promoter of her husband's high-profile career and not a fan of Hofmannsthal, who obliged by avoiding her almost entirely during his twenty-eight-year-long collaboration with Strauss.

As with any creative partnership, Hofmannsthal and Strauss had roles to play that differentiated them from one another dynamically, investing the relationship with drama of its own. The idea-rich aristocrat and the workmanlike, middle-class musician assumed their parts as naturally as their breeding dictated. The contrast generated energy, even at the expense of feelings and the occasional bruised ego. To complicate matters further, Hofmannsthal himself was a fascinating bundle of contradictions, a staunch defender of tradition who was also deeply aware of the need to move ahead to embrace Modernism. On the page, he could howl and snarl with the darkest of the Expressionists, but contemporaries and later generations have preferred his anachronistic brand of Baroque sweetness and light. His greatest creations remain the elegant Meissen centerpieces of *Der Rosenkavalier*: the Marschallin in her satin and lace and young Count Octavian, immaculate in white and silver silk brocade and bearing the silver rose signifying a marriage proposal to a fifteen-year-old commoner, the daughter of a dreaded nouveau riche Viennese. It is delightful to think of how diligently scholars combed the annals of eighteenth-century Austria and further back in time to find the origins of this quaint custom of the nobility, only to concede that Hofmannsthal had made it all up from whole cloth, with a little assistance from his elegant friend, Count Kessler.[3] It takes an adroit student of aristocratic rituals to pull off a fake as convincing as that.

Like the silver rose by which he trumped the most code-conscious of all audiences, the opera *Der Rosenkavalier* is a splendid throwback to the eighteenth century and is also the somewhat autobiographical creation of the pampered darling of a prosperous family, who grew up in a small palace in Vienna. His doting parents made sure he attended the opera at the Burgtheater as well as concerts by Liszt, Clara Schumann, von Bülow, Artur Rubenstein, Brahms, and Joachim at Bosendorfer Hall. Hugo von Hofmannsthal arrived on the literary scene a superbly educated nineteen-year-old prodigy, blazing with the glory of his first book of precious, polished lyric poems. His mother, a Catholic, was of the "bagatelle" nobility based on her descent from wealthy landowners (other possibilities included officers and bureaucrats as well as wealthy merchants or industrialists recognized by the empire, as was the case of the Wittgensteins). Most of her considerable family fortune was lost in the stock market crash of 1873. On Hofmannsthal's father's side, he was partly Jewish, and scholars, notably Carl Schorske, believe that the assimilationist trend among wealthy Austrian Jews of the period made his father all the more eager for Hugo to play both the role of the artist and that of the aristocrat.

He was treated specially at home and at school. At the Akademisches Gymnasium his teachers and schoolmates granted particular attention to the "von" in Hugo's name. As the great Austrian novelist Herman Broch (author of *The Sleepwalkers* and *The Death of Virgil*) pointed out in a powerful, prescient study, written in exile in New Haven from 1947 until 1950 but never completed, "the aristocratic particle had a nimbus about it that instilled respect."[4] Broch's penetrating analysis is, like Hofmannsthal's work for the most part, a disguised elegy for the last days of the Austrian empire and a way of life, aesthetic and social, that both acknowledged had already vanished. Broch paints a romantic picture of Hofmannsthal as a schoolboy:

> Every child lives in dream-like imaginings; every child's a fairy-tale figure to himself. But whereas other children's experiences of reality cause them to feel like Tom Thumb or Cinderella so that they may likewise become prince or princesses in their fantasies, young Hofmannsthal was already in reality—in any case his reality—a thorough fairy-tale prince, singled out by beauty and spiritual triumph, singled out by his own seclusion, singled out by the emperor himself as a "nobleman," to the point where he felt a closer identification with the emperor, that ornately costumed figure gazing down at him from the portrait on the classroom wall, than he did with his teachers and peers. And in this way, unchecked, admitting no proof—if, indeed, without counterproof—and unnoticed, the dream and dream solitude was incorporated into everyday reality.[5]

Broch asserts that this personal fantasy of imperial glory was a sustaining factor in Hofmannsthal's creativity throughout his life, and one certainly feels that this is the case in works in which aristocratic characters are brought onstage, particularly Octavian, the courtly young dreamer, and the Marschallin, his nostalgic lady love, in *Der Rosenkavalier*.

Broch also points out that Hofmannsthal was keenly aware that his life coincided with the twilight of the imperial era—the plush red velvet emperor's box at the opera house was dark those evenings he went with his parents—but in art he might succeed in finding a way to extend the dream. Broch is not alone in his assessment of Hofmannsthal's retrospective stance. Schorske opens and closes his monumental history of fin-de-siècle Vienna with a similar view. He considers Hofmannsthal to be an emblem of the artistic class of the period because of his mixed background and complete devotion to art. According to Schorske,

> The Hofmannsthal family was the living embodiment of the bourgeoisie's aesthetic-aristocratic tradition. Hugo's father was a Viennese patrician of the purest dye, a true aristocrat of the spirit. Unlike Schnitzler's father, he had no idée fixe concerning his son's choice of career, his function in society. What alone mattered was that the boy cultivate his faculties for the optimum enjoyment of refined leisure. The gifted son was consequently reared in a virtual hothouse for the development of aesthetic talent. Small wonder that the adolescent Hofmannsthal became a young narcissus, "early ripened and tender and sad." Quickly absorbing the fashionable poetic and plastic culture of all Europe, his language glowed darkly with purple and gold, shimmered with world-weary mother-of-pearl. Small wonder, too, that he became the idol of Vienna's culture-ravenous intelligentsia, young and old.[6]

There is no historian better equipped than the interdisciplinary master Schorske to delineate the social and cultural situation that prompted Hofmannsthal to set out to preserve the heritage he had been so lovingly given by his family. Broch etches a picture of a culture in rapid decline, drifting toward a "vacuum" of values and taste, with Hofmannsthal feverishly holding onto the vestiges of traditional meaning. Schorske, however, holds a relatively brighter view:

> If the Viennese burghers had begun by supporting the temple of art as a surrogate form of assimilation into the aristocracy, they ended by finding in it an escape, a refuge from the unpleasant world of increasingly threatening political reality. . . . Elsewhere in Europe, art for art's sake implied the withdrawal of its devotees from a social class; in Vienna alone it claimed the allegiance of virtually a whole class, of which the artists were a part. The life of art became a substitute for the life of action. Indeed, as civic action proved increasingly futile, art became almost a religion, the source of meaning and the food of the soul.[7]

This idealism and simultaneous awareness of its futility is embedded in Hofmannsthal's greatest works and manifest in his life. The starting point for an appreciation of his noble quest is the fascinating and prescient essay "The Letter of Lord Chandos." For scholars of Modernism and Postmodernism who focus upon the crisis of representation, particularly as manifest in language, it represents a milestone. Its value as a guidepost to Hofmannsthal's thinking and future dramas cannot be overestimated. A profoundly personal and sincere cri de coeur, reminiscent in its way of the great yet despairing *Heiligenstadt Testament* (1802) of Beethoven, it is all the more remarkable for its date: written at the very end of 1901 and published in 1902. The issue it lays out, albeit under the cloak of a fictive historical voice, is the same as the central problem that powered the debates over both Structuralism and Deconstruction, namely, what linguists beginning with Piaget and De Saussure called the collapse of the denotative value of language. Hofmannsthal dramatizes the harrowing experience, undoubtedly genuine, of a young writer blessed with great gifts and incipient glory yet losing his grip on his medium and thence his life. Until the time he wrote it, Hofmannsthal was enjoying dazzling success, a young literary comet streaking across the Viennese café scene, publishing widely and to great acclaim and reveling in precisely the pleasant if relatively recondite life that his family had envisioned for him. Despite its defeatist tone, the essay did not mark the end of that promising start. It became the fulcrum upon which Hofmannsthal leveraged the rich literary, musical, and artistic background that was his birthright to gain a broader, more public, and therefore more active role in Viennese cultural life.

That sense of noblesse oblige married to the obvious impossibility of returning to the Golden Age of Maria-Theresa prompts sympathetic feelings of admiration, particularly among those who hope for the triumph of art over adversity. This is precisely the heroic part in which Schorske casts Hofmannsthal, closing his magnificent history of the period by returning to the figure who played such an important part in its opening pages: "Hofmannsthal's attempt to break out of the solipsism and cultured isolation of the life of art was then two-pronged: On the one hand, he returned to revitalize a traditional morality of personal responsibility; on the other, he thrust forward toward depth psychology and the affirmation of instinct. . . . Hofmannsthal had rescued the function of art from the hedonistic isolation into which his class had carried it and had tried to redeem society through art's reconciling power. But the rifts in the body social had proceeded too far. Society could tolerate tragedy or comedy, but not redemption through aesthetic harmonization. It was left to a new generation to formulate the intellectual consequences of that cultural fact."[8] In a way, Hofmannsthal's earnest and principled art carried out the essence of an aristocratic code of honor. Art had been in need of a rescuer, and he was willing to answer that call.

The public phase of Hofmannsthal's maturity, taking hold of his writing as he emerged from an overprotected chrysalis of lyric poetry, resembles many of the other figures in this study (Russell, Bacon, Balthus, Liszt, Delacroix, Sand, Puvis de Chavannes, Lautrec), who deliberately expanded their audiences by moving away from the specialized, academic, or narrowly elitist circles in which they started their careers to seek a broader arena. In Hofmannsthal's case, what might have turned into a career similar to that of Mallarmé or Pater, spent polishing short and beautiful if labyrinthine essays and lyric poems, was turned first toward the more accessible materials of folktales and then to that realm of action and interaction with the public, the theater. One noteworthy parallel to the change made by Hofmannsthal is a similar progression through Celtic mythology to the Abbey Theatre made by William Butler Yeats (who ended up debating in the Irish Senate) or the translations from Italian folktales and best-selling fiction of Italo Calvino, to pick an example closer to our own time. Another parallel is offered by the life of Samuel Beckett, whose poetry had delighted a handful of connoisseurs in Paris and whose novel *Murphy* had sold only six copies in 1946 when he decided to try his hand at writing plays, a medium that brought him a vast audience. Certainly, the popularizing of philosophy by Russell, as well as his political activism, also bear comparison with Hofmannsthal's transition to the theater, and Lautrec's posters were, of course, not only early examples of billboard advertising but of theater announcements, although it must be said that Hofmannsthal and Lautrec were worlds apart in their approaches to their subject matter.

Hofmannsthal's works were destined to become the proverbial instant classics they are, not just because they were so masterful but because they had that patina about them, similar to the masterpiece effect that Balthus strove for in painting. As exciting as they were in their time, when they consistently made their successful debuts, they are in a specifically Mannerist way examples of avant-garde opera. However Modern his idiom, the core of Hofmannsthal's thinking remained a spiritual allegiance to the tradition. He once observed that the activity of modern poets "stands under the decree of necessity, as though they were all building on a pyramid, the monstrous residence of a dead king or an unborn god."[9] This admission, read in the wake of a major body of scholarship devoted to the burden of the past, instigated by Harold Bloom's slim but important book *The Anxiety of Influence*, has a particularly ominous ring. Following the arguments of Broch and Schorske, the dead king can be as literal and recent as the emasculated Austrian emperor or as deep-seated as the overall need of an artist for a god or king to reign somewhere, however dimly in the background. It would take a mighty pen indeed to redeem a vow as challenging as this. As Schorske comments, "With his Habsburg traditionalism and his daring quest for a new politics of sublimation, he seemed to be at work on both."[10] In addition to Broch and Schorske, at least one other powerful literary historian accords a similarly high honor to Hofmmansthal. At the end of his own masterpiece on cultural memory and heritage, *European Literature and the Latin Middle Ages*, E. R. Curtius turns to Hofmannsthal as a leading figure in the "protest against forgetting" that his own book enjoined. Curtius insists, apropos of Hofmannsthal's legacy, "there is nothing more pressing than to restore 'memory' in the sense of a European cultural tradition."[11]

Taking upon himself the nearly impossible burden of being simultaneously traditional and original, it is no wonder that Hofmannsthal suffered a cataclysmic moment early in his career. He turned to the fictive identity of Philip Lord Chandos, the younger son of the earl of Bath, who writes a letter dated 22 August 1603 to the philosopher Francis Bacon, later Baron Verulam Viscount of St. Albans, grandson of the duke of Exeter. Chandos has maintained two years of silence and is now twenty-six, as was Hofmannsthal when he wrote the essay. At nineteen—the age when Hofmannsthal had celebrated his first success as a poet—Chandos had written a highly praised pastorale for Queen Elizabeth, then set off on the Grand Tour. His downfall bottomed out in a sudden attack of paralysis that is specifically linguistic in its symptoms. The scholar cannot even recognize his own Latin treatise, much less continue writing—it is, he realizes, "a disease of my mind." How fascinating that this young Austrian poet would elect as his persona an English aristocratic intellectual of the seventeenth century and proceed to reveal all the distress he feels at being unable to make his words mean anything—referring to all the prevailing languages of the time, including Latin but excepting German.

Chandos is sick of rhetoric and facile literary evasions. His lapse into silence has been precipitated by a harrowing confrontation with "that deep, true, inner form which sin can be sensed only beyond the domain of rhetorical tricks; that form of which one can no longer say that it organizes subject matter, for it penetrates it, dissolves it, creating at once both dream and reality."[12] Like a graduate student despondent over completing the dissertation, Chandos doubts he will ever fulfill his ambitions when nothing has meaning: "I feel as though I myself were about to ferment, to effervesce, to foam and to sparkle. And the whole thing is a kind of feverish thinking, but thinking in a medium more immediate, more liquid, more glowing than words. It, too, forms whirlpools but of a sort that do not seem to lead, as the whirlpools of language, into the abyss, but into myself and into the deepest womb of peace."[13] Nearly half a century before Beckett or Joyce's *Finnegans Wake*, and a generation before Wittgenstein, this premonition has a familiar ring. As Schorske comments, with regard as well to the plays and their ability to reconcile class differences, "Hofmannsthal accepted the breakdown of language itself. Like a Baroque man, he affirmed a polylingual reality. In his plays, as in life, every character has his own dialect. The problem is not to find and save the single truth of pure language, but to adapt the voices, dialects all, to each other, as, in letter writing, one tempers one's diction to the person addressed. The social potential of language was in its adaptability, its capacity to adjust to otherness, its plastic power for interpersonal bonding."[14]

Verging on the silence of Mallarmé and Swinburne, considered elsewhere in this study, Chandos writes, "the language in which I might be able not only to write but to think is neither Latin nor English, neither Italian nor Spanish, but a language none of whose words is known to me, a language in which inanimate things speak to me and wherein I may one day have to justify myself before an unknown judge."[15] In terms of Hofmannsthal's own career, this essay, so ahead of its time, signaled an important shift from writing in the esoteric vein (mainly his polished poetry and essays on aesthetics) to the public sphere of writing for the theater, through which he determined he could accomplish more toward his goal of restoring some of the values of an Austria either gone by or rapidly going by. The paradox that lies at the heart of this assumption involves the necessity of using language, albeit in a different vein but somehow facing the same dreaded problem as the Chandos letter poses. The confessional vein of the essay is in the line of Rilke's *Malte Laurids Brigge*, and similarly, the blend of theology and genealogy is linked to Hofmannsthal's own sense that his presence echoed that of distant ancestors.

As Hofmannsthal expert David Miles notes, there is a strong presence of the contemporary philosopher Ernest Mach as well in this vitally important essay, which has been underrated by literary critics: "Behind these words lies not only the existential despair Kierkegaard had prophesied for the aesthetic existence once it had become conscious of itself, but also a pathologically Machian revolt against such specious abstractions as ego and body: Chandos suffers from an 'inexplicable uneasiness' at even uttering the words 'spirit,' 'soul' or body. What Mach preaches, 'the self must be given up'—Chandos is forced to live, and life thus becomes for him a succession of isolated moments, the self an array of pointillistic fragments."[16] Others place the Chandos letter and what followed, the movement into theater, in a more nationalistic perspective. In Broch's not altogether admiring terms, "With his Salzburg morality plays and his well-intentioned but misguided cultural criticism, Hofmannsthal had elevated the baroque gestures of his youth from lyric poetry to the *lebende Bilder* into a cultural vocabulary and ideology for Austrian revival."[17] Compensating for an absent emperor, the artist takes responsibility for reinstating cultural identity through the interweaving of paradigms and principles in the fabric of literature at its most refined level.

Hofmmansthal was not immune to the charms of contemporary art. An encounter with what was then considered to be one of the most outré examples of Postimpressionism, the paintings of Van Gogh, led to the deeply appreciative epistolary essay "Colors," written in May 1901 and intriguingly subtitled "From the Letters of a Man Who Returned" as though the proper art lover could retreat from his accidental and exhilarating brush with the art of the future. Rapturous and impressionistic, it offers some of the most memorable writing in the vast body of Van Gogh criticism. The little drama Hofmannsthal sets up is familiar: a self-made millionaire on a business trip arranging a major deal is suddenly gripped by a panic he attributes to a "poisoning . . . lying in the European air" that robs all around him of its reality. To escape, he ducks into a small gallery and for the first time in twenty years spends some time with art. Here is a sample, cited to show Hofmannsthal not just as a sharp-eyed lover of painting but as one who is deeply receptive to the power of a new and untamed force in art:

> Shall I tell you about the colors? There is an incredible blue, most powerful of blues, which constantly reappears, a green like that of molten emeralds, a yellow that deepens into orange. But what are colors if the innermost life of objects doesn't break through them! And this innermost life was there, tree and stone and wall and gorge gave of themselves their innermost, almost casting it at me—not, however, the voluptuousness and harmony of their lovely inanimate lives, as sometimes, in days gone by, like a magic atmosphere it had flowed towards me from old paintings: no, only the impact of its existence, the ferocious wonder of its existence surrounded by incredibility, made a dead set at my soul. . . . It was in a storm that these trees were born under my eyes, were born for my sake, their roots stretching into the earth, their branches stretching against the clouds; in a storm these earth rifts, these valleys between hills surrendered themselves; even in the bulk of the rock blocks was frozen storm. And now I could, from picture to picture, feel a Something, could feel the mingling, the merging of formation, how the innermost life broke forth into color and how the colors lived one for the sake of the others, and how one, mysteriously powerful, carried all the others; and in all this could sense a heart, the soul of the man who had created it, who with this vision did himself answer the spasms of his own most dreadful doubt.[18]

That Hofmannsthal was ready to venture a ringing endorsement of Van Gogh's passionate painting decades before popular approbation made him a safe bet should not be altogether surprising, given his close personal acquaintance with Schiele and Klimt. He was also on top of the literary scene through his café contacts and wide reading. Yet he had a mechanism for staying above the messier battles over shock value, the breaking of rules and the necessary debunking of ancestors. His impersonality, much like Eliot's, consisted in maintaining a distance from even his closest ally, Strauss, as well as the audience. It is fair to assume that this was partly due to his aristocratic attitude, conveyed in a revealing essay, "Shakespeare's Kings and Noblemen" (1905), in which he praises a sense of nobility that is "the Atmosphere, the air of life, *ce grand air* pervading everything."[19] Hofmannsthal revels in the dignity and even "defiance" of characters who sport the aura of greatness.

> This light, this air, is around them in such abundance and with such intensity that it cannot be ignored. A noble consciousness—nay, deeper than that—an existence of almost conscious nobility, a noble breathing, and closely connected with it a remarkable tender and strong feeling for the other person, a mutual almost impersonal affection, a tenderness, reverence for the human. . . . Their equilibrium is one of the most beautiful things I know. Like graceful, well-built ships they lie rocking to and fro above their own shadows on the flood of life. Round them there is something exultant, something expansive overflowing into the air, an abundance of life, a glorification of life itself, something definitely welcoming life, something that evokes the Pythian and Nemean odes of Pindar, those radiant salutations of victors.[20]

The reverence for an aristocratic equilibrium, cool but caring, larger than life, lies behind the aspiration Hofmannsthal held for all his principal characters, as we will see.

He himself may have been aloof, but Hofmannsthal read contemporary Austrian culture with the perspicacity of an orthopedic surgeon examining an x ray, diagnosing the hairline fracture that was developing under the pressure of European progress and determined that an inventive invocation of the tradition would be in order. That is where devices such as the artificial custom of the silver rose—Hofmannsthal's trick but easily taken for an archaic and authentic detail from generations past—are so effective. Another example of this deliberate manufacturing of a tradition is his "medieval" morality play, *Jedermann* (Everyman) written in 1911, then revised for the Salzburg Festival of 1920 and played each year during the festival as the official commencement ceremony, not unlike the military tattoo that is the emotional high point of the Edinburgh Festival each year. Like many pageants, it is concocted to defy time, and those who don't know the background to the work may be excused for assuming that it had been put on annually in the same way in Salzburg for centuries. In fact, Hofmannsthal and the great stage impresario and director Max Reinhardt, the genius loci of the Salzburg Festival, put together the *Jederman* in conditions that make it easy to understand their belief in their own ability to turn back the clock. Reinhardt's still-elegant castle, just twenty minutes' walk from the center of Salzburg, is a Baroque fantasy; originally built in the eighteenth century, it was turned into a fairy-tale environment in which to create and to play, a veritable theater set reaching back further in history. The Schloss Leopoldskron, once a bishop's residence, has a mirrored Venetian dining room, marble ballroom, secluded chapel, and most enticing of all, a dark, elaborate library, completed in 1927 as a replica of the library in the Abbey of Sankt Gallen in Switzerland. Book-lined and gas-lit, with a sinuous upper gallery reached by a hidden spiral staircase, it was the perfect place to sit together and concoct a theatrical spectacle that would simultaneously speak to the present generation of Austria and echo the past. Just as Broch had pointed out with respect to Hofmannsthal the schoolboy, the dramatist was a dream peddler who, like Reinhardt, was comfortable living outside the present.

The need to escape was understandable. Beyond the civilized confines of the *Schloss* and its rich library, the twilight of the empire was giving way to a fearful darkness. The Nazis would commandeer the Schloss Leopoldskron as a convenient stop on the way to the nearby Berchtesgaden. As Broch, with the benefit of hindsight, wrote,

> No doubt Hofmannsthal knew from the very beginning that he was himself ultimately assimilating to the vacuum. But he could do nothing else. He could not dispute his fate; all he could do was intensify its ultimate meaningfulness—a transcendence of fate was the ultimate meaning—and because it was a final meaning, it was realized in *The Tower*. Yet to that end he had had to pursue his entire experiment in life and death, an experiment into which he was compelled by his heritage every bit as much as by his specific and almost ominous talent, in short his fate, and one which he was thus forced to take upon himself, even though the agonizing insecurity of wisdom would now never leave him. He saw all too clearly that he stood everywhere on desolate ground: there were no prospects for the continued existence of the Austrian monarchy, which he had loved and never stopped loving; there were no prospects for his fondness for a nobility that had become little more than a caricature; there were no prospects for the stylistic integration of a theater whose greatness now rested on the shoulders of a

few surviving actors; and there were no prospects of bringing about a renaissance of this entire vanishing legacy of the splendor of the Marie-Theresian eighteenth century, now reduced to a Baroque-tinted opera. Hofmannsthal's life was a symbol, a noble symbol of a vanishing Austria, a vanishing nobility, a vanishing theater—symbol within the vacuum, yet not of the vacuum.[21]

The heroism of Hofmannsthal lay in his resistance to that "vacuum." At a time when much of Modern art and thought either embraced the chaotic devaluation of values, offered elegies for the old order, or set out to destroy the artistic forms that reflected it, Hofmannsthal studiously applied himself to advancing the good of the tradition by bringing fresh invention to those forms. Opera in full regalia explored through witty dialogue and edgy music the latest ideas about time and desire arising from psychology and contemporary philosophy. A good old-fashioned drawing room comedy offered the chance to raise, in a refreshingly straightforward manner, the touchy questions of what is expected of the aristocrat with what is now called post-traumatic stress disorder, or shell shock as it was known after World War I.

The "Baroque-tinted opera" to which Broch refers is *Der Rosenkavalier*, the high point of Hofmannsthal's career. Before its premier in 1911, he used a pair of plays, *The Tower* and *The Difficult Man*, and an unfinished novel, *Andreas*, to flesh out the philosophical drama that germinated in "The Letter of Lord Chandos," traces of which find their way into every one of Hofmannsthal's works. The Graeco-Freudian extravaganza of his first play, *The Tower*, begun in 1902, taps that tradition of Symbolist fantasy that includes Maeterlinck, Villiers de l'Isle Adam, and Huysmans and even reaches back to the aristocratic William Beckford's *Vathek* and the murky, moody opening scene of *Hamlet*. An odd work that is remarkably different in tone from the quicksilver sophistication of *Der Rosenkavalier*, the play lies closer to the inner life of the young Hofmannsthal than the refined and courtly opera. As the translator Michael Hamburger writes in the introduction to the English edition of the plays and libretti, noting that the playwright took as his starting point Calderon's *Life Is a Dream*, "It is the one completed work of Von Hofmannsthal that fully engaged all his disparate faculties and energies—the mystical and the worldly, the visionary and the analytical, the adventurous and the conservative—and coordinated his many-sided experience in a single imaginative structure."[22] Schorske uses *The Tower* as an example of Hofmannsthal's plea for the culture of grace and proceeds from it to Karl Kraus's satires and finally Arnold Schoenberg's opera *Moses und Aron* as the ultimate Modern word on the redemptive enterprise of art:

"Hofmannsthal and Kraus each memorialized in their dramas the failure of their own efforts to revitalize society through the cultures of grace and the word, respectively. It remained for Arnold Schoenberg to dramatize the failure of those two traditions in their relation to each other. . . . It is a victory of the word, but one that is de-socialized, removing the word from the world. It marks an end to the attempt of Austrian liberal culture to unify the two conflicting elements in Austrian cultural tradition, to build a rationalistic *theatrum mundi* with the help of art."[23]

The airless, dank atmosphere of *The Tower* seethes with the tension of a power struggle between Prince Sigismund and his father, King Basilius of Poland, as well as the governor of the tower, Julian, charged by the king with keeping the prince away from court in the fear of a coup. As Hofmannsthal admitted, the historical trappings are "more legendary than historical," but the hierarchy of nobles, recalling his essay on Shakespeare, is firmly in place. From the beginning, the autobiographical aspect of Sigismund is evident. One of his jailkeepers says of him, "Why, he knows Latin and can get through a fat book as though it was a side of bacon. But sometimes a word sticks in his mouth, and he can't get it out."[24] Early in the play the prince wonders where the world is. "The boundary between what's within and what's without has been blurred," answers his jailer.[25] Later, Sigismund muses, "The whole world is only just enough to fill our minds when we look at it through the little peephole, secure in our own houses! But woe when the partition crashes."[26] While the scenario and tone are reminiscent of *Axel*, which had been the talk of Paris only six years before *The Tower* was written, the impending sense of personal crisis is once again distinctly related to the situation of the mute Chandos.

The dramatic high point of the play is the confrontation between the prince and the king, and again the language of the scene recalls the early philosophical essay. Julian calls the prince "a blank sheet of paper" to allay the fears of his suspicious father. The prince has been immured so long he is on the brink of insanity. Asked who he is, he answers, "They said to me, you were dreaming, and again and again, you were dreaming. And that way, as when someone puts an iron finger under the hinge of the door, they lifted a door from before my eyes and I stepped behind a wall from where I can hear everything you say, but you cannot reach me, and I am safe from your hands."[27] Always in Hofmannsthal you find this stately remote figure, maintaining his or her distance and observing the sad progress of events. The most mysterious of them is the Maltese Knight in *Andreas* and the most lovable of them is the wise Marschallin in *Der Rosenkavalier*, because she is the warmest and most sympathetic. Sigismund arrives at his noble bearing innately, and in his quiet confidence the voice of Hofmannsthal himself is heard: "A man needs a space no smaller than the whole world, to exist in truth—but for twenty years I lived in a hollow stone, and there was one word I did not know: the word *longing*. For wherever I am, I permeate with my being, am present, and rule."[28] The sense of power implicit in this statement is extraordinary, especially in a literary age dominated by the antihero, ignoble and unsure. One of the great Austrian novels of the time, for instance, is Rober Musil's *The Man without Qualities*, the title alone suggesting the vast difference from Hofmannsthal's consummate man of quality. Even Joyce's princely Stephen Daedelus, who also emerges from a tower and contends with a type of imprisonment (in Ireland) as well as the anxiety of a nation in decline, does not have this degree of self-assurance or self-sufficiency, filled as he is with longings of many kinds. Hofmannsthal has presented what Nietzsche would call an "untimely" hero at a moment when Austria was in need of such a figure. How much of his character is drawn from the mirror is a matter of conjecture.

Of the many aristocratic characters that Hofmannsthal created, perhaps the most intriguing, baffling, and in the end, pointless souls is the Knight of Malta, who graces one of the few complete sections of *Andreas*, a youthful novel set in Venice. For various reasons, not just the setting but the troubling nature of its encounters, it invites comparison with Thomas Mann's *Death in Venice*. The mysterious Knight surfaces again several times in the jottings, posthumously published, in which the resolution of the novel—the unification of the eponymous character's spiritual and sensual polarities—is sketched. The first time the young gentleman, Andreas, sees the solitary knight, he is so enraptured with his dignity that he volunteers to carry to him a letter that has dropped from his desk at a café in the square. It is a superb description of the excitement of the moment when a bagatelle noble meets the real deal and a typically sophisticated Hofmannsthal situation in that he often pairs nobility of slightly different rank in one scene as a means of exposing the nuances in behavior that the hierarchy necessitates. We see the same deference in the way the count admires the baron in the play *The Difficult Man*, and, for comic effect, in the strained relations between the Marschallin and the Baron in *Der Rosenkavalier*. Here the Knight of Malta is introduced through the admiring eyes of an inferior:

> There was more than grace, there was a really inimitable distinction, in the way the Knight listened to him and took the paper, and Andreas thought he had never seen so wonderful a harmony between the bearing of a human being and the sound of his voice. "You are very kind, sir," came from his lips in German, perfectly pronounced. His genial and at the same time spiritual

> face seemed to express a profound kindliness arising from his soul. In the space of a moment Andreas felt himself received with benevolence, caught up into an atmosphere which ennobled every fiber of his being, and then dismissed. He stood before the stranger as if inanimate, he felt his body clumsy, his attitude uncouth. But there was in every limb an awareness which imprinted deep within him the image of the tall figure stooping slightly towards him, in easy assurance, in gracious civility, as flame stoops quivering to flame.[29]

A gesture of deference and desire, of aspiration and identification (one leans toward a mirror), this simile of the two flames draws one of the most intense scenes in the novel to a close, a passage more engaging than any of the love scenes. This is the way the torch is passed, one generation to the next. The romantic sense of the aristocracy's spiritual beauty, which was probably instilled in Hofmannsthal by his parents, is powerfully present. Among the fragments collected by editors in lieu of an ending to *Andreas*, which Hofmannsthal abandoned in 1913 after two years' work, and which was published posthumously in 1920, there is a snippet that is immensely helpful in understanding the need for that Eliot-like impersonality in Hofmannsthal's work: "Andreas (at bottom) goes to Venice chiefly because the people there are always masked."[30]

It is a dreamlike novel, full of desires and disguises, extremes of sensualism and idealism, and a general failure to believe in the reality of what is happening at any one moment. In this way, time, one of the great themes in Hofmannsthal's work, becomes detached from historical chronology. Just as his own writings and operas can be viewed in a timeless manner (the parallel with Balthus's paintings is striking), the volume of Ariosto that Andreas receives is not a period piece: "The Knight gives him Ariosto to read on account of the wonderful world-sense that is his. He does not read Ariosto with an eighteenth-century mind. He understands what the Knight means when he says that there is no such thing as the past: everything that exists is present, is even born at the present moment (feeling when listening to Bach)."[31] The modernity of Hofmannsthal is dependent upon this immediacy that art engenders, be it Ariosto or Bach or his own work.

Even the characters seem dislocated from the temporal context. The anachronistic severance of the person from the proper historical setting is a standard Modernist tactic, seen in the sudden appearance of Tiresias, for example, in Eliot's *Waste Land*, of tunic-clad classical figures in the Rose period paintings of Picasso or De Chirico (who has a steam locomotive chugging past in the background), or the time warps by which composer Phillip Glass and his librettist David Henry Hwang introduced, in rapid succession, contemporary physicist Stephen Hawking, Christopher Columbus, and a futuristic flight crew of astronauts in their opera *The Voyage*. For Surrealism and the theater of the absurd, the more jarring these discords, the better. The Knight has an abstracted, elevated quality: "He moves in a time which is not quite the present, and in a place which is not completely here. For him, Venice is the fusion of the classical world and the Orient, impossibility, in Venice, of relapsing into the trivial, the unmeaning."[32] In *Der Rosenkavalier*, the Marschallin is raised to much the same level of both wisdom and world-weariness, and it is remarkable to note that these works are the products of a young man still in his twenties. Even then Hofmannsthal knew that one of the best uses of historical settings would be the ability to loosen the hold of the present, to allow his imagination to move more freely through the philosophical questions that attracted him. These did not slide "into the trivial, the unmeaning" but cleaved to issues of such weight that his works belong in the same league as those of the past that similarly undertook matters of gravitas. Every serious playwright in German is another Goethe in terms of what he or she takes on conceptually, and it is no coincidence that he is the standard by which Hofmannsthal measured himself and others: "We have no literature of modern times. We have Goethe, and attempts."[33]

In the little-known play *The Difficult Man*, the eponymous character, Hans Karl Buhl, is a count, a war hero, a bachelor, and is psychologically tender from an experience that, the play divulges, involves a dreadful experience during his military service. In a sense, his quiet life—after a year and a half as member of the Upper House, the Austrian answer to the House of Lords, he has yet to utter a word in any debate—is what distinguishes him, much like the taciturn Knight of Malta. Late in the play he explains, "Everything one utters is indecent. Merely to put anything into words is an indecency. And when one looks at it closely, my dear Aldo, except that men never look closely at anything in the world, there is something positively shameless in our daring even to experience some things."[34] Suddenly, the Chandos syndrome is once again present—this time with a firmer etiology in that it is a symptom of what we now know as post-traumatic stress disorder. The count is also elegantly holding at bay the manipulations of his sister Crescencem, who is determined to bring him out into society and help him find the sort of bride who would be appropriate to his station. His life is spent in the salons and clubs of Viennese high society in the 1920s. The stage directions stipulate that most of the scenes at home are to be set in "a rather old Viennese palace." The sadness of the count is far more specific than the malady of Chandos or the mystery of the Knight of Malta. "There is a sacred truth which I know—I must always have known it, but it was only at the front that it first became clear to me: there is the accident of chance, which apparently does with us what it will—but in the middle of being thrown hither and thither, dazed and in fear of death, we are also aware of, and we know, that there is also a Necessity which chooses us from one moment to the next, which comes, so quietly, so close to our hearts and yet cuts keen as a sword," he says.[35] The grandeur of his mien and the respect for his rank is mainly felt through the comments of those around him. His ambitious nephew comments, "A gentleman like you makes himself felt by his mere presence. . . . You never go out for anything and never try to talk people into anything, that's just what's so elegant in you."[36] Baron Neuhoff, an admirer who has just had his portrait painted by Bohuslawsky, beseeches the count to have his own done. The invitation recalls an insight of Broch's into the juvenile magic of Hofmannsthal's creativity: "What is it that makes real dignity so inimitable? Because there's a residue of the childlike in it. By way of this childlike quality Bohuslawsky would get round to imbuing your portrait with something which is extremely rare in our world and distinguishes you in the highest degree: dignity. For we live in a world that lacks dignity."[37]

In this, we recognize the lament of Hofmannsthal for the vanishing Vienna he seeks to preserve, as well as a sly self-portrait. The childlike quality, as remarked by Broch and others, remained a key to Hofmannsthal's art through the end of his career. During a party in an eighteenth-century drawing room, the character Neuberger complains, "Intellect and these people! Life and these people! All the people you see here ceased to exist long ago. They're nothing but shadows now. Nobody who circulates in these rooms belongs to the real world in which the intellectual crises of this century are resolved."[38] Hofmannsthal sends up this snobbery but not without seriously raising the question of what makes one character genuinely superior to others. The count is approached in the midst of an elaborate scheme for an elopement that goes awry. The tone is one of "people like us," with the addition of an observation that sets the "difficult man" on a plane above: "You are a true, good friend; people like me are simply not able to extricate ourselves from the meshes of the destiny prepared for us by the smiles or frowns of women, but you have lifted yourself once for all above that atmosphere. (*HK gestures him to stop*). You can't deny it, you have that aura of superiority around you, and as in the long run life never stands still but must always progress or regress, you simply can't help having round you from day to day the increasing loneliness of the superior man."[39]

There is too much variety in Hofmannsthal's characters and narratives to accuse him of adhering to a formula. Nonetheless, his deep-seated beliefs do often lead him to similar solutions to dramatic problems, like a painter who uses a particular palette or structural matrix to resolve the individual problems of different canvases. Hofmannsthal was a great proponent of propriety, within which he was not averse to offering glimpses of the emotional mess that lay beneath the attractive veneer. When the romantic misfire at the end of *The Difficult Man* threatens to bring chaos and conflict, the count falls back on tradition. "For this kind of situation, the right and proper forms have existed for a thousand years. What we have experienced here tonight was, for good or for ill, if we are to call things by their right names, a betrothal. A betrothal culminates in an embrace between the betrothed parties."[40] There is an abiding sense that tradition will be a trustworthy guide, in one's behavior and in art. In a letter to Marie Taxis of the still influential (in the arts) Turn und Taxis family, Hofmannsthal explains that the goal of artists is "to multiply the present by assimilating the lives of others and by living the present to the full, the rough reflection, through recalling the past. For since time is something highly relative, a more perceptual category of the mind, one can actually fill a moment with infinite meaning."[41] It implies a sense of the vertical depth of time and heritage that makes real the mystical kinship with ancestors, somewhat as in the novels of Henry James. This is where the count in *The Difficult Man* draws his self-assurance. His reliance on gesture and good form looks ahead to the delicate if artificial ritual of the presentation of the rose that is the centerpiece of *Der Rosenkavalier*.

When it comes to genres and modes, Modernism plays favorites. Prose takes priority over poetry. Painting, photography, and collage nudge sculpture out of the gallery's central spot. The short piece for orchestra or chamber group supplants the symphony and the sonata. The full-length Romantic ballet cedes the stage to bursts of expressive lyricism or prolonged Minimalist variations on a theme, while the trend in drama and film is also toward more compact formats. Sifted out in this winnowing process, opera in the twentieth-century took on a museum atmosphere that persists to our time, even though the medium exerts as vibrant and irresistible an allure as ever for composers and dramatists. Arguably for economic reasons involving the sheer difficulties of supporting the avant-garde, "grand" opera has not kept pace with such musical forms as, for instance, the string quartet, which has just as venerable a provenance yet bends, with a suppleness that opera does not seem to have, to contemporary styles and ideas, from Schoenberg's Pantonalism to Philip Glass's Minimalism, John Harbison's and John Corigliano's Neo-Romanticism, to Olivier Messiaen's and Arvo Part's Mysticism and beyond. Even in the hands of Glass and avant-garde director Robert Wilson, or other quirky directors such as Patrice Chereau and Peter Sellars, a full-length, ritual-laden night at the opera struggles to offer the type of experience—strangeness, shock, novelty, and most important, originality—that is often encountered in the recital hall when fresh chamber music has its debut.

This raises the stakes for Hofmannsthal and Strauss as Moderns. They gloried in the traditions of opera, cheerfully confining their efforts to its elaborate formal matrix. Their voluminous correspondence offers constant reminders of how closely they hewed to their solid grounding in the great effects they had absorbed from performances in Vienna, Paris, Prague, Milan, and the other grand houses of Europe. Bouncing allusively from readily identifiable sources such as Mozart's *Nozze di Figaro* and Wagner's *Meistersinger* (which played a huge role dramatically and musically in the shaping of *Der Rosenkavalier*), they fashioned "new" works that challenged the audience with unusual dramatic and musical ideas but also satisfied the seasoned operagoer's yearning for a touch of the familiar. This is the reason they still play to full houses in cultural capitals. As with Puccini, another twentieth-century composer whose works are now among the "war horses" (lamentable term) of the standard repertoire, the secret of their continued success lay partly in their ability to build the illusion that the operas they created were of an earlier vintage.

The courtly Austrian poet and businesslike German composer and conductor were such an unlikely pair that they rarely came together face to face in the twenty-eight years of working together, so broad was the gap between their upbringing and manners. This was not a meeting of coevals like Russell and Wittgenstein or a mutual admiration society such as the compatible circle of Sand. One anecdote in particular illustrates not just the great social divide between them but the distinction made by the whole package of details and attitudes Hofmannsthal brought to the relationship, permitting him to depict with certainty and authenticity the noble characters they placed onstage. The differences between them came to a head during a minor dispute over just that sort of detail. Partway through their progress on *Der Rosenkavalier*, a question arose regarding how the noble Marschallin would react when her young lover, Octavian, chose the younger girl. Hofmannsthal wanted Strauss to understand why the Marschallin would calmly retain the lightness of their earlier exchanges, whereas Strauss, tipping his hand to show his middle-class morality, bade him give her stronger language. Hofmannsthal played his strongest card, directly from personal experience. He sent Strauss a letter he had received from his close friend, Princess Lichnowsky (careful to ask for its return, of course, as a letter in the wrong hands is a particularly sensitive issue among members of this class, as readers of *Liaisons Dangereuses* will confirm). "The whole opera would suffer," Hofmannsthal wrote Strauss in 1910, "if the personality of the Marschallin were to be deprived of her full stature." Strauss was unconvinced. Hofmannsthal produced the evidence. "A letter from Princess L, which I enclose and would ask you to return sometime, will show you how strongly women feel this—how they, who make up such an important sector of our public, look upon the whole vivid unfolding of the action from the point of view of the Marschallin."[42] In the end, the librettist won this battle. How many princesses did Strauss know personally, after all?

Hofmannsthal used his royal connections to help Strauss. When their *Elektra* failed to make it to the stage in Vienna after success in Prague, Hofmannsthal offered to pull a string with Prince Montenuovo, who was the *Obersthofmeister* of the Vienna Opera House. These incidents are characteristic of the relationship. Throughout their collaboration, Hofmannsthal took the part of the worldly, conservative, tasteful traditionalist, from whose pen the words of counts, countesses, barons, and minor nobility issued with precision and accuracy. In exploring their work as Modernists it is important, however, to appreciate the sophisticated ways in which Hofmannsthal infused centuries-old forms and what appear to be familiar court intrigues with the fast pace and often jagged emotions of his time. That is the secret of the *meisterstück* of the Strauss-Hofmannsthal collaboration, their comic gem, first performed in 1911, *Der Rosenkavalier*. The action is set in Vienna of 1740, and naturally one of the heartstrings it plays upon is nostalgia for those halcyon days of imperial order and sumptuousness. Who better than a nobleman and avid historian such as Hofmannsthal to set this down on paper in 1911, together with a composer who produced the interwoven waltzes that are the plum moments of the score for lovers of that other Strauss? In terms of Bloom's theory of the anxiety of influence, the notion of a later Strauss taking on the Viennese waltz king in his own genre is already rich.

The work's genesis unfolds in the pages of the correspondence like a time-lapse movie of a blooming rose. Strauss initially wanted an opera about Savonarola, which Hofmannsthal discouraged (secretly, because he distrusted Strauss's taste in literature and painting); instead the poet, working at a small baroque palace at Rodaun on Vienna's outskirts, concocted the plan for a "pellucid" opera "almost like a pantomime," according to a letter dated 11 February 1909. As the (aristocratic, no less) editor of the letters, Sackville-West, observes in his introduction, "We seem to be watching a Siamese cat working out a modus vivendi with a Labrador."[43] One of the first elements they agreed upon was the need for the seductive little waltz that laces the work like perfume, in Strauss's words, "an old-fashioned Viennese waltz, sweet yet saucy, which must pervade the whole of the last act."[44] In fact, it appears far earlier in the final version of the opera as a preview, capturing the audiences' yearning for a melody and giving Baron Ochs an irresistible love charm that he wields like Papageno's magic glockenspiel (one of many Mozartean devices in the opera). Once it returns in full glory in the final act, one can imagine the forceful effect it must have had, not only upon Hofmannsthal when he first heard it but upon the Viennese audience.

The waltz was Strauss's deft play upon archaism. The poet also provided gems that blended beloved echoes of old Austria with sharp-edged lines that only a Viennese acquainted with Freud or Rilke would have at hand. Once the libretto was on the table, the composer was thrilled, and expressed his delight in terms guaranteed to appeal to the elitist predisposition of the poet and testifying to the courage of their convictions: "It really is charming beyond measure: so delicate, maybe a little too delicate for the general mob, but that doesn't matter."[45] As the pages of the score began coming back his way, they initially elicited from Hofmannsthal a strong, conservative reaction that suggests the sort of "anti-Modernism" that Robert Storr has described in the visual arts. The specific target is Wagner and his *Tristan und Isolde* (today we have all but forgotten what a pathbreaking work this was), but the basic fear is that his assiduous evocation of eighteenth-century clarity, exemplified by Mozart, would be threatened by music that was too Modern. As Hofmannsthal wrote, near the halfway point, "I was obviously very much tied down by the metre scheme which you prescribed for me, but in the end I found it rather agreeable to be bound in this way to a given tune since I felt in this something Mozartian and a turning away from Wagner's intolerable erotic screaming—boundless in length as well as in degree; a repulsive, barbaric almost bestial affair this shrieking of two creatures in heat as he practices it."[46] The discrepancy, not just socially but intellectually and aesthetically, between Strauss and Hofmannsthal begins to show. Fortunately, at this early stage of their creative partnership, manageable antithetical tendencies served to fuel the process, giving it the necessary friction instead of bringing it to a grinding halt.

The dual portrait is also under the strain of the difference not only in character but in social rank. Even after rising to a position of great prominence in European musical circles, particularly as a conductor, Strauss was regarded as a professional performer and, rather unpoetically, a bit of a hustler when it came to money. Hofmannsthal, although no less worldly when it came to cashing his royalty check and arguing for his fair share, managed to maintain the air of the noble amateur who was above all that. An even more important point of contrast involved who was in charge of a project. There is one way to consider these differences: as a power struggle. The dispute over the priority of words or music is a great theme in opera, and Straus and Hofmannsthal brought it to the stage most literally in *Intermezzo*, which opens with a debate on the subject. As in any close relationship, the balance tilts one way and then the other as they come to grips with various problems in their collaborative efforts, and it is not surprising that Hofmannsthal, though younger and certainly less central to the business needs of the opera house management and music publishing industry than Strauss, often had the upper hand, winning the smaller battles and directing the composition of the music according to the flow of the words. The ultimate resolution of this question, however, lay with time.

Hofmannsthal certainly knew how to depict rank onstage, often to comic effect. The sophistication of *Der Rosenkavalier* lies not just in its contrast between the servants and the aristocrats, but in the sharply accurate way in which the mid-level aristocrats and nouveaux riches address one another. By no means the equal of either the Marschallin or Count Octavian, the crude Baron Lerchenau nonetheless knows he can chew out her servants ("Where did you learn your manners? A Baron Lerchenau doesn't hang about waiting-rooms," his first words in the opera, are far from impressive to the audience, which immediately shares the Marschallin's embarrassment over his crudity). When he loses his wig and then tries the same tone with the police, his authority is questioned, and it remains for the Marschallin to save his face. The passion for delicious detail concerning the aristocracy is in the work, however. When the elegant young Count Octavian, covered in silver and looking like an angel, appears to the overprotected bourgeoise, Sophie, she surprises him by telling him all sorts of trivia she has read about him in her *Ehrenspiegel Oesterreichs* (Austrian almanac of honors, that nation's equivalent of *Burke's Peerage* in the United Kingdom), which she keeps on her nightstand and uses to look up her "future ducal and princely relations." One can be sure Hofmannsthal had one in his library (he was in it), whereas Strauss probably joked about it.

These are the charming touches that, like a staging that makes the opera a period piece down to the dueling scars on the cheeks and the elaborate jewelry the stars wear, thrill opera audiences hungry for spectacle. A "class-conscious" reading of the opera would focus on such moments as Octavian's parody of the lower-class dialect, the tongue-in-cheek jibes at the self-made nouveau riche (the ingenue Sophie's father), and the abuses by Baron Ochs of his aristocratic privileges. Leave that to the Marxist interpreters. Social commentary, for one thing, provides the weakest link in the chain of the opera, and even for those who love the work, the moment Ochs leaves the stage and the supposedly funny business at the inn comes to its conclusion never comes soon enough. "My sense of humor must not be sufficiently Germanic," laments one friend of mine, an opera expert and otherwise a fan of the work, after even the most convincing performances. More substance is found in the characterization and the poetry that Hofmannsthal built into the opera, which is far too sophisticated to be read as a pastiche of Mozart.

At the end of the first act, the Marschallin drifts into a meditative mood in which she contemplates the *ou sont les neiges* theme (literally, "*such dir den Schnee / vom vergangenen Jahr*") and wonders at the unmarked passage of time that could have brought her so rapidly and unknowingly from the "little Resi" fresh from the convent to the "old woman, the Field-Marshall's wife, the old Princess Resi." The libretto far surpasses most works of its kind in its logic and poetry:

How does the dear Lord do it?
While I always remain the same.
And if He has to do it like this,
Why does He let me watch it happen
With such clear senses?

In Verdi, Rossini, or the model Mozart, a crucial confrontation with age often occurs, but the treatment is far different, as the countess's role in *Nozze di Figaro* demonstrates. The audience knowingly follows her plight as she focuses upon the pain of losing her husband to a younger woman. Hofmannsthal adds a layer of self-conscious irony and detachment. To make it all the more poignant, especially for those who frequently attend the opera, the part of the Marschallin is frequently sung by a soprano who has been known on stage for years, first in the youthful trouser roles such as Octavian or Cherubino, then as the great tragic heroines of the repertory. Late in her career, when she appears as the Marschallin to reflect upon the passage of time, the nostalgic effect has a real-life dimension for fans that can be overwhelming. Hofmannsthal proves a master of this trap, because it has been his theme from the Chandos letter: the inability to hold onto and control meaning as time passes. When the Marschallin cautions Octavian not to hold her too tight, not to behave boorishly, like all other men, including her husband and Ochs, she cites her own ability to let go:

I am in the mood when I really sense
The weakness of all temporal things.
In the depths of my heart I sense
That one should keep nothing,
That one can grasp nothing,
How everything runs between the fingers,
How everything we grasp at dissolves,
How everything disperses like mist and dreams.

The main difference from the situation of the poet in "The Letter of Lord Chandos" arises from the fact that, rather than language and the problem of words, the Marschallin is baffled by time. The libretto rises to a new level of poetry in this passage from the end of the first act, and the music, too, finds a way to shed its earth-bound tonalities—the big brassy sound that often accompanies Ochs or the rich harmonies that Octavian and Sophie find in their duets—and reach a higher plane. The Marschallin's meditation continues, culminating in the unforgettable image of her stopping the palace clocks late at night so she can sleep again without worrying over the ravages of age:

> Time is a strange thing.
> When one lives heedlessly, time means nothing.
> But then suddenly,
> One is aware of nothing else.
> It is all around us,
> It is also inside us.
> It trickles in our faces,
> It trickles in the looking glass,
> It flows through my temples.
> And between me and you
> It flows again, silently, like an hour-glass.
> Often I hear it flowing—unstoppably
> Often I rise in the middle of the night
> And stop all, all the clocks.
> And yet one should not be afraid of it.
> Time, too, is a creation of the Father
> Who has created us all.

The unbearable lightness permeates the other characters. As though infected, Octavian, in the final act, begins to tell the Baron of the hopelessness of life. "Time goes, / and the wind blows / and soon we'll be gone too. / We're simply human." With that gesture, like the passing of the rose, Hofmmansthal conveys the sense that a new generation of Viennese aristocrats will continue the graceful manner and thoughtful existence of the Marschallin. While Octavian and Sophie launch into a dreamy love duet, the Marschallin releases her hold. In terms of narrative alone and the manipulation of eighteenth-century and twentieth-century mores that Hofmannsthal is performing, this gesture is the recognizably Modern solution to the problem. It offers a moment of sophistication that is not unlike what W. H. Auden (to the music of Igor Stravinsky) provided in his reinterpretation of an eighteenth-century classic, William Hogarth's suite of paintings *The Rake's Progress.* Auden etched his libretto with acid; Hofmannsthal's flows like wine:

> I vowed to myself to cherish him
> in the right way,
> that I would even love his love
> for another woman!
> I certainly did not think
> That it would so soon overtake me.
> The majority of things in the world
> Are such that one would not believe them
> If one were told about them.
> Only those who experience it believe it
> And do not know how—
> There stands the boy and here I stand,
> And with that strange girl there
> He will be as happy
> As men understand happiness.

These two scenes present the most ravishingly beautiful moments in the operas of Hofmannsthal and Strauss and arguably the most affecting moments in all twentieth-century opera. Of all the formidable writing on the part of critics and scholars that these glorious passages have inspired, some of the most worthy found its way to the editorial page of the *New York Times* around the turn of the millennium, a time and forum in which thoughts on time were a nickel a bushel and mostly banal, if not execrable. This meditation, penned by *Times* commentator Verlyn Klinkenberg, obviously quite soon after attending a performance of *Der Rosenkavalier* at the Metropolitan Opera, captured the "psychological delicacy" perfectly. As with the performances of Dame Kiri Te Kanawa in the 1980s at the Met, the appearance of a longtime favorite diva, Rene Fleming, in the role of the Marschallin gave the work even greater resonance. Klinkenberg focuses on the dramatic high point of the first act in "What the Marschallin Makes of Time":

> I found it hard to free myself from the force of that scene in Act I, even as I left Lincoln Center in the deep cold after midnight. Music so often seems like a way of realizing the movement of time, of coloring it so that its current becomes audible. It flows, as the Marschallin says, all around us, and yet as those words form onstage, sustained by Strauss's music, it seems as though that pure vocal line, the very breath with which Ms. Fleming forms the notes, becomes the lone point in the Metropolitan Opera House where

> time is advancing. That is an illusion, of course, an example of the disruptive stillness that great art always creates. The nimbus of James Levine's head moves, as does his baton. The tips of the violinists' bows can be seen quivering. Pages turn inaudibly in the orchestra pit, and the audience breathes. If you could suspend the Marschallin's meditation on time and read over the shoulders of the horn section, move feely around the set and through the wings, look into the backstage machinery, the rigging of ropes and cables that supports the scenery and curtain, you would begin to grasp the intricate architecture of that instant, all the conspiring it takes to create a scene of such persuasive simplicity. But the music moves and time divides, between the Marschallin and Octavian, between us and the people we were before the opera began. It is a coincidence that Strauss and Hofmannsthal began to create the Marschallin just four years after Einstein published the scientific paper that destroyed the idea of absolute, independent, unvarying time. Yet our knowledge of that proximity is not a coincidence. The Marschallin voices an ancient anxiety about time—"suddenly one is aware of nothing else"—and yet she seems to be saying something utterly new, something that marks her not as a creature of Maria Theresa's Vienna, but as a witness of our modern lives, where space and time bend together.[47]

It is time to turn our attention from the words to the music. Perhaps the most graceful, suggestive mark on a musical page is rather prosaically known as the slur. A long curving line over the staff, it arches, often across several measures, and is sometimes accompanied by the Italian expression *legato*, meaning "tied together." For pianists who seek to master phrasing, violinists searching for the endlessly spun melodic line of a concerto, or singers hoping to sustain the mounting effect of a dramatic climax, there is no more important challenge than producing a secure legato. The score of *Der Rosenkavalier* makes generous use of this mark in the Marschallin's passages, and the interpretive liberties taken by various sopranos often extend this to its musically viable limit (within the constraints not only of the voice's capability but of the tempo and momentum of the scene). Strauss carries the passage off to perfection. The hallmark is the attenuation of the vocal and instrumental lines, the matching of two violins and two soprano voices (the Marschallin and Octavian) in a ravishingly lyrical line emerging from good old-fashioned Mozartean structures and suddenly looking ahead to all kinds of later twentieth-century sonorities, including not just Schoenberg and Webern but even Copland and Grieg.

Masterpieces have their focal moments and their passages of development, and each commands the viewer's or listener's attention in a different way. A fascinating telescoping effect takes place in the grand opera of *Der Rosenkavalier* that leaves the audience at a distance in some scenes and then pulled up very tight and close in others—notably the Marschallin's meditations. Even in the massive, lavish productions favored by contemporary opera houses, this transition from a busy stage with an abundance of extras and scenic details to absorb to the close-up, emotional identification between audience and principal can be fascinating. The Marschallin's last line consists of just three soft words in a prayer of withdrawal that takes us back to her earlier invocation of God in the contemplation of time: "In God's name." There are some who feel that with those words Hofmannsthal's greatest achievement as an opera librettist came to a close, a sad thought in that several more works followed in the course of the next two decades, under the tremendous pressure that the success of *Der Rosenkavalier* had created.

If time is the tragic note in *Der Rosenkavalier*, it is the repeated joke in *Ariadne auf Naxos*, a one-act opera staged as dinner entertainment in that it must be concluded by nine in the evening. This is a knowing spoof of the classical unities of time and place. Hofmannsthal edits and arranges Molière's *Le bourgeois gentilhomme* in a way that insidiously suggests a certain disdain, not only for the nouveau riche of Vienna but possibly for Strauss as well. Monsieur Jourdaine, as in the play, is trying to impress the Marquise with a coat that has been the labor of twenty tailors. The in joke for the audience is that the marquise and count agree to attend his pretentious soiree only because he's loaned the count 15,800 livres. Having keenly observed the efforts of the bourgeois to entertain himself and others of his rank, Hofmannsthal puts cold observations to their best comic effect. The butt of the humor is Jourdain.

Reciting his greeting he starts sputtering, and his syntax devolves into nonsense. The German text is so funny at this juncture that it is worth quoting for the repetition: "Gnädige Frau . . . dass Ihre Gnäden die Gnäde für mich haben und so gnädig . . . sind, dass sie mir die Ehre antun, mich mit Dero gnädigen Gegenwart zu beehren (Honored Lady, it is a great honor for me to have the great happiness and good fortune to be so happy that Your Honor shows me the honor of honoring me with your honor's honorable presence"). After the opera is over, his guests leave laughing at him, and he says to himself as if in a trance (*wie entruckt*): "Everyone keeps on at me about my association with people of quality—but I can't imagine anything nicer. They have such finesse, such an incomparable air of easy, relaxed courtesy; I would gladly have given, if not my right arm, then a few fingers at least to have been born a count or marquis and to have had that certain something which confers such grandeur on all they do." It's a vicious satire, and reading between the lines one wonders how Strauss felt upon reading it. The letters between them, our customary source, stay on a technical level as the long period of collaboration on the work, fraught with difficulties, continued from year to year. Given the pragmatism and swiftness with which the two generally dispatched their commissions, the long slog was unusual.

The answer to the question of what could delay them so long lies in the music. While Hofmannsthal offered psychological insights and moments of irony that are this side of the threshold of Modernism, he did not move on technically in the same way that Strauss did. The starting point for this divergence is *Ariadne*. Remember the injunction against Wagner in Hofmannsthal's letters regarding the composition of *Der Rosenkavalier*? In *Ariadne* there is a direct quote of the infamous, wild "Tristan" chord that musicologists cite as a landmark in the liberation of tone color that signaled Modernism. This sign of rebellion had been foretold in the work of Strauss. The critic Derrick Puffet points out that Strauss would quote from Wagner in the original key and lift passages note for note from *Die Meistersinger* or *Tannhauser*. He was liberal, too, in his borrowings from Brahms and Liszt. Yet the Tristan chord, which Puccini had also invoked in his *Tosca*, was an especial act of rebellion in that there is no question that it was the Wagnerian opera that Hofmannsthal had in mind when he railed against the operatic depiction of sexual ecstasy. According to Puffet, from this point on, Strauss occupies a singular position in Modern music:

> It is idle to look for connections with Hindemith or other fourth-obsessed composers of the 1920s, even when Strauss is at his most 'modern,' as in the skat party from *Intermezzo*, he never sounds like anyone but himself. Some of the sonorities in the later operas (*Daphne* in particular comes to mind) are marvelously distinctive—really quite original—and could perhaps become the basis of an expanded tonal language, similar to those suggested by Busoni in the more adventurous parts of *Doktor Faustus*, by Shreker in *Christophorus*, and by Weill in some of this works of the 1930s. But Strauss at this time had no interest in "expanding the language." His concern was increasingly with refinement, with a purification of his harmonic style, which makes parts of *Capriccio* sound like late Fauré.[48]

Other critics, including the great Wagnerite Alfred Newman and the philosopher and Schoenberg disciple Theodor Adorno, agree that Strauss occupies an important and unique position in the history of early Modernism. That story today is being rewritten to include more lyrical, less pantonal composers. The recent acceptance of such Neo-Romantic operas as those of Corigliano, Harbison, and others has readjusted the balance between pantonalism (Schoenberg's system) and harmonies that the ear is more accustomed to, from Verdi or even Wagner. In this regard, Strauss and Hofmannsthal stand to music much as Francis Bacon and

Balthus do to painting, as champions of figural or harmonic work in a time devoted to abstraction or dissonance and their defenders. As Puffet writes, "The stylistic alternatives of Modernism and Neoclassicism may not be adequate or accurate in describing the two stylistic tendencies of Strauss. Musical modernism persists. It is perhaps the modernism of the spirit, of ego assertion, which has been defined as Strauss's modernist style tout court. But the two tendencies of modernism as the assertion of the spirit, indistinguishable from the will, and an ascetic withdrawal from the world, may speak more to the point. The later musical modernism suggests a withdrawal into the security of sensibility, first in the Hofmannsthal operas and then in the works that claim a withdrawal from politics."[49]

Where Hofmannsthal may have pulled back from world events and Modernism, Strauss pressed bravely forward, responding to them. His symphonic *Metamorphosen* was a lament for the destruction of German culture, written just after the bombing of the Munich Staatstheater in October 1943. Those who met him in his later years, including the pianist Alfred Kalisch, were impressed by his advanced views and interest in the latest movements in aesthetics. The concluding comment regarding the emperor, a patron of the composer's, is historically noteworthy if seemingly dated. "He is modern in all his artistic tastes, as the pictures on his walls testify. This love of all that is new and of this century is part and parcel of himself, and is not a mere accidental accretion, as some would have us believe. He is a convinced believer in the *Ubermensch*, and respects all who, though they may be his opponents, display the qualities connoted by this word. Hence his admiration for the German Emperor, who is, intellectually and artistically, at the opposite pole, and though they can never agree on any musical topic."[50] Other contemporary impressions confirmed the aspect of a thorough Modernist. Julius Korngold, who succeeded Eduard Hanslick as the preeminent critic of the time (and was notorious for boosting the reputation of his son, the composer Erich Wolfgang Korngold), wrote of Strauss in May 1907: "He's always had his eye out for anything that was contemporary. A musician who is modern through and through, including keeping up with literary modernity, with all its moods and fantasies, and heeding the currents of the times."[51] Newman credits Strauss with advancing the cause of Modernism, and it is clear that he is referring to the Strauss who went on independently of Hofmannsthal: "He has already enriched music with more new ideas than any musician since Wagner. He has made music realistic, not only in the coarse sense of material imitation, but in the high sense that with him musical character drawing has become extraordinarily poignant and veracious. Such humor and such pathos as those of Don Quixote, for example, represent a quite new phase of musical psychology. He has got away from the wigs and tights and the stage apparatus of Wagner, and by his music alone paints for us the kind of men and women we see around us day by day."[52]

The fact that Strauss's music, though Modern, was accepted as rapidly and readily as it was in his own time is remarkable, as is its persistence as an influence on contemporary composing, particularly in the case of Thomas Ades and John Corigliano. The particular dissonances and chromatic combinations, as well as the orchestration, that made a distinctive Strauss sound, both in the dramatic tone poems (which always seem to have as their heroes men, while the operas focus on women, a weird parallel to the division between Hofmannsthal's plays and novels about men and the self-same operas about women) and in the songs are rich in the types of innovations that give musicologists good reason to place Strauss, as they did Liszt and Chopin, among the early Modernists. One important voice is that of the philosopher Theodor Adorno, who feels that Strauss approached but did not answer a core issue in Modernism. As his writings on Schoenberg show, Adorno valued a type of spontaneity and "honesty" in musical composition, as opposed to rhetoric. He underlines the "restless" quality in Strauss:

> We do not have a musical representation of a struggling or confessional consciousness, as we do in a Mahler adagio, for example. We do have a series of perfect musical forms, hovering between composer and world. There is little true thematic development, variation or metamorphosis. Themes lead into one another with expert fluidity, and without authorial commentary. . . . Strauss does not ask, in music, *the* question that musical modernism asks, and that is whether a musical subject can engage in dialogue with the world legitimately. What remains is not a self or a subject but a mode of movement and interaction with the world. Neither Strauss nor the restless music finds a self but only continued and ever-ingenious movement—belated and inadequate confrontation with self and history, in other words, but an honest one, in which self and world remain ill-defined and dynamic, distant from the aesthetic and political temptations of cultural myths: the myth of the spirit and the myth of the theater.[53]

The formal perfection that so appealed to Adorno was a shared value that bound Strauss and Hofmannsthal. As with so many other figures under consideration in this study, especially Swinburne with his long swooping variants on classic metrical lines, the formal underpinnings make many kinds of innovation possible. In Adorno's eyes, it is the thorough appropriation of the tradition that allows Strauss to take the next step, the quintessentially Modern measure, in breaking the mold. His version of the history of music offers a surprisingly close relationship between the subject and the matter. The identity of the composer assumes greater significance in this view. Adorno writes:

> The music of the psychological subject corresponds to the subject. The world it designates is the creation of the subject, and its content derives from the relationless "I." Thus the music of the psychological subject is not capable of breaking out of its sphere directly upward at any point. In the nineteenth century, as this phenomenon was taking shape, Mendelssohn's shivering classicism and Chopin's dazzling play, Schumann's blind repetition of the sonata, and Bruckner's congregationless chorale are all equally tragic attempts to conjure up once more the power of forms. But to all of them was given a share of real participation in lasting forms, for the collapse of the "I" is not yet complete, and Beethoven's mastery beckons from a not-unreachable distance. Beethoven is all person; he achieves this by wrestling with forms that extend challengingly into his world. In Strauss the reality of forms has vanished for good; it continues to exist only as appearance. Strauss lives neither with the forms nor against them; he establishes the forms of the past for himself.[54]

Looking at the polar opposition of Hofmannsthal and Strauss, it is difficult to say who ought to have been in the ascendancy, but there is a logic in the notion that Strauss should progress to become the more Modern of the two masters. Hofmannsthal, with his observance of rites and traditions, dominated the relationship, but winning an argument is often a matter of having the last word. It is hard to think of a composer more identified with endings and finality than Strauss, partly because he was so adept at the mode. Like Samuel Beckett, he made most of a career out of saying good-bye, including the meditations of the Marschallin in *Der Rosenkavalier*. The most famous of Strauss's endings are the *Four Last Songs*, virtually deathbed pieces of glorious beauty that are very close musically to the music of the Marschallin, not simply because they are for soprano but because of the interplay between voice and violin in long, sinuous lines of extraordinary lyricism. They were among three masterpieces Strauss created during what he called the "Indian Summer" of his last year, 1949, spent at his country home in Garmisch. In addition to the *Four Last Songs*, he created the oboe concerto and the *Metamorphosen*, a lament for twenty-three solo strings that, as mentioned before, was prompted by the destruction of the Dresden and other opera houses during the war. The effect of a soaring voice, such as that of Jessye Norman, rendering the *Four Last Songs* is awe-inspiring. These may be late creations, but they have a quality that is wholly Modern in the sense that Abstract Expressionist paintings by Jackson Pollock and Franz Kline are Modern: power. The tidal surges of sound build to crescendi that, Strauss knew, pound down upon the traditional harmonies and cadences of music. They bring to mind a profound aphorism of the Romanian philosopher E. M. Cioran: "Music, a system of farewells, evokes a physics whose point of departure is not atoms but tears."[55]

4

Members of the Club

ALGERNON CHARLES SWINBURNE AND FREDERICK, LORD LEIGHTON

Until the Bloomsbury phenomenon, the most tidily packaged, neatly defined movement in English arts and letters that could be called Modern was the Pre-Raphaelite Brotherhood. Clubby and self-reflective, the tight circle of painters, poets, and obligingly enthusiastic critics stands out from similar contemporary groups (notably the Impressionists, against whom they aimed their strongest invective, as well as the Barbizon School and the German Nazarenes, from whom they adopted many of their narrative ideas) in part because of the members' relative affluence and genteel lineage and also their deep-rooted sense of the historic basis of their work.[1] It culminated in a neo-medievalism that imbued their conversation and writing, their showy homes, the workrooms of William Morris's craftsmen, and the studios of painters who were pleased to be directly compared with Cimabue, Giotto, Mantegna, and Boticelli—unlike most artists of our time who look at you cross-eyed if you suggest their work is anything but sui generis. As the name implies, the retrospective quality of their stylistic and thematic revolution took its cue from an age they felt represented an early innocence in the history of art and literature. They viewed the renewal of original aims and techniques as a radical and necessary departure from the cheap, exhausted aesthetic of their era, and it is difficult not to read their turning away from England's rapid industrialization as a gesture of escapism as well.

The fervor with which they went about this redirection of aesthetic history, including the formation of a secret society or "brotherhood" that gave the whole group the kind of cachet that in the present day would be construed as a public relations coup, was exactly like the excitement of any other avant-garde. By the time the international art scene took them up in group exhibitions that drew thousands (particularly in Paris and the United States), they had the benefits of the buzz that in our time was generated by young lions of the English avant-garde, including Damien Hirst, whose recent group show was simply dubbed *Sensation* and whose impact, like that of the Pre-Raphaelites, was swift and controversial. It is paradoxical to think of a phalanx of Moderns that rode into battle under the banner of an aesthetic that had flourished centuries before. Perhaps it is no more odd than the importance of Arcadian symbolism to Puvis de Chavannes (a contemporary admirer of the Pre-Raphaelites), the romance of Gauguin's Tahiti, the impact of African tribal carvings on later painters such as Picasso, the influence of early Greek dance upon Ruth St. Denis and Martha Graham, Pound's choice of Provençal lyrics for allusive materials, or the powerful echoes of plainsong and medieval chant in the work of recent composers such as Arvo Pärt. The rallying point in all these cases is a restorative link to the "primitive" as a means to refresh the vocabulary and outlook of a medium. The essential gesture is the rejection of the prevailing styles and idioms of the current age.

As in our own time, the word *quality* was a rallying point for the Pre-Raphaelites, who felt that after Raphael the making of art had declined, largely through a loss of technical skill and respect for training. Their rigorous test for a well-made painting invoked the highest standards of draftsmanship as well as the jewel-like application of saturated color. The obsessive attention to detail that gives these paintings their photographic finish has had a curious effect upon their reception. With each foreground leaf and blossom as crisply defined and correct as seems humanly possible, the usual response of all but the most jaded viewers is one of awe. Even though the founding principles of the Pre-Raphaelites sound elitist (would the miners in Yorkshire know who Raphael was?), the popular appeal of such realistic paintings is undeniable. Their photographic accuracy is today a big hit among mass museumgoers and lowbrow collectors who overpay to the tune of millions for them at auction, such as Sir Andrew Lloyd Webber. The forthright message of their overtly religious or storybook subject matter also helps to make them palatable to viewers put off by abstraction or the darker psychological uncertainties of Expressionism. One way in which it diverges from most of Modern art as we know it is the utter lack of irony in the delivery of these narratives. There is a giant emotional gap between the sweetness and light of the paintings by Lord Leighton that young Francis Bacon grew up looking at in his family home and the acidic nightmares of Bacon's own paintings.

The broad popular appeal of Pre-Raphaelite art was in part a strategy. Morris and critic John Ruskin were advocates of reaching the workmen of the time with a message of beauty and education. The stained glass commissions for which Edward Burne-Jones was famous were populist translations of homilies into light in that great tradition of church glass, offering the lay audience their Scripture in a form that they could understand. Irony leaves the uninitiated behind, and the idea was that even for those who might never know who Giotto was the power of the message would not be lost. Even as they sought to distance themselves from the art establishment, the Pre-Raphaelites did not want their painting to seem arcane to the ordinary viewer. The complex relationship between the Pre-Raphaelites and the Royal Academy, as well as that between Swinburne and Oxford, reflects this dual nature. On the one hand, these artists insisted upon being accessible to the lower social echelons whose betterment appealed to their sense of noblesse oblige. On the other hand, the style and allusive nature of their work was as academic as could be. The most recent scholarly study of Leighton, a collection of essays that aims at establishing his essential modernity, points to his advanced thinking on public arts education and policy as one of the key aspects of his legacy.[2] One important historical fact that cannot be overlooked is the strong commitment to the nineteenth-century English socialism of William Morris, the forceful presiding spirit in the decorative arts who was one of the most outspoken figures associated with the Brotherhood. The egalitarianism of Morris, Leighton, and Ruskin ensured that the pictures would be legible to a working-class audience. The enemy, as in the case of Sand and her circle, was the dread bourgeoisie, especially the nouveau riche in England, whose competitive collecting had, ironically enough, driven the art market to its heights.

Art as anachronism has been a theme of this study, and the repudiation of time present through the evocation of time past that is the nominal premise of Pre-Raphaelitism involves a rationale that accords well with a strong tendency in twentieth-century art and thought. With so much talk of Postmodernism and what Harold Bloom has called the "belatedness" of the contemporary artist, it is strange to come across an ideologically charged group that calls itself Pre- anything. The yearning for the "innocent eye" (the phrase is Ruskin's) is a subplot in the history of Modern art, embracing phenomena as diverse as the highly finished paintings of the Pre-Raphaelites and the wild, rough expressiveness of Art Brut and Jean Dubuffet or other Primitivist painters, notably Henri Rousseau. Plagued by the challenge to be original when so many ideas have already been realized and, some would say, exhausted, one possible interpretation of the importance of the yearning for innocence is a desperate hope to bypass the shadow of being derivative. It can also be read in terms of Eliot's theory of the selective use of the tradition, much as he returned to the Metaphysical poets for license to create a more complex, layered Modern poetics. One of the most rewarding studies of this question is Roger Shattuck's *The Innocent Eye*, which takes an interdisciplinary approach.[3] By comparison with the world-weary, cynical regard of Lautrec, for example, or even Bacon, both of whom seem to have seen all, the Pre-Raphaelites invoke a naïveté that is closer to the pure lyricism of, for example, Puvis or Balthus.

The Pre-Raphaelites formed as a distinct group in September 1848 in the home of one of the most affluent of their number, John Everett Millais. He would eventually become too rich and successful for their blood and, under pressure, voluntarily split from the group a few years later. The original bond was art historical and critical. Over a folio volume of Carlo Lasimio's engravings, made after the frescoes by Benozzo Gazzoli at Campo Santo at Pisa (which, incidentally, inspired Liszt's *Totentanz*), and Taddeo Gaddi's *Life of Job*, they, joined by William Holman Hunt and Dante Gabriel Rossetti, excitedly mapped out an aesthetic program to overthrow the stiff taste of British art under the sway of Sir Joshua ("Sloshua") Reynolds and the Royal Academy. The idea was to reinvigorate painting with the freshness and power it once had. Hunt, Millais, Rossetti and his brother William Michael, along with Thomas Woolner (1825–92), a sculptor; James Collinson (1825–81), a painter and now all but forgotten; and the critic F. G. Stephens (1828–1907), were the first to sign their canvases and letters to the editor with the mysterious initials "PRB," a coded answer to the official FRA affixed by the Fellows of the Royal Academy to their work. As with any elite order, they modeled their organization upon the historical aristocracy, which makes it all the more apt that two of their most prominent figures would be veritable gentry.

As with any hard-charging artistic movement that delivers a style or subject matter that is novel, the Brotherhood encountered initial critical resistance and resentment. The in-house code that was so much a part of their day-to-day excitement alienated art-world professionals even as it intrigued the curious. Particularly in the earliest phase of the movement, detractors found the fantasies that fueled both the poetry and the painting too private to decipher. From Rosetti's *House of Life* sonnet sequence to Swinburne's long dramas based on Greek themes, with the paintings and drawings that would then comment on the poetry—or vice versa with poems written to celebrate and interpret the paintings—the movement seemed to circle on itself too tightly, which gave the subject matter a recondite and homogeneous quality. Ancient Greek and Roman themes, along with obscure Bible stories, were favorite narrative sources. The approach to them was often imbued with the thorough and enthusiastic study of ancient and Renaissance thought and painterly techniques. The members of the Brotherhood in general were blessed with what today would be considered magnificently well-rounded educational backgrounds, leaving them fully conversant with the classics in literature, art, and music. It was a historically informed avant-garde movement that reached back far beyond its immediate precursors. Both Swinburne and Lord Leighton forged their styles from alloys of Renaissance and Classical models that they knew intimately from direct study of the originals. In Leighton's case, extensive travel and training abroad, particularly in Italy and Germany, had a direct impact upon his technique, and Swinburne's immense knowledge of Greek and Latin versification helped shape his distinctive style. While French painters such as Corot and Delacroix were almost obliged to spend an apprenticeship in Rome, Leighton was unusual among British painters for his commitment to study in Italy.

The artists of the Brotherhood were young and headstrong and, particularly when inflamed by the wit of Swinburne, as on a couple of occasions when they gathered at Oxford for one supposedly solemn event or another, they had a tendency to stand apart and snipe at the establishment, as young Turks are wont to do in any period. Not surprisingly, there was a moral outcry from outsiders in response to their work and their well-known "secret" society, which in the case of Swinburne never ended, partly because of his own wild, usually drunken high jinks, the forerunner of the better-known antics of Whistler and Wilde. Some of the adverse reaction to the Pre-Raphaelites is difficult to fathom today. For example, critics found *The Carpenter's Shop* by Millais blasphemous for its near-photographic depiction of the young Christ at work for his father. The high moral dudgeon with which their work was greeted was a match for the ethical tone of the art itself, which in turn reflected the religious ardor of the Pre-Raphaelite approach to art. As in France during the same period, Aestheticism was a creed, and there was not much moderation in the way in which Swinburne, Leighton, and most certainly the Rossettis presented themselves.

The group's paintings in the Royal Academy exhibition of 1850 took a pasting from critics. They needed a break, and three years after banding together, the Brotherhood received its biggest boost: a pair of letters to the *Times* in May 1851 from the potent pen of John Ruskin, just on the brink of becoming the reigning critic of the day. The rigorous examination of natural detail that still appeals to lovers of Photo-Realism in painting in our day, and the sharpness of contour with which individual leaves of a foreground shrub, for example, were delineated, followed perfectly Ruskin's exhortations to paint with close attention to the particulars of nature. Nothing could be less in keeping with the painterly styles of the time, in either Paris or London, and part of the Modern quality of the group was their willingness to strike out on their own in terms of this instantly recognizable (to this day) style. Their publication, *The Germ*, which appeared in 1850 and lasted only three issues, was first subtitled *Thoughts towards Nature in Poetry, Literature, and Art.* Another point of convergence between Ruskin and the Pre-Raphaelites was the moral tone that gave his writings their evangelical élan and the paintings their emotional charge. To dismiss this as merely a "Victorian" quirk is to miss a possibly significant tendency in aesthetics. Postmodernism has carried Modern irony to the point where faith in art and artists is nearly untenable. Before this emptiness there was plenitude. Romanticism was brilliantly if acerbically characterized by T. E. Hulme as "spilt religion." The substitution of art, music, and poetry for theology was a near-cataclysmic shift in belief that occurred in the nineteenth century, when museums and concert halls became the churches of the time, and Wagner's Bayreuth could attain the status of a shrine. The next such change led toward science, so that Cubism, logically oriented philosophy, and mathematically determined musical composition became the basis for belief—until that began to be whittled away by the sort of further doubt that Russell wielded like a chisel. In general, the figures under consideration in this study, particularly Swinburne and Leighton, held fast to art as a system of belief, blessed by its purity and the unimpeachable validity of its Classical and Renaissance foundations. For the generations that followed, particularly in the face of World War I, the resiliency and tenacity of this faith in art offered a vital connection to the original impulse to make art in the first place. Considerably advanced from the Romantics (although the lyric Swinburne was incessantly compared with Shelley, partly for their aristocratic backgrounds), Leighton and Swinburne carried on the hope that their work could effect the spiritual benefits that still echo in the Formalism of our own time.

The end of the Brotherhood's first phase was nigh by the time Millais was elected to the Royal Academy in November 1853, becoming a baronet in 1885 and so successful as a painter that he became fantastically wealthy. His swift rise was reflected in the acclaim and success of the others. Crowds turned out to see Holman Hunt's *Light of the World*, which toured the United States and Australia in 1854, about the time when biblical scenes by Hunt were selling for 5,500 guineas each, a vast sum. The peak may have been the Royal Academy exhibition of 1856, when crowds filed by *The Light of the World* by the thousands. A similar phenomenon was caused by certain Hudson River School paintings of the time, notably, *The Heart of the Andes* by Edwin Church, which used its monumental scale and potent depiction of light to dazzle American spectators much as special effects wow the audiences in movie theaters. The dazzling speed and breadth of Swinburne's poetry and conversation, as recorded by Henry Adams (the "wild Walpurgisnacht of Swinburne's talk") and others, is the verbal equivalent of this powerful virtuosity, recalling the impact of Liszt or Chopin in recital.

The defection of Millais was not by any means the end of the story, however. The movement was revived by a group of Oxford undergraduates led by Edward Burne-Jones (1833–98) and William Morris (1834–96), who had studied the work of Rossetti. Their decoration of the debating hall of the Oxford Union Society in 1857 was a high point of the movement's second wind. This rear guard built the bridge to Aestheticism, Art Nouveau, Symbolism, and various other early stirrings of Modernism with direct connections to Aubrey Beardsley, Oscar Wilde, Ernest Dowson, Lionel Johnson, Yeats, Whistler, and eventually Pound and Eliot. This was the generation that took a serious swerve into the applied arts, including stained glass, tapestry, needlework and mosaics, book and type design—all tinged with medievalism in terms of style and subject and yet wholly Modern in their response to the decorative needs of the middle classes. The Pre-Raphaelites took it upon themselves to refashion the arts and design for Modern consumption. In 1864, Morris founded his decorating firm, in which Rossetti, Burne-Jones, and Ford Maddox Brown were all partners, and Morris, Marshall, Faulkner and Company applied the Pre-Raphaelite ideology to, for lack of a more glamorous term, home furnishings.

Two figures at the periphery of this dynamic and internationally influential group—Algernon Swinburne, second son of the earl of Ashburnham, and Frederick, Lord Leighton, baron of Stretton—pursued their own marvelous directions in poetry and art, extending the frontiers of the movement to the borders of Modernism and beyond. Leighton became the guardian of high art at one of its most prestigious gates, as the active and vocal president of the Royal Academy. In later decades he was wrongly maligned in art history for having kept Impressionism at bay in England, when in fact there were certain British Impressionists whose careers he helped. As both an arbiter of taste and a practitioner, he was a public figure, an artist and an aristocrat on the London scene.

Swinburne came on board as a student at Oxford when he met Dante Gabriel Rossetti during the painting of the murals. If Swinburne, like Rossetti, had one quality that was both his greatest strength and his most annoying failing, it was the excitement with which art and ideas would possess him. After university he left the massive family estates at Capheaton and Ashburnham (both his mother and father were descended from still powerful, land-rich families) to move into Tudor House in Chelsea with William Rossetti and George Meredith and, once a week as

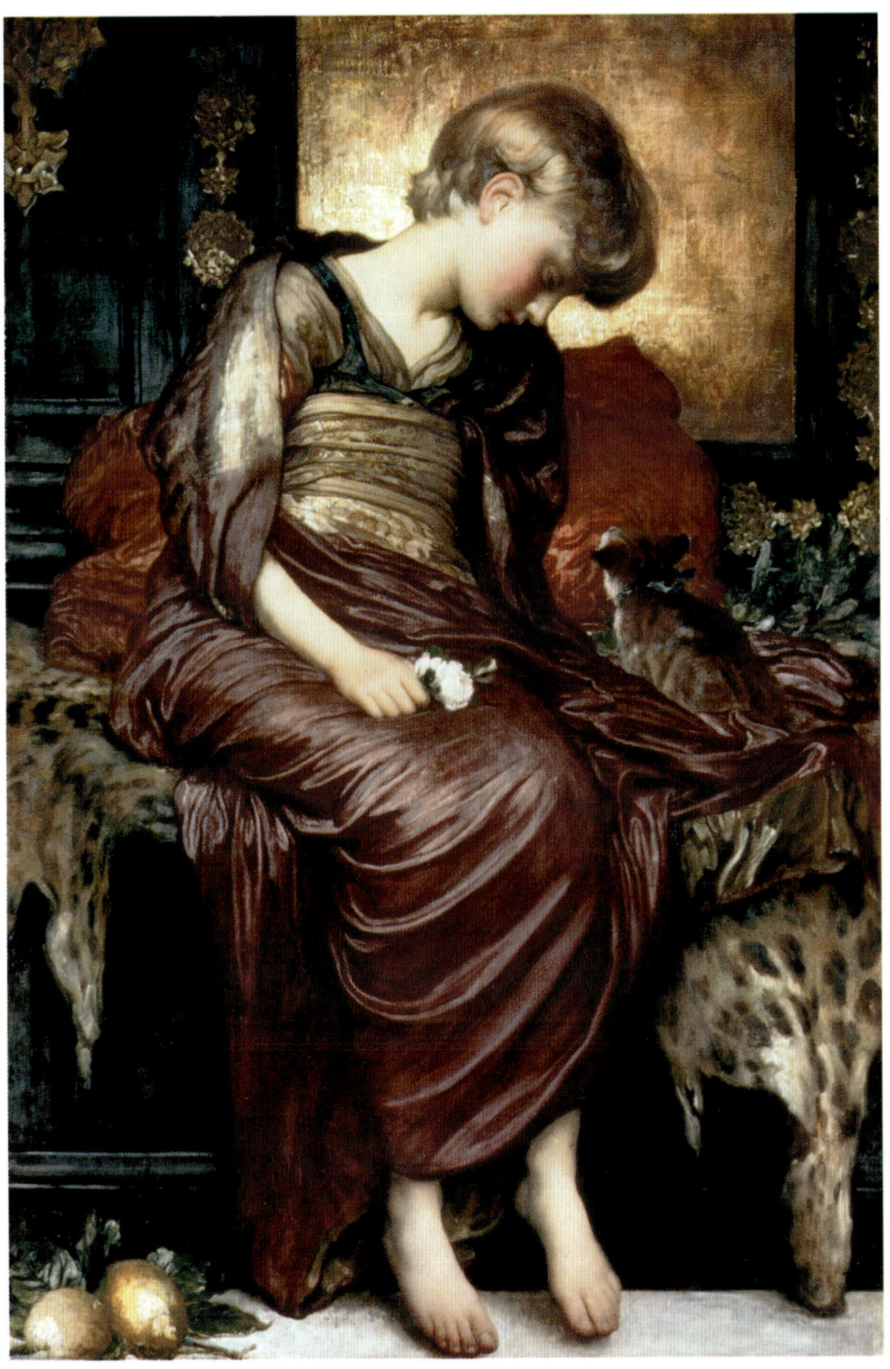

Frederick, Lord Leighton, *Kittens*, circa 1883, oil on canvas, 48 in. x 31 ½ in.
Courtesy of Christie's Images, New York

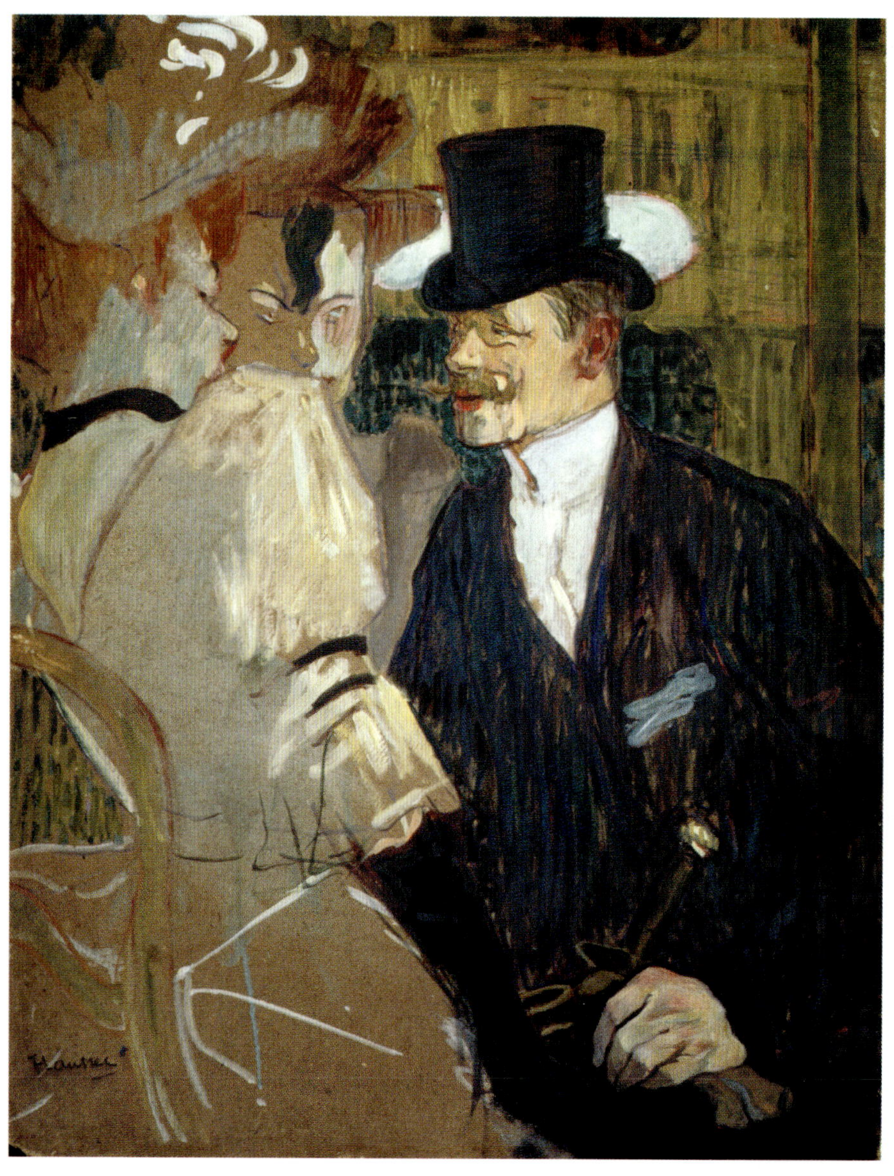

Henri de Toulouse-Lautrec, (French, 1864–1901), *The Englishman (William Tom Warrener, 1861–1934) at the Moulin Rouge,* Study for a color lithograph commissioned in 1892, Oil and gouache on cardboard, H. 33 ¾ in. W. 26 in. The Metropolitan Museum of Art, Bequest of Miss Adelaide Milton de Groot (1876–1967), 1967. (67.187.108) Photograph © 1979 The Metropolitan Museum of Art

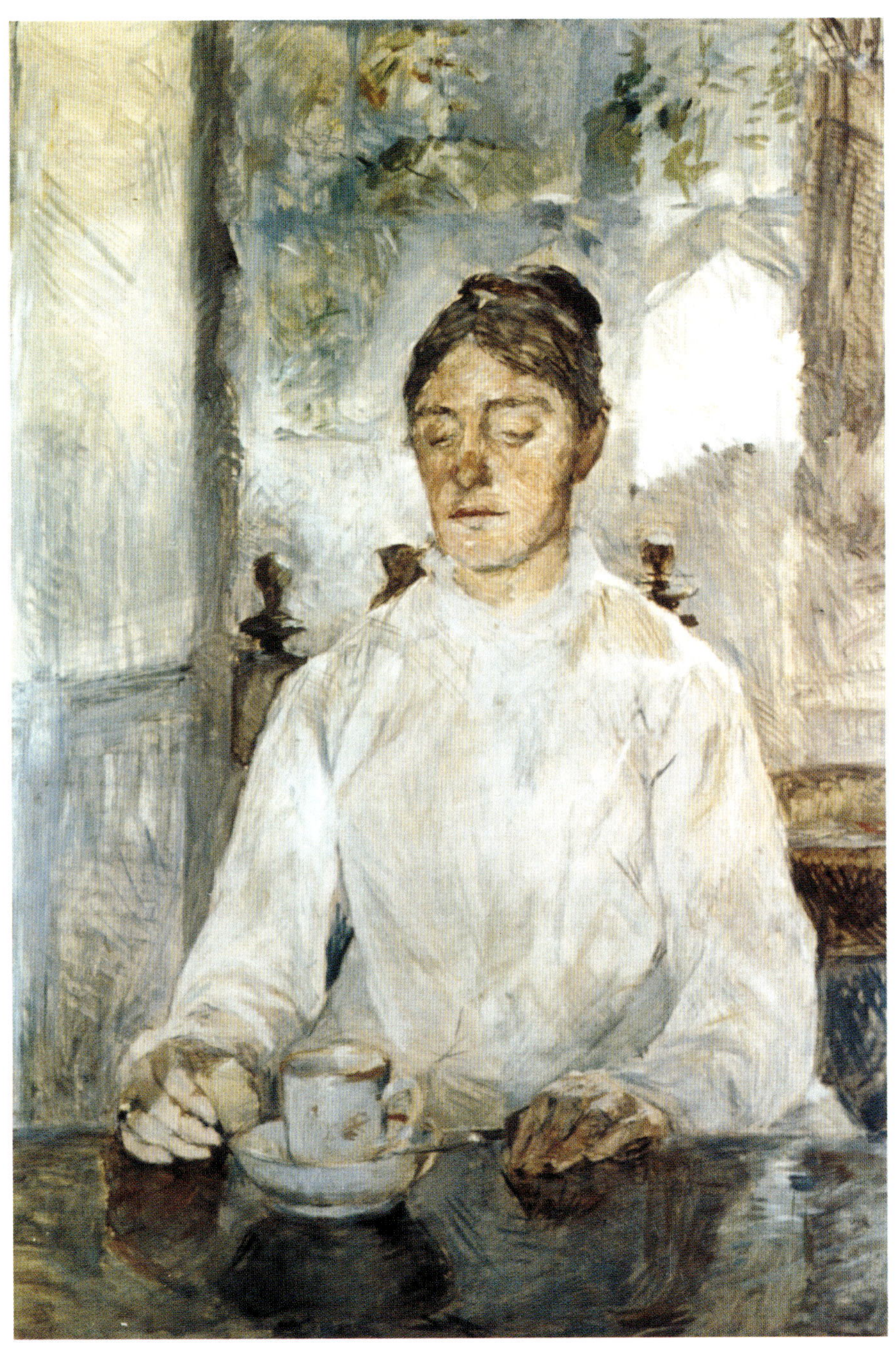

Henri de Toulouse-Lautrec, *La Comtesse Adèle dans le Salon du Château de Malromé*, 1881, oil on canvas, 24 in. x 38 in.

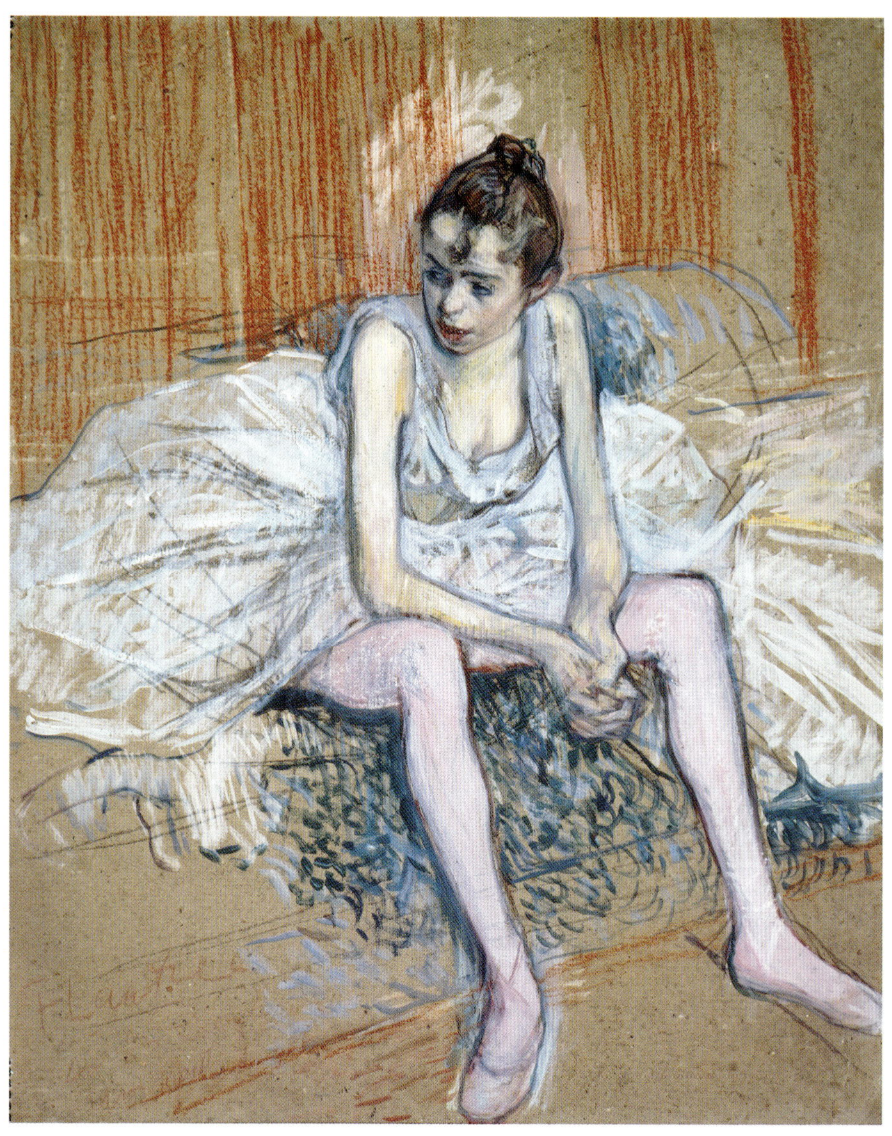

Henri de Toulouse-Lautrec, *Danseuse assise aux bas roses*, pastel, 1887, pastel, 14 in. x 26 in. The John Langeloth Loeb and Frances Lehman Loeb Collection.
Courtesy of Christie's Images, New York.

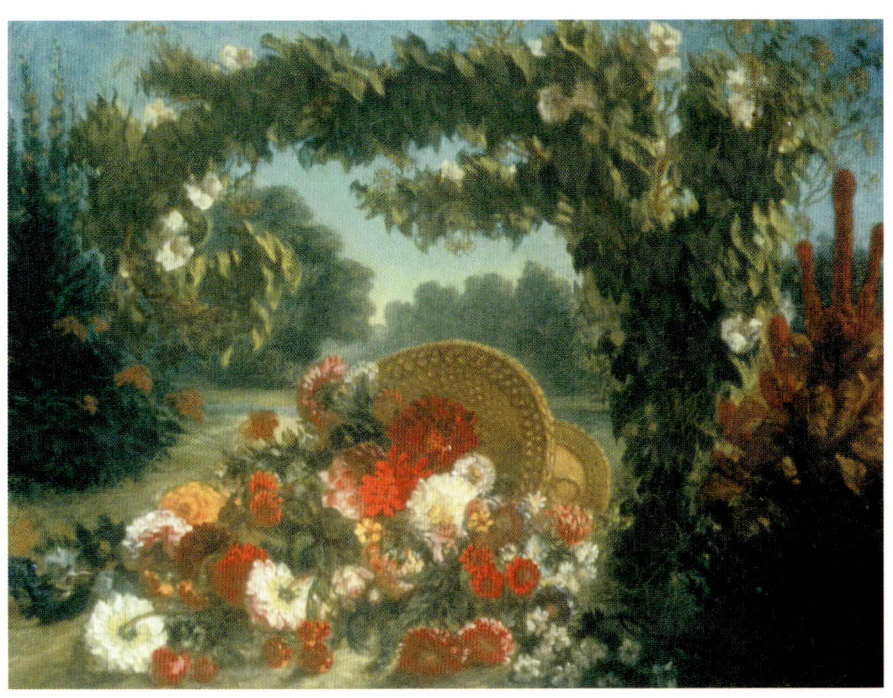

Eugène Delacroix, *Basket of Flowers Overturned in a Park*, 1848–1849, oil on canvas, 107.3 cm. x 142.2 cm. Courtesy of the Metropolitan Museum of Art.

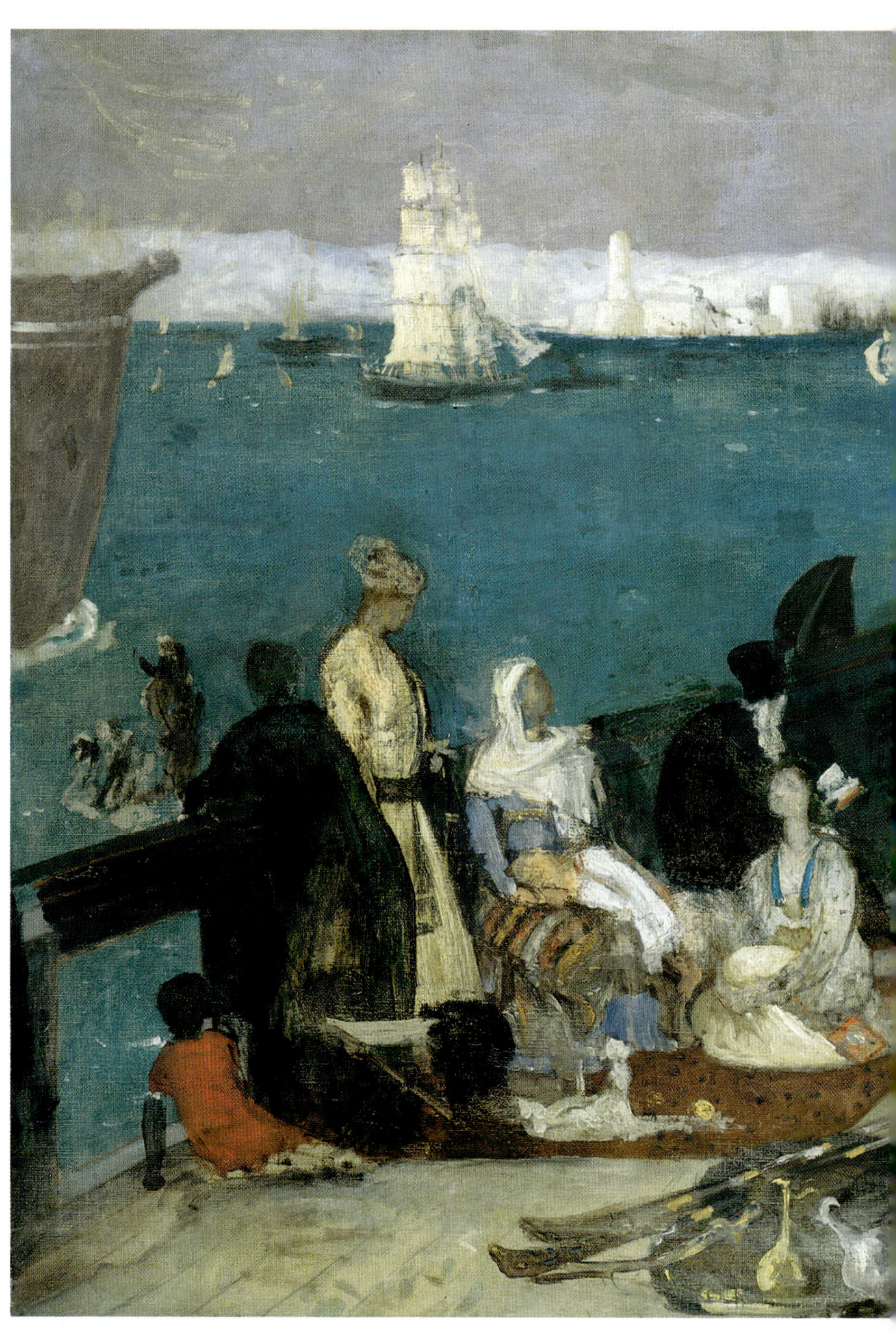

Pierre Puvis de Chavannes, *Marseilles, Gateway to the Orient*, c. 1868–1869, oil on canvas, 38 ¾ in. x 57 ⅝ in. Acquired 1923. The Phillips Collection, Washington, D.C.

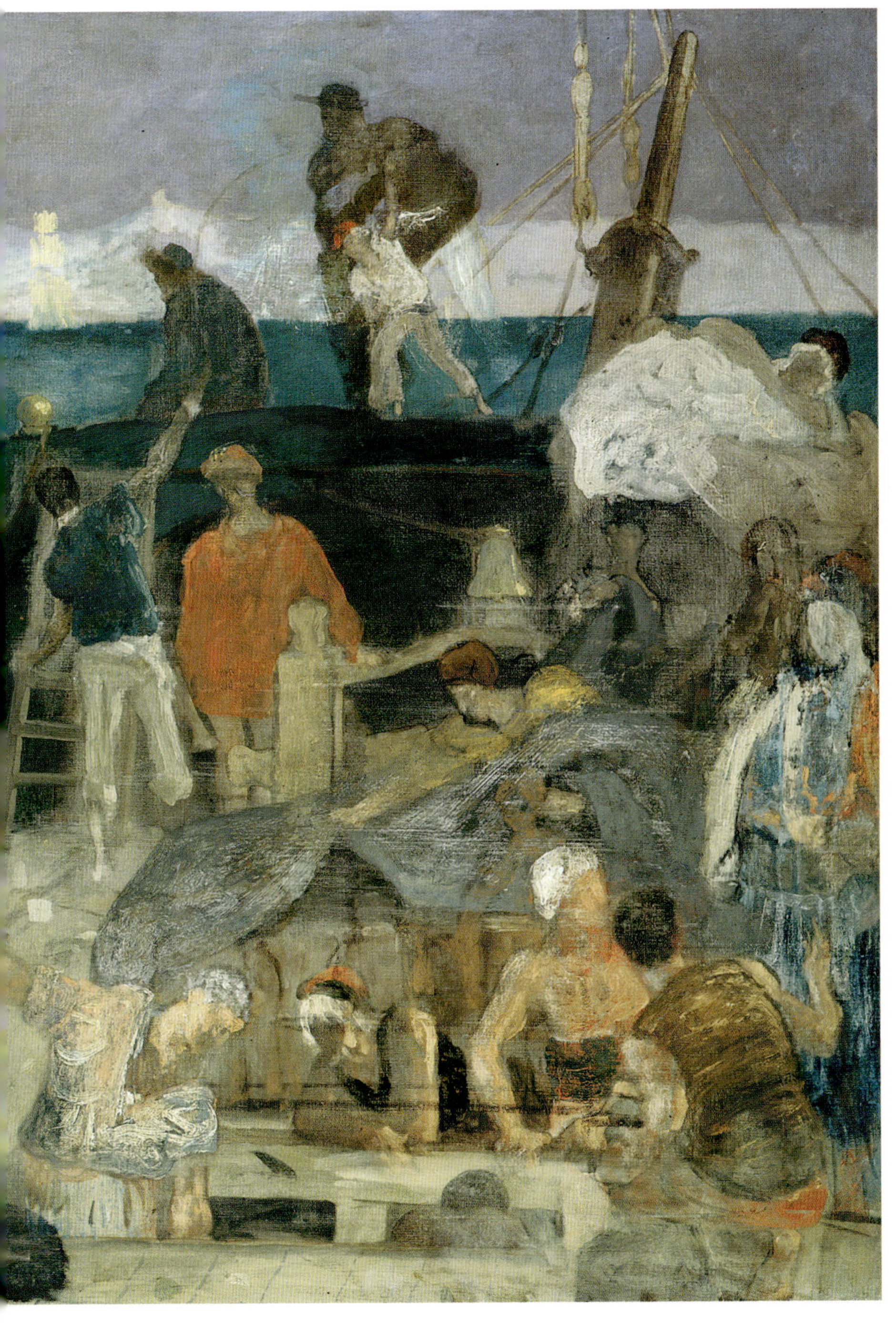

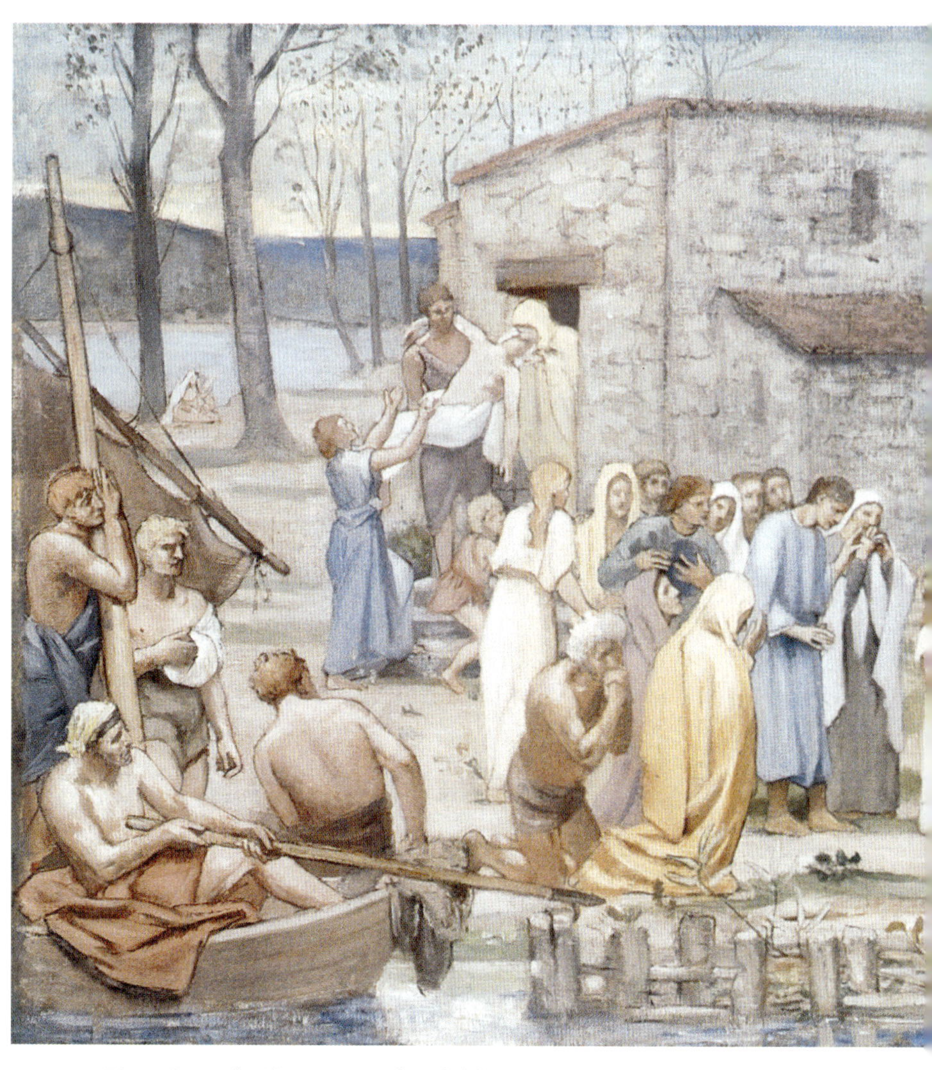

Pierre Puvis de Chavannes, *The Childhood of Saint Genevieve*, 1874, oil on canvas 20 ½ in. x 40 ¼ in. Courtesy of Christie's Images, New York.

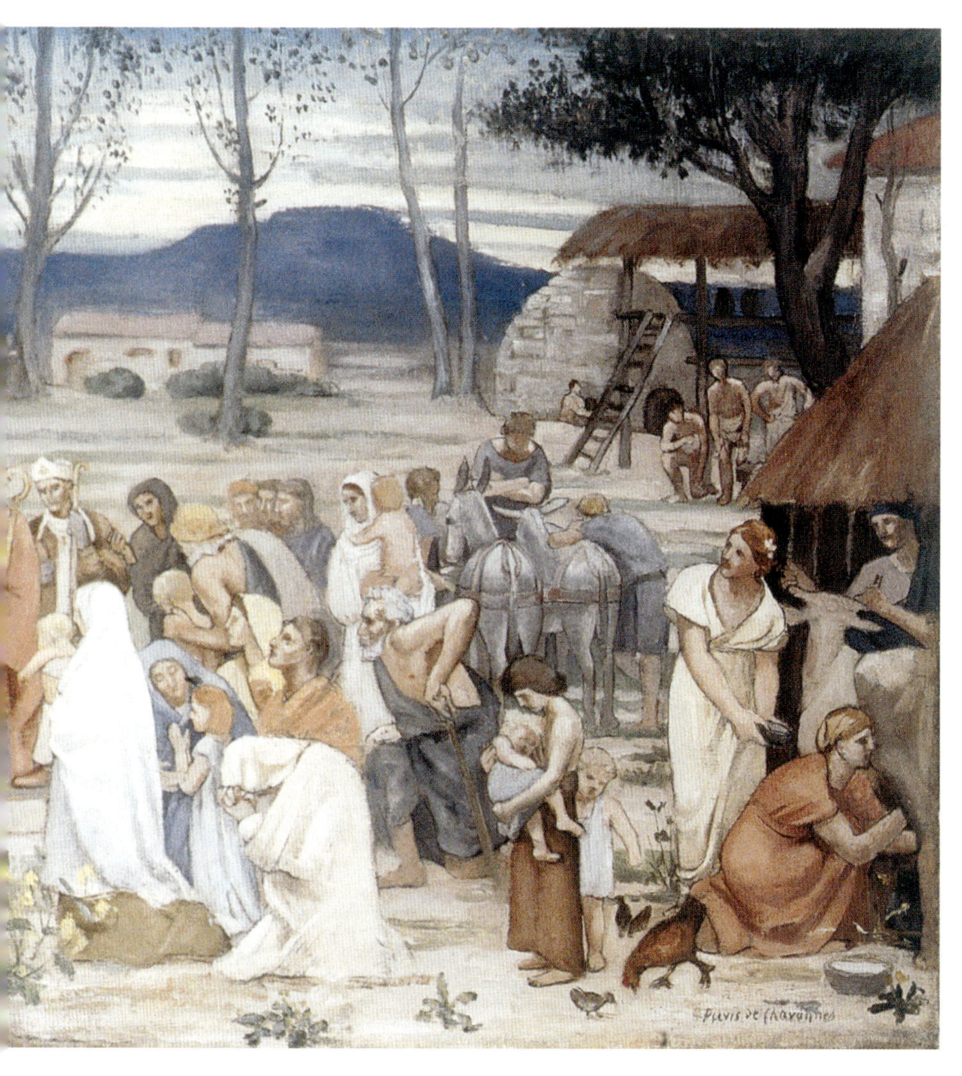
Puvis de Chavannes

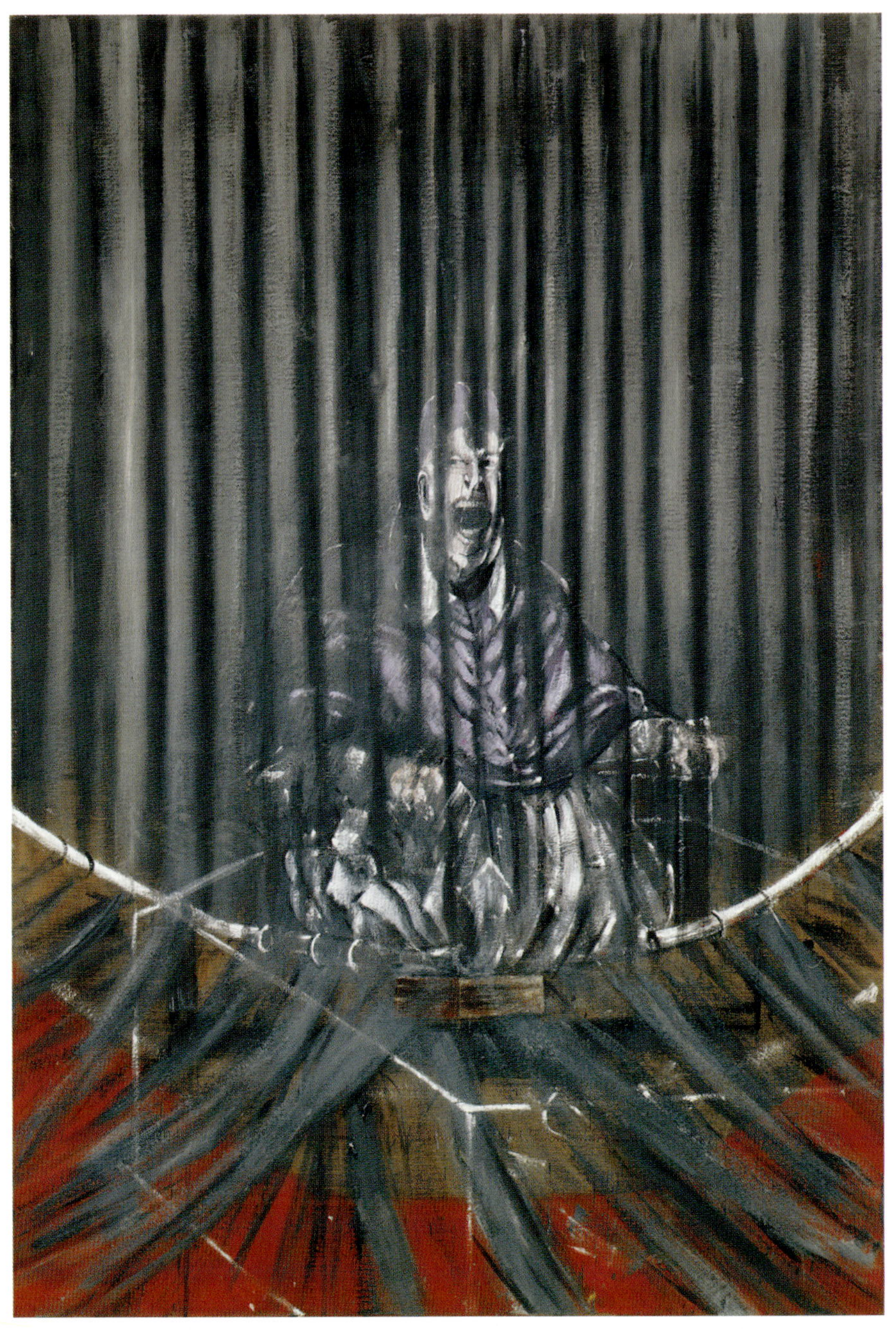

Francis Bacon, *Study after Velazquez*, circa 1950, oil on canvas, 78 in. x 54 in.

The Estate of Francis Bacon. Courtesy of Tony Shafrazi Gallery, New York.

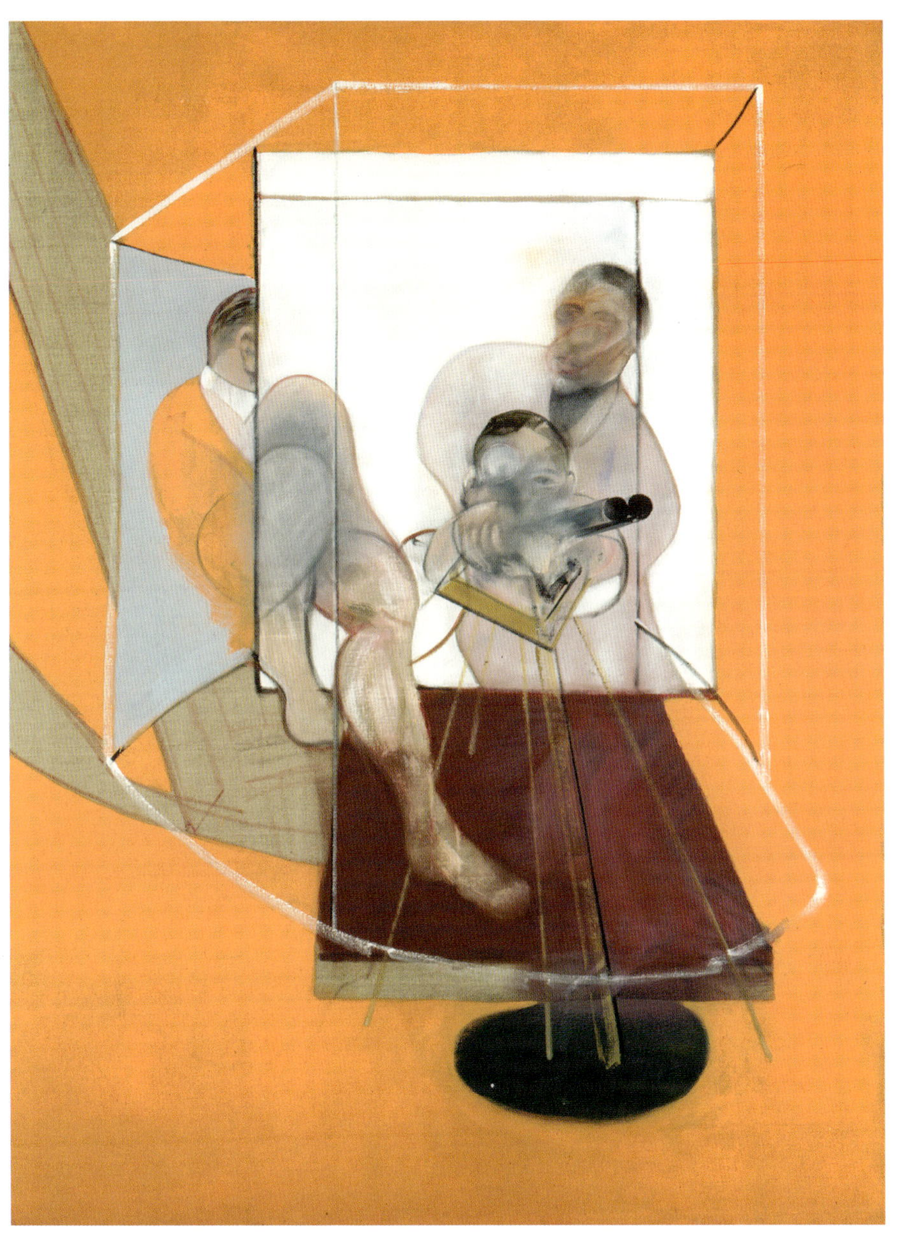

Francis Bacon, *Three Figures, One with Shotgun*, 1980, 78 in. x 54 in.

The Estate of Francis Bacon. Courtesy of Tony Shafrazi Gallery, New York.

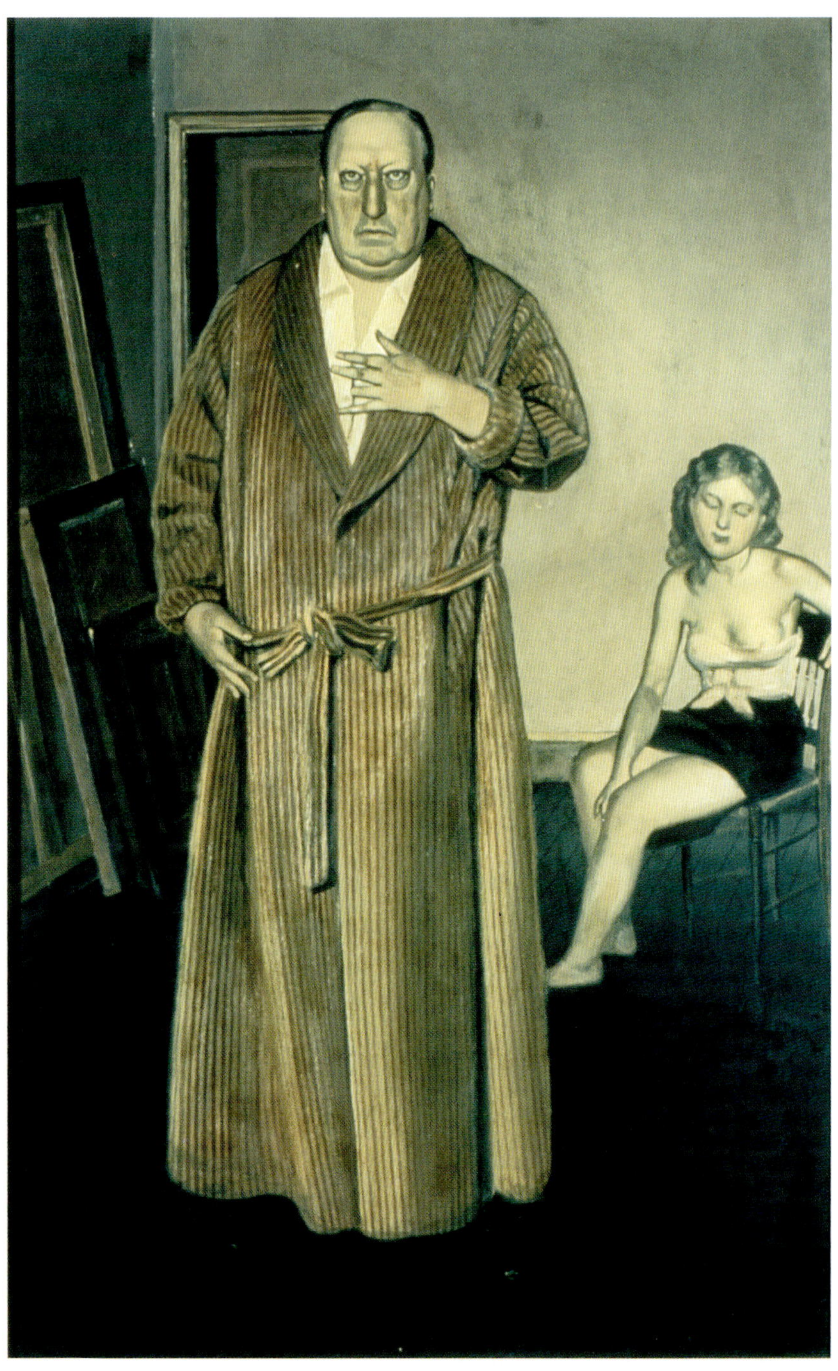

Balthus, *André Derain*, 1936, oil on wood, 44 ¼ in. x 28 ½ in. (112.7 cm. x 72.4 cm.). The Museum of Modern Art, New York. Acquired through the Lillie P. Bliss Bequest. © Artists Right Society (ARS) New York/ADAGP, Paris Photograph © 2000. Courtesy of the Museum of Modern Art, New York. From *Making Choices: Modern Art despite Modernism.*

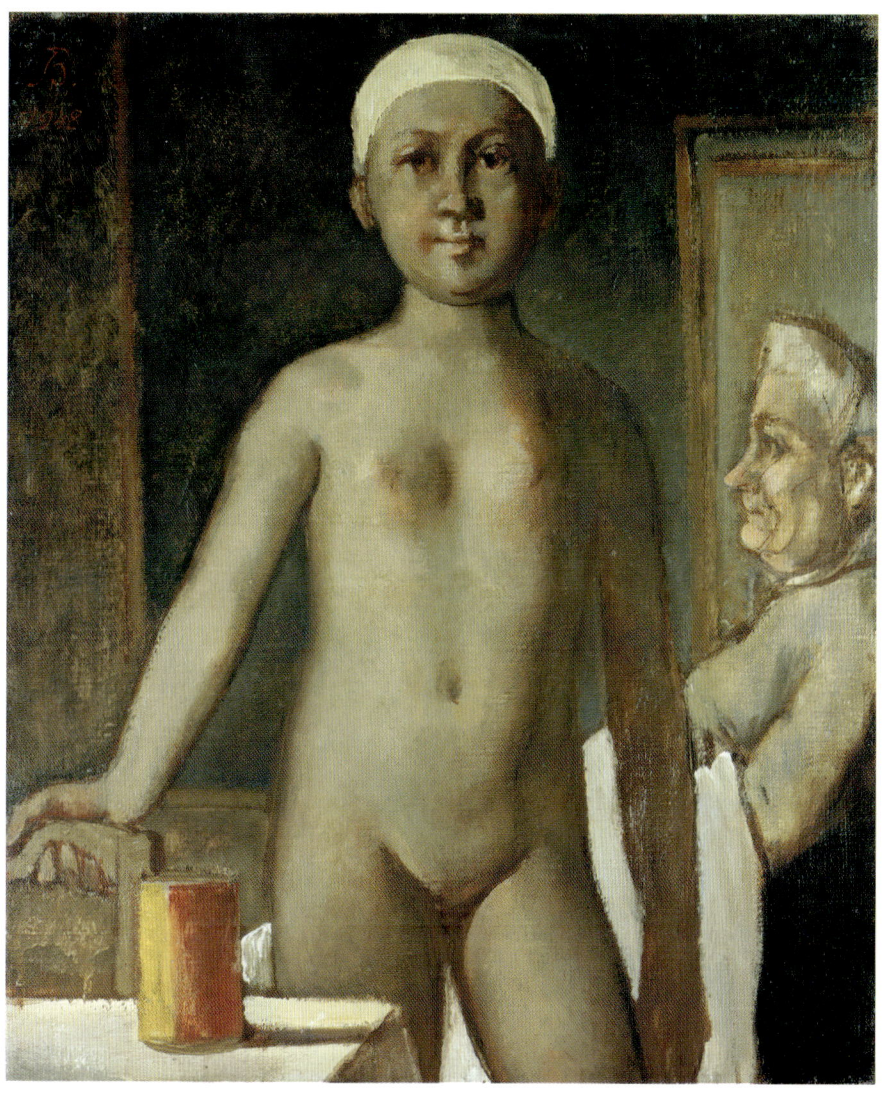

Balthus, *Jeune Fille a sa toilette*, 1948, oil on canvas, 22 ½ in. x 18 ⅛ in.
Courtesy Jan Krugier Gallery, New York.

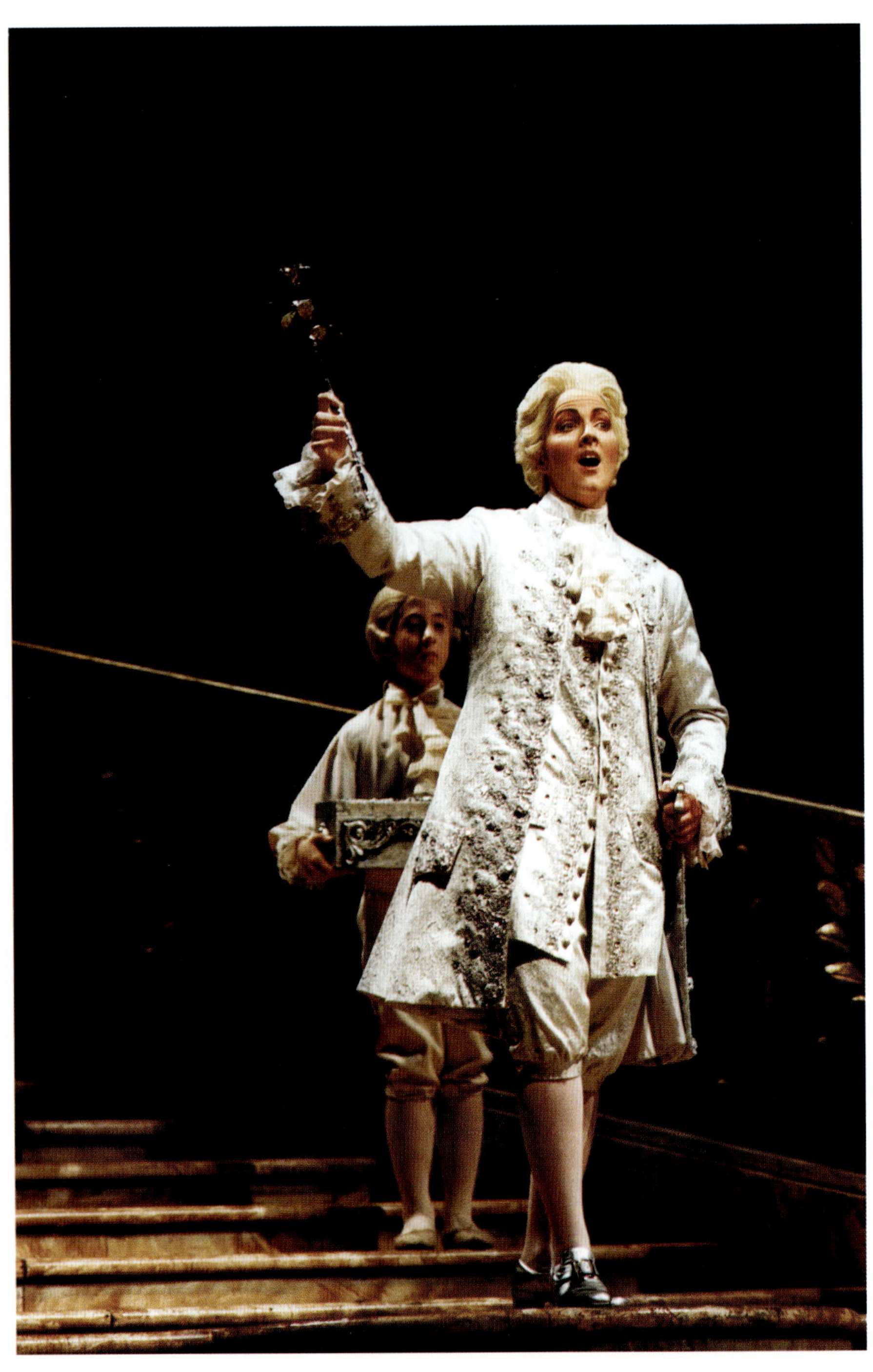

Margaret Lattimore as Octavian in *Der Rosenkavalier*, April 2000.
Photo: Courtesy of Michigan Opera Theatre.

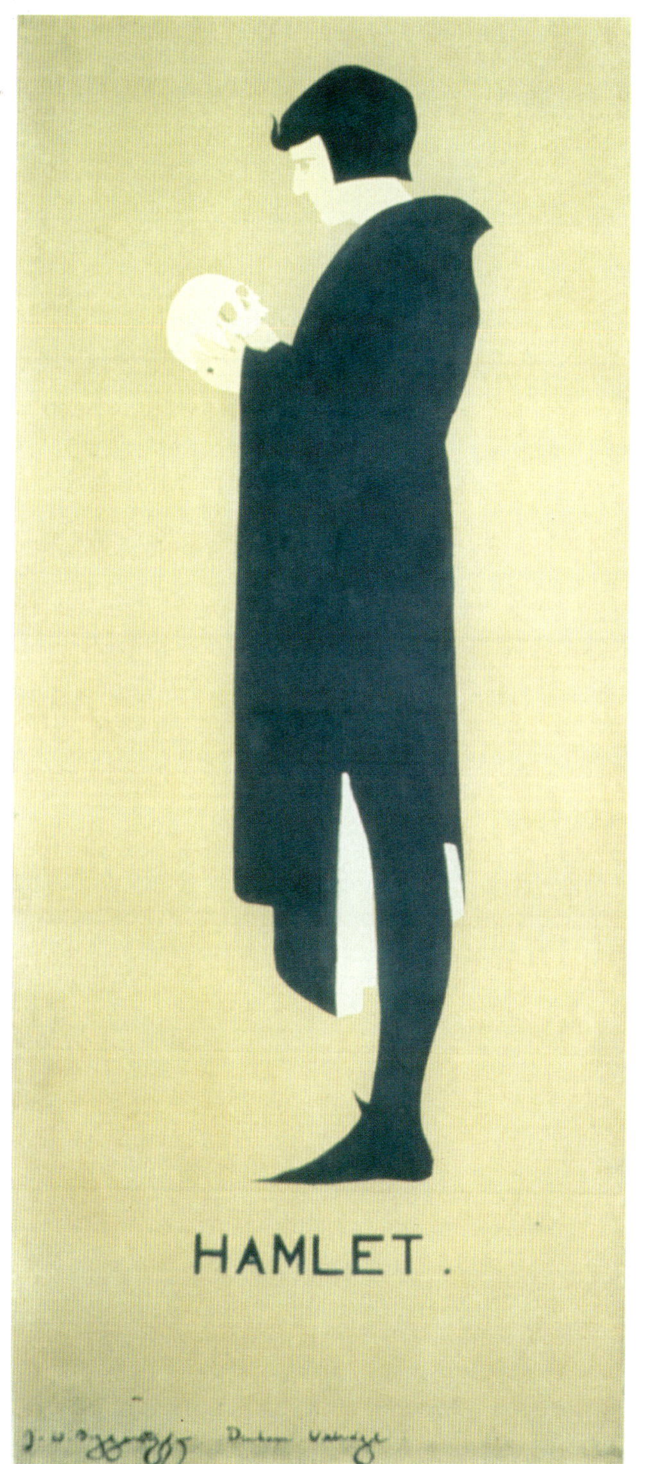

The Beggarstaffs (William Nicholson and James Pryde), *Hamlet*, 1894, 67 ⅜ in. x 28 ⅞ in. Museum of Modern Art, New York. Gift of the Lauder Foundation, Leonard and Evelyn Lauder Fund, Jack Banning and by exchange. From *Modern Starts: People*.

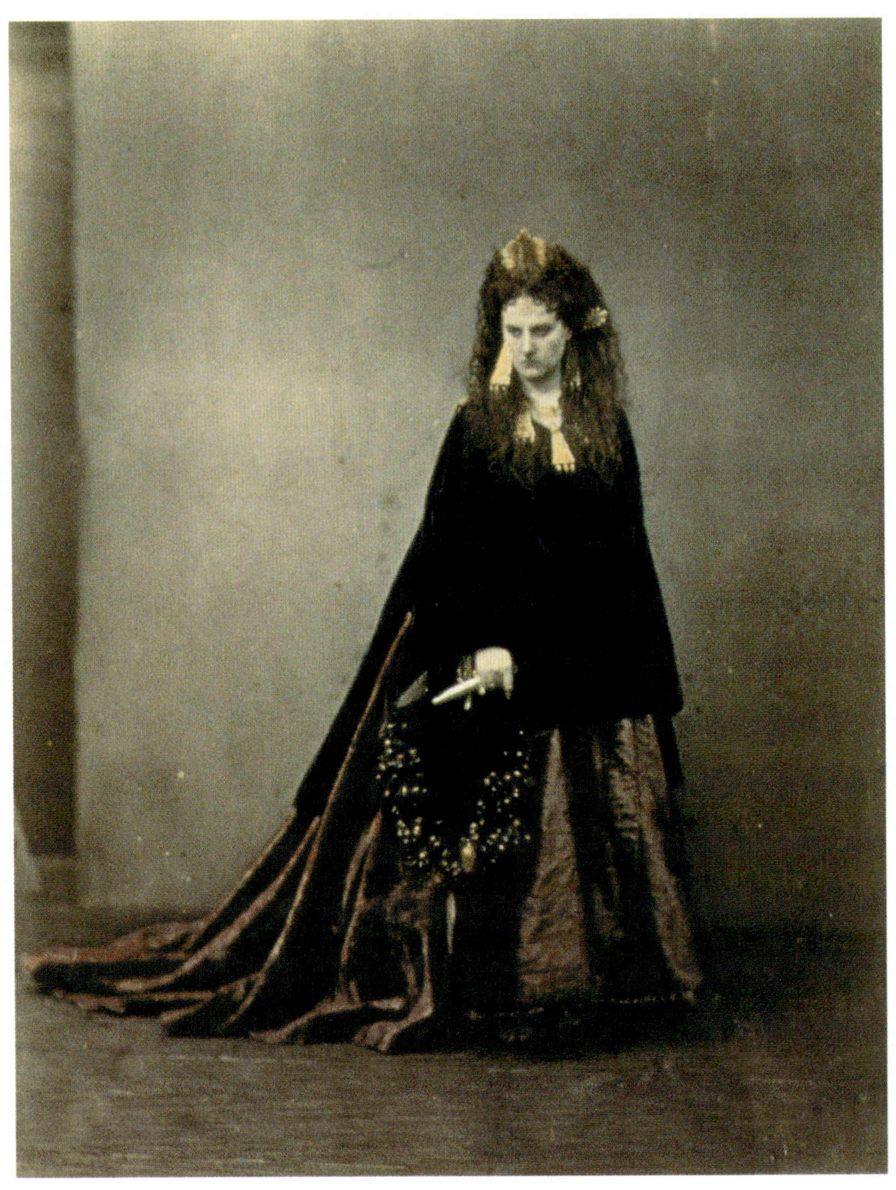

Pierre-Louis Pierson, *Vengeance*, 1863–1867, albumen silver print retouched with gouache, 24.4 cm. x 19.2 cm. Martini di Cigala Collection, San Giusta A Rentennano. Courtesy of the Metropolitan Museum of Art. From *La Divine Comtesse*.

a paying guest, Dante Rossetti. The wild times there, including nude chases down the banisters, a menagerie of exotic animals, and chaotic drinking bouts, are odd enough to be the stuff of legend but too well documented to be anything but at least partly true. The notoriety became part of Swinburne's rise, à la both Byron before and Bacon or even Hirst after, setting the pattern for the success-guaranteeing position of the "bad boy" of British arts and letters. He may have been closest, however, to Lautrec in the circumstances surrounding his early years and choice of career. Physically slight and frail, Swinburne was also the son of a military man (in this case, an admiral) whose passion for hunting and outdoor sports, as well as his deep desire to hold onto the family estates, was entirely lost on an artsy heir. Like Lautrec, Swinburne sought the most rigorous training in his vocation by studying literature at Oxford and, to descend to a lower level, like Lautrec, Swinburne's sexual cravings were answered in bordellos. His sadomasochistic tastes were similar not only to the more lurid moments in Lautrec but to Bacon as well.

Leighton, by contrast, was the very picture of respectability. Refined and ostentatiously proper, if somewhat shy, he had made the most, intellectually and socially, of his family's decision to give him a few years abroad in Germany and Italy for a thorough academic grounding in his chosen career. While monarchs have been absent from this study until now, it is impossible to dodge a brief reference to Queen Victoria as a factor in the careers of both Leighton and Swinburne. Leighton fared much better with the regent, whose more than competent if traditional watercolors (Prince Charles follows in her footsteps in this passion) helped attune her to leadership in the arts in her domain. She became one of Leighton's champions, solidly backing his work as a patron and endorsing his administration of the Royal Academy, where he pursued an active course in promoting the careers of a select group of English artists. As with Hofmannsthal and Yeats, Leighton's efforts bore a nationalistic stripe. Just the day before his death in 1896, Queen Victoria raised his title to baron, making him the first artist in England ever to attain that level of ennoblement. His standing among painters was comparable to that of Alfred, Lord Tennyson in the literary set, and the composer Sir Edward Elgar, whose favorite dynamic marking on a score was *nobilmente*.

By contrast, Swinburne's reputation and radical associations politically cost him the queen's patronage. At the death of Tennyson in 1892 (after forty-two years of holding the laureateship conferred by Victoria), it was widely expected that Swinburne would become poet laureate. "I am told that Mr. Swinburne is the best poet in my dominions," Edmond Gosse reports her as having said to her prime minister, Gladstone.[4] He discouraged her by referring to the exuberance of Swinburne's political verses as well as of the rowdy young college men who took them up as anthems. Swinburne's candidacy was undermined, and a complete stiff, Alfred Austin, was appointed. Late in his life, Swinburne vented his frustration in a letter to William Michael Rossetti that is right on target vis-à-vis the sheer dullness of Austin's poetry, referring to Austin only as "the present laureate . . . who has spared me the trouble of not acknowledging his books, since his promotion."[5] It may be that, by basking in the glow of royal admiration, Leighton wielded more power of the conventionally institutional kind than Swinburne did, but the latter comes off as the more Modern of the two in part because of his unruly and rather dangerous status. While the androgyny of Leighton's youthful sitters has been noted by recent scholars, even his nudes are cloaked in academic propriety that deflects attention from the erotic heat of, to pick one notable example, his torrid *Flaming June*. Swinburne, on the other hand, was protected by his rank from the kind of legal and social ramifications that his obvious homosexual liaisons would have leveled upon Pater or Wilde, although Swinburne was not nearly as brazen or political as Wilde was in such matters.

The connection between poet and artist was close during the period when Swinburne lived in London. As Swinburne made his social rounds, one frequent stop was Leighton's extraordinary home on Holland Park Road. Like the later Bloomsbury set near the British Museum and the circle of Sand in Paris, the Pre-Raphaelites and their Aestheticist successors tended to cluster in particular neighborhoods. There was a strong Chelsea contingent (Swinburne, Whistler, W. M. Rossetti), and there was the more posh set. Leighton's elegant studio and townhouse, an important address for London's musical as well as artistic life, was not far from William Burge's Tower House and Holman Hunt's elegant residence. Leighton lived there from 1866 through 1895 and in his studio painted many of his most important works, including *The Garden of the Hesperides* and the wildly popular *Flaming June*, one of the most frequently reproduced works of the nineteenth century. The home was designed by Leighton's friend George Aitshicon, who pulled out all the stops in terms of Orientalism and materials, some of them collected for him by the adventurer Richard Burton, who returned from sorties to Damascus, Rhodes, and Cairo with Islamic tiles and lamps for the Arab Hall or silks and rugs. The entry was dominated by an immense statue of a peacock as well as one of Icarus by Alfred Gilbert. Under a golden dome a fountain played, Japanese goldfish swam, and guests circled on a floor of solid black marble. A frieze of peacocks by Walter Crane decorated the halls, and calligraphic inscriptions from the Koran were part of the decor. Leighton House, which is now a museum somewhat like the Moreau Museum in Paris or Church's Orientalist Olana on the Hudson River, was itself a work of art. It may seem over the top for a private residence, but its function was more of a public showplace, the first of its kind and a prototype for others, not just in London in that age but for later manifestations of the studio and home as places of commerce and entertainment, another aspect of Leighton's Modern legacy.

The close relationship between Swinburne and Leighton was both personal and professional. Highly regarded as an art critic—his essays on Renaissance painting were a counterpoint to those of Ruskin and a strong influence on Pater—Swinburne was one of Leighton's most notable champions, particularly through an essay published in 1868. Another firm supporter was Henry James, who wrote of Leighton: "It is impossible to be more graceful and elegant and more keenly artistic than Mr. Leighton; he strikes me as one of the few English painters who have had an artistic training that would be considered thorough by a high French standard. . . . But in Mr. Leighton's plasticism there is something vague and conciliatory; it is as if he thought that to be more plastic than that would not be quite gentlemanly."[6] It is a riveting observation, no less so for being Jamesian in that both artists are Moderns of the same stripe, acutely conscious of borders and thresholds of propriety they will not cross.

A recent collection of essays on Leighton moves from his debt to Classical sources through his infatuation with the Renaissance to conclude with a section on his particular contribution to Modernism. To some, that would seem to be pushing it, to take a stalwart Victorian like Lord Leighton and make a case for him as Modernist. Yet there is a compelling logic to the study, which points out that Leighton's views of education and the social mission of art are well ahead of their time, and his championship of contemporary artists now indubitably considered to be Modern, including Sickert, Clausen, Degas, and several British Impressionists, also qualified his inclusion in this category. As the volume's editors point out in their introduction,

> It would be reactionary to call for a return to the values of nineteenth century Aestheticism, or uncritically to revive the post-Kantian rhetoric of transcendence. Yet the study of Leighton's work may help to break the stalemate between a discredited Modernism and a historicism that evades questions of value. If Leighton's work has never been comfortably accommodated within the critical discourses of either the nineteenth or twentieth centuries, that might be precisely its virtue. We cannot claim to have invented a new language to substitute for that embarrassing word "beauty" nor do we pretend to have decided the dispute between high art and kitsch.

> But by treating Leighton's art seriously, we open the discussion to issues neglected or occluded in recent art history.[7]

In addition to beauty, that problematic term in a Postmodern context, the clarity of his painting is distinguished by the "luxury" and "elegance" that have been discussed in this study with respect to Delacroix. They figure prominently in the portraits—imagine the distinction of having one's portrait done by the president of the Royal Academy. One who sat for him had a strong tie to Chopin. Mrs. James Guthrie, whose portrait Leighton painted in 1864–5, was Ellinor Stirling (1838–1911), daughter of James Stirling, governor of Australia and distant relative of Jane Stirling, Chopin's benefactor and possibly lover toward the end of his life. The work can best be described as a large Baroque painting, its background crowded with flowers, although the format also suggests contemporary formal portraits by Manet and Whistler. The focal point is a transfixing pair of doe eyes through which Leighton effects that purification of emotion that is the hallmark of so many Pre-Raphaelite portraits.

As another example of Leighton's virtuosity, consider the large, ravishingly luxuriant work entitled *Kittens*, painted in 1883 when Leighton was at the height of his power as president of the Royal Academy (he was appointed in 1878 and held the post until his death). The work was actually lost to scholars from 1925 until it was sold at Christie's London in 1998, in an era when the figure was being reconsidered in contemporary art. Viewers may be excused, however, for fixing their initial attention on its dazzling background. Its use of sumptuous textiles and a leopard skin as well as its gold ground gives Leighton the chance to steal a Klimt-like sensuality. Beardsley, too, would use this elaborate patterning to meld figure and ground, and Matisse, who knew Leighton's work in this genre, also might have been influenced by the rhythmic and colorful use of the background. But the figure is exquisitely delineated. The dangling feet casting their shadow on white marble are an ideal example of Leighton's forte, modeling, and the rhythmic folds of the maroon silk robe in which the boy is wrapped are captivating. As with many Pre-Raphaelite paintings, there is a calculated drama involved in the lighting. It rises from richly tinted shadows to evenly bring out the colors and finer points of the setting up to the boy's shoulder, neck, and face, at which point it is turned up a notch to accentuate the perfect English complexion of the child. It casts an angelic nimbus around his head and long, curled hair upon the gold silk damask panel behind him. By an arch that begins with the boy's right hand and wrist and proceeds along the arm and over the head descending again to the upturned nose of the kitten, Leighton ties together the two figures.

This is by no means the only great painting in which Leighton depicts a child. An early work presents a young girl listening to the sound of a blackbird singing behind her and the trickling water beside her. It is entitled *Songs without Words*, after the popular piano pieces of Mendelssohn. An early work, it was completed shortly after one of his first tours of the Continent. Leighton wrote, "I have endeavored, both by color and by flowing delicate forms, to translate to the eye of the spectator something of the pleasure which the child receives through her ears." That blending of the visual and aural offers one technical tie with the work of Swinburne, who was famed among the French Symbolists, for whom synesthesia was a particularly important effect, for his skill in this area.

This is but one similarity between Leighton and Swinburne. Classicist and ardent student of Renaissance painting, the poet was actually a cut above the painter socially. Raised by a doting mother and indifferent father, Swinburne was given the finest possible education at both Eton and Oxford, as well as at the family's vast country house at Ashburnham and various other residences, notably a mansion in Cornwall called Capheaton, where Swinburne could be by his beloved sea. A linguistic prodigy, there are many accounts of him as a small boy reading for hours, sitting cross-legged with huge and rare folio volumes in his lap from the family's wonderful collection as well as the school libraries. He was a legend at Oxford, where he corrected the professors. When he headed to London as a young poet, it was, again as in Lautrec's path to Paris, to make something of himself as an artist rather than simply to inherit the family's holdings and carry on the tradition. His father was appalled not only by his son's artistic bent but his homosexuality and was later concerned about his alcoholism. As gruff as his father was, at his death, Swinburne wrote "Inferiae," a memorial that does not bear his father's name (as do others of the period to Gautier, Hugo, and Barry Cornwall) but has a gentle reverence that is surprising given their estrangement:

> Past, all things born with sense and blood and breath;
> The flesh hears nought that now the spirit saith.
> If death be like as birth and birth as death,
> The first was fair—more fair should be the last.[8]

It may be just a snippet of occasional verse, but it has many of the distinctive characteristics that Moderns either love or abhor in Swinburne. Here is the meticulously balanced phrasing within lines that arises from repetitions some found unnecessary and confusing ("If death be like as birth and birth as death"). The master prosodist could launch a stanza with a spondee ("Past, all . . .") and then knock out a gripping series of iambs ("the flesh hears nought that now . . .") with such sure-fire technical skill that it made him, along with Gerard Manley Hopkins, a distinctive voice in late-nineteenth-century poetry. The addition of variation directly upon theme could extend a thought for stanzas at a time ("The first was fair—more fair should be the last"), unleashing long torrents of words that drew the ire of arch-Modernists, notably Ezra Pound, who were fighting for economy of diction. Like Sickert under Leighton's wing, Eliot and Pound were among many whose early careers were profoundly influenced by Swinburne, as we will see toward the end of this chapter.

As fashionable as it has been to knock Swinburne's overblown and long-winded lyricism from the time when he was still alive down to the present, he has also had his champions, among them Yeats, Pound, Crane, Stevens, and in his own day, Mallarmé, Baudelaire, and Henry Adams (a gem of *The Education* is a long account of Swinburne at a country house weekend hosted by Monckton Milnes, which ends in a Scottish guest calling the lord of Ashburnham "a cross between the Devil and the Duke of Argyll"). He was in fact the unlikely scholarly progeny of two hardy English aristocratic families, one an ancient Border clan of Northumberland whose peerage was dormant from the thirteenth century and had controlled vast tracts of land from Swinburne Castle, lost during the reign of Edward II. The baronetcy due to the poet as eldest child was conferred in 1660 upon John Swinburne, the first of three baronets to marry wives of royal descent. The poet's mother, Lady Jane Henrietta, was the daughter of the third earl of Ashburnham, a Sussex family known for its allegiance to Charles I (they helped conduct the king from Oxford to safety during an uprising). The earldom was created in 1730, and Swinburne's mother was but one of several in the family to be connected by marriage to the dukes of Northumberland.

Before going off to Eton, the young poet spent most of his days at one of several vast country houses, including the magnificent seaside mansion of East Dene near Bonchurch on the Isle of Wight and The Orchard, home of his uncle, where he had "the sun to sport in and the cliffs to scale," as he wrote later. Not surprisingly, much of Swinburne's greatest poetry is linked to the beauty and power of the sea. In late summer and early autumn the family decamped to Capheaton in Northumberland, where the rough, cold climate was meant to instill manliness in him, according to his father. While at Eton, where his intellect blossomed through his ravenous consumption of European classics virtually on his own in the library, his parents took him to meet the aged Wordsworth at Rydal Mount in the Lake District, just six months before the great Romantic poet died. Edmund Wilson, who identified the play *Axel* by the aristocratic Philippe Auguste Villiers de L'Isle-Adam as the starting off point for Modernism and Symbolism, dwells on Swinburne's aristocratic parentage in his introduction to a 1962 edition of the novels: "The point is that Swinburne was unique among English writers of the nineteenth century in that he belonged to the top nobility."[9]

Swinburne spent three years, between his graduation from Eton and his matriculation at Balliol College, at the family estates, scaling the massive cliffs to the sea, body surfing, and being tutored in the Classics. At Oxford he was, in 1856, one of the founding members of the Old Mortality Society, along with John Addington Symonds and Walter Pater. As with the Apostles at Cambridge, to which Russell and Wittgenstein belonged, the tastes of the secret society were advanced for the time, including long discussions of Browning, logic, and Italian Republicanism (Swinburne was from the start a great supporter of Giuseppi Mazzini, to whom he addressed an ode, one of the reasons he was bypassed as laureate later). There is something about those last weeks at the end of an academic year that brings unusual energy and unforeseen connections to students' lives, often changing them and offering new directions. Just before the long vacation of 1857 arrived, Swinburne was taken to Pembroke College by Edwin Hatch, an Oxford personality and head of a belletristic society that Swinburne also participated in, to meet William Morris and Edward Burne-Jones, who were just starting their ambitious decorative scheme for the bays of the Debating Room at the Union; and that is how Swinburne arrived at the point where we began this chapter, with those heady days of the Pre-Raphaelite Brotherhood. In 1863, as the publication of his two major books neared, he remained in London and at Holmwood, one of the family's estates, most of the year. Then in 1866, all hell broke loose, much as it had when Byron's *Don Juan* appeared, when *Poems and Ballads* became the anthem of a generation that included Wilde, Lionel Johnson, Ernest Dowson, and the young W. B. Yeats, as well as more conservative poets like John Betjeman, eventually the poet laureate. The poems were chanted by undergraduates who marched to their mesmerizing cadences, arms linked, around the quadrangles of Oxford and Cambridge. The impact of these two slim volumes upon the poetry and criticism of the time was massive. They roused English letters from the torpor of the long echo of Wordsworth and Coleridge.

It was an Oxford man who wrote the article in the *Saturday Review* of August 1866 that sealed Swinburne's reputation as a dangerous rebel, even before the controversial volume of *Poems and Ballads* hit the shelves. "We are in the midst of fire and serpents, wine and ashes, blood and foam and a hundred lurid horrors," wrote the anonymous reviewer.[10] The original publishers withdrew the book in panic, and it was issued by Moxon, which also arranged to publish Swinburne's criticism. Their appetites whetted by the charges of paganism and by the snatches of rhapsody quoted in the review, undergraduates at Cambridge and Oxford, as well as the literary avant-garde, made the slim volume a best-seller.

The shortcut to Modern poetics in a consideration of Swinburne is his unquestionable contribution to Decadence, mainly by reference to what was construed then as his rampant interest in sexuality ("unclean imp" was but one of the insults flung at him by that first anonymous reviewer). Even before Swinburne's passion for the writings of "the divine Marquis" was well known through published letters, in his own time Swinburne was branded with the label of "mystic" and deviant by Max Nordau in a lengthy diatribe in his infamous book, *Degeneration* (1895). Nordau links Swinburne not only with the Pre-Raphaelites but with Baudelaire (for his "diabolism and Sadism" as well as the "ego-mania of decadentism" and, of course, the depravity of his homosexuality and the "megalomaniacal contempt for men and its exaggeration of the importance of art"). In the end what bothered Nordau the most was the impenetrability of the code:

> Language has no word for that which one believes he sees as through a mist, without recognizable form. The mystic, however, is conscious of ghostly presentations of this sort without shape or other qualities, and in order to express them he must either use recognized words, to which he gives a meaning wholly different from that which is generally current, or else, feeling the inadequacy of the fund of language created by those of sound mind, he forges for himself special words which, to a stranger, are generally incomprehensible, and the cloudy sense of which is intelligible only to himself, or finally, he embodies the several which he gives to his shapeless representations in as many words, and then succeeds in achieving those bewildering juxtapositions of what is mutually exclusive, those expressions which can in no way be rationally made to harmonize, but which are so typical of the mystic.[11]

Separating Swinburne from Rossetti and Morris, Nordau ironically calls him a "higher degenerate" as opposed to Rossetti, whom he deems an "imbecile." Nordau was not the first to find the arcanum of Modernism frustrating, and the impenetrability of aristocratic codes, created in the first place to keep prying eyes away, also provoke this kind of anger.

Nordau's vicious book had its echo in one of the most sensational critical studies in our own era of controversial criticism, Camille Paglia's *Sexual Personae*. With individual chapters on Swinburne and the Pre-Raphaelites, Paglia extends the pagan categorization and shows how they can claim their place in our contemporary attitudes toward sexuality in the arts. She is particularly enchanted by Swinburne, who "restored to English literature the sexual frankness it lost after the eighteenth century."[12] Nothing if not quotable, she also hopes to redeem Swinburne from neglect and describes him as an essential bridging figure: "Swinburne demonstrates the great continuity of western culture, that brazen union of pagan antiquity with imperial Hollywood. Swinburne is a Hollywood poet. His pagan sexual personae, Dolores and Faustine, are blazing projections of Decadent cinematics. Through his voice, the sensational female superstar dominates space and time. . . . Swinburne's poetry demolishes Victorian society and plants matriarchy amid patriarchy. Swinburne is a female monarchist."[13] Since sexuality is her agenda, Paglia dwells lovingly on Swinburne's taste for flagellation, the appetites of those female characters ("love machines") of his poetry such as Dolores and Faustine, the androgyny of the male and female characters in verse dramas such as *Atalanta in Calydon*, and the fear, hostility, extreme pain, and isolation associated with sexual pleasure. "Swinburne's poetry is one of the most comprehensive modern attempts to turn sex into epistemology," Paglia ventures.[14]

With sensitive readings of several of the major poems and plays, Paglia probes the linguistic and stylistic basis for her judgments regarding his revolutionary and important role in Modern poetics. One observation that certainly strikes home, not just vis-à-vis Swinburne but with respect to Bacon, Balthus, Wittgenstein, and Lautrec as well (the thread of cruelty pulls them together), invokes an element that is familiar to any aristocrat: a code. As Paglia writes, "Now earth-cult is given a new liturgy and body of prayer. Hence Swinburne's peculiar incantatory style, parodied from the moment it appeared. I would defend that style, admired by so many young Englishmen, by arguing that in Swinburne the ritual origins of art are recovered and restored. Swinburne's poetry shows paganism as it really was, not idleness and frolic but a severe code of ritual limitation, curbing the dangerous daemonism of sex and nature."[15] The studio practice of painting, the writing of poetry, the practice of professional philosophy all exert their strictures, through which meaning is both found and expressed. However odd it seems, try Paglia's sentence with "Formalism" substituted for "paganism," and the rigorous art of many of the figures under consideration here, including Bacchantes like Bacon and Swinburne, will fit the definition like a glove.

Paglia is not the only recent critic to revisit Swinburne in a Modernist light. One of Swinburne's most adroit explicators, the French critic George Lafourcade, wrote seventy years ago that Swinburne "is far more akin to Proust and Gide, Lawrence, Huxley, or Joyce than either Tennyson, Browning, Leconte de Lisle, Zola, Meredith or Hardy. . . . And by the way in which he embodied this sensibility in perfect works of art he is the superior of most moderns."[16] Later critics, including Victorian specialist William Buckler, Romantic expert Jerome McGann, and Modernist John Rosenberg, as well as experts in the problematic border between Victorian and Modern, such as Carol Christ and Linda Dowling, concur in the opinion that Swinburne takes his place as an early if eccentric Modern who kept alive the Romantic vine stock of Byron and Shelley that produced such heady vintages.[17] Taking this thought one step further, Leslie Brisman and Nicholas Tredell confer on Swinburne a Postmodern consciousness in its privileging of sound over conventional sense.[18] In a critical environment that is still reeling from the narcotic effect of Derridean prose and still making its way through *Finnegans Wake*, Swinburne's white-water cascades of puns, oxymorons, alliteration, assonance, and abstractions seem far closer to the lingua franca of today. In this passage that opens "The Sailing of the Swan," a section of the long poem, *Tristram of Lyonesse*, the powerful effect of "eros and high rhetoric" pushes the limits of language:

> Fate, that was born ere spirit and flesh were made
> The fire that fills man's life with light and shade;
> The poser beyond all godhead which puts on
> All forms of multitudinous unison
> A raiment of eternal change inwrought
> With shapes and hues more subtly spun than thought,
> Where all things old bear fruit of all things new
> And one deep chord throbs all the music through,
> The chord of change unchanging, shadow and light
> Inseparable as reverberate day from night;
> Fate, that of all things save the soul of man . . .[19]

It is almost impossible to move in to cut off the flow of poetry as momentum-charged as this. Circling upon itself, swooping into multisyllabic phrases of indeterminable meaning ("multitudinous unison"?) and shifting the terms of its analogies so quickly as to make tracking the subject all but impossible, it becomes a private language. Like the roman-fleuve of Proust, its priority is to keep moving. The echo effect, not just of the repeated monosyllable "Fate" but within lines such as "Where all things old bear fruit of all things new," is a signature Swinburnean device that reminds many critics of Poe, although the English poet takes it further. There are two ways to look at Swinburne's language in light of the aesthetics of our own era: it is abstract, and it is private. In terms of current theory, he is "post-philological" in the graphic opacity of his language and artificiality of his diction, although the subtle etymological puns and metrical allusions have to be admired for their deep acquaintance with the roots of English. The brilliant critic George Steiner, writing about Modern poetry, particularly that of Mallarmé, observes that it is syntactically and semantically difficult to track: "There is also a strain of autism in such poetry. Language is focused as language, as in a circular room of mirrors, and by modulation the principal subject or agonizing myth of the poetic enterprise is poetry itself."[20] This self-reflective, inward-turning quality is matched in Swinburne's poetry by a syndrome, diagnosed as part of his narcissism by his severest critics, called echolalia—the repetition of sound, the interior rhymes and refrains that make Swinburne's longer poems in particular into vast echo chambers that often seem to present more sound than sense. Another quality that endears him to the devotees of Postmodernism is his natural gravitation to images of destruction, emptiness, and most importantly, silence. He and Mallarmé are the two greatest poets of silence in the Modern canon.

Swinburne's "season in silence" (to borrow a phrase from his poem "The Triumph of Time") is that epoch of denigration that his reputation entered even before his death in 1909; the last years of his life were spent in deafness. Silence is a recurring theme, a link to the poetics of Mallarmé as well as of Crane and even to later writers such as James Merrill and John Ashbery. From the orchestral pedal point of "deep silence answers" in "The Lake of Gaube" to the final words of "Epicene," "silence takes the psalm," it is an ultimate condition, a higher tone that his character Althea maintains in her stoicism. Swinburne's flaunting of mimetic rules with melic and rhythmic patterns struck Ruskin, to name one admirer (who famously detested Whistler), as "consummately pure." Swinburne submitted his rhythmic, rhetorical, and musical talents to silence in the public admonitions of the chorus in Swinburne's reworking of Euripedes' *Meleager*: "For words divide and rend; / but silence is most noble in the end." In Swinburne's work, silence is also associated with the ascetic retreat, sterility, the impairment of the senses, destruction, and peace at the limits of pain and pleasure (the two were closely linked in his eyes).

While silence has a long and distinguished provenance (Classical tragedy, ancient Chinese philosophy, Shakespeare, Marvell, Pascal, Hegel, Novalis, and to choose a figure much closer to Swinburne, Carlyle), it plays into the context of the modern "aesthetic of purity" and perfection—John Cage's "thirteenth tone," Mallarmé's "musicienne du silence," the embodiment of the blank page so dear to Derrida. In "L'Azur," Mallarmé reaches for the hypostasis of "un grand plafond silencieux," which anticipates Susan Sontag's brilliant essay "The Aesthetics of Silence" and the "mood of ultimacy and the furthest extension of that reluctance to communicate, that ambivalence about making contact with the audience which is a leading motif of modern art."[21] Swinburne's own strategy of silence was a prophecy and an attempt to achieve transcendence. Modernism problematizes (and thematizes) the limits of language, the border zone of silence, like Swinburne's dramatic cliffs at which land plunges into sea (his passion was battling the waves off Cornwall as a swimmer, skinny and short and seemingly powerless as he was in the surf, and deriving a wild ecstasy from being rolled by the waves). The Modernist topos of the central silence, the "clearing" of Heidegger or Flaubert's desire to write a book "about nothing" are all engaged in this aesthetic of blankness that Swinburne and Mallarmé conceived long before the whispering white brushstrokes of Robert Ryman's monochrome paintings or Cage's notorious four minutes and thirty-three seconds of nothing became the scandal of the music world.

Swinburne's articulation of the ascetic ideal may be found in both the prose and the poetry. In the apologetic "Notes on Poems and Reviews," published in 1866 in response to the zealous attacks of John Morley, Robert Buchanan, and others upon his *Poems and Ballads*, he describes the "total pause of passion" that his "Hesperia" and "The Garden of Proserpine" are intended to capture. The language is reminiscent of Schopenhauer's definition of "nobility of character" in denial:

> The worship of desire has ceased; the mad commotion of sense has stormed itself out; the spirit, clear of the old regret that drove it upon such violent ways for a respite, healed of the fever that wasted it in the search for relief among fierce fancies and tempestuous pleasures, dreams now of truth discovered and repose attained. Not the martyr's ardour of selfless love, an unprofitable flame that burnt out and did not service—not the rapid rage of pleasure that seemed for a little to make the flesh diving, to clothe the naked sense with the fiery raiment of faith; but a stingless love, an innocuous desire . . . it is not without design that I have slipped in, between the first and second part, the verses called "The Garden of Proserpine," expressive, as I meant they should be, of that brief total pause of passion and of thought, when the spirit, without fear or hope of good things or evil, hungers and thirsts only after the perfect sleep.[22]

As early as the poem "The Triumph of Time," the conflation of the sea, silence, and asceticism may be found in Swinburne's poetry of renunciation, a lyric of thanatos in response to a loss of eros. The sadique pleasure of being battered by waves and chill spray is one form it takes, and in "The Triumph of Time," Swinburne invokes the sea, "Cold and clean as her faint salt flowers." The foam-flowers at the wave's edge are images of impotence and "unmaking" or "dis-formation," which can be associated with a Modern notion of the world dismantled. This idea of renunciation is strongest in a pair of consecutive stanzas that deal with a farewell to music:

> I shall never be friends again with roses;
> I shall loathe sweet tunes, where a note grown strong
> Relents and recoils, and climbs and closes,
> As a wave of the sea turned back by song.
> There are sounds where the soul's delight takes fire,
> Face to face with its own desire;
> A delight that rebels, a desire that reposes;
> I shall hate sweet music my whole life long.
>
> The pulse of war and passion of wonder,
> The heavens that murmur, the sounds that shine,
> The stars that sing and the loves that thunder,
> The music burning at heart like wine,
> An armed archangel whose hands raise up
> All senses mixed in the spirit's cup,
> Till flesh and spirit are molten in sunder—
> These things are over, and no more mine.

In "Laus Veneris" a similar gesture of renunciation leads to a closely related stanza that invokes silence. The pilgrim's invocation of silence is not made without pain, and the unmistakable element of sadism can be related to the loss of the senses, the anesthesia that is the negation of Swinburne's renowned synesthesia. It was written long before he became deaf.

> Would God my blood were dew to feed the grass
> Mine ears made deaf and mine eyes blind as glass,
> My body broken as a turning wheel,
> And my mouth stricken ere it saith Alas!

Through the early lyrics, most often discussed in terms of sadism (including "Anactoria," "Felise," "Faustine," and "Dolores"), the same pattern of renunciation can be observed. These songs about "the mystery of the cruelty of things" typically end, after the obliteration of the sense, in the "season in silence" that follows "the whitening wind of the future, the wave of the world" as he wrote in the "Hymn to Proserpine." The emptying out of "Sapphics" is evident from the beginning. It opens with a silent vigil that the poet endures through the course of the night until the advent of a vision:

> All the night sleep came not upon my eyelids
> Shed not dew, not shook nor unclosed a feather,
> Yet with lips shut close and with eyes of iron
> Stood and beheld me . . .

The visit of Aphrodite and Sappho is the reward, and the song the sensual compensation for a night of deprivation. In the last stanzas, as the song of Sappho fades, asceticism takes the place of luxury:

> Then the Muses, stricken at heart, were silent;
> Yea, the gods waxed pale: such a song was that song,
> All reluctant, all with a fresh repulsion,
> Fled from before her.
>
> All withdrew long since, and the land was barren,
> Full of fruitless women and music only.
> Now perchance, when winds are assuaged at sunset,
> Lulled at the dewfall,
>
> By the grey sea-side, unassuaged, unheard of,
> Unbeloved, unseen in the ebb of twilight,
> Ghosts of outcast women return lamenting,
> Purged not in Lethe,
> Clothed about with flame and with tears, and singing
> Songs that move the heart of the shaken heaven,
> Songs that break the heart of the earth with pity,
> Hearing, to hear them.

The persona of the solitary poet wandering by the sea, as in "The Last Oracle," "Neap-Tide," "In the Bay," and "By the North Sea," is one of the most readily identifiable ascetics in Swinburne. In "The Lake of Gaube" the autobiographical element is strongly evident as it describes a plunge into the deep cold water identical with the swimming Swinburne loved. The wanderer is often described as "the last, least voice" of a departed chorus, as in "By the North Sea," in which he seeks serenity beyond the "veil of Maya" and the turmoil of "Earth and all its thoughts." The tone is particularly reminiscent of Keats's "When I have fears" sonnet:

> Slowly, gladly, full of peace and wonder
> Grows his heart who journeys here alone.
> Earth and all its thoughts of earth sink under

Deep as deep in water sinks a stone.
Hardly knows it if the rollers thunder,
Hardly whence the lonely wind is blown.

Another Modern topos in Swinburne is the forsaken garden, which prefigures Yeats's "ancestral houses" by decades. Emblems of aristocracy, silent stages where the decayed images of the gods are reflected in neglected pools, they are the ideal background to a Modern drama of mortals mocked by the gods. Their most fitting counterparts in the visual arts would be Eugène Atget's images of the Parc de Sceaux, the Parc Delessert, or St. Cloud, desolate landscapes of what Hugo called the aristocratic *bainlieu*, the emptiness and very monochromaticism of which capture the spirit of decay. In Atget's views of the park surrounding Colbert's seventeenth-century Chateau de Sceaux, at the nadir of its decay when Atget visited in March 1925 (it has since been restored), its crumbling masonry and overgrown walks are as allegorical as they are documentary. In the early series of poems on this theme in *Poems and Ballads*, "A Forsaken Garden" stands out for its drama. It opens in a familiar Swinburnean setting, the *hortus closus* of Renaissance pastoral. The poet ironically evokes a sense of domestic safety in which the hazards are hidden. The perils of the desert are conveyed in a chain of modifiers, however: steep, abrupt and broken, dense, hard, strait, waste, sheer, and wild. Colors fade, and the "ghost of a garden" loses its form as it is overgrown, with "the rose-red seaweed that mocks the rose." It is not just chromaticism that gradually disappears, but sound, smell, and touch as well, as the garden more closely approaches the grave. The "blossomless bed" is a sign of sterility, and the "edge" between land and sea is an eschatological image of the verge of oblivion:

In a coign of the cliff between lowland and highland,
At the sea-down's edge between windward and lee,
Walled round with rocks as an inland island,
The ghost of a garden fronts the sea.

A girdle of brushwood and thorn encloses
The steep square slope of the blossomless bed
Where the weeds that grew green from the graves of its roses
Now lie dead.

The fields fall southward, abrupt and broken,
To the low last edge of the long lone land.
If a step should sound or a word be spoken,
Would a ghost not rise at the strange guest's hand?

> So long have the grey bare walks lain guestless,
> Through the branches and briars if a man make way,
> He shall find no life but the sea-wind's restless
> Night and day.[23]

The sleepless wind is one of the agents of annihilation, along with the sea. Images of time and the wind come straight from Shelley's "Sensitive Plant" and move directly on from Swinburne to become the "levelling wind" in Yeats's volume *The Tower*, as well as Paul Valéry's neglected masterpiece "La Cimetière Marin," which may have been a response to Swinburne. Certainly, its "masse de calme" and palatial edifice of silence that succumbs to the waves is similar, as is Eliot's *Four Quartets*, particularly "Burnt Norton," set in a country house destroyed by arson in the eighteenth century and situated near other ruined manor houses, at Chipping Campden, and Lord Falkland's Great Tew, as well as Hidcote Manor, all of which Eliot knew well:

> So we moved, and they, in a formal pattern,
> Along the empty alley, into the box circle,
> To look down into the drained pool.
> Dry the pool, dry concrete, brown edged,
> And the pool was filled with water out of sunlight
> And the lotos rose, quietly, quietly,
> The surface glittered out of heart of light
> And they were behind us, reflected in the pool.
> Then a cloud passed, and the pool was empty.[24]

As stage settings, these gardens of Swinburne, Yeats, and Eliot induce more thoughts of the past than of the present or future, and "the waste of time" is succeeded only by emptiness. Another Shelleyan element is the "dreams of its wintry rest." George Meredith called Swinburne the "greatest lyrical poet of the world" but complained that his work lacked "an internal center," a comment sure to endear Swinburne to adherents of Deconstruction and Modernism.[25] Abstraction, which is all too often mistaken for obscurity, plays a major role in a consideration of Swinburne as Modern. One of the leading, most advanced art critics of the day, he preferred Whistler's "rapid rendering of a rough interior" to the finished English watercolors popular in his day, an apt introduction to his own talents to rapidly launch into passages of such facility, recalling the rhapsodies of Chopin and Liszt, and accelerate the momentous progress toward nihilism in language as well as belief. As a literary critic, he was an advocate of masters of movement and rhythm (Whitman, Blake, and

Hugo). Working in an era when the boundary between poetry and prose was shifting (an important condition of Modernism in its early stage), Swinburne perpetuated the poetic tradition.

Swinburne may be regarded as a Modern not just for his poetry but for his criticism, which has quietly proved, through its advocacy of Whitman and Blake among others, to have been admirably ahead of its time. For this reason, Swinburne's high reputation in France among Mallarmé and his followers is more significant than his place as the odd man out in English letters (although he was regarded by many, as late as the turn of the century, as having the inside track on the laureateship). Along with poets in English who acknowledged his powerful influence (Gerard Manley Hopkins, Yeats, Eliot, Pound, Joyce, Wallace Stevens, and Hart Crane), the French avant-gardists, from Baudelaire and Mallarmé to Verlaine and Rimbaud, made him a pivotal link between Romanticism and their lyrical Modernism. There are literary historians who find this branch of the genealogy of Modernism empty or eccentric, too polished and "pretty" to be strong poetry, just as many adherents of abstract painting and sculpture eschew the figure. But Bacon and Lautrec, among others, were the poets of the body in art, whereas Swinburne was a master of the song and narrative in poetry.

Swinburne excited a tremendous response in France and became a contributor and frequent topic of critical debate in a short-lived but highly charged and powerfully written avant-garde journal called *La République des lettres*. What Poe was to Baudelaire and his generation, Swinburne was to Mallarmé and his tight circle of poets and critics. In his day, Swinburne was often linked with Poe, and it is easy to see why the two hard-drinking, echo-happy poets might go together, although Swinburne was given to point out to one of Poe's editors, J. H. Ingram, as well as to his translators (including Mallarmé) that Poe was of an earlier generation, "the old set," including Gautier and Baudelaire. Swinburne was a devoted reader of Baudelaire (the first record of his reading *Les Fleurs du mal* is in 1862, five years after it first appeared), and Swinburne's poem "Laus Veneris," begun that year, reflects his reading of Baudelaire's essay, published in 1863, on Wagner's *Tannhauser*. In March 1863, he visited Manet's Paris studio in the company of Whistler and Fantin-Latour, and from that moment his friendship with critic Alphonse Legros dated. Swinburne was a frequent visitor to the Symbolist hotbed of the Paris salons during the time when his revolutionary volumes *Poems and Ballads* and *Atalanta in Calydon* were in preparation. He was in Paris with Lord Houghton (Monckton Milnes) in 1869, before visiting Walter Savage Landor in Florence (bridging two eras in one European swing, from the survivor of the high Romantic era to the harbingers of Modernism). He makes cameo appearances in the journals of the Goncourt brothers as well as the memoirs of Hugo and Guy de Maupassant. In 1869 he met Gautier and Flaubert, just a few months before *L'Education sentimental* was published.

As a measure of Swinburne's popularity among the avant-garde, when Gautier died on 23 October 1872, Swinburne was invited by the committee that organized a memorial volume to write two sonnets, an ode and elegies in both Latin and Greek. Of the 172 pages of the Festschrift, 155 were occupied by Swinburne's prodigious contribution, and no other poet had more than two pieces in the collection, published as a supplementary edition of the influential journal *Le Parnasse contemporain*. Others involved in the *Tombeau de Gautier* included Hugo, Leconte de Lisle, Banville, Anatole France, and Mallarmé. The volume was significant not merely as an occasion for the collaboration of so many rising stars of the avant-garde but as a mark of closure to the era of the Parnassians.

As Mallarmé's reputation grew, Swinburne joined the campaign to bring more recognition, particularly on behalf of the long meditative poem *L'Après-midi d'un faun*, which Mallarmé "traded" with Swinburne's elegiac "The Last Oracle," another long lyric on a Classical theme. Both poems offer sustained lyricism and the tension between a distant, absent stimulus and the responding subject. Swinburne's deep regard for *L'Après-midi* should be viewed as a convincing sign of the modernity of his tastes. A litmus test of avant-garde sensitivity, it has appealed to interpreters (Manet, Debussy, Nijinksy, and more recently, Jerome Robbins) whose command of the Modernist principles of their media has enabled them to adapt it successfully. It was in its time a poem ahead of the critical vocabulary by which it could be widely understood, for another generation at least, in the words of an admirer, Albert Thibaudet, "Le morcea des connaisseurs et le point central, parfait à la fois simple et raffiné, ou viennent converger toutes les directions inflexibles, toutes les époques deson talent."[26]

Swinburne at this time became an important player in the founding of *La République des lettres*, an avant-garde journal that Mallarmé, Flaubert, Catulle Mendes, and others were organizing. The early numbers demonstrated its international outlook, with pieces by and about Wagner, Poe, Pushkin, and Turgenev; articles about Italian Renaissance painting; and book advertisements that indicated where titles were available not only in Paris but in London (at Baillier, Madall and Cox, Williams and Norgate, and Trullmer & Co.). Printed in an elegant font on heavy stock, the thirty-two-page first issue included new writing by Flaubert, Mallarmé, and Leconte de Lisle, as well as a prose translation of Swinburne's "Pilgrims" made by Augusta Holmes, admirably preserving the echo effect of the original through liberal use of repetition and refrains. The editors' preview of coming attractions refers to more contributions by Swinburne, and the little gossip items also mention him. In short, no other writer, French or English, played so prominent a role in the debut of this exciting new publication. Back home in England, Swinburne was ecstatic. In a long letter of 1 February 1876 to John Morley, editor of *The Fortnightly*, he mixed gossip about George Moore, Trollope, and Browning and an amusing account of a recent Parisian enterprise in which he had become involved: "I, as a French poet of the day, have been solicited to help in setting it on foot, together with Leconte de Lisle & Flaubert, and younger men of note."[27] In the years that followed, Swinburne and Mallarmé diplomatically edited one another's work, and the English poet was one of the first to see a manuscript of the revolutionary *L'Après-midi d'un faun*. With Mallarmé's fine touches, Swinburne's "Nocturne" appeared in the second issue, followed by an essay on Blake. Certainly, the interplay of allusions to both Chopin and Whistler adds an interdisciplinary depth to "Nocturne," and in its opening lines one has a glimpse of the mastery of French prosody that inspired Mallarmé's (and Hugo's) admiration:

> La nuit écoute et se penche sur l'onde
> Pour y cuillir rien qu'un souffle d'amour;
> Pas de lueur, pas de musique au monde,
> Pas de sommeil pour moi ni de séjour.
> O mère, o Nuit, de ta source profonde
> Verse-nous, verse enfin l'oubli du jour.[28]

It all fell apart when the journal began to serialize Zola's *L'Assomoir* in July 1876, running for six issues until the following January. Swinburne was joined in the boycott by an equally indignant Victor Hugo. Swinburne called the novel "loathsome," and the fallout caused an unfortunate break with Mallarmé, whose British friends became Wilde and Whistler. However, as late as 1893, Mallarmé wrote to Eugene de Castro, a Portuguese poet, that he kept a photograph of Swinburne along with ones of Baudelaire, Maeterlinck, and the Portuguese poet Joao de Vens over his desk.[29] When Mallarmé visited Oxford and Cambridge in 1893 to offer a lecture on poetry that was a tour de force, he made no effort to reach Swinburne, nor did Swinburne attend, although Swinburne was mentioned by Mallarmé in a conversation with G. E. Moore at Pembroke College, in the same breath as Verlaine, Huysmans, and Maupassant.

Swinburne's deafness in part forced him to isolate himself in the London suburb of Putney. His admirers included all the major figures we now consider the pillars of Modern literature. As biographer Richard Ellmann relates it, when Yeats and Joyce first met, they discussed Oscar Wilde, Homer, Shakespeare, Balzac, and Swinburne, at whose name Joyce supposedly burst out laughing and made the others in the café turn around to look at them.[30] Joyce was fascinated with Swinburne's homosexuality. He is in a sense the poet laureate of *Ulysses*, a literary figure as the leading lyric voice of his generation and a prominent Shakespearean and as a type of the hermaphrodite (particularly in the "nighttown" episode). In the opening scene, set in the Martello tower, only Yeats and Swinburne are cited, and Swinburne is first with a phrase from "The Triumph of Time" that becomes a leitmotif in the novel, associated with Stephen's guilt over defying his mother's dying wish the he pray for her: "I will go back to the great sweet mother, / Mother and lover of men, the sea."

Both Eliot and Pound were fervent admirers, devoting essays to Swinburne's poetry and echoing him in their own. "Only a man of genius could dwell so exclusively and consistently among words as Swinburne. His language is not like the language of bad poetry, dead. It is very much alive, with this singular life of its own. But the language which is more important to us is that which is struggling to digest and express new objects, new feelings, new aspects, as for instance, the prose of Mr. James Joyce or the earlier Conrad," wrote Eliot.[31] His later works (particularly *The Four Quartets*) possess a Swinburnean aural richness, suggesting that the path of the new veers from the lyric effusions of Swinburne into the prose of Conrad and Joyce, where Swinburne's influence is also felt.

No poet is more readily identified with Modernism than Pound, and his ambivalent fascination with Swinburne is felt in both essays and in some of his greatest poetry. During his early years in London, like Picasso in Paris searching for Lautrec, he longed to meet Swinburne but never did. Swinburne was being kept under virtual house arrest by his friend and a family conspirator, Theodore Watts-Dunton, in Putney. Pound's assessment of Swinburne's poetry is very like Eliot's, focusing on diction:

> He neglected the value of words as words, and was intent on their value as sound. His habit of choice grew mechanical, and he himself perceived it and parodied his own systemization. He habitually makes a fine stanzaic form, writes one or two fine strophes in it, and then continues to pour into the mould strophes of diminishing quality. . . . There is, underneath all the writing, a magnificent passion for liberty—a passion, dead as mutton in most of his contemporaries, and immeasurably deader than mutton in a people who allow their literature to be blanketed by a Comstock and his successors; for liberty is not merely a catchword of politics, nor a right to shove little slips of paper through a hole. The passion not merely for political, but also for personal, liberty is the bedrock of Swinburne's writing. The sense of

tragedy, and of the unreasoning cruelty of the gods, hangs over it. He fell into facile writing, and he accepted a facile compromise for life; but no facile solution for his universe. His belief did not desert him; no, not even in Putney.[32]

Swinburne is in Pound's poetry and in his letters. The early volume, *Ripostes* (1912), includes "Salve O Pontifex," a tribute to Swinburne as "lifter of the heads of men." Pound uses Swinburnean flourishes and the persona of Swinburne in the early lyrics to enliven them as criticism, much as Dante's meetings with other poets in the *Commedia* add a dramatic dimension to literary criticism. Swinburne plays a heroic role, not only in "Salve O Pontifex," written three years before his death, but in "Swinburne: A Critique," another early lyric on that utterly Swinburnean theme, the crossing between the Classical to the Christian era, when the term *modernus* was coined. Pound's poem is even set on the border between land and sea, Swinburne's favorite territory, on the margin. The silence in which the high priest of Iacchus departs might refer to Swinburne's recessed reputation, rapidly headed to oblivion in the eyes of Pound's generation:

One after one do they leave thee,
High priest of Iacchus,
Toning thy melodies even as winds tone
The whisper of tree-leaves, on sun-lit days.
Even as the sands are many
And the sea beyond the sands are one
In ultimate; So we here being many
Are unity. Nathless thy compeers
Knowing thy melody,
Lulled with the wine of thy music
Go seaward silently, leaving thee sentinel
O'er all the mysteries,
High priest of Iacchus.[33]

Pound's "Swinburne: A Critique" misspelled Swinburne as "Swinbourne" in typescript, as though he were an exotic place removed in time. The poem's opening is similar to that of "Salve O Pontifex," and the phrase "ruler in mystery" echoes the "manifold mystery" of the cult of Iacchus:

Blazes of color intermingled,
Wondrous pattern leading nowhere
Music without a name,

Knights that ride in a dream,
Blind as all men are blind,
Why should the music show
Whither they go?
I am Swinburne, ruler in mystery.[34]

As in the earlier poem, the critical issue is Swinburne's obscurity, and Pound selects suitably Daedalian imagery to represent the problem. The errant paths of "knights that ride in a dream," suggesting as well the early Kandinsky with his cossacks, illustrate the ambiguity of "wondrous pattern leading nowhere." The insistence on Swinburne's mastery of craft is apparent ("pattern" and "paint"), and, like the master, Pound uses the oneiric mode, shared by Swinburne's "Laus Veneris" and the dream sequences of *Tristram of Lyonesse*, both derived from romance sources.

Pound invokes Swinburne in the *Cantos* more than once. He takes a swipe at the Pre-Raphaelites and Tennyson, including Swinburne, but is kinder at the end of Canto LXXXI, when he switches to a tone of lament. It is by far the most touching in the many instances of Swinburne's appearance in Pound's poetry:

To have gathered from the air a live tradition
Or from a fine old eye the unconquered flame
This is not vanity.
Here error is all in the not done,
All in the diffidence that faltered.[35]

There is a biographical anecdote behind this passage. It reveals itself in the next canto. The "fine old eye" is Swinburne's, and like Yeats, Ford Madox Ford, and others who recur in this section of the *Cantos*, the heroic figures of the artists are historical. Pound reveals that, as a young American in London trying to gather all he can from those who were there, he failed to meet Swinburne, who died in April 1909:

Swinburne my only miss
And I didn't know he'd been to see Landor
And they told me this that an' tother
And when old Matthews went he saw
The three teacups
Two for Watts Dunton who liked to let
His tea cool,
So old Elkin had only one glory
He did carry Algernon's suit case once
When he, Elkin, first came to London.[36]

The satirical tone in which Pound depicts the fawning idolatry of Elkin Matthews, the renowned London bookseller, does not completely dispel the envy of Pound at knowing that he had not met Swinburne. Was the third teacup for Pound? The suitcase is a wonderful image for the burden of the past. Pound admits his regret for not having paid his respects in person. The arch-Modernist was in need of that contact that would ensure continuity. Nobody reads Swinburne any more. It would be rare even to find graduate students reading Browning. If he were in the anthologies, however, he'd most likely be represented by one of those great gusts of language that took Oxford by storm in his day and that rattled around persistently, however transformed, in the more lyrical Eliot and Pound, as well as in later "silver age" poets such as John Ashbery, James Merrill, and William Matthews. They would immediately feel the force of the first chorus from *Atalanta in Calydon*, once gently mocked in the gag line of a James Thurber cartoon, with its irresistible, completely correct Anglicization of Greek rhythms:

> When the hounds of spring are on winter's traces,
> The mother of months in meadow or plain
> Fills the shadows and windy places
> With lisp of leaves and ripple of rain;
> And the brown bright nightingale amorous
> Is half assuaged for Itylus,
> For the thracian ships and the foreign faces,
> The tongueless vigil, and all the pain.[37]

5

Peer Review

BERTRAND RUSSELL AND LUDWIG WITTGENSTEIN

Their childhood spent basking in the last rays of Europe's final great empires, Bertrand Russell (1872–1970) and Ludwig Wittgenstein (1889–1951) began life as two little princes destined to be Apostles at Cambridge University. Eventually, with each other's help, they became philosopher kings. Because Russell wore his heart on his sleeve, the direct link between his work and his aristocratic sense of identity is often a matter of record. Although he was the second son, his brother renounced the earldom, and Russell ascended to the title. With Wittgenstein, the more Modern, less noble of the two, the will to distance himself from his privileged past—manifest in his relinquishing of considerable wealth and refusal of family string-pulling while he was interned as a prisoner of war—was strong enough to keep Russell and others from initially guessing his background. The role of his upbringing in his philosophy is more subtle because the autobiographical element of his writings is often disguised. Inevitably, for both, who they were determined what they thought. The fact that these mirroring figures became intimately connected and consciously, together, set the course of what they knew to be Modern philosophy suggests that their compatibility in rank and intellect counted for more, perhaps, than biographers, historians, and many commentators have allowed.

Rather than begin in the conventional way with parallel images of the two boys in sailor suits cavorting in the elegant gardens of their family mansions, let's start with a delicate episode, more exciting and intimate, from Russell's life. The analytic powers for which he was famed were also trained upon moments of particular vulnerability, even culpability. This scene takes us to the core of Russell's feelings about being the scion of one of England's great families. Suitably enough, it is set in the drawing room and probably the bedroom of a lavish townhouse in London's fashionable Bedford Square. Although Russell was to succeed to the title of earl of Bedford, the mansion actually belonged to Lady Ottoline Morrell and her husband, Phillip, a member of Parliament and close friend of Russell, who was conveniently visiting his constituency in Burnley that night, 19 March 1911, when Russell and Lady Ottoline bade adieu to her two other dinner guests and allowed their months-long flirtation to advance to its next stage. It was the first time Russell cheated on his first wife, Alys. He was also betraying his friend Phillip, who had enlisted Russell's help on his Parliamentary campaign during the past year. Russell slipped out of Lady Ottoline's door around four the next morning. Biographers smugly assure us they did not have intercourse until a later encounter—their affair lasted eleven glorious years, his best as a thinker, during which she was his muse and confidante.

That night coincided with a liminal moment in Russell's career. He was on the verge of sailing for France to deliver three of his most important early lectures on the relationship between philosophy and mathematics. Thanks to Russell, the line of demarcation between the two disciplines swiftly blurred. The past nine years of his marriage to his American wife had been insipid, and Russell's descent into illicit love was precipitous. It is fascinating to note, in this passage from his autobiography, how importantly Ottoline's background figured in the formation of their attachment: "We were both earnest and unconventional, both aristocratic by tradition but deliberately not so in our present environment, both hating the cruelty, the caste insolence, and the narrow-mindedness of aristocrats, and yet both a little alien in the world in which we chose to live, which regarded us with suspicion and lack of understanding because we were alien. All the complicated feelings resulting from the situation we shared."[1] This note of alienation is not insignificant in the story of Russell and Wittgenstein. It offers the first deviation from the plumb line of genealogy and English traditions to the international, intellectual, and Modern path Russell would follow.

As fascinating and seductive as Lady Ottoline was (enough to have similar affairs with the painters Augustus John and Henry Lamb, as well as with the critic Roger Fry and William Butler Yeats, earning her satirical immortality as the basis for Hermione in D. H. Lawrence's *Women in Love*, written in 1916), Russell had a strikingly eagle-eyed view of her charms. The liaison also reveals much about Russell's picture of his own situation. As with many artists, the oddity of his position, not only as an anachronism but as a reluctant representative of his class and as a twentieth-century liberal, conferred self-conscious alienation. On the opposite side, we have Ottoline's nobility—she was the half sister of the duke of Portland and lived in Welbeck Abbey in Nottinghamshire, where she played hostess for her MP's political cronies as well as artists and intellectuals—and her ambivalence regarding the behavior of her class, offering grounds for sympathy. One could almost say she was uniquely qualified to be his mistress.

The panache of the aristocratic artist was one of Russell's weapons from the start. His confessions are beset by minimal internal conflict due in part to that self-assuredness of a mighty intellect fed by enormous family resources (and expectations). When the philosopher George Santayana met Russell at Cambridge in 1891, he observed that the Englishman had been given a "perfect princely education" and had clearly been raised to be prime minister, as his grandfather, Lord John Russell, twice had been.[2] All this meant that Russell knew that a career in academe would be considered a grave disappointment to his family. "When I finished my student years at Cambridge, I had to decide whether to devote my life to philosophy or to politics. Politics had been the habitual pursuit of my family since the sixteenth century, and to think of anything else was viewed as a kind of treachery to my ancestors."[3]

Fortunately for Russell, there was a pronounced strain of rebelliousness amid the family baggage, along with an immense amount of self-possession. For all his stylish assertions and occasional snobbishness, his memoirs and letters are also filled with sniping remarks about his own class. In Rome in 1894 in the company of formal English aristocrats, he observed in a letter to his young American sweetheart, Alys, "I do wish I could go about with her all day long instead of with these stiff, inartistic aristocrats. Whatever else might have been to be hoped from my never having met thee, my grandmother might always have despaired of my marrying an aristocrat: their icy reserve (though I feebly try to ape it) would kill me to live with. And I do believe the frivolous life of society and idleness kills out every particle of seriousness from all the girls who were at all attractive, it is only the Mary Bensets among aristocrats who read great books and make extracts."[4] This is not to say that, as with all of us, Russell did not have moments of impatience with family matters. In a letter to Lucy Donnelly he wrote, "Yes, one's people are very trying: they are a living caricature of oneself, and have the same humiliating effect that is produced by the monkeys in the Zoo: one feels that here is the unvarnished truth at last."[5] Russell's biographers are certainly right in noting the resentment roused by the way Russell's grandparents and uncles tried to scare him away from what they deemed an unsuitable marriage to Alys, an American, by using the new science of eugenics to prove to him that their children were likely to inherit genes causing madness from both his side of the family and hers. Madly in love with Alys at the time (Ottoline was not yet in the picture) and inflamed by an equally strong inherited tendency toward subversion, Russell defied them. That is why he once wrote, in a mock obituary, that his life "had a certain anachronistic consistency, reminiscent of that of the aristocratic rebels of the early nineteenth century."[6] Sifting through the Russell canon for moments when the polish of his noble upbringing and the grit of his iconoclastic attitude served him in good stead, one arrives at such gems as this passage from the essay "Knowledge Behavioristically Considered":

> An entomologist perceives vastly more beetles in the course of a country walk than other people do. The subtlety with which connoisseurs can distinguish among wines and cigars is the despair of youths who wish to become men of the world. Whether this increase of sensitivity can be accounted for by the law of association, I do not know. In many cases, probably, it can, but I think sensitiveness to form, which is the essential element in the more difficult forms of abstract thought as well as in many other matters, cannot be regarded as derivative from the law of association, but is more analogous to the development of a new sense. I should therefore include improvement on sensitivity as an independent element in the advancement of knowledge. But I do so with some hesitation.[7]

Russell was born with the kind of confidence that perfectly suited the philosophy he would pursue, which strove, almost impossibly, to deliver the final word on the most overarching questions. "I had when I was younger—perhaps I still have—an almost unbelievable optimism as to the finality of my own theories."[8] It is well known what became of the young man who spent an agitated night on Lady Ottoline's couch in 1911. Fifty years later he had grown into the role of elder statesman of an international movement in the analysis of mathematical as well as philosophical thought. Moreover, he emerged as an outspoken human rights advocate and ethicist, what would today be known as a political pundit, weighing in with global impact—frankly, exceeding the reach of his illustrious grandfather—upon a wide range of issues, including woman's suffrage, religion, nuclear proliferation, and the cold war. This ardor for the most public arena in which to test his powers of argument can be viewed as hereditary. He was the descendant of prime ministers and Parliamentarians back to the rebellious Lord William Russell, executed in 1683 for plotting to assassinate Charles II and his brother James II in the so-called Rye House Plot. Of more immediate impact was the example of his grandfather, Lord John Russell (1792–1878), third son of the sixth duke of

Bedford, who twice served as prime minister and had also, it should be noted, studied philosophy at Edinburgh. Along with many other aristocrats of his rank, he was a radical Whig, who served in Lord Grey's cabinet and advocated religious freedom, public education, and the elimination of the death penalty. His greatest achievement was the passage of the Parliamentary Reform Act of 1832, which extended the franchise to men of the middle ranks. From him, Bertrand Russell received his fiery sense of identification with the underdog, often at the expense of sympathy with his own class.

The two generations prior to Russell's were especially dear to him, figuring prominently in his autobiographical writings. Russell's aristocratic legacy was not solely a matter of paternal inheritance. Lord John first married Lady Ribbesdale, who died in childbirth, and then Frances Anna Maria Elliott, second daughter of the earl of Minto and a powerful influence upon young Bertrand, along the lines of the stately grandmother with whom George Sand played harpsichord duets. Their son John, Viscount Amberley, who was born in 1842, was slightly dour (perhaps due to his Scottish heritage) and blessed in his marriage to the high-spirited Kate Stanley, the daughter of the second Lord Stanley of Alderley. As Russell wrote in his autobiography, "I loved the Russells and feared the Stanleys. . . . I owe to the Russells shyness, sensitiveness, and metaphysics; to the Stanleys vigor, good health and good spirits."[9] Lord John combined these apposite qualities in an appealing way. Like Cincinnatus (or Bill Bradley), he served when he felt the state needed him but then preferred to retire to his massive country house rather than cling to office as his power slipped away. There, in the splendor of Ravenscroft, a huge, well-staffed, eighteenth-century pile near Trelleck, with ten bedrooms and forty acres of park lands, he labored daily, the epitome of the enlightened noble amateur, on a book that would have been destined for instant obscurity had he completed it: "An Analysis of Religious Belief." His son, of course, would stun his audience in 1936 with the book *Why I Am Not a Christian*. An ardent scholar of both Buddhism and Christianity, the elder Russell paused in his writing to welcome such visitors as John Stuart Mill, Bertrand's godfather and a dear friend of the family; Thomas Carlyle; and Ralph Waldo Emerson. As with the circle of Sand or the Pre-Raphaelite Brotherhood, the Russell household offered a mix of heady company in which the term "genius" was bandied about with almost unfair abandon. As an undergraduate and then a young professor at Cambridge, Russell was also a fixture of the Apostles, a secret society, many of whose members became part of the Bloomsbury circle, yet another epitome of an elite, closed society in which both rank and artistic or scholarly achievement counted for a great deal.

Bertrand was the third and last child, born 18 May 1872, three years after the first son, Frank, who ascended to the title but relinquished it, and an ill-fated daughter named Rachel. Before Bertrand was three, in a calamitous string of circumstances, his mother, father, and sister all died within the course of a year. In 1875, Russell was sent to Lord John's home. Queen Victoria had appointed Lord John to an earldom, and he lived in Pembroke Lodge in Richmond Park near London, the house and grounds given by the queen. It had eleven acres and a glorious view of Epsom Downs toward Windsor Castle. Bertrand lived there until adolescence. When he gained legal maturity at twenty-one, he inherited twenty thousand pounds, from which he derived an income of six hundred pounds a year, which offered him a lifelong safety net and emboldened him in 1894 to defy his family's wishes and marry Alys Pearsall Smith. His monetary inheritance was not all that he owed his family. A strong sense of tradition as well as a feeling of being out of the ordinary came with the name. Snooping in his father's diary he felt strongly the grip of the past as pattern: "This gave me an uncanny feeling that I was not living my own life but my father's over again, and tended to produce a superstitious belief in heredity."[10] No matter how Modern Russell's thought would become in terms of the philosophical and political movements it enjoined, a profound sense of tradition was its foundation. By counting John Stuart Mill as "family," Russell also chose his intellectual forebears and seriously counted his allegiance to Mill until the point where the older philosopher seemed dated.

Russell's idyllic life had another effect. It tended to lead him away from reality, into abstraction: "The garden seemed to remember the days of its former splendor, when foreign ambassadors paced its lawns and princes admired its trim beds of flowers. It lived in the past, and I lived in the past with it."[11] Like Hofmannsthal in his youth, Balthus in his old age, and Yeats in his imagination, there is in this lyrical reminiscence an enviable sense of living an anachronistic life, out of the present and blessedly separated from the cares outside the wall. The same quality is found in his description of his grandmother: "She was completely unworldly and despised those who thought anything of worldly honors."[12] In truth, the notion of any of the Russells being "unworldly" is ludicrous, given the family's immense wealth and constant, deep involvement in the affairs of the day in British politics. Yet the knowledge that Russell would become absorbed by the most rarefied and pure discipline of the academy—mathematics—dovetails perfectly with this idea of hovering above or beyond reality. Like so many other artists, including some under consideration here, that utopian inclination developed early in life has a specific influence upon the kind of thinking and art they make. Swinburne with his sunken kingdoms off the coast of Cornwall, Balthus in his dreamy world of adolescence, Hofmannsthal in his romance with the well-run households in the Vienna of Empress Maria Theresa, Puvis in the Arcadia he painted over and again—all were inclined to address the Modern age obliquely, through poetic constructions that were closer to the ideas they hoped to convey.

The yearning for an absolutely harmonious realm in which all makes sense was all the more entrancing for Russell. Here was order in a time besieged by chaos. "The world of mathematics, which you condemn, is really a beautiful world; it has nothing to do with life and death and human sordidness, but is eternal, cold and passionless," he wrote to Lady Ottoline. While Russell dismisses Byronic Romanticism, he extols "emotions that are beautiful to the possessor" and finds them in his mathematics. The bond of isolation he shared with Ottoline, that ability to hold the world at arm's length, is a clue to Russell's habits of thought. It also figured heavily in the later work of his protégé, Wittgenstein, who made pointed use in his *Philosophical Investigations* of a famous citation from Spinoza: "Mens aeterna est quatenus res sub specie aeternitatis" (The mind is eternal insofar as it conceives things from the standpoint of eternity). Both Russell and Wittgenstein, along with Leighton and Hofmannsthal, favored quality in the form of the well written, the well made, and the technically competent. In a letter from Russell to Lucy Donnelly in 1903 (a time when many of his missives were addressed from Castle Howard, the gorgeous eighteenth-century country house owned by his mother's family that became internationally famous as the star locale of the television series based on Evelyn Waugh's *Brideshead Revisited*), he wrote: "It is very interesting the way you care for good prose: it is the way one ought to care about the thing that makes the value of one's work. It is in that way that I value certainty and system, which are, in the end, what most of my life is devoted to."[13]

Russell's massive life work, so consonant with the prodigious output that his family's energy and character produced, was nonetheless based upon a tradition in English thought so Modern that they could scarcely have understood it. A. J. Ayer was a noted English empiricist and authority on Russell whose account of his philosophical genealogy leads back through British empiricists such as Locke, Berkeley, and Hume, as well as Mill. Ayer views Russell's position in philosophical history as being far closer to this predominantly British line than to the circle of Rudolf Carnap, Wittgenstein, and Moore (the latter two were close friends and colleagues at Cambridge). They privileged questions over answers, and Russell preferred arrivals. As Ayer explains, the primary aim of Russell's work kept the definitive as its true north: "The motive for his search for definitions is that successful definitions reduce ontological commitments."[14]

This may seem a contradiction, leading in the opposite direction from that impulse to withdraw, but at about the time of his affair with Lady Ottoline, Russell became more and more determined to write for a popular audience. Some have suggested this was a competitive reaction to Henri Bergson's popularity or even an attempt to engage Lady Ottoline in his work. The effect was to shake Russell loose from the cloistral power struggles of Cambridge and, like Noam Chomsky or Richard Rorty in our time, make him a media figure in areas that ranged far beyond his discipline. A common thread among the artists under consideration in these pages, all of whom could well have enjoyed the splendid isolation that was their birthright and that remains the option of many nobles, is their yearning for the limelight. Chopin and Liszt could complain all they wanted to about the headaches of being idolized by thousands of fanatics, but they created spectacles of mass hysteria when they played. Hofmannsthal was most at home taking his bow along with the conductor during the last curtain call in the opera house, and Balthus and Bacon presided over openings of their exhibitions that were the highlights of the social season in London, Paris, or New York. By accepting the public responsibilities of leadership that an artist or thinker incurs, they act in the tradition of public service that a nobleman traditionally bears. In the twentieth-century, particularly, this entailed a willingness to perform, since the roles of both artist and aristocrat are considered so anachronistic or extraordinary and since the idolatry of celebrities is inevitably linked to showmanship. It was not necessarily their "job" to be public figures in an age when the aristocracy was no longer expected to command or lead.

Russell took on the role of public figure independently, correctly anticipating that his extroverted ways and far-reaching stratagems would bring the resentment of his academic colleagues and misunderstanding from his family. Privately, he joked about churning out his "shilling shocker" mass-market books, vastly more literate antecedents to the lightweight "Philosophy for Dummies" titles that crowd genuine books off the shelf today. The dichotomy between the nobleman and the Ruskinian populist adds an intriguing tension to many of Russell's texts. In an elegant essay, "The Cult of Common Usage," for example, Russell's back straightens at the notion of the mystique surrounding "common sense." Within the context of an argument for a specialized language or notation for philosophy, he writes, "It is not the function of philosophy—so they maintain—to teach something that uneducated people do not know; on the contrary, its function is to teach superior persons that they are not as superior as they thought they were, and that those who are really superior can show their skill by making sense of common sense. It is, of course, a dreadful thing in these days to lay claim to any kind of superiority except in athletics, movies, and moneymaking."[15]

Elsewhere, his musings on politics and society take him right to the heart of his privileged background, as in the following passage on the aristocratic ideal. Ranging from history to sociology, ethics, religion, and politics, this brief meditation on class derives its authority in part from Russell's vast knowledge of these fields and in part from his experience. One feels that he knows at first hand these "admirable conversationalists" whose claims to the "good life," construed in its Socratic sense rather than in the way that today's Wall Street masters of the universe might use that phrase, are false. Ironically, this paragraph is directly followed by another on the aristocratic Shelley as a prophet of the new millennium:

> Certain good things, such as art and science and friendship, can flourish very well in an aristocratic society. They existed in Greece on a basis of slavery; they exist among ourselves on a basis of exploitation. But love, in the form of sympathy, or benevolence, cannot exist freely in an aristocratic society. The aristocrat has to persuade himself that the slave or proletarian or colored man is of inferior clay, and that his sufferings do not matter. At the present moment polished English gentlemen flog Africans so severely that they die after hours of unspeakable anguish. Even if these gentlemen are well-educated, artistic and admirable conversationalists, I cannot admit that they are living the good life. However nature imposes some limitation of sympathy, but not such a degree as that. In a democratically-minded society, only a maniac would behave in this way. The limitation of sympathy involved in the aristocratic ideal is its condemnation. Salvation is an aristocratic ideal, because it is individualistic. For this reason, also, the idea of personal salvation, however interpreted and expanded, cannot serve for the definition of the good life.[16]

Excellence of style and the pursuit of the good life are paired in a way that suggests the valorization an artist might make. Russell often alluded to "the retreat from Pythagoras," not only in his career but as a trend in early Modern thought, referring to the way in which he, Wittgenstein, and others found themselves in territory, such as the aesthetic or psychological, that had been traditionally removed from mathematics (which he described as having "beauty, cold and austere, like that of sculpture"). In a similar way, he found himself taking positions that were anti-Hegel and anti-Aristotle, distancing his approach from classical categories. It was an age when the gap between mind and body, as inherited from Descartes, was suddenly narrowed by Einstein's equations among space, time, and matter. In the Cambridge of today, Russell would find an even more extraordinary embodiment of the redefined Cartesian duality in the person of Stephen Hawking. Russell's gaze was often turned toward the stars. As he considered Nature in its totality, as an entity that we can imagine and appraise, he placed man in the position of being the arbiter of value (a loaded philosophical term) by virtue of the ability to embrace what can be thought. The language of his conclusion is particularly interesting from an aristocratic perspective: "It is we who create value and our desires which confer value. In this realm, we are kings, and we debase our kingship if we bow down to nature. It is for us to determine the good life, not for Nature—not even for Nature personified as God."[17]

From essays on his profession and education to confessional passages about falling in love, Russell's writings lay bare a mighty intellect gripped by conflicting impulses. Even his astonishingly open indiscretions became grist for the analytical mill and part of his writer's capital. As recondite as much of the work on logic and mathematics can be, volumes of his writings, including the autobiographical works, are accessible to a lay audience. Russell's ardor for the public arena in which to test his capable powers of argument can, of course, be traced to previous dukes of Bedford, prime ministers and parliamentarians going back to the time of Henry VIII. The autobiography, in which one can follow this play of private and public impulses, is a hodgepodge, miserably edited with too free a hand. It includes too many of his early academic papers and other documents yet offers a fascinating glimpse into the refining process by which a great mind is formed. It is similar in tone to *The Education of Henry Adams* and at times reminiscent of Proust's *A la Recherche*, although this is less a bildungsroman than the documentary record of a gradual dispersal of ignorance with the pruning tools of logic and mathematics. It includes the well-known encounters with Boole's *Laws of Thought* (1854) and the theories of Giuseppe Peano, Leibniz, C. S. Peirce, Frege, and of course, Russell's close friend and coauthor, Alfred North Whitehead.

Like many British bluebloods of the era, Russell sided with the liberals politically, and he and Lady Ottoline took delight in slamming the life of privilege that they had enjoyed (they had known each other since childhood). What some might call hypocrisy others would more charitably view as the often messy attempt of a multifaceted man, living in a confusing, transitional moment in history, to pursue his many passions without either abandoning tradition or relying entirely on its models. It is no wonder these internal conflicts would surface in his essays. A professional philosopher in a field so abstruse and theoretical as to be, more than most, identified with the ivory tower aspect of Cambridge, he was so involved politically as to spend time in jail for his beliefs and to resign a lectureship that brought not only income but the academic affiliation that most scholars need for publication and "legitimacy." He also balanced his writing between voluminous tracts for a specialized audience, such as his *Principia Mathematica*, with accessible clear writing on ethics, religion, contemporary issues (a quick book, *The Problem of China*, practically completed before he left the country), and the best-selling *History of Western Philosophy*.

The Nobel Prize in Literature of 1950 spotlighted the paradoxical role of the earl of Bedford, one of the world's preeminent mathematicians, as Promethean bringer of sophisticated philosophical explication to common men. One of the unifying aspects of his life and career, however, was his insistent desire to be at the forefront of whatever issue he took on, and this propensity to be in the avant-garde kept him self-consciously on the edge of Modern thought. As his historically important friendship with Wittgenstein showed, it seems at times childishly competitive. He would come away from an evening of talk with the victor's satisfaction of having bested all others in a kind of mental arm wrestling, almost a parody of academic rivalry—just like poets vying for the laureateship, composers secretly yearning for knighthood, or Balthus titling his self-portrait *H.M. King of the Cats*. There is no *Burke's Peerage* for artists, but a pseudo-aristocratic pecking order is always discernible in every period and discipline.

Arguably, the most challenging area of conflict for Russell was the split between mathematics and philosophy and where along that boundary he might position his thoughts on logic as well as metaphysics. It took courage to saunter into these widely different and highly specialized fields, and it helped to have had a first-rate education at Eton and Cambridge. Just as Russell's upbringing encouraged him to think that he would be universally welcome whether in the presence of royalty or of the estate gardener, he also felt endowed with an intellectual passe-partout, a license that led him into many avenues and disciplines, making the task of the serious student of Russell particularly delightful or tricky, as the case may be. This is a trait he shared with Wittgenstein, who hesitated between psychology and logic in categorizing his later writings and who was instrumental in luring Russell's interests from pure mathematics toward linguistics and psychology. As Russell observed, in a statement that is autobiographical and philosophical, "Logic is the youth of mathematics and mathematics is the manhood of logic."[18] All this genre-bending is part of the modernity of both Russell and Wittgenstein. The concern for being Modern is evident from the very first sentence of the preface to Russell's *Principia Mathematica*, which was begun in 1900 and took a turn toward a consideration of inductive theory in 1910. That was the first time that Russell took on the problematic role of the theory of types. One of the reasons that he would turn from the hard-edged path of mathematics was that Wittgenstein himself had raised the obstacles that deflected him. As Russell wrote in the preface to the second edition, dated 1925, "Even if it is flawed the stricture of what is reared on it is sound—the tendency of later mathematical propositions to be more true than earlier." This difficult sentence refers to the axiom of reducibility about which he concedes: "But clearly it is not the sort of axiom with which we can rest content."[19]

What happened to Russell's vaunted certainty? His own protégé had intervened. Wittgenstein had demonstrated that functions of propositions are always truth functions, and a function can occur in a proposition only through its values. The tidy theory of the well-ordered series collapses, and the existence of irrational and real numbers breaks down. Adopting a note of resignation, Russell is conscious of the historical passing of mathematics and logic into a new phase, less involved in measure or quantity and more in class relations, propositions, and forms. To use a comparison within the scope of this study, it is not unlike the emphasis of Swinburne on form and syntax in his critical writings. Russell thought long and hard about this question in a variety of contexts. One essay, "Physics and Neutral Monism," considers aesthetic form from the rapidly changing viewpoint of the new physics:

> We are often asked to concede that the beauties of poetry or music cannot result from physical laws. I should concede that the beauty does not result from physics, since beauty depends in part upon intrinsic quality; if it were, as some writers on aesthetics contend, solely a matter of form, it would come within the scope of physics, but I think these writers do not realize what an abstract affair form really is. I should concede also that the thoughts of Shakespeare or Bach do not come within the scope of physics. But their thoughts are of no importance to us: their whole social efficiency depended upon certain black marks on the white paper. Now there seems no reason to suppose that physics does not apply to the making of these marks, which was a movement of matter just as truly as the revolution of the earth in its orbit.[20]

By 1919, in the introduction to *Mathematical Philosophy*, the tone of Russell's core philosophical writings had shifted, becoming one of contingency and hesitancy, consonant with the fractured modes of Freud or analytic Cubism: "For the moment I do not know how to define 'tautology.' It would be easy to offer a definition which might seem satisfactory for a while; but I know of none that I feel to be satisfactory in spite of feeling thoroughly familiar with the characteristic of which a definition is wanted. At this point, therefore, for the moment, we reach the frontier of knowledge on our backward journey into the logical foundations of mathematics."[21] He includes a footnote, melodramatically referring to Wittgenstein's influence and the fact that, as a prisoner of war, with the manuscript of his *Tractatus* in his knapsack, he was out of touch with Russell and other supporters, including John Maynard Keynes: "The importance of tautology for a definition of mathematics was pointed out to me by my former pupil Ludwig Wittgenstein, who was working on the problem. I do not know whether he has solved it, or even whether is alive or dead."[22] There was no immediate way around this impasse, erected by Wittgenstein, through which Russell's yearning for an adequate medium persists: "Because language is misleading, as well as because it is diffuse and inexact when applied to logic (for which it was never intended), logical symbolism is absolutely necessary to any exact or thorough treatment of our subject."[23] Russell, at the instigation of Wittgenstein, had just opened the path to a language-based core of thought that would shape the future course of aesthetics, literary criticism, art, and of course, philosophy down to our own day.

By way of understanding how Russell placed this development in historic context, we turn to a few of the more eccentric volumes of his oeuvre in which his views of the family legacy are spelled out. In a tone and on a scale completely similar to George Sand's long paean to her ancestors in the opening chapters of *The Story of My Life*, Russell and his third wife, Patricia, undertook an extensive editing project that resulted in *The Amberley Papers*, published in 1937. Culled from the family letters and documents going back a century and supposedly locked in privacy by a will that Russell felt free to defy, it is an eccentric and completely charming profile of Russell's ancestors that invites interpretation for its link to his life's work. His later volume, *My Philosophical Development*, may be more directly autobiographical, but *The Amberley Papers* sheds romantic light upon Russell as heir to a rich and complex legacy that was both intellectual and political. The two volumes also make delightful reading. If you ever want to slip away from the coarse and banal mass media of our time to become lost in another world, take down *The Amberley Papers*, brew a pot of Earl Grey tea, and immerse yourself in this elegantly atmospheric cedar chest of letters, diary entries and press clippings. They are punctuated by funny comments and snippets of history by Russell himself. Deep in these pages, throughout which articulate, lively individuals address one another with passion and civility, you'll suddenly feel the urge to pull out a sheet of your best stationery and a fountain pen to write a letter to your beloved, sealing it with wax and a family crest.

In this world so unlike our own, Lord Amberley and his equally aristocratic wife, Kate Stanley of Alderley, play the leading roles, joined by such unforgettable characters as the high-toned Rosalind, Russell's aunt, who, in a fit of teetotaling piety, poured the great vintages in the wine cellars of Castle Howard and Naworth, her estate, down the drain. These were lives touched directly by great art as well as events, as in the case of so many other figures in this study. The Amberley home had frequent visits from the eminent Pre-Raphaelite painters Frederick, Lord Leighton and Edward Burne-Jones, the philosophers Carlisle and Mill, as well as numerous brushes with royalty. Even if some of the anecdotes are not much direct help in elucidating Russell's philosophy, they're too charming to resist. When Russell's father was a boy, one of his dearest chums was the Prince of Wales, and in a letter to his mother he recounts a play date at neighboring Windsor Castle during which he and Prince Albert enjoyed a bit of football in the palace gardens, fed the ducks, and were briefly honored by a royal pat on the head from Queen Victoria and Albert, the prince consort. "I liked my Royal Visit very much indeed,"[24] he wrote to his mother. Another delightful moment is offered by a love letter from Lord Amberley to Kate during their courtship, dated 25 October 1864: "You shall work by my side, you shall fight with me and for me, and your task will be even higher, a greater one than mine."[25]

Then there are moments when the distinguished mien of the next generation seems to be prefigured, as for instance in this letter from Thomas Sanderson, a close friend of Amberley's from Cambridge, who at one point was to be Bertrand's guardian and teacher. In a letter to Kate he extols the welcome feeling of having a companionable spirit in the room while one writes: "There is a sense of fullness in the room and work goes much better when someone dear is by the while. Doubtless Amberley will corroborate this by experience. I only speak deductively from the idea, a priori, or perhaps rather from imaginated experience. From the bareness that sometimes comes round and through me when alone; and makes the walls look hard and superficial and not, as it were, of infinite depth."[26] This is the sort of observation that is tossed off casually in the letters that makes the crabbed e-mail style of today look so paltry. There are even references to other figures in this study, such as Sand. As Lord Amberley writes to Kate, "I like many of George Sand's novels. It is said the reason of the great difference in their sentiments one can hardly call them principles was the way she was influenced by her various lovers—her style is always beautiful. Whether the demoralization of France may not be owing to their favorite teachers ever putting enjoyment above duty one does not feel sure of."[27]

It is not the fashion among today's biographers and Russell scholars to view his family life in a positive light. The stuffy Victorian atmosphere, particularly its puritanical spirit of denial and control, offers an incongruous and inconvenient backdrop for a portrait they want to present of a hard-edged, analytic philosopher, England's answer to the Viennese dominance of philosophy and psychology. Implicit in this approach is the attitude that a leader of the avant-garde could never emerge from the comfortable cocoon of nobility. Most suggest that Russell was crippled emotionally by his family. As one psychobiographer writes, "It is clear, however, that a distressing feature of the aristocratic system of paid caretakers for children was that these persons, who sometimes inspired great fondness, were temporary. Like Russell's parents they too were loved and lost, renewing a sense of bereavement which was not given time or occasion to work itself out."[28] To emphasize the "poor little rich boy" element of Russell's story helps to explain the callous treatment of women. Though by no means another Picasso in his degree of cruelty, Russell was a rascal and far too interested in the pain he inflicted on his rejected girlfriends. Yet the assumption that he rejected his upbringing as overbearing and alien to him cuts off an overlooked and rewarding path of inquiry for students of Russell's thought.

Russell himself dwelled on this issue in a self-reflective (occasionally self-aggrandizing) mode. He made the analysis and partial rejection of his legacy a springboard for his originality and a sturdy source of motivation in a life that was in every way the antithesis of the stereotypically comfortable, intellectually vapid style of the superfluous English aristocrat (particularly that bunch of underachievers associated with the House of Windsor in our day). Certainly a major aspect of his tight relationships with such academic cronies as G. E. Moore, Whitehead, and Wittgenstein consisted of a powerful sense of their crowning positions in contemporary thought. That included division according to rank, into a hierarchy with a constant sense of who stood in first place and the responsibility for offering the paramount solution to problems that had defied or stumped other philosophers until their time. Russell, who wrote eloquently and often on the topic of power, consciously gauged the teacher-student hierarchy and the relative standing of his colleagues, not according to the petty criteria that dominate tenure battles and academic backstabbing in our time (totals of publications and footnotes, number of smiles from the provost) but according to subtly assessed encounters between thinkers in which one clearly bests the other. Russell took pride in "blowing away" his students and peers, and that is why he was pleasantly astonished by Wittgenstein, who did not roll over and die in debate.

Russell also was keenly aware of the transition from one generation to the next and of his place in the momentous intellectual and social shift into the twentieth century. He rather cherished the notion of straddling the epochal divide between the nineteenth century and its strong beliefs and the next wave of English thinkers, from whom he also relished a certain distance. In this regard he is similar to Winston Churchill, another aristocrat who found himself in a position of leadership in a world significantly changed from that of his father, Lord Randolph. As Russell wrote,

> The tone of the generation some ten years junior to my own was set mainly by Lytton Strachey and Keynes. It is surprising how great a change in mental climate those ten years had brought. We were still Victorian, they were Edwardian. We believed in ordered progress by means of politics and free discussion. The more self-confident among us may have hoped to be leaders of the multitude, but none of us wanted to be divorced from it. The generation of Keynes and Lytton did not seek to preserve any kinship with the Philistine. They aimed rather at a life of retirement among fine shades and nice feelings, and conceived of the good as consisting in the passionate mutual admirations of a clique of the elite.[29]

Here is Russell the superior historian and egalitarian at his best. Given the fuss over the inverted Bloomsbury set ever since, it is refreshing to see how he distances himself from their "clique of the elite." Frankly, he outranked them socially and outgunned them as a writer. It is also amusing to consider this historic tidbit: The dukes of Bedford, thanks to a charter granted by James I, owned Bloomsbury (as well as Covent Garden) and derived much of their wealth from its rents. Although nothing could be more exclusive than the tiny club of thinkers who can understand all that Russell has written in his mathematical and philosophical vein, making his achievement decidedly elitist in at least that respect, his intentions in other regards were democratic. There is a sensitivity to his audience and its connection to the wider world, especially in the phrase "though more of us wanted to be divorced from it." The same connection to his origins, coupled with the effort to at least appear on the outside as a regular chap, is shown in the modest professorial digs he lived in. When Russell and his wife, Alys, set up house in a quaint garden cottage called the Millhanger, near Friday's Hill in Cambridge, their friend and frequent visitor, Helen Thomas, described it in this way: "The inside is extremely sophisticated and, I noticed to my no small amusement, Bertie, although he pretends to think nothing at all of his family has hung his walls with pictures of the Dukes of Bedford, the Stanleys of Alderley and so forth."[30]

Russell was both a cold-eyed futurist and a romantic historian. On the one hand his vision of a three-dimensional abstract space was a wonderful, Einsteinian preview of not only Cubism but cyberspace. On the other, he was pleasurably but persistently burdened with the rich legacy he inherited. One day in July 1902 he visited his Aunt Agatha at Pembroke Lodge for ten days' rest. The sojourn was spent in conversation over tea about "tragedies in which all the actors are gone," as Russell later wrote. "All the life of the present grew to me dreamy and unreal, while the majestic Past, weighed down by age and filled with unspeakable wisdom, rose before me and dominated my whole being. The Past is an awful God, though he gives Life almost the whole of its haunting beauty. I believe those whose childhood has been spent in America can scarcely conceive the hold which the Past has on us of the Old World: the continuity of life, the weight of tradition, the great eternal procession of youth and age and death, seem to be lost in the bustling approach of the future which dominates American life. And that is one reason why great literature is not produced by your compatriots," he wrote to an American friend, Lucy Martin Connelly, on 6 July.

Three years later, that same Aunt Agatha gave Russell an heirloom that was a permanent and tangible reminder of his family's power and expectations. It was a gold pocket watch and chain that had been worn by Lord John when he was prime minister. As Aunt Agatha wrote (under the legend PRIVATE) to Russell in March 1905, "Dear dear Bertie I should like to feel that you will always try to be worthy—you will try I know—of being his grandson for he was indeed one of the best men the world has known—courageous—gentle—true—and with a most beautiful childlike simplicity and straightforwardness of nature which is most rare—I like to think that you remember him—and that his last words to you 'Good little boy,' spoken from his deathbed with loving gentleness,—can remain with you as an inspiration to goodness through life; but of course you cannot remember and cannot know all that he was.—But if you will have it I should like you to wear and treasure this watch in memory of him—and of the long ago days in the dear home of our childhood."[31]

A pocket watch is a pocket watch, and philosophy is a profession, as we are constantly reminded by professors in graduate seminars. What could possibly justify the link between the two? It may seem a novel notion, but the theme of legacy, heritage, or tradition is involved on both levels. The leap from the anecdote of the watch to the philosophical writings is no small hop, but the concept of heritage is a stepping-stone. Why shouldn't philosophers, like poets and novelists, be subject to the type of analysis that identifies their voice? Just as stylistics can be used to help decipher the argument of a poem or establish the telltale signature methods of a novelist, it can also be used to examine the writings of a philosopher. Both Russell and Wittgenstein operated in the field of language philosophy, drilling deep into questions of grammar and semantics, so there is even more reason to ponder the question of voice in a consideration of their work. In the case of Russell, who won his Nobel for literature in

1950 (Churchill, by the way, also won his Nobel for literature), the apparent ease with which he composed translates into a fluidity for the reader that is notable. In his autobiography he confides that this was a vital concern from childhood: "The construction of prose rhythms was the only thing in which I found any real consolation."[32]

As fresh, original, and distinctive as Russell's style is, there are echoes in it not just of the prevailing authorities in English philosophy (Moore and Mill, above all) but of other voices. That note of lofty indignation, the meticulous diction, even the offbeat humor all bear traces of the family style: the eloquence of the father, which stood him in good stead on so many occasions in Parliament; the frequent and exquisitely phrased letters; the rapid and effective questions and ripostes that were the staple of dinner conversation. His diction on occasion rose to lyrical heights of undeniable grandeur, as in this brief excerpt from "The Essence of Religion" (1912): "The finite self, impelled by the desire for self-preservation, builds prison walls round the infinite part of our nature, and endeavors to restrain it from that free life in the whole which constitutes its being. Sudden beauty in the midst of strife, uncalculating love, or the night wind in the trees, seem to suggest the possibility of a life free from the conflicts and pettinesses of our everyday world, a life where there is peace which no misfortune can disturb."[33]

The language of Russell's philosophical texts is sprinkled with terms that have double meaning within the context of a consideration of him as an aristocrat: *class*, *power*, *identity*, *legitimize*, the half-joking use of "the present king of France" as an illustrative example of someone who does not exist yet, can all be named. Even the adjective *ignoble*, one of his apparent favorites, gains resonance.

> It seems to me now that mathematics is capable of an artistic excellence as great as that of any music, perhaps greater; not because the pleasure it gives (although very pure) is comparable, either in intensity or in the number of people who feel it, to that of music, but because it gives in absolute perfection that combination, characteristic of great art, of godlike freedom, with the sense of inevitable destiny; because, in fact, it constructs an ideal world where everything is perfect and yet true. Again, in regard to actual human existence, I have found myself giving honor to those who feel it is a great tragedy, who think truly about Death, who are oppressed by ignoble things even when they are inevitable; yet these qualities appear to me to militate against happiness, not only to the possessors, but to all whom they affect.[34]

It is easy to take this punning too far, but on occasion the diction is very suggestive. "The chief task I have to maintain is the legitimacy of analysis," he writes. In Russell's life, whether in connection with his assuming the title of the third duke of Bedford upon his brother's renunciation or the frequent worries over a pregnant girlfriend while still married to Alys, "legitimacy" is a loaded word.

Philosophical rivals, spoiling for a fight, were attuned to the aristocratic accent. A particularly colorful example of how Russell's background could be dragged into a debate is presented by a testy exchange in the late 1930s with the American philosopher and educational expert John Dewey, a darling of today's vibrant revival of pragmatism. It was a time when Russell abhorred superstition and metaphysics, which he linked. Writing on Dewey's logic in 1939, he asserted, "In every writer on philosophy there is a concealed metaphysic, usually unconscious, even if his subject is metaphysics, he is almost certain to have an uncritically believed system which underlies his explicit arguments."[35] Then Russell picked apart Dewey's work as an extension of a peculiarly American metaphysic. Dewey was quick to take exception and turned to an ad hominem argument that invoked Russell's lineage. "Mr. Russell's confirmed habit of connecting the pragmatic theory of knowing with obnoxious aspects of American industrialism . . . is much as if I were to link his philosophy to the interests of the English landed aristocracy." Russell backed off. He responded: "For my part, I am accustomed to having my opinions challenged (especially by Communists) as due to my connection with the British aristocracy, and I am quite willing to suppose that my views, like other men's, are influenced by social environment. But if, in regard to Dr. Dewey, I am mistaken as to the social influence concerned, I regret the mistake."[36]

At a certain point, the analytic approach that Russell was rapidly pursuing found itself in a cul-de-sac. The philosopher had exhausted the rivals at hand and was in need of fresh stimulus. Enter Ludwig Wittgenstein, the son of one of Europe's wealthiest industrialists and, like Hofmannsthal (a distant relation), a member of the bagatelle nobility, those minor members of the aristocracy whose titles were bestowed by the emperor within the past two hundred or so years. Like the *noblesse de robe* of France, they were dutiful bureaucrats and business leaders upon whom the court had smiled, earning the titles of count and baron that could be passed on from one generation to the next, unlike the life peers of the United Kingdom. Russell first mentions Wittgenstein's appearance at Trinity in a letter to Lady Ottoline of 18 October 1911: "An unknown German applied, speaking very little English but refusing to speak German." The student soon became "my German" in his letters to Ottoline, which track the rapid progress of their friendship. Anyone who teaches is familiar with the stages through which a particularly promising student is tracked on the radar. Not long afterward, Russell wrote, "I am much interested by my German and shall hope to see a lot of him."[37] Wittgenstein followed Russell home from a lecture, and they argued until dinner. The charming and often retold account of the spontaneous combustion between them that led to one of the great intellectual bonds of the twentieth century remains a vital narrative in philosophy because it so clearly presents the transfer of a legacy from one moment in history to the next and literally from one school of analytic thought to its successor. Gears mesh this smoothly only when they have been fitted with precision, and the Russell-Wittgenstein alliance is more than a fortunate coincidence of academic interests. The similarities between their family backgrounds and life stories helped prepare this perfect fit. As Russell remarked to Lady Ottoline in March 1912, "He even has the same similes as I have."

Just before Russell and Wittgenstein there had been the strikingly different team of Russell and Whitehead. Their highly productive collaboration was tense and probably as dependent upon their differences as people as upon their similarities as thinkers. Whitehead, older and far less fortunate financially as well as socially, was the Cambridge don who spotted Russell's talent amid the crush of entering freshmen completing their placement examinations. As student became teaching colleague and then coauthor of the massive project of the *Principia Mathematica*, their lives became intertwined but never as equals. Russell quickly leapfrogged Whitehead intellectually through his breathtakingly incisive and quick critique of the inconsistencies in Whitehead's logic. Meanwhile, the struggle of Whitehead and his wife with her illnesses and the general indignities of being an impoverished academic drew Russell's pity and interference. While their book was in progress, Russell visited their home daily, and his deep concern for Evelyn Whitehead, the mathematician's wife, who battled depression and heart disease, led to an epiphany that revealed to Russell what he afterward felt as the tragic condition and isolation in which each individual resides. The book that Whitehead and Russell produced—plodding, monolithic, solidly hewn from their rigorous questioning of one another, and in the end (by Russell's own admission), flawed—reflects an entirely different kind of thought from the quicksilver conversational style of rapidly mounting, Socratic debate he enjoyed with Wittgenstein.

As with Hofmannsthal and Strauss, the Russell-Whitehead relationship was complicated by the difference in class, and as with the librettist and composer, the rift was occasionally reflected in their work. Russell's horizon always seemed wider and less interrupted simply because, as at a coastal hotel, the view was better from a higher floor. He tended to lord it over Whitehead in matters having to do with the overarching questions of why they would view philosophy a certain way at all. With Wittgenstein, the nature of the dialogue was no less a contest, but these are two eagles at high altitudes, and their greater intimacy, stemming from parity, fostered a looser, more speculative, and wider-ranging exchange. Although Russell provided an introduction to Wittgenstein's first publication, the two did not copublish. Their agendas in this regard were vastly different. Wittgenstein did not easily release his work for publication, and most of what we know as his books was collated from transcripts made by devoted students. Russell, on the other hand, was prolific and completely unfazed by the prospect of letting a book go out to meet its public as the ink was drying, even when its conclusions were interim.

Russell and Wittgenstein formed a deeper bond, and perhaps because of it they rose to more impressive levels in the thoughts they drew from one another. There is a way in which this high-voltage affinity parallels the precisely contemporary and obviously stimulating romance between Lady Ottoline and Russell, and the closest account of the early phase of his acquaintance with Wittgenstein is found in the letters to Ottoline. At first, Russell does not even seem to know that Wittgenstein is even Austrian, much less the member of a distinguished and powerful family. The younger man's intellectual capital is more important to Russell than the fact that the Wittgensteins, thanks to the rapidly assembled steel and iron fortune of Karl, Ludwig's father, were so important to the cultural and economic life of Vienna that Karl was known as the "Carnegie of Austria-Hungary," and the adjective *wittgensteinisch* was coined to describe the tasteful if aggressively masterpiece-hungry grandeur of their art-rich lifestyle. Johannes Brahms, Pablo Casals, the conductor Bruno Walter, and the great violin virtuoso Joseph Joachim and his string quartet were visitors to the mansion on Vienna's Alleegasse where Ludwig was raised. The painter Gustav Klimt and the designer Josef Hoffmann were the beneficiaries of major commissions, and the Wittgensteins were a force as patrons of the Secession—even to the extent of paying Klimt for his fresco, *Philosophy*, after the faculty of the University of Vienna voted to reject it.

Both families had their rebellious side, but the Wittgensteins had the edge for their role in the growth of Modernism in the arts. The family collection, assembled between 1870 and 1910, included works by fashionable portraitists such as Laszlo and Kramer but also paintings and sculpture by Rodin, Segantini, Rudolf von Alt, Max Klinger (a bust of Beethoven), and of course, Klimt. The predominant quality of the art was its air of calm and what Wittgenstein's beloved older sister called the "ethical" play of vertical and horizontal compositional structures. There was, underneath, a hum of Expressionist passion waiting to burst out. As an astute biographer of Wittgenstein observes, there is a strong connection between this atmosphere and his lifelong habits of thought: "There was something very *wittgensteinisch* in the idea of an intense and even febrile nervous energy channeled and contained in an apparent spontaneity. It appears again and again in Ludwig Wittgenstein's life and in his work, in the exhortations to his sister and his friend's daughter Mareile Hansel to draw honestly and decently, in his admiration for the sunniest and least forced works of Schubert written in the most miserable circumstances, in the obsessive rephrasing and rearrangement of his philosophical remarks in order to find the most natural and least professorial expression and sequence of thought."[38]

When it comes to the modernity of Wittgenstein, in addition to his legacy via contemporary literary theory and aesthetics, there are other, early signals of how far ahead of his time he was. One of the most fascinating involves a house he designed for his sister Gretl in 1926 (the plans are actually stamped with Wittgenstein's name along with that of the architect, Paul Engelmann, and Wittgenstein for years after was listed as an architect in the Vienna directory). The house he meticulously helped to create was a forerunner of the International Style and Minimalism, decades before a house was ever described by Le Corbusier as "a machine for living." Wittgenstein was adamant about making the details perfect, focusing his attention upon the locks, radiators, windows, and doors and browbeating the manufacturers to conform to his specifications with a degree of precision they were not accustomed to meeting, reducing one of the engineers to tears. While the house suited Gretl perfectly, his other sister, Hermine, found the "house-embodied logic" too austere. As with the wooden furniture Wittgenstein later designed for his own Cambridge digs and for colleagues, ornament was strictly forbidden, as were luxuries such as carpets and curtains. Biographer Ray Monk explains: "The house was designed with little regard to the comforts of ordinary mortals. The qualities of clarity, rigor and precision which categorize it are indeed those one looks for in a system of logic rather than in a dwelling place."[39] As with Eliot and the poetics of objectivity, Wittgenstein was wary of the dangers of personification and moved, as did Eliot, in the direction of a dissociation of emotion from the analysis of sensation, language, ethics, and science. Russell, too, for all the luxuriance of his diction, had his ascetic side, particularly in the way he wielded Occam's Razor as a means of reducing philosophical questions to their essentials ("it was a principle of parsimony as regards to entities," he once wrote).[40]

Not only was Wittgenstein au courant in his taste in Austrian art, but he was remarkably fluent in the aesthetics and thought of Europe in general. As with Russell, whose French was excellent thanks to his year of working at the British embassy in Paris and whose German was already fluent when he studied at Berlin University in 1895, Wittgenstein was blessed with the ability to use the languages in which the day's philosophical questions were debated. The conversation with the twenty-six tutors engaged to teach the eight children in the gardens of the country houses or the galleries of the mansion was customarily conducted in French or English:

> All his family, not just those who spent years in England or America, could write it all their lives and speak it with that out-of-date purity and refinement of accent and vocabulary that is now heard only from survivors of their generation or middle-aged members of foreign royal families. Their German, too, was of a beauty and elegance not often heard now—the German of culture and the stage in the Austria of that time, recognizably different from the German of the empire but in no sense a dialect. Indeed they had little contact with the people except as servants and dependents. Their contacts at children's parties or dancing schools were with the upper classes. Their outlook and all their habits were those of Austrians, indeed, but Austrians of those classes. Education in the home accentuated this remoteness: the normal way of life of most Austrians—not just of *das Volk* but of those that became writers and scientists—was alien to them. Ludwig, for example, always wrote in a bold Latin hand: when he became a schoolmaster he had to struggle to teach himself the customary *Kurrent*. Their education, then, was typical enough, but typical of a particular class at a particular time.[41]

Ludwig was sent to the Realschule at Linz, where, staggering thought, he was a contemporary of Adolf Hitler in 1904–5, although Hitler was two years behind him and there is no evidence the two had much contact. Wittgenstein addressed his schoolmates using the polite form *Sie*, according to Monk (biographer of both Russell and Wittgenstein, whose principal source for a hefty section of the Wittgenstein biography on the early days at Cambridge is Russell's published letters). The children knew Wagner's *Die Meistersinger* by heart and were splendidly musical. Ludwig was a superb clarinetist and mediocre, unenthusiastic pianist, leaving that to his brother Paul, a concert artist who continued to perform and commission compositions even after the loss of his right arm in World War I.

Although Russell seems, at least according to his letters and memoirs, to have been unaware of Wittgenstein's wealth and social prominence, many at Cambridge viewed the young Austrian with his noble carriage and his fine equestrian skills as a personage even before classes began. He spent liberally to furnish his rooms and headed to London for concerts and luxurious stays at the Grand Hotel. When Wittgenstein's father died in 1913 during Christmas holiday, obituaries in the *Neue Freie Presse* and in the *Times* of London revealed to Russell and others at Cambridge just how important Wittgenstein's family was. According to one biographer, "Russell and the others had not known how important a man he had been in the world."[42]

Wittgenstein was courted by both the musical and the philosophical elite of Cambridge, coming under the wing of not just Russell but John Maynard Keynes, who stood by him and helped during brief difficulties, official and emotional, through the 1930s. While Russell was suspected of trying to keep Wittgenstein to himself, Keynes arranged for Wittgenstein to join the Society of Apostles, which drew not only students and young faculty but alumni from Bloomsbury. A premium was placed upon flash, and first impressions and conversational brilliance, as in the salon performances of the circle of Sand, betokened genius. Wittgenstein certainly fit the bill, correcting not just Russell but Moore as well on their writing and lectures, behaving like the young Swinburne at Oxford with Benjamin Jowett. Wittgenstein's earnest simplicity won him respect among his peers and the faculty. He was elected to membership in the society in November 1912 but rarely participated. He viewed the proceedings as frivolous.

It would be a grave disservice to Wittgenstein as thinker to imply that he talked a good game, leading influential and prominent figures like Keynes and Russell to promote his books and secure his career in academe. That was anything but the case. Unlike the chattering class of current intellectuals, whose dinner partners are called into service the next morning as agents and publishers, Wittgenstein held himself aloof from the social scene and displayed excessive modesty with regard to both the publication of his work and the type of posts he held. One unforgettable episode in his life saw him teaching at a grade school in Trattenbach, a town in rural Austria south of Vienna, in a position of extraordinary humility and in a region deliberately chosen for its poverty (when he arrived at his first posting, Maria Schultz am Semmering, he refused to stay because the small mountain town had the luxury of a fountain). However, the conversational aspect of Wittgenstein's philosophical practice is of vital importance, and there is no question that it was shaped by the close encounters with Russell. Much of Wittgenstein's legacy is precisely his way of talking, as preserved by students and young lecturers, who were devoted to him. This reminds us of the tradition from Socrates through Jung and Jacques Lacan in psychoanalysis, Hans Hofmann and Barnett Newman in the painting studio, Igor Stravinsky (as recorded by Robert Craft), Walter Savage Landor's "Imaginary Conversations," and of course, paradigmatically, Samuel Johnson and the "table talk" of Samuel Taylor Coleridge from which the "conversation" poems grew.

Wittgenstein's Socratic mode of teaching and thinking wove together uncertainties, divagations, repetition, and linear pursuits of questions, sometimes languid and sometimes compressed, that unfolded in his mind. This was Modern not just because it was original, but because, as with Chopin's music, it reflected the process of thinking itself. The genres of philosophy included the dialogue, of course, but by Wittgenstein's day they were dominated by the monograph, which pounds at a single question through a book-length exposition that traditionally starts with a review of the existing literature and moves on to a critique, proposes an original thesis, explicates and defends it, and pushes on toward a q.e.d. ending that brings closure in the certainty of a point well driven home. That is not the experience of reading Wittgenstein. One characteristic of his style, to complement the remarks on Russell's, is the degree of uncertainty it permitted. The care and punctilious elegance of Wittgenstein's talk was crucial to the substance of his thought, and it was derived from his upbringing. Wittgenstein was correct—in his speech, his probing questions, and his evenly paced, careful, overly qualified answers. This is just what we expect from the little boy taught to pronounce his English in a prim, grammatical, measured way.

Wittgenstein's seriousness made him more than a match for Russell. As McGuinness notes, "His whole background led him to see life as a task, to demand of himself some achievement. He was conscious of exceptional abilities, yet discontented with the work he was producing. On another side, he wanted to give and receive affection, which for him meant to have some positive and productive relation with others, and yet constantly found himself put off by them and constantly himself put them off."[43] His ambition also made him a match for Russell. Theirs was a conversation between charged equals. In March 1912, Russell wrote to Ottoline: "We had a close equal passionate discussion of the most difficult part in mathematical philosophy. I think he has genius. In discussion with him I put out all my force and only just equal his. With all my other pupils I should squash them flat if I did so."[44]

Like Francis Bacon, Wittgenstein had a reckless disregard for the material benefits of his family background. In 1913, shortly after the death of his father, he simply gave away all his money. The most magnificent and art historically important gesture was a series of private grants, including twenty thousand kronen each to the poets Georg Trakl and Rilke, as well as to the artist Oscar Kokoschka and the architect Adolf Loos, and one hundred thousand kronen in all to the "Kunstler" of Austria. Unfortunately, it will not help the argument to include Wittgenstein among the Modernists to learn that of Trakl's poems he once wrote: "I do not understand them, but their tone makes me happy. It is the tone of true genius."[45] The gift coincided almost precisely with the end of the Austro-Hungarian empire, when Hungary declared war on Serbia. When World War I came, he never took advantage of his social rank in the army as a recruit, although he befriended educated officers. The experience changed him and his thought, and even Russell realized that Wittgenstein brought back from the war the capacity to carry philosophy into areas that Russell himself could not cover.

That is how, in effect, Wittgenstein became the more Modern of the two, somewhat as Strauss moved on past the tradition-bound Hofmannsthal in a similar collaborative situation. Under fire, close to death, he gained new perspective on the relationship between technical philosophy and reality. "But now, in this the worst summer of danger and defeat, somewhere between the shells and the bullets, he began to feel that the two were connected; that grasping the essence of propositions or of an operation had something to do with adopting the right attitude toward life. No longer does his attitude toward his philosophy merely exhibit the same structure as his attitude toward life: the two are now identified. The critic of Russell is fused in the reader of Dostoevsky."[46] At the end of hostilities in 1917, Wittgenstein was taken prisoner and sent to a camp at Cassino, where Franz Parak saw him in dire straits: "He had a thin face and a noble profile, was of middle height, and, to judge by his figure and general appearance, was not yet thirty years old. . . . But the really striking thing about him was his manner of speaking: it conveyed an extraordinary definiteness. There was a characteristic movement of his head too: usually it was bowed, but from time to time he would throw it back and direct his gaze into the distance. This was Ludwig Wittgenstein."[47] He refused to let his family extricate him, and his first action upon returning from duty was to give away more money to his brothers and sisters and take up residence in modest quarters. In 1926, when his inheritance was supposed to come to him, he made sure he received none. "He would not like to see his family poor, because in their case they would be losing such power as they had. It is implausible though that Wittgenstein meant to renounce power for himself: rather he wanted only what power he could produce for himself from his own personality."[48]

The famous story of Russell's arranging for Wittgenstein's brilliant *Tractatus* to be published while he was still in the prison camp has been told many times. At this point, Russell knew that his heir-apparent had been found. "Perhaps the most perfect example I have ever known of genius as traditionally conceived—passionate, profound, intense, and dominating," he said of Wittgenstein. "I have the most perfect intellectual sympathy with him. . . . I love him and feel he will solve the problem that I am too old to solve. All kinds of vital problems that are raised by my work, but want a fresh mind and the vigor of youth. He is the young man one hopes for." Russell was cranking out his *Theory of Knowledge* at the breathless pace of ten pages a day when Wittgenstein delivered the critical remark that pulled it up short—the problem with applying mathematical certainty to philosophy. The two of them contrived a way to pass the crown and honor the dynasty of Russell's thought in what rapidly became, and has remained to this day, the era of Wittgenstein. "The idea that Russell repeats again and again of handing over the subject of mathematical logic to Wittgenstein was taken perfectly seriously by both of them, and, if it was felt as a relief by Russell, it was, correspondingly, felt as a great burden of responsibility by Wittgenstein. He had to solve the problems he was working on, he felt, because nobody else either could or would deal with them. It was as if he had been given an important and difficult task by God Himself, and he refused to take it lightly."[49]

Then the predictable denouement occurred. Wittgenstein suddenly bolted for Iceland and took up a life of ascetic withdrawal, violently breaking with Russell. In a letter of 27 May 1913, Russell wrote: "We were both cross from the heat—I showed him a crucial part of what I have been writing. He said it was all wrong, not realizing the difficulties—I feel in my bones that he must be right, and that he has seen something that I have missed. Well, well,—it is the younger generation knocking at the door."[50] Decades later, while never disavowing the contribution of Wittgenstein's early work, Russell decried the imperious posturing and metaphysical tenor of Wittgenstein's musings before his acolytes in the 1940s: "He, himself, as usual, is oracular and emits his opinion as if it were a Czar's ukase, but humbler folk can hardly content themselves with this procedure."[51]

After such synergy, the differences between Russell and Wittgenstein become more important. Russell believed that there was always a key to a unified knowledge of the world, feeling at one stage that logic, then mathematics, and even physics offered the answers to the science and philosophy of the time, as biology had been Darwin's answer. With tremendous enthusiasm and the exuberant confidence in being right that he had from the start, Russell embraced one paradigm after another. Another way to describe Russell's theoretical universe is "luxuriant" in that in his mind it exceeded all there really was. The term recalls the premium Delacroix placed on luxuriance, or the ornamental opulence of a Hofmannsthal opera. Wittgenstein and, it will be seen, Balthus took a different approach to the precious objects of their thought and art. They veered toward Minimalism by austerely stripping away the old-fashioned clutter of overelaboration to conduct their examinations in a crisper, more focused light. The contrast between Russell and Wittgenstein can even be felt in hefting the tomes of the former and comparing them with the slim volumes of the latter. The tone of their inquiry often starts in a similar way, exemplified by this passage from the opening of Russell's *Problems of Philosophy*: "Is there any knowledge in the world which is so certain that no reasonable man could doubt it? This question, which at first sight might not seem difficult, is really one of the most difficult that can be asked. When we have realized the obstacles in the way of a straightforward and confident answer, we shall be well launched on the study of philosophy—for philosophy is merely the attempt to answer such ultimate questions, not carelessly and dogmatically, as we do in ordinary life and even in the sciences, but critically after exploring all that makes such questions puzzling, and after realizing all the vagueness and confusion that underlie our ordinary ideas."[52]

The luxuriance of Russell is found in his love of generality and the view of the whole, far more freedom than Wittgenstein would ever allow. Russell laid the foundation for a tradition in contemporary thought that led from Wittgenstein through A. J. Ayer, W.V.O. Quine, Otto Neurath, Rudolf Carnap, and Kurt Gödel among mathematicians, as well as Alan Turing (credited with inventing the binary computer), John von Neumann, Gilbert Ryle, Saul Kripke, and a strong line of philosophical followers devoted to logical and analytical approaches to problems. As one historian summarizes his legacy, highlighting his modernity:

> In a sense, there has always been an "analytical philosophy" and Bertrand Russell's achievement was to dress it for the twentieth century. In the same sense, however, there has always been a "phenomenology," and Husserl did for it what Russell did for the analytical. In both cases, though, it was the concentration on the meaning of a thing or object as distinguished from another thing or object that distinguished their philosophies from those of their predecessors. This is the twentieth century in philosophy. Now at the end of the century, like the two Ways—Swann's and Guermantes'—in Proust's novel, Russell's analysis and Husserl's phenomenology have found themselves meeting in a new discipline called cognitive studies. Atomic logic provides the digital hardware required for understanding and modeling the mind's basic operations. Phenomenology provides the goal of exploration. And all to answer the twentieth century's favorite question, What was I thinking? And logic and arithmetic are still where the two men left them—untrustworthy as a Pentium chip.[53]

The reason Wittgenstein seems so much closer to us as Postmoderns is the negative construction he opposed to Russell's assurance. Rather than a unified theory amassed in one tightly argued opus, his books, gathered by students and editors after his death for publication, are fragmented, raising more questions than they answer, circling the solutions to basic problems only to abandon the ground in favor of meticulously rephrasing the question over and again. This negative cast is a matter of Wittgenstein's method, but it also applies to the grim and purposeful view of his life's work: "I ought to have done something positive with my life, to have become a star in the sky. Instead of which I remained stuck on earth and now I am gradually fading out."[54]

For all their differences in style, Wittgenstein was similar to Russell in that he focused on the totality of what could be known and thought. Inevitably, in both cases this ambition involved their upbringing as well as their writing. The urge to alter all applied to their mediation between the past and the aristocratic tradition in which they were raised and a future in which that reliable order would be just a memory. As Monk observes, "Wittgenstein was attempting to change everything. His pessimism about the effectiveness of his work is related to his conviction that the way we look at things is determined, not by our philosophical beliefs, but by our culture, by the way we are brought up. . . . Wittgenstein had a tradition—one that he loved dearly: the German/Austrian literature, art and (especially) music of the nineteenth century; but he was acutely aware that, for the greater part of his life, this tradition was no longer alive. In this sense, he was not so much unhappily in love, as desperately bereaved."[55]

Whether the hierarchy was one of noble titles, wealth, academic titles, or military rank, most of Wittgenstein's life was spent in an uneasy tension with an existing order. For all the attention that is paid to his possible homosexuality and *ex post facto*, long-distance diagnoses of his depression, one phase in his life is neglected in the exploration of the relationship between his biography and his philosophy: his five years of military service. Wittgenstein, who rose through the ranks from *korporal* to *leutnant*, was fired upon and stood his ground at the front, earning a recommendation in June 1916 for bravery for holding his point. During precisely that time, not in the walled gardens and silent libraries of Cambridge, he wrote his *Tractatus*. Ostensibly a dissertation on logic, it held a message between the lines. Even if it is read from the simply biographical viewpoint, as the intensified meditations of a sentry on duty, the opening of the *Tractatus* has powerful resonance:

> I know that this world exists.
> That I am placed in it like my eye in a visual field.
> That something about it is problematic, which we call its meaning.
> The world is everything that is the case.[56]

Many forces converge in this epochal passage. Wittgenstein becomes a nearly powerless witness to the demise of the old world order and his beloved empire—the historical becomes personal. An already acute reflexivity about perception is sharpened by survival instincts and military discipline. Fighting the temptation of complete passivity under the circumstances, he concentrates upon the nagging problem of meaning and ventures an astonishingly broad proposition about the world and how it may be construed. In strict philosophical terms, Monk points out, Wittgenstein synthesizes the realism of Frege, the idealism of Schopenhauer, and the solipsism of Otto Weininger.[57] We might add to that the echo of an important Modern principle of poetics, adapted from Baudelaire by both Mallarmé and Eliot and summarized by the phrase, "to purify the dialect of the tribe." Monk hits the nail squarely on the head in identifying a rare moment of identity in the work: "It is as if the personal and the philosophical had become fused; ethics and logic—the two aspects of the 'duty to oneself'—had finally come together, not merely as two aspects of the same personal task, but as two parts of the same philosophical work."[58]

If Wittgenstein's personality resembled anybody in the history of philosophy, even to the circumstances of his birth, it was Michel de Montaigne. Born to a wealthy Jewish mother, Antoinette de Louppes (Lopez) of Toulouse, and a minor nobleman of a very distinguished house in the Dordogne, Montaigne was superbly educated, first at home in Latin and then at the University of Guyenne in Bordeaux. Like Wittgenstein, whose friend (possibly lover) David Pinsent was a catalyst in his development as a philosopher, Montaigne's greatest work was composed as an elegiac response to his great friendship, from his days at court, with Etienne de la Boetie. Conspicuous modesty and a passion for propriety were characteristics of both Wittgenstein and Montaigne: "I correct the faults of inadvertence, not those of habit," Montaigne wrote to a critic.[59] Although Montaigne's retreat, at age thirty-eight, was neither permanent nor absolute (he served two terms as mayor of Bordeaux and was gentleman-in-ordinary to Charles IX and Henry III, ending as a supporter of Henry of Navarre), it set a tone and precedent. An aristocrat withdraws from a world in which his name as well as his capabilities confer power upon him. He learns to approach philosophical and literary questions in a probing yet not nearly so scientific way as his predecessors. In this, the points of resemblance to Wittgenstein begin to mount. Twice in his life, Wittgenstein disappeared without warning to Norway to give himself a set of serene conditions under which he could complete his circling style of rumination. Both Montaigne and Wittgenstein were inclined to the "essay" as opposed to the treatise. They also drew extensively upon their aristocratic backgrounds for material.

As one anecdotal example, we move ahead in Wittgenstein's career to a series of seminars and conversations on aesthetics and culture offered not in a classroom but in private rooms at Cambridge in 1938. Wittgenstein held spellbound a knot of students that included Yorick Smythies, Rush Rhees, and James Taylor, each of whom helped to assemble his thoughts in book form, published posthumously. It is vintage Wittgenstein material, elegantly phrased yet laborious in its tenacity regarding the correct use of every word. This passage catches the eye because, uncharacteristically (Wittgenstein's philosophy is anything but autobiographical), it does touch upon his upbringing. They are talking about taste, and the problem that Wittgenstein will not relinquish to an easy formulation is an elaborate contextualization. Probing the meaning of the words *taste* and *tradition*, rather than creating guidelines or establishing rules of connoisseurship (which his students would have accepted, gladly), Wittgenstein pursues a language-oriented course of analysis. He progresses from what is familiarly known to what is alien: "In describing musical taste you have to describe whether children give concerts, whether women do or whether men only give them, etc., etc. In aristocratic circles in Vienna people had [such and such] a taste, then it came into bourgeois circles and women joined choirs, etc. This is an example of tradition in music."[60] The topic is ideal. It brings the Modern thinker face-to-face with the question of tradition and focuses upon the present after tracing briefly how Wittgenstein reaches it.

Then the talk takes a bizarre turn as Rush Rhees, one of Wittgenstein's disciples—would he have had so many devoted young transcribers if he hadn't been an aristocratic presence?—asks if there is a tradition in "Negro art" and whether Europeans would be equipped to appreciate it. Suddenly Wittgenstein, renowned for his poise, falls apart. He is at a loss as he moves from terra firma to what we now recognize as the province of multiculturalism, what was in his own time purely theoretical. He spins his wheels for a moment (this is after all a transcript, a fact we further apprehend while perusing the footnotes), and they grip only when he gets back to European roots:

> What would tradition in Negro Art be? That women wear cut-grass skirts? etc, etc. I don't know. I don't know how Frank Dobson's appreciation of Negro Art compares with an educated Negro's. If you say he appreciates it, I don't yet know what this means. He may fill his room with objects of Negro Art. Does he just say, "Ah!" Or does he do what the best Negro musicians do? Or does he agree or disagree with so and so about it? You may call this appreciation. Entirely different to an educated Negro's. Though an educated Negro may also have Negro objects of art in his room. The Negro's and Frank Dobson's are different appreciations altogether. You do something different with them.

It is one of the most awkward moments in Wittgenstein's usually seamless flow of thought. Fortunately, the conversation shifts. Wittgenstein changes topic to "a cultured taste in painting" of the day as opposed to that of the fifteenth century: "There are lots of people, well-offish, who have been to good schools, who can afford to travel about and see the Louvre, etc., and who know a lot about and can talk fluently about dozens of painters. There is another person who has seen very few paintings, but who looks intensely at one or two paintings which make a profound impression on him. Another person who is broad, neither deep nor wide. Another person who is very narrow, concentrated and circumscribed. Are these different kinds of appreciation? They may all be called 'appreciation.'"[61]

Coincidentally or not, the conversation takes another twist and within a few pages, at least, becomes rather despondent as Wittgenstein and his disciples contemplate the "deterioration" of culture and specifically of intellectual life. If only they knew. "An old style can be translated, as it were, into a newer language; it can, one might say, be performed afresh at a tempo appropriate to our own times. To do this is really only to reproduce. That is what my building work amounted to. But what I mean is not giving an old style a fresh trim. You don't take old forms and fix them up to suit the latest taste. No, you are really speaking the old language, perhaps without realizing it, but you are speaking it in a way that is appropriate to the modern world, without on that account necessarily being in accordance with its taste."[62] That is a superb rationale for Neo-Classicisim.

Acquainted with the old order and brought roughly into the new by his experience in the war, Wittgenstein here gives us a prime example of an elegant mind attempting to cope with that change, right in front of his adoring students. He accomplishes this with style, and he manages to articulate a set of problems general and complex enough to keep subsequent generations talking and writing, even painting, without surpassing him, including the artist Jasper Johns, who incorporated Wittgenstein's infamous duck-rabbit paradox in several paintings; Jean Francois Lyotard; Stanley Cavell; and the philosopher and novelist Maurice Blanchot. In an essay entitled "Wittgenstein's Problem," Blanchot returns often to the idea of a luxuriant philosophical universe and shows how Wittgenstein's philosophy can become a part of literary theory. Blanchot's homage is made complete by the imitation of Wittgenstein's style as well as the direct approach to a question that haunted French literary theory of the 1970s and later, the problematic adequacy of language to thought. It begins with the shortfall of "forms," and Blanchot invokes Flaubert and Levi-Strauss to help place the issue in a literary and cultural, rather than exclusively philosophical, context: "'Too many things' is the Other of language, which is itself, then, regarded as 'forms,' the latter being assumed to be merely finite in number (as Flaubert and Levi-Strauss postulate), while things would correspond to some kind of infinity (or indefiniteness)."[63]

As the passage continues, Blanchot redirects the argument along the lines of current French literary theory, specifically the adroit way in which the *nouvelle romanciers* constructed texts upon a minimal premise. The origin of this was in a famous letter of Flaubert to Louise Colet, widely cited by Modern French writers, that he hoped to write "a novel about nothing." A connection both historical and critical can be made here to the work of Swinburne, which flowed around an absent center. Swinburne's work appeared side-by-side with that of Flaubert, as mentioned in a previous chapter. Blanchot brings Wittgenstein's thought into this tradition of the discourse on nothingness and turns the formula around:

> But the characteristic of a form of language is that it only contains something as long as it contains nothing. Which amounts to concluding that if there are "not enough forms," this is true only for a language in that it only contains something as long as it contains nothing. Which amounts to concluding that if there are "not enough forms," this is true only for a language that considers form to be already and merely a thing. In other words, even if there is only a finite number of structures, that is, a determined number of kinds of relations, as long as just one of them is such that it expresses (holds) the infinite, Flaubert's statement can be turned around, and one should not complain about "too many things" but rather "never enough things," the entire universe, then, being not enough to fill the Danaids' barrel.[64]

For Blanchot, the "Other of speech" is a vital question, particularly in his capacity as novelist. He continues, albeit with a slight historical innacuracy: "At this point we come very close to Wittgenstein's problem, as corrected by Bertrand Russell: that every language has a structure about which one can say nothing in that language, but that there must be another language dealing with the structure of the first and possessing a new structure about which one cannot say anything except in a third language—and so forth."[65] It is worthwhile to reflect on how much, thanks in part to his background, Wittgenstein understood this Chinese box of languages within languages, codes within codes. The trick is an awareness of rank and hierarchy. Think of how fluently he changed from German to English to French even as a schoolboy, when this notion of an infinite series of languages may have had its birth.

6

The Irish Ascendant

WILLIAM BUTLER YEATS AND FRANCIS BACON

Before the grim nightmare of council houses and city streets penned by barbed wire, Ireland knew, even as late the prewar twentieth century, a twilight of Anglo-Irish society based in vast estates, where an uneasy ambivalence about both Crown and country fostered a courtly alienation from both. In that elegant if troubled world, two leading figures of Modern aesthetics had their beginnings. One rhapsodized about the beauty and heroism of the nobility, and one desperately hated the whole scene, fled, and spent a lifetime covering up the fact that he was of it. The first was William Butler Yeats, who knew the civility of country house life as a "poor relation" and guest. The man who escaped was the painter Francis Bacon, most of whose closest friends (a problematic term in his case) never even knew that he was to the manor born, having grown up on a great estate and come within a whisper of being titled.

There are many eloquent portraits of the last days of the Anglo-Irish aristocracy in literature and memoirs, but the most endearing and enduring are the elegies of the house poet of Coole Park, William Butler Yeats. Although Bacon is identified more with the poetry of T. S. Eliot than of Yeats, thanks to paintings that are titled after Eliot poems, it was Yeats who knew Bacon's origins best, and it is a very powerful poem by Yeats—"The Second Coming"—that Bacon proclaimed his favorite, ranking it alongside the *Oresteia*. Bacon was heir to a great estate, but Yeats was more romantically drawn to the gentility of the Anglo-Irish country house life. As a child, Yeats summered at the mansion of Major Pollexfen, the distinguished, thoroughly Edwardian cousin on his mother's side whose aristocratic blood gave later fantasies of the poet's own nobility at least a dim foundation in reality. For all his Wordsworthian celebrations of the wisdom of the wandering indigent, Yeats's highest lyrical instincts were roused during the two decades of guesthood, on and off, at the vast estate of Coole Park, where he indulged his taste for "all lovely intricacies of a house," such as "the old sun-broken trees / That cast their shadows upon road and bridge," the riding to the hounds (he never mounted up), and the hunting exploits of the noble Major Gregory ("Soldier, soldier, horseman he, / And yet he had the intensity / To have published all to be a world's delight.") As with Sand's reverent hagiography of the renaissance woman her grandmother represented to her, so Yeats's portrait of the all-round talents of Major Gregory underscores his deep respect for the superiority of the cultivated gentry: "And all he did done perfectly / As though he had but that one trade done." In sum, Major Gregory was the model that the aristocracy is meant to be: "Soldier, scholar, horseman, he, / As 'twere all life's epitome." Along with his patron, Lady Gregory, Yeats compiled a collection of Celtic tales that informed his poetry and lent narrative and symbolic structures to his plays. She was the typical aristocratic amateur, bent on preserving the history and wisdom of the cottagers of her own vast estate with the future Nobel laureate at her side as she gathered oral history door-to-door. Yeats's transformation of this "low" source into "high" lyric poetry functions in much the same way that Hungarian dances and folk tunes did as rough materials for Liszt.

The pure originality of traditional Irish legends is far easier to apprehend as grist for Yeats's mill than the ambiguous legacy of opulence that informs late poems such as "Coole Park and Ballylee" and "Meditations in Time of Civil War." The problem is that as an Irishman and a would-be nationalist he is already near-guilty about his feelings of allegiance to the Anglo landowners. Beyond that, his sense of wonder and delight about the aesthetics of the typically eighteenth-century or nineteenth-century Anglo-Irish country house is mixed with the desire to be Modern. In the "Ancestral Houses" section of "Meditations in Time of Civil War" (1923), Yeats paints a watercolor elegy of "selectness" and "gentleness," and then hangs a questioning cloud over it with the suggestion that the "indifferent garden deities" that preside are also powerless, emptying the scene not just of its human players but of the divine as well. There are just a few too many instances of the word *rich* for the tone of resentment to be missed:

> Surely among a rich man's flowering lawns,
> Amid the rustle of his planted hills,
> Life overflows without ambitious pains,
> And rains down life until the basin spills.

Within this depiction of the fountain "in which shadows the inherited glory of the rich" is a haunted emptiness, a suggestion that the patrician ease, alien from Yeats's own nagging ambitions as both artist and politician, is gone. Hence the repeated "what if" in these lines:

O what if gardens where the peacock strays
With delicate feet upon old terraces,
Or else all Juno from an urn displays
Before the indifferent garden deities,
O what if leveled lawns and graveled ways
Where slippered Contemplation finds his ease,
And Childhood a delight for every sense
But take on greatness with our violence?
Escutcheoned doors, polished floors,—
Portraits—those things the greatest of mankind
Consider most to magnify, or to bless
But take our greatness with our bitterness?

For Yeats, Wilde, Beckett, Joyce, Heaney, Bacon, and other Modern Irish figures in the arts, greatness comes at a price. The bitterness arises from the struggle between the Irish and English, a conflict of baffling endurance in which few heroes can be acclaimed. Its gray, banal annals, unlike the dramatic tragedies and triumphs of conquest in other wars, rob poets and painters of the best materials for traditional genres. The siege mentality is never ideal for the arts, although some have made the most of it. Samuel Beckett certainly is identified with the theme, and when Susan Sontag directed *Waiting for Godot* in Sarajevo during the hostilities, she made that aspect of the play all the more literal. Others have found turmoil to be fertile creative territory. Bacon's family, for example, was caught on the wrong side of this conflict both in terms of their own safety (their home came under attack by Irish nationalists) and if one subscribes to the notion that an artist should be "politically correct." Bacon's motives for leaving Ireland, as we will see, were more personal than those of Beckett or even Joyce, who also yearned for a setting more understanding of his sexuality. Bacon told biographers in later years that the "violence" faced by his grandmother in particular, who was married to the local (Royalist) chief of police, was a powerful influence upon his young mind. The searing explosiveness of his paintings, the fear and pressing sense of enclosure, can be attributed in part to the boyhood worries shared with the siege mentality of the aristocracy during the Troubles.

Yet for Yeats this theme leads to the elegiac equation of beauty and aristocracy, both fading as the modern age moves on. His love of the Anglo gentry's way of life shows, and the ambiguity involved is rich soil for poetry. There is room here for one anecdote about the Nobel laureate, so smitten with the ceremony of the Norwegian court that he, like Balthus, as well as Beethoven and so many others, craved an aristocratic lineage badly enough to lie about it. According to a reminiscence of George Moore published first in the *English Review* of 1913, Yeats bought a coat of arms for his bookplate, pursuing his connection to Mary Yeats of Lifford (died 1673) as well as borrowing a motif from a Jacobean cream jug with the Butler crest. As Moore mockingly recalls, "We asked ourselves why Willy Yeats should feel himself called upon to denounce the class to which he himself belonged essentially . . . with so admirable a parentage it did not seem necessary that a man should look back for an ancestor, and we had laughed at the story . . . that on one occasion Yeats was crooning over AE's fire he had said that if he had his rights he would be Duke of Ormonde, and that AE had answered, 'In any case, Willie, you are overlooking your father.' "[1]

This love of the aristocracy is the basis for his passionate tribute to the sisters Eva Gore-Booth and Con Markiewicz in "their old Georgian mansion." It stirs in the "intellectual sweetness" of "Coole Park, 1929," through which an honor roll of heroes brings together artists and aristocrats, including the playwright John Millington Synge as well as Henry Hyde and upper-class figures such as Hugh Lane or Shawe-Taylor that people "a scene well set and excellent company." The same drawing room mise-en-scène lends its richness to "Coole Park and Ballylee, 1931," which opens with a view down the long gallery of ancestral portraits found in every country house, including Bacon's homes: "Old noble heads, old pictures everywhere / Great rooms where travelled men and children / Found content or joy."

The estate itself becomes a sacred "spot whereon the families lived and died" and the "gardens rich in memory glorified," yet the loss of that grandeur ("all that great glory spent") leaves a quandary. The family becomes nomadic ("some poor Arab tribesman and his tent"). Here is a Modern, Joycean theme (it will figure prominently in our consideration of Bacon, too). For Yeats, it is resolved in part only when he restores an ancient Norman keep that is the setting and subject of his great pair of late volumes, *The Tower* and *The Winding Stair*. In the final lines of "Coole Park and Ballylee, 1931," as the annals come to a close, he rises to a philosophical height from which a vantage is gained over his own situation as Modern thinker:

> We were the last romantics—chose for theme
> Traditional sanctity and loveliness;

Whatever's written on what poets name
The book of the people, whatever most can bless
The mind of man or elevate a rhyme
But all is changed, that high horse riderless,
Though mounted in that saddle Homer rode
Where the swan drifts upon a darkening flood.

The issue is succession, and the problem is a discontinuity from one generation to the next. By proclaiming the advent of the "last romantics," Yeats poses the closing of an era and a tradition, asserting with the "riderless horse" that the laureateship of this lyricism is empty. As Harold Bloom and others have shown, the persistence of Romanticism in Modern poetics is due in part to Yeats and his nostalgic capacity for clinging to the recent past. This is similar in feeling to the role of the "noble rider" in Wallace Stevens's essay, "The Noble Rider and the Sound of Words," its title adopted in turn from an iconic watercolor of a hard-riding Cossack by Wassily Kandinsky. For both Yeats and Stevens, the advent of the Modern era brings bitterness and uncertainty, as is particularly figured in "the darkening flood" of that last line. It anticipates an even greater catastrophe in "The Second Coming," a poem that Bacon loved and discussed with biographers and critics. In particular, Bacon was enamored of that brutal ending, the advent of the "rough beast." In conversation with Michael Peppiatt, his most recent and reliable biographer, within the context of the ability of his pictures to shock the sensibility, Bacon points to the prophetic quality of the Yeats image to grab and immobilize an audience: "They are violent and yet it's not enough. Something much more horrendeous is the last line in Yeats's 'The Second Coming,' which is a prophetic poem: 'And what rough beast, its hour come round at last, / Slouches towards Bethlehem to be born?' That's stronger than any war painting. It's more extraordinary than even one of the horrors of war pictures, because that's just a literal horror, whereas the Yeats is a horror which has a whole vibration in it, a prophetic quality."[2]

Bacon is a far more difficult nut to crack, both biographically and critically, than Yeats, in part because the place of Yeats in the history of literary Modernism is so secure and that of Bacon is just now being redefined by art historians eager to redress the error of leaving figural painting out of the canon. In his recent study, written to accompany the rehanging of the Museum of Modern Art's permanent collection in a manner that for the first time offers emphasis to Bacon's place in history, curator Robert Storr numbers Bacon among his "anti-Modern Moderns." He also contends that Bacon was a Postmodernist long before the term was coined, for his appropriation not just of works by Cimabue, van Gogh, and Velázquez but of photographs by Eadweard Muybridge and John Deakin and film stills from Sergei Eisenstein's *Potemkin* (1925). Storr writes:

> Eye-catching, gut twisting, and arch, those paintings were rituals of eroticized violence in which no real damage was ever done to the fastidiously maintained integrity of Bacon's pictorial conception. Like the sadomasochist relations they frequently portray, his art was predicated on an unspoken contract, a pact between the painter and tradition that precluded irrevocably destructive acts, even as Bacon transgressed the rules governing the kind of plush, gilt-framed Salon pictures his output superficially and subversively resembled. Although elegantly morbid, Bacon's work is a hex against the death of painting at the hands of the hard-edged abstract painters who preferred geometric forms to the human figure. As much as Bacon enjoyed the role of social outcast—gambler, drunkard, homosexual outlaw—he enjoyed playing bad-boy antimodernist even more.[3]

As with Balthus, Storr views Bacon as a "literary expressionist," and since his thesis is still untested in the arena of criticism and scholarship, he feels compelled to add a cautionary note about Bacon's weaknesses ("the formal repetitiousness and shrieking emotional monotony of his work").[4]

Bacon is not easy. The first problem is the glass. Between you and the lush, virtuoso essays in paint and pastel is this annoying, inexplicable barrier imposed by the artist, not by some fastidious museum curator or a cautious collector afraid of vandalism when a painting goes on loan. From the mid-1960s to the end of his career in 1982, Bacon had every finished painting securely fronted by heavy glass and encased in a gold frame. It was a time when the galleries were hanging large, unframed canvases that deliberately used the relationship between their own physical edges and the wall as part of the composition, to the extent that connoisseurs would press their heads to the wall and examine the edge of the stretchers for the painted marks there and the layering of the surface. Bacon, ever the contrarian, sealed those edges off. He offered this cryptic explanation in an interview in 1974: "I don't believe art is available; it's rare and curious and should be completely isolated; one is more aware of its magic the more it is isolated."[5] This distancing posture is an unusual attitude for a painter, and the complete opposite of Balthus, who forbids glass in front of his paintings. In other ways, however, Balthus and Bacon, who knew one another well, are similar, particularly with regard to the way they fooled people about who they were. With diagonally opposite agendas (one wanted to be thought of as a Cockney tough guy, the other as a Polish gentleman) they wound up twisting art historians by blurring their personal history.

Bacon lied about who he was. "I had no upbringing at all. I used simply to work in my father's farm near Dublin. I read almost nothing as a child—as for pictures, I was hardly aware they existed," he told Peppiatt, with whom he feigned cooperation.[6] As Peppiatt is compelled to note, "To be thought of as a totally natural, uncultivated talent apparently suited Bacon's purpose, no doubt allowing him more freedom; and for that reason, perhaps, the fragmentary information he offered about his early years presented them as disaster-ridden and dangerous, with little comfort and no culture."[7] Nearly the same problem is presented by Balthus, except that while Bacon began life in comfortable surroundings with a distinguished lineage and later denied this life of privilege, Balthus acquired wealth and concocted an illustrious family heritage to go along with it.

When Francis Bacon was a miserable little boy finishing his pudding in the huge dining room of Enwood, Herfordshire, once the home of the earl of Oxford, as he emptied his plate under the stern eye of his disapproving father, he would reach the family crest of Sir Francis Bacon, first Viscount of St. Albans and, in the eyes of some fanatics still, the author of Shakespeare's plays. Bacon's father commissioned the plates, claiming descent from Sir Francis's half brother, Nicholas. The Baconian lineage was far more important to his father than it was to the artist, although in later years as he caroused in London or Monte Carlo, Bacon bragged with relish of his link to the Elizabethan pederast, supposed author of Shakespeare's plays, who at his death in 1626 stiffed his creditors for some £22,000 in gambling debts. Given the brouhaha over Bacon's estate and the alleged swindling of his Cockney boyfriend and heir by the Marlborough Gallery, news of which surfaced in the spring of 2000, there does seem to be some sort of hereditary propensity toward messy inheritances. Bacon's father was a very English trainer of race horses in County Kildare, Ireland, who lived in one gorgeous country house after another. He revered the viscount but was forced to sell a cache of his letters to the duke of Portland to pay his own immense gambling debts—a habit his son would also develop.

The philosopher-viscount was not by any means Bacon's only hereditary connection to aristocracy in the arts, as Lords Byron and Leighton figure in his inheritance and upbringing as well. The artist's great-grandfather left Eton to join the Hussars, becoming one of Wellington's top generals (the youngest officer on the field at Waterloo) and then assembling his own private army in the service of Don Pedro of Portugal. His wife, Lady Charlotte Harley, was the colorful daughter of the fifth earl of Oxford and the woman to whom Byron, her lover, dedicated *Childe Harold* (calling her Ianthe, for whom Bacon's sister was named). When

Lady Charlotte eventually emigrated to Australia, her carriage bore the crest and motto "Crede Byron." Bacon himself, had circumstances been somewhat different—that is, had his father not caught him trying on women's underwear and thrown him out of the house at age fifteen—might well have inherited the earldom. There was one problem, though. Queen Victoria offered to restore the rank of earl of Oxford to the family, but his grandfather, a Boer War veteran with that hereditary penchant for gambling, demurred for fear of exposing himself to suits from his creditors.

On his mother's side, immense wealth garnered from the making of shell casings for the military created a world of aristocratic splendor at Jesmond Towers, a vast Gothic mansion built in the nineteenth century near Newcastle, where the young artist spent his holidays. During World War I he visited often, and his grandmother became a powerful influence upon him. There Bacon wandered long dark hallways adorned with paintings by Frederick, Lord Leighton as well as other fashionable Pre-Raphaelites, including William Etty and Charles Mitchell. Decades later, the first and most congenial of his London studio-residence-showcases would turn out to be the former townhouse and studio of the Pre-Raphaelite eminence Sir John Everett Millais. There are two valid reasons for pausing to ponder the details of life at Jesmond Towers and their relation to Bacon's art. The architectural ideas and idiosyncrasies he encountered found their way into his compositions by way of direct and inventively transformed quotations. An overlooked episode in Bacon's life is his brief stint, before he turned to painting, as an interior designer, albeit one who tended to use stainless steel furniture (some of which also makes its appearance in the paintings). The other aesthetic stimulus in his formative years that brought about a late response was the drama and technical wizardry of the Pre-Raphaelite paintings in particular. Bacon would become a painter of large, potent narratives and portraits. Finally, and practically speaking, as the nephew of a patron and collector, he knew the collectors' patter and the psychology of owning and acquiring major works of art.

Bacon recreated in the background of his agonizing paintings of screaming popes and vicious dogs the graceful architectural curves of Jesmond Towers, its bow windows and arches drawn from memory. Even by comparison with Bacon's own childhood home in Kildare, with its eighteen rooms and nine grooms (with more than a few of whom Bacon experienced his earliest sex) and five indoor servants and where the boy Bacon was only expected to be seen at teatime, the elaborate splendor of Jesmond Towers was spectacular and lavish enough to be intimidating. One of Bacon's biographers, David Farson, discussed the artist's upbringing with Earl "Gray" Gowrie, who grew up in almost identical circumstances in the same village as Bacon and is now one of the most elegant and powerful figures in the art world, thanks in part to his high rank at Christie's (before the scandal) in London and his service on the Arts Council. Gowrie reacted to the dramatic contrast between the distinguished lineage and the image of himself projected by Bacon: "I became increasingly bemused by the discovery that he had been brought up in luxury and style. This cast him in a different light, as a man whose background conditioned him to expect the best. It explained something about the grand style of his personality. People who are deraciné never entirely break free."[8]

While Farson's is an irresponsible, gossip-laced account of Bacon's wild exploits in London's East End and Europe's pleasure palaces (the parallels with Lautrec and the demimonde of Paris are irresistible), his sources are often insightful and he is capable of occasionally shedding light on the most obscure aspects of the study of Bacon. He notes that Bacon's "Pope series" may be related to the paternal connotations of Il Papa, highly charged territory for the artist, whose father mercilessly tried to "make a man of him." Until the moment he was expelled, Bacon lived according to a grand style and the aristocratic codes of the Anglo-Irish landowners that he later in life derided violently in anecdotes. Bacon's identity has always been approached through issues other than Irishness, as critics key in on his homosexuality or his self-abuse through alcohol or even his disability (chronic asthma).

With the growling canines, shrieking baboons, and scowling sphinxes of his most nightmarish paintings, Bacon shows that he has more than one "rough beast" in his repertoire. Like the blurry threat of Yeats's poem, Bacon's beasts are distinct enough from the particulars of history, one conflict or another, to inspire a deeper, more general anxiety. The Baconian bestiary has its beginnings in some of the earliest paintings to come down to us (the artist destroyed hundreds of works, including most of his drawings). The monster who chomps at a bouquet of red roses, poised on one vestigial leg that emerges from a patch of long grass, in an untitled painting of 1943–34 has a powerful hunched back and shadowy, cavernous underbelly. In 1952, upon his return from Africa, Bacon made three paintings of snarling dogs, in part based on the photographer Eadweard Muybridge's motion studies of a mastiff walking, entitled *Dread Walking*. Bacon indicates motion with the trace of paw marks both before and after the white-blue figure of the dog, its red mouth open, the same dark concavity under its hips as Bacon used with the monster, one leg splayed as though it were lame. The dog patrols the Nazi rallying ground patterned after a press photo of Nuremberg, with a light-absorbing dark sky above a band of blue for the horizon. It acts with the elongated shadow of the dog to make the nocturnal tableau all the more menacing. The third painting places the mastiff in a flower bed, with a hint of the trim, level lawns of Yeats's ancestral houses in the lightly brushed green ground, still within the hexagon of the Nazi parade ground motif and against that inky black sky.

Speculating on the connection, one reading would suggest a link between fascism and the hold of the ruling elite over Ireland. As a recent biography of Diana Mosley, one of the Mitford sisters, reveals, the sympathy among British aristocrats for Hitler was not just bizarre but prevalent. Bacon might have been using this, as he did any pretext, to attack his own class. It may have been even more pointed than that if you recall that his mother's family was involved in making weaponry, and one of his most searing experiences was pulling the dead from London buildings after the blitz. A late painting against his hot signature orange ground has an astonishing, threatening image at its center. Aimed right at the viewer is the barrel of a shotgun that thrusts itself from the whirling center of the composition. We have commented earlier in this study upon the distancing gesture of many of the artists under consideration, but this intimidating effect exceeds them all.

Even the recurring urge to destroy his own work may be read in a number of ways. It fits hand and glove with the Modernist questioning of the permanence and fetish status of the art object. By ruining canvases that even in their day were considered expensive, now phenomenally so (in the millions of dollars), he was philosophically attacking the traditional reverence for the work of art. Psychologically, the rage and self-loathing that spurred such violence must indeed have been powerful, however obscure it is today—necessarily, in the absence of journals, letters, and other first-hand documentation. Some artists have, on occasion, found a healthy purgative in ridding their studios of massive quantities of older work, especially in such cases as a brilliant early start, in one style or idea, that has veered in a less than popular direction, making the earlier work a distraction to both the artist and studio visitors or dealers. One artist of my acquaintance slashed every canvas on the premises when his wife left him, and another lost thousands of drawings in a warehouse fire. Both contend that it was the best of all possible events as a means of clearing and unburdening. Few artists make good self-editors, and too often an early idea becomes stale with repetition, so Bacon's instinct, like the periodic forest fires that bring new growth, was primarily healthy. It was also in strict accord with his tendency to disguise origins, whether they were his aristocratic roots or his preliminary studies for paintings in progress.

The pinnacle of this series is a Whistlerian nocturne, *Man with Dog* (1953), in which the addition in blurred grays and greens of a man's legs from the waist down (it would seem in a suit, although that may be the knowledge of another series of Bacon portraits interfering) puts a human element in the picture. The upper curtain of black now slants across the canvas at a precipitous angle, and the landscape is no longer the stadium at Nuremberg but a London street. The mastiff, braced against moving to the black curb of the sidewalk above a fluvial blue street, is created by a pair of stiff forelegs making a gothic arch in the front, with a blur of motion behind. From its collar to the unseen hand of the man walking it flashes an exquisite linked leash of white dabs, hurrying back and forth just as the light chain and tassel does in the papal portraits. The motif invokes, as the curators of the retrospective point out in the exhibition catalog, an influential Futurist work, *Leash in Motion* (*Guinzaglio in Moto*) by Giacomo Balla, painted in 1912 and seen by Bacon at the Tate in 1952.

The London street is conjured by the solid aspect of the drain and the curb, as well as the man in the suit and the leashed dog. The heavy grays on green offer an almost metallic effect, rather like what you obtain by using hard repeated strokes of a pencil to build up a sheen of blue-black (an effect that Brice Marden brilliantly attains in his drawings). The current of blue in the street is caught by the subtly curving strokes, counter to it, of the drain's grate. The virtuoso touch, however, is that dangling trail of light that constitutes the leash, as compelling as its antonym, the smoky shadows cast by the dog (one scholar suggests that the man's legs are shadows cast on a wall).

In August 1953, the same year he created the series of the dogs, Bacon completed his *Study of a Baboon*, which shares many of the same compositional devices as the dog paintings—specifically, the dense black upper rectangle of the canvas, the nearly centered image of the animal in an opalescent, brushy knot of black, white, blue, and gray, and the open mouth in a yawn or cry. Where the black horizontal of the curb in *Man Walking Dog* or the blue horizon of the earlier paintings served to mediate between the illuminated and shadowed parts of the dog paintings, the firm black horizontal of the supporting bar of the cage plays the same role in the baboon painting. In both, the horizontal barrier separates one dense, even region of strong color from another across which a swiftly moving brush has rhythmically and lightly left, in curved strokes arching downward as they travel from the painter's left to right, a river-like current or windblown meadow grass. The baboon painting departs from the dog series in the level of innovation and virtuosity to which it pushes the handling of the paint. Just when Bacon was at work on the painting, he was gaining sufficient ground as a rising star on the London contemporary art scene to be asked by dealer John Rothenstein for exhibition catalog essays; and in the context of his praise of Matthew Smith, an English

Fauvist, Bacon explains why Smith takes his place beside Turner and Constable for his ability to make "idea and technique inseparable": "Painting in this sense tends towards a complete interlocking of image and paint, so that the image is the paint and vice versa. Here the brush stroke creates the form and does not merely fill it in. Consequently, every movement of the brush on the canvas alters the shape and implications of the image. That is why real painting is a mysterious and continuous struggle with chance—mysterious because the very substance of the paint, when used in this way, can make such a direct assault upon the nervous system; continuous because the medium is so fluid that every change that is made loses what is already there in the hope of making a fresh gain."[9] Spoken like a true gambler!

This immediacy of "image and paint" through which form is built with brushstrokes is nowhere better demonstrated than in the rendering of the chain-link cage overlaid on the upper half of *Study of a Baboon.* The thick, glossy ridges of black form an impasto pattern completely at odds with the dry, brushy lightness of both the tree and the baboon. Moreover, the downward, swooping, grasslike curves to the painter's left of the baboon's tail sweep diagonally to the right, flowing across the bottom half of the canvas. The left and right extensions of the branches are also gesturally and materially different from those tightly spaced, relatively straight, mechanically regular lines of black that Bacon uses to delineate the cage's steel. Here, as in so many of his paintings, the one-time designer of steel and chrome furniture takes pains to depict a metallic cage around a living creature. The ghostly blue, white, and purple calligraphy of the baboon is a fitting introduction to the cool, transparent evocations of popes, businessmen, lovers, and athletes of later years. Swept and smudged into a disembodied, nervous, glowing torso, the loosely brushed animal suddenly gathers solidity and focus in the tight rendering of its cavernous upper mouth, fangs, and sneering upper lip.

The same contrast between a spontaneous, brushy treatment of the lower figure and a substantiated, "worked" head is seen in the *Study for Figure* and *Man in Blue* series. In the former, from the neck to the shoulders, Bacon already diminishes the detail, as well as the heaviness of the paint, progressing to a sketchy and almost nonexistent pair of crossed legs on a sofa. The blue, black, and green face, with black mouth agape and ringed in individually defined white teeth, begins to seem almost independent of the hastily brushed, pale body. The same disembodied, floating effect is what makes *Man in Blue III* such a haunting picture. After a delicate white line makes the turn from collar to shoulder to arm, it trails off into the night below, so that only the white shirt, enveloping a dark tie, connotes the businessman's body, while his pink and blue face, though interrupted by a burst of white around the left eye, is strongly built, with a very firm rendering of the jaw line, ears, solid cleft chin, and assiduously parted coiffure. This *Man Trapped*, as it became known, is one in a series of seven painted rapidly between March and early June of 1954. The model may have been a man Bacon met at the Imperial Hotel at Henley, where he was staying, or it may have been poor Peter Lacy, Bacon's much-abused bourgeois businessman lover. Critic Sally Yard points out that Bacon painted it from life, making the series somewhat unusual in that he was more inclined—particularly later in his career, after Cecil Beaton made disparaging remarks about a portrait of him in the studio—to work from photographs.[10]

The concentration of detail and density in the face, in counterpoint to rapid, sketchy rendering of the body, is nothing new in Modern art of course. One sees it in nineteenth-century masters of portraiture, from Manet and Cézanne through Sargent, but there are two artists in particular whose technical similarities to Bacon are enlivened by historical links. One is Lautrec, whose paintings so often anticipate Bacon and whose life parallels Bacon's so closely. Lautrec's lightning strokes of powdery white on a dark ground, his rhythmic explorations of the play of drapery or costume, his detached theatrical settings and propensity for figure studies of the body in motion, and even his sense of scale and the placement of the figure on the sheet or canvas, all closely suggest similar practices in Bacon's studio. Lautrec arrived in Paris from the large country estate of an aristocratic father addicted to riding and hunting who alternately ignored and abused his son for his disability and "un-manly" intentions in the arts. Bacon was no different except that he did not head to London or Paris as a student of traditional techniques; he was as ambitious as Lautrec, but he was in much more of a hurry. Lautrec was more attached to his family. Both relished the demimonde from which so many of the characters that people their novelistic art could be taken. It may not be such a remarkable coincidence that both were alcoholics from their twenties on, given the historical propensity of artists to imbibe, nor is it surprising that both were openly reliant upon prostitutes for their sex lives.

Bacon took this a notch lower by bragging about his exploits as a prostitute in Berlin and London's East End, even at one point advertising himself on the front page of the *Times* of London as a "gentleman's companion," allowing his Nanny Lightfoot, a member of his household for decades until her death, to choose the applicants with whom Bacon would go out on his assignations.[11] As Peppiatt reports, the complex motivations behind this partly involved raising cash for his phenomenally expensive lifestyle at Quierndern Mews studio, where Bacon lived and worked, with his "alderman lover" as some sneeringly called Eric Alden, the businessman who was Bacon's longtime companion in the 1970s, along with the nanny. Yet making money was only partly the motivation for this dangerous occupation. Bacon undoubtedly suffered from a deep desire to wreak revenge upon his father and, more touching, his desire to have his boyish good looks affirmed by the attention of his clientele: "I was always very pleased to have someone new, because my parents had told me I was awful looking and that nobody would like me. . . . I've worked on myself a great deal—I've tried in all kinds of ways to remake myself. In that sense, I'm artificial—I'm probably the most artificial person there is."[12] This telling remark about artifice and the remaking of the self, in perfect harmony with the effacement of his aristocratic origins, is borne out by the elaborate ritual Bacon followed before going out. As friends recount, he labored long and hard before the mirror to apply makeup, including rouge and shoe polish to color his hair, and the particulars of this involved toilette are close to the daily studio rite of the preparation of the palette and the mixing of colors.

Leaping ahead in history and selecting as postfiguration an artist whose work is in many ways a continuation of Bacon's own, we may turn (perhaps surprisingly) to the enigmatic deceptions of Jean-Michel Basquiat. He also took pains to hide his upper-middle-class background, presenting himself as the bad boy graffiti artist from the ghettto who sold his services in New York's Washington Square to support a $300 per day drug habit as well as a lifestyle that was the 1980s version of what Bacon was doing in London three decades earlier, including the expensive clothes and trips, the big studio, the trappings of the highly successful and socially sought-after artist. To compound this oddly manifold link, there is also the related presence of Andy Warhol, whose cold, even mercenary approach to portraiture is oddly akin to Bacon's, however different the results. Those unmistakably physical brushstrokes in Bacon's messy studio, gestures straight out of El Greco, are a far cry from the mechanical application of color, particularly through silkscreen, at The Factory. Both used photographs directly, including news shots (for Bacon, those of Woodrow Wilson, Canadian prime minister Louis St. Laurent, and English politician Sir Austen Chamberlain; for Warhol, just about any celebrity he could get hold of). They were ascetic in their ability to remain at a distance from the subjects they painted, but there is a compelling reason behind the fact that the Museum of Modern Art in New York, where Picasso is still king, has placed the works of Bacon in a far more prominent spot than those of Warhol in its current interpretation of the tradition. It harks back to the "rough beast" in the prophetic works of Yeats or the howling prisoner at the start of Hofmannsthal's *Tower* or any of the many other great tragic masterpieces by figures in this study. Bacon's violent vision, sealed in glass and framed in gold, proves more than a personal outburst, more than a symptom of the age (which is where it leaves Warhol and his ilk behind). In Bacon, the recurring cry of the feeling soul before the onset of chaos resonates for the ages.

7

King of the Cats

BALTHUS

The improbable life and work of Balthus—Balthusz or Balthazar Klossowski, Count de Rola and self-proclaimed descendant of Lord Byron, the Romanov czars, or the last king of Poland, depending on whom he talked to and when—defies all sense of historic and aesthetic reality. That Balthus, the only contemporary figure under consideration in these pages, continued to paint into the twenty-first century is in itself a minor miracle. After a stroke, a wheelchair user who was reportedly in the studio daily, he died in 2001 at age 92, at work on a major painting that he had shown, partly completed, in Paris, Japan, and New York. How he maintained throughout his life an extraordinary pretense regarding his origins is also the matter of high drama, taking us to the core of the identity problem right at the outset.

So it is important to make it clear from the start that, of all the artists and thinkers under scrutiny in these pages, Balthus has by far the least claim on aristocratic status. Born in Paris on 29 February 1908 (the oddity begins with his being a leap-year child and prone to playing games with his age), Balthus inherited far more artistically than aristocratically. His father, Erich, was an art critic, historian, and competent painter; his mother, Baladine, was a flamboyant painter and, as the lover of the poet Rilke, a well-connected figure on the arts scene. Poles in exile, Erich and Baladine Klossowski were, frankly, just minor nobility, rather in the manner of Chopin, and the invention of the mask of the Count de Rola was entirely the artist's own. The artist's detractors assert that there is no such title as the Count de Rola. When World War I began, his parents, German citizens, were forced to flee to Berlin, separating in 1917. Balthus and his older brother, Pierre, went with their mother to live in Geneva, where Rilke became a surrogate father.

As a measure of Balthus's nebulous social standing, consider the story of his courtship, in the 1930s, of a beautiful young aristocrat, Rose Alice Antoinette de Watteville, whose parents initially shunned Balthus, not simply because he was a struggling artist but because his family background was inadequate. His brilliant portrait of her, *The Bernese Hat* (now at the Art Institute of Chicago), is stunning in its frankness and austerity. As with other portraits of aristocratic subjects, notably of the Countess de Noailles, Balthus strove to deliver the power and attraction of a formidable character (the great Ingres portrait of the Countess d'Houssainville comes to mind), yet unlike the work of his nineteenth-century predecessors, stripped of the trappings and conspicuously severe in its setting. Even the title is a gesture toward anonymity. The work was one of a series of major paintings he finished in the 1930s with the intention of paying the bills and impressing her family with his success (the parallel with Degas is noteworthy), presenting the paintings as tableaux rather than as lucrative portrait commissions. Balthus married her in 1937 and completed the painting the following year. They were separated in 1946 after the birth of two sons, one of whom, Thadée, married a veritable princess, Loulou de La Falaise, the daughter of a real count (Comte Alain de La Falaise), whose mother was Maxime Birley, daughter of the queen's portraitist, Sir Oswald Birley. It is irresistible to mention that Loulou, Yves Saint Laurent's factotum, remains one of the reigning stars of the fashion world, and her wedding ball at the Chalet des Iles, a castle on an island in a lake in the heart of the Bois de Boulogne, was hosted by Saint Laurent. Included among its four hundred guests was a parade of celebrities, both *fashionistas* and aristocrats: the Rothschilds, the Klossowskis, Karl Lagerfeld, Bianca Jagger, and others from the Andy Warhol set.

Critics of a literary bent are apt to focus on the Surrealist side of Balthus. Guy Davenport, in a an elegantly slim collection of aperçus about a few favorite paintings, concentrates on the arrogantly Surrealist coding used. He compares the portrait of the Countess de Noailles, a major patron of the Surrealists, to Wyndham Lewis's unflattering portrait of Edith Sitwell, likening the figure of the countess, sitting in a bare room, to "a third-grade schoolteacher, surely, resting between classes."[1] Davenport beautifully describes the portrait's most arresting and surprising quality: its austerity. "This portrait illustrates as well as any of Balthus's his ability to take the bare minimum of a subject and bring it to the highest pitch of clarity, of presence. This rich spareness contrasts with the century's aesthetic of merging figure and ground in a dazzle."[2] The other figure in this study it brings to mind is Wittgenstein, who, lean and handsome, would have made a superb model for a similar treatment. The sharp angles of the countess's figure and the unadorned wooden table and chair are consonant with Wittgenstein and his designs. You can't help thinking the philosopher would have approved of the clear-minded treatment of the countess and of Davenport's aphoristic treatment of subject and symbol in the painter's work: "Great art is always eloquently tautological; the world in Balthus is a metaphor of itself."[3]

The genealogy of Balthus was far more distinguished in the arts than in the conventional aristocratic way. The apartment on the rue Boissonade in Montparnasse, where he was raised, was book-lined and hung with paintings by not only his mother and father but by Cézanne and Delacroix, as well as Japanese woodcuts (a salient detail in light of his later marriage to a woman he claimed, falsely, was a Japanese princess). In addition to the hovering presence of Rilke, Balthus was a protégé of both André Derain and Pierre Bonnard. His homage to Derain is a large portrait, now in the collection of the Museum of Modern Art in New York and a pivotal work in the recent *Modern Art Despite Modernism* exhibition. It presents the artist staring sternly at the viewer in an uncharacteristically confrontational pose, in a striped robe, his sharp-fingered hand pretentiously tucked into the open shirt beneath. Like Lautrec's portrait of *The Englishman at the Moulin Rouge*, the work presents the artist as nobleman. Those who know Balthus by his reputation rather than his face might be excused for mistaking the work for a self-portrait. A youthful model, in dishabille and seemingly ravished in the very recent past, sits in the background.

Although Derain was far from a domineering figure in real life, the erotic scenario suggested by the painting is the aftermath of the artist exercising his *droit du seigneur* in the manner of the nobleman. The setting is the studio (the stacked canvases, some facing the wall as any artist with a work in progress would have them, are just behind Derain), yet the massive folds of the striped robe could be a parody of a courtier's formal attire. Deeply disturbing for its sexual innuendo as well as the unsettling gaze of Derain toward the intruding viewer, it is without question a powerful example of Balthus's capacity to endow a contemporary figure with the majesty of a Renaissance duke. The magic of Balthus is his ability to bridge the distant past and our own time in a style that melds the majesty of the former with the avant-garde bite of a Modern who perpetually poses the question of which character in his enigmatic dramas is the victim and which the figure in control. It is in the psychological dimension of what the artist himself called "surrealism after Courbet" that his work belongs in the category of Picasso and Giacometti, two of his most fervent admirers.

In the case of Balthus, it is the artist as well as his work that defies time. Timelessness is a quality perhaps too often assigned to works of art. It implies the physical permanence we dare hope for in the art's objecthood. This is a characteristic that is, for some, less than essential in an age of sculpture and even painting that is intended by its maker to decay before our eyes, as in the case of large paintings with straw attached to them by Anselm Kiefer, photographic works on distressed paper by the Starn twins, melting icicles arranged by Andy Goldsworthy or the now submerged *Spiral Jetty* of Robert Smithson, a watershed in the earth art movement. We also live in a more sophisticated era with regard to the condition of an art work and the effects of time as well as to the practice of conservation. All this considered, one quality that is prized by most people in the work of art is its ability to outlast us, to continue visibly unchanged through the course of coming generations, physically taking its place in the legacy of our families, our universities, our museums, and our culture. It is the complement to our other great demand upon art, that it be ahead of its time, prophetic as prototype of the truths that more laborious or rational thinkers will reach in due course. This removal of art from the natural processes of change in decay is a notion as old as early Greek sculpture or the copying of Chinese calligraphy from ink on paper to stone.

Ars longa, vita brevis. The axiom invokes the defiance of time. It issues an aggressive challenge to the inevitable alteration of the views and contexts of those who in the future would stand before the object charged with the responsibility of interpreting it for themselves. In a Postmodern age, it is considered an old-fashioned attitude toward the atemporal virtues of art, romanticized in Keats's ode "On a Grecian Urn" and made banal by the appetite for "appreciation" on the part of greedy investor-collectors. Generally attributed to the object, timelessness also can be associated with particular genres or media. Any opera or ballet created today struggles with the problem of the theater's having become a "museum" for archaic forms. In literature, the survival of the sonnet or three-act comedy stems from the longing for continuity with a strong tradition, as much as from convenience. The contemporary sonnet sequences of John Berryman, Robert Lowell, and James Merrill, among others, bargain with immortality by staking comparison with those of Spenser, Sidney or—dread notion—Shakespeare. When Anton von Webern and Elliott Carter touch pen to paper to begin a new string quartet, they cope with the echoes of Haydn, Beethoven, and Mendelssohn, among too many others. Recent forays into fresco by contemporary artists, including Donald Sultan and Francisco Clemente, offer examples of the deliberate attempt to achieve fresh effects in what strikes some as an archaic medium with a vast body of masterworks preceding them, including those of Delacroix and Puvis. Even artists who work in oil on canvas, particularly in genres such as the portrait, landscape, or still life, sometimes apologize for and other times take pride in the fact that a painter of any era could walk into their studio, grab a brush, and start working in an entirely familiar setting.

The continuity of art is embedded in its materials, methods, and masterpieces. Occasionally, it resides as well in the character of the people who make it. Balthus was a throwback to the golden days of Paris in the years *entre deux guerres* when he and Giacometti, Picasso, Matisse, Miró, Calder, and others knew and supported each other's work day by day. The identity of Balthus has been shaped in part by association with this heroic crew, now considered to have brought Modern art to its summit. He was, if anything, a member of this distinguished club with a difference and remains outside the standard accounts of art history as it covers this period. Besides his role as sole survivor, he was also the product of the construction of an elaborate personal mythology around his pretensions to a nonexistent title as the Count de Rola. As a recent biographical study makes clear, amid genuine frustration on the part of author Nicholas Fox Weber (who lived with Balthus in Switzerland in part to attempt to extract any semblance of veracity from what seems to be a compulsive liar), the artist invented a series of aristocratic liaisons to bolster his claim to the title. One of the most colorful of these ties is by way of his mother's supposed descent from Lord Byron through the clan Gordon. The entire Byronic fantasy is in all likelihood based on a pleasant memory of a Scottish nanny that Balthus had in Paris.

Another story he told links him with the Raginet family in Russia, who were Romanovs. Later, at about the time he became a quasi-ambassador of culture to Rome as André Malraux's appointed director of the French Academy, he suddenly became the descendant of the last king of Poland, Stanislaw August Poniatowski, who abdicated in 1795 and was renowned as a great patron of the arts. The king's restoration of the glories of the Warsaw castle and his creation of the palace of Lazienki spurred the efforts of Balthus to restore the Villa Medici during his tenure there as head of the French Academy. Weber spends page after page assiduously reporting and refuting these claims, citing the disgust with which Balthus's estranged brother, Pierre, views the whole Count de Rola masquerade, as well as the mockery of friends. "There was no precedent for Balthus's title in his family. Not surprisingly neither Balthus's father nor his older brother was ever anything but Erich or Pierre Klossowski. Although any attempt to meet Pierre through an intermediary failed—as I expected it would because of his well-known reluctance to discuss his brother—I have been told by mutual acquaintances of his and Balthus's that he considers the title of 'Count' to be nonsense not only factually but unjustifiable, but also embarrassingly pretentious."[4]

By insisting on being addressed as count and thrusting this persona to the forefront while vigorously denying scholars' and journalists' basic biographical details on the occasions of major exhibitions or publications, Balthus directed the world's attention to an image of the artist as aristocrat that had its endearing as well as absurd qualities. He even invented an elaborate lineage for his beautiful Japanese wife, Setsuko, three decades his junior, who, he said, is descended from a great Samurai family (she's nothing of the sort). They met when Balthus was sent to Japan by André Malraux on a mission for the ministry of culture, and she served as his translator.

It would suit this study perfectly well were Balthus to be a real count. But what may be even more telling is the eagerness with which he embraced his exaggerated aristocratic identity. This is not another Bacon, reluctant to own up to his background. It's the inverse. Balthus's eagerness to be seen as an aristocrat can be taken as a compelling indication of the way in which one prominent painter identifies the status of the artist with that of the nobleman, making a statement about what it means to be an artist by staking it on an embellished genealogy. In this regard, and in his paintings, Balthus imposed a metaphorical distance, an air of superiority, between himself and the public.

Yet the aristocratic pretense is not merely a reflection of Balthus's exalted sense of the role of the artist. The mirror is hung to block our view of a situation that is more complex. As the world first learned in 1984, when a major retrospective was held at the Metropolitan Museum of Art in New York and the attendant catalog and publicity turned up the fact, Balthus's maternal grandfather was the cantor of the Orthodox synagogue of Kovelitz in Novgorod. His name was Abraham Beer Spiro, a variant on Shapiro, and he moved his family to Breslau, where he became the cantor of the Old Storch Synagogue and also became locally known as a composer. For Balthus, whose anti-Semitism offended his Jewish biographer Weber on more than one occasion, this was yet another motivation for deceit. Pressed by his biographer, he insisted that Spiro was a close family friend called "uncle." The lengths to which Balthus was prepared to go to obscure this fact may seem dubious these days. In Europe in the 1930s, when the habit was formed, this ruse was different, because denying one's Jewish past was in part a matter of survival.

This clouds the issue of the aristocratic pose and its importance to Balthus as an artist. It is one thing to avoid reprisal and another to adopt a fake title as a philosophical gesture. The former is a matter of fear; the latter looks like calculation. As his biographer points out, Balthus arrived at the stage where he believed in the legend. He harbored an almost touching adherence to the title, by which friends and servants were obliged to address him, as well as the press (*Time* magazine, the newspaper *Le Monde*, and the major art magazines obliged). It is tempting to pose a straightforward correlation between his self-election as Count de Rola and his development as an artist, along the lines of Yeats's fabrication of an aristocratic identity as a springboard to creativity. Balthus, like Bacon, reached his peak, producing his most heroic work, in the 1950s and 1960s, when aspects of both style and subject were in part attributable to his aristocratic stance. It is possible to read his paintings in terms of his passion for the past as played out in his own dramatization of life as the lord of the manor. The eccentricity of this role was enough to guarantee Balthus a degree of originality, and this was compounded by how he painted.

One aspect of Balthus's reputation as an artist is his admirable ability to steer his own course. Picasso's often-cited remark that he was the "only artist around not painting Picassos" can be taken as a starting point. It is interesting that Picasso was among the earliest collectors of Balthus's work, buying an early portrait and for the most part speaking of Balthus's paintings with uncharacteristic approval, which we can understand in part because the two were far enough apart that Picasso could afford to be lavish in his praise. He recognized in Balthus a highly original take on Modernism that stood apart from the technical or conceptual tendencies of the time. Balthus eschewed the prevailing movements, from the entreaties of the clubby Surrealists to the various types of abstraction—the geometries of Delaunay and Braque and the biomorphs of Miró, Giacometti, and Arp. As his biographer has written, "Balthus is one of the great loners of twentieth-century art; he belongs to no school, no 'ism,' but his own."[5] Abstraction was emphatically out of the question. In a particularly nasty critique of the work of Jean Arp, he sniped, "I too could have done the sort of things he did—you just have to paint like a blind man."[6] He may have kept their influence at bay in his work, but all were friends and allies with whom Balthus was in steady and intellectually engaged contact.

An artist does not have to be of a certain group to be influenced by them, since even critique or rejection is a response to an idea that is in the air. To avoid Picasso or Miró is to swerve around substantial obstacles en route to an individualized approach to art. Flip through a book of Balthus's work, though, from the earliest to the massive final work, *Still Life with Cat before a Mirror*, and you will be struck by the integrity of his style, its resistance not only to change but to acquiescing to the tidal pulse of the enormously exciting artistic and literary ideas of Paris in that era. Over and again the paintings show the steadfast adherence to the well-muscled figure, the dramatically lit interior, or in the case of *The Street* and *Passage du Commerce Saint Andre*, a quiet corner of the city, rendered in a style that the artist discovered early in his career. Its Modern qualities include a powerful illusionism by which, to take one famous example, he perplexed viewers for decades with the stiff, inanimate figure of a man in *The Street* that was regularly taken by critics for the depiction of a wooden sign, a cutout figure, until the artist himself explained it was another of the living characters in the scene. Like the masks of Picasso, the direct if distant stares of the figures in a Balthus painting have an unnerving aggressiveness. As Davenport writes, "Picasso painted in the Latin of the Principate, when portraiture became big-eyed and staring, the human form became stiff and heavy, and the world was fascinated by but weary of violence. Braque painted in Greek. Balthus paints in the patrician French of Henry de Montherlant, aloof from vulgarity."[7]

Balthus painted Balthuses for seventy years. The effect of setting himself above so many was one of placing himself away from others and enforcing a productive isolation in which his highly original style could flourish. If there was an exterior force at work in his makeup, it would have to be described as the legacy of past masters into whose ranks Balthus fits as easily as he does into any contemporary collection. As T. S. Eliot chose the metaphysical poets for company and Lord Leighton nominally placed himself and his tightly knit group within the framework of Giotto, Duccio, and others who preceded Raphael, Balthus chose Piero Della Francesca, Poussin, and Puvis as progenitors. The kinship between his work and theirs is solidly based on technique, from the style of draftsmanship to the method of painting. The narrowed eyes and small mouth of a Piero and those of a Balthus might be mistaken for one another out of context, if details from each were reproduced without captions in a book. The closer you look, as in any family resemblance, the stronger the similarity. At the Detroit Institute for the Arts there is a painting by Poussin, an Arcadian scene, that from a distance has that stillness of atmosphere that Balthus seizes in his landscapes (notably, *The Mountain*). Even if the Poussin is the more tightly grouped, there is an extraordinary similarity between the way the two are executed. To take but one example, the brief, soft brush strokes in crossing diagonals at the edge of the bare knee of the central figure in the Poussin and the nearly identical brush work found at the border between the knee and background in the Alpine scene suggest that Balthus went to school on Poussin to achieve just that effect. While Balthus took pains to steer his biographers and critics clear of too close a comparison between specific figures in his paintings and those in Piero's that he seems to have drawn on directly, the material similarities are powerful enough to lead to a strange thesis: Balthus ascended to the first rank of Moderns by continuously painting Old Master pictures.

Concomitantly, he devoted his ninety-two years to becoming a living anachronism, fashioning an opulent and protected modus vivendi in his vast chalet in the Suisse Romande where servants, sycophantic art dealers, and his famously obedient wife protected him from the unpleasantness of the world of affairs, allowing him to work, think, and enjoy himself according to the rhythms of a baronial existence not far removed from the daily routine of an aristocrat of four centuries earlier.

This raises a problem. What if Balthus's defiance of time and change was so successful that he ought no longer to be considered Modern? If there is such a thing as a Modern Old Master, Balthus would be the paradigm. There is a deliberate resistance of Modernism in Balthus as he lived, which brings us back to the difference Robert Storr perceives between Modernism and being Modern. Weber recounts a telling anecdote from firsthand observation during his days at the Grand Chalet. Balthus and Setsuko may have withdrawn to their mountain retreat, but that did not mean they were not subject to a daily deluge of invitations to openings and requests for interviews. As Weber relates, they took a dim view of the contemporary art scene: "He and Setsuko sometimes opened their morning post in front of me. Looking at the announcements they received from the Centre Pompidou and other showplaces of modernism, they acted as if it were all one big joke. Why deliberately create such ugliness?"[8] In Storr's recent study of anti-Modernist Moderns, Balthus looms large as a figurative painter (and draftsman of the school of Ingres) as well as a personality with obvious inclinations toward the ancien régime. It is undeniable that in certain paintings or at certain moments in his life, Balthus was more Modern than at others. As a test of this, Weber points to the close friendship with Antonin Artaud, who wrote of the painter in an important early essay that he had painted Lady Iya Abdy "the way a primitive might have painted an angel; with as sure a technical mastery, with an identical understanding of the spaces, lines, lights and hollows which constitutes space."[9] Balthus and Artaud found common ground in sexual and oneiric subject matter, stylishly probing the darker levels of consciousness. Where Artaud took a turn toward barbarism, anticivilization, and disorder, Balthus elected the other path, and Weber feels he undermined the power of his art: "As in the artistic production of those non-European cultures embraced by Artaud, primal forces dominate undisguised. Balthus's work joins the seemingly barbaric side of the human mind with the decorous. By now denying the violence of his art—indeed, by succumbing, as the Count de Rola, to complete Europeanization—Balthus is effectively negating one of the great merits of his work. For his art is a celebration of anger and turmoil as much as of grace and tranquillity. Its achievement is in showing the degree to which opposite forces commingle. Uncontrollable cravings thrive in the most ordered, unruffled settings. In keeping with Artaud's mandate, Balthus could reconcile these polar opposites of human existence. Fantasies of murder enter the drawing room."[10]

The greater adherent of the Expressionism of Artaud was Pierre Klossowski, the artist's brother, a noted translator of Kafka, Kierkegaard, and Sade and author of sadomasochistic fantasies. Pierre was associated not only with Rilke and Gide but with George Bataille, André Breton, Michel Leiris, and Michel Foucault, who wrote a thoughtful appreciation of his novel *The Baphomet* (1965), a *Vathek*-like reworking of the gnostic theme of the interaction between gods and men, using the story of Diana and Actaeon. In his essay, Foucault pounces on Klossowski's portrayal of evil and the danger of the "synthesis of the different." He writes, underscoring a type of modernity that is felt as well in the darker paintings of Balthus: "Klossowski's experience lies here, more or less: in a world where reigns an evil genius who has not found his god, or who might just as well pass himself off as God, or who might even be god himself. Such a world is neither Heaven nor Hell, nor limbo; it is, quite simply, our own world."[11]

Balthus made the choices that set him apart from Artaud and others involved in the Modernism that tore down the past. Camus once wrote of him, "One must select, not destroy." For many Modern painters, the first obligation was the elimination of the figure, landscape, and still life and the re-creation of the painting in terms of its purest elements. The difference between Balthus and, to choose one example, Mondrian lies in the program or ideology of Modernism chosen by the latter as opposed to the independent, and still wholly Modern, approach of Balthus. Storr gives particular prominence to the alternative line of painters, including Balthus's mentors Derain and Bonnard (rather than Picasso and Braque). In terms of MOMA's canon, the exhibition turned out to be a promotion of Balthus to a more prominent place, exemplified by the prominent hanging of the portraits of both Derain and Miró along with the permanent collection's great masterpiece, *The Street.* Storr pokes fun at the "studied perversity" and intentional immaturity of Balthus and calls the artist "one of the last surviving examples of the classic Baudelarean dandy in whom the avidity of childhood is allied to adult perseverance, with both shielded from outside scrutiny by a feigned indifference to the everyday world."[12] In this, Guy Davenport agrees: "There is the ungiving understanding that what's of value in life is inherited from the past. In the present we have healthy bodies and their fate, nothing else. Our century's events do not exist in Balthus."[13] Citing the conservatism of Poussin, De La Tour, Chardin, David and the "stiff genre paintings" of two Swiss artists, Joseph Reinhardt and Henry Fuseli, Storr points out that the satirical cruelty and shock value of the work attracted the avant-garde, including Artaud and the Surrealists. It still does.

Despite his lofty contempt for the avant-garde, many artists, both "hot" and obscure, emulate Balthus. Amid the torrid ranks of the young British artists gathered in the *Sensation* exhibition that exploded on the scene in London and at the Brooklyn Museum, the duo of Dinos and Jake Chapman, with their wildly erotic sculptures of preadolescent boys and girls provocatively posed and endowed, offer one example of an homage to Balthus (in the theoretical materials they appended to their work, they specifically cite him as a source for their imagery). Per the debate on high and low, the Chapmans are emphatically anchored to the low end of popular culture, making Balthus even more of a high Modern by contrast. For some, one of the obstacles to an appreciation of Balthus was the nagging charge that his portrayal of adolescent girls was pornographic. Before the controversy over Robert Mapplethorpe's nude portraits of children in the 1980s, when the debate at least forced a few art critics to rigorously apply themselves to the applicability of that label in the visual arts, the firmest guidelines to the distinction between art and pornography were offered by legal cases involving literature, from Flaubert and Baudelaire through the American court system's rulings on Joyce's *Ulysses* and Nabokov's *Lolita*. In all likelihood, no matter how familiar or revered the great paintings of Balthus are liable to become over the years, they are also bound to remain, as in the case of Caravaggio, somewhat suspect in the eyes of an uneasy minority.

A salient example, however, of how art that is similar to and derived from his can be pornographic, and why his own does not fit into that category, is offered by the far more pointed and explicit work of the Chapmans. This is low art, traipsing along the borderline that Jeff Koons also skirts with his pseudo-porn. A measure of the difference is offered by their source materials. Where Balthus is drawn from Caravaggio, Koons and the Chapmans are perhaps too directly tied to pornographic magazines and comic books, pop culture of extremes. One can't help wondering if that will not limit their permanent significance as art. These are not the only enfants terribles who claim Balthus as a father figure. During precisely the same season that the Chapmans were in town as part of the British *Sensation* exhibition, in galleries within a few paces of one another in New York's SoHo, Bo Bartlett and Judy Fox had one-person shows of strikingly similar large-scale portraits of children and sculptures staring directly at the viewer with a sophistication that, again, invokes Balthus. The perdurance of the figure in the work of Tom Wesselman, Alex Katz, Eric Fischl, and others cited in Storr's new account of Modern art also owes much to the long-standing example of Balthus, even without the frisson of sexuality that the avant-gardists overly rely upon.

Like many of the dignified fathers mentioned in this book, Balthus was loath to acknowledge the artistic pretensions of those who claimed to be his progeny. His categorical rejection of cutting-edge developments placed him in a curious position art historically. That is why the scholarly term high Modern, a favorite of Clement Greenberg and others, is at hand. Just as we attach the "Classical" seal of approval to the severe practitioners of Minimalism in the 1970s (specifically Judd, Morris, and Andre) or use it to frame the rigor of Cubism and the severe painterly styles of the Surrealists (de Chirico, nearest in tenor to Balthus, particularly in his use of Classical imagery, and Morandi, a handy point of reference in terms of influence and technique, whose influence upon the still-life passages in Balthus has been acknowledged by the artist), so too the rigor and grand manner of Balthus's large-scale compositions demands a more serious critical vocabulary than the sarcasm of a Bruce Nauman, Mike Kelley, Kiki Smith, or certainly the cynical Koons. This is not wholly due to the chosen medium either, even if the substantial body of work in oil on canvas presented by Balthus, Bacon, Freud, and in the United States, Fischl, Katz, Alice Neel, and others does lay claim to the qualities that prompt critics and the public to experience it as high rather than low.

Balthus is a textbook example of the rigorous painterly techniques and draftsmanship, the compositional Formalism (pyramidal or otherwise balanced figure groupings, Renaissance ratios, tightly framed geometries), and the conceptual complexities of Modern art at its peak. In this regard, although the two are infrequently paired, he resembles Fernand Leger, to name another painter whose reputation, thanks to some recent retrospectives and critical reassessment, is making a comeback. His populist devotion to the worker and the machine certainly distances him from Balthus, but examine the treatment of the female nude and compare it with Balthus, particularly in the direct stare of the face and the strength of the figure, and the similarities begin to emerge. As with Balthus, Leger had his disciples, most notably Roy Lichtenstein. Later in his career, Leger improbably became a favorite of "elitists" who preferred the highly stylized painting of the figure. Both Leger and Balthus were prominent in MOMA's *Modern Art despite Modernism* show. As its curator, Robert Storr, points out, "For literary painters such as Balthus, the literature of the image must be good if a painting is to succeed, or else narrative must be minimal so that plain, yet revealing, appearances can speak. The mystery of *The Street* puts it in the first category. The two portraits (Miró and Derain) exemplify the second."[14]

Oddly enough, it is rare to hear the term *masterpiece* in discussions of contemporary art, in part because it takes time for that judgment to congeal but also because the fragment, parody, and irony have made it difficult to stake that claim in the first place. More often than not, masterpieces are the target of contemporary art as commentary. Contrary to this rejection of the grand statement, it often seems as though Balthus could do nothing less than set out to paint masterpieces, one after another, up to and including the huge, final canvas, that most avow to be a noble failure. Certainly *The Mountain*, *The Street*, the portraits of Miró and Derain and *The Golden Age* are intentional essays in the tradition of masterpieces, the sort of works that, when seen at gallery openings, are tagged "museum pieces" as opposed to those that a private collector would take home. This unabashedly Romantic yearning for the grand gesture on a scale of Delacroix or Rubens, like the hunt for the Great American Novel among embarrassing flops by Mailer, Styron, Bellow, Updike, and Pynchon or contemporary grand opera that can hold its own with Puccini and Verdi—this ambition also can be dangerous.

It is not for the faint of heart, in other words. It takes a Balthus to summon the self-assuredness for the task. His adherence to the role of the aristocrat had a direct bearing upon this aspect of the intentional assumption of a style, a scale, and subject matter that transcends the private painting. As Hofmannsthal and Russell would key their language to the public arena of the stage or large lecture hall, or Puvis would calculate the effect of a color combination as it would appear in a vast mural, Balthus reached for bold statements in all that he did. One biographical note that illuminates this dilemma is offered by his legacy as director of the French Academy in Rome from 1961 through 1975, an appointee of André Malraux charged with the revitalization of the ailing institution. Although he was revered as a teacher of the Prix du Rome winners in residence there and maintained a studio where he completed a handful of superb paintings, including *The Turkish Room* and *Japanese Woman before a Black Mirror* (both portraits of Setsuko, who became his wife during that time) and the Cézannesque painting *The Card Players*, he gained fame for restoring the sixteenth-century villa and reviving it as an outpost of De Gaulle's ambitious campaign to promote French culture.

Balthus inherited an institution steeped in tradition. Ingres had been its director from 1835 through 1842, and visitors included Velázquez, Montaigne, Caravaggio, Boucher, Fragonard, Hubert-Robert, and Corot. For years before Balthus's arrival it had been identified with stodgy academicism and its reactionary defiance of all forces of change in art, including, quite famously, Impressionism. The French Academy in Rome was anti-Modern, and Malraux, ironically enough, dispatched the sensation of the Paris art scene to inject a bit of life and Modernism into it. During his tenure, Balthus not only presented his version of Modernism, a Classical canon of paintings and sculpture that started with Courbet and extended through such friends as Picasso and Giacometti, but preserved and recreated the past through the restoration of the Villa Medici, in which he took an active hand, not only presiding but at one point dabbing paint on the richly colored walls. Room by room, he created one Balthus after another, with austere but dramatic arrangements of antiques and works that he collected on the modest budget of the Academy, throwing out many of the dated plaster casts that tied the place too tightly to its academic roots and arranging stagy groupings of other sculpture and objects. Along with the lavish entertaining, the project returned Balthus to his adolescent stint as a theatrical set designer in Paris—a key to the studied deployment of figures and furnishings in his paintings.

The bifocal agenda of his assignment—to expound Modernism and restore Renaissance grandeur—seems inherently at odds with itself. Not for Balthus. The reasons it coheres are found in the art and in the life and directly draw upon his claims to royal blood, however spurious. Balthus represents the supreme example of an artist who views Modernism as a tradition rather than a break with tradition, and as long as he was alive he embodied those continuities without which great art forms die. He was like the great opera diva, passing on to her protégée the subtleties of a performance tradition, grounded in the details—how the knife is picked up and concealed in *Tosca* just before the assassination of Baron Scarpia, the secrets of going against the breath while singing in a laryngeal way, the age-old mystery of the "open throat" and other arcane lore. Pianists and violinists and performers of all stripes cherish their direct connections to illustrious predecessors—notably, Chopin and Liszt—to whom or in response to whom particular inflections (rubato is often a test case) are dedicated. For all the rhetoric of iconoclasm that attends so much of Modern art as polemic, this passing along of essential knowledge remains the subtext.

As caretaker of the Villa Medici, Balthus selectively brought back what he considered to be the greatest assets of its past, exiled others to oblivion, and then added his own austere, precious aesthetic, which we can call its Modern element. Photographs of the salon-library of the villa after Balthus had applied his ideas are remarkably fresh and contemporary even to this day for the uncluttered, open spaces he created and the precious placement of an eighteenth-century chair against a monochrome wall with a generous expanse of polished floor leading up to it, just as the Minimalist Robert Wilson in his home or his studio campus at Water Mill will take a similarly exquisite chair (his collecting obsession) and make it all the more precious for the quiet context in which he places it. Balthus's curatorial vision brought to Rome the finest examples of his favorites' and dear friends' works, thanks to the enormous power Malraux wielded in the art world. The exhibitions are all of a piece. They are bracketed by Rodin and Giacometti, two magnificent examples of artists whose high regard for the tradition is reflected in mode and materials (the figure in bronze), and balanced by an approach that eliminates or distorts dramatically enough to make the work Modern. This balancing act is maintained in the middle shows of Ingres and Courbet, leading to the Classical rigor of Braque and, to lighten the mix, Bonnard. As Weber observes in his analytic summary of this period in Balthus's career, "In 1961, Balthus's canvases began to acquire the same muted patina he was applying to the villa's walls and an elegance bordering on decadence. This premeditated look of antiquity, this deliberate courtliness, the mannerist formality were evident in the building he redesigned at the same time he was redesigning his art and himself."[15]

As had Delacroix, Balthus savored elegance in art. His paintings couch disturbing issues of power and eros in a manner so refined, so patinated, that they hang in museums almost unobtrusively, like ticking time bombs waiting for the victim to turn a corner and draw near. The Modern element is the exploration of power relationships between man and woman, teacher and student, older and younger—those burning dramas that turn so many viewers away. The patina of warm tones and traditionalism functions in the same way as the heavy glass and golden frames in which Bacon (a frequent guest at the Villa Medici) sealed his monstrous creations. Balthus, by the way, bristled at protective glass, or worse, Plexiglas, in front of his meticulous surfaces because he felt it kept viewers from experiencing the paintings fully.

Skeptics might drive us to a pretty pass where Balthus's status as both Modern and nobleman could be challenged. The challenge then is to reach the mind of the creator to show that it was important to Balthus that he could balance both. Some paintings disclose the inner thinking of the artist. Standing before a big, gestural canvas by Franz Kline, to take one obvious antithesis, it is possible to feel what it may have been like to make that huge brush stroke, to be the artist before the easel. Before a large-scale Balthus, partly because of the way it was executed and partly for the forbidding stares of the figures in it that return one's gaze so frankly, the precisely opposite effect is felt. The maker of the art seems remote, a denizen of another era and culture, and the characters in his mise-en-scène are also distant and defiant. The laying on of paint and the underlying drawing are evident but only upon close observation. Paradoxically, this is the case even when Balthus is the model for the figures, as he often is, including the women. Weber, who is also expert in picking out the face of Baladine, the artist's mother, in the paintings, points out that the painter used his own face for the (female) teacher in *The Guitar Lesson*

(1934) and the male figure in *Cathy Dressing* (1933) as well as in his self-portrait as *The King of Cats* (1935).

Balthus had referred to himself as His Majesty The King of Cats (using the English phrase) back in his twenties, and throughout his art the disconcerting, aloof presence of a cat in a scene charged with sexual tension became a signature motif. The feline squint he used in the painting, in which his chin and nose begin the metamorphosis into cat's features, is found in many of his portraits. In the self-portrait, one hand is clenched in a fist, the other rests on a hip far above a real cat rubbing his trouser leg adoringly. On the small stool where the tablet declaring "A Portrait of H.M. The King of Cats, painted by Himself, MCMXXXV" there is a whip. The background to the painting is empty, and crisp shadows drift across a stony floor. Although the shirt, tie, jacket, and pressed pants might suggest a dandy, another role comes to mind. His head and shoulders drawn up straight, his long legs spaced like a regimental officer, he assumes a pose as remote, disdainful, and even arrogant as can be. The straight lines by which those legs are created point the way to the rigid silhouettes of Jasper Johns, as well as the rectilinearity of Leger's mechanical figures, and invoke the prim, vertical postures of Seurat. Balthus had a way of tightening the outline of a figure to introduce a feeling of stiffness and emphasize the impersonality. The result is a portrait of a cavalier who considers himself the best painter in Paris, and so the best artist in the world.

That deliberate distancing follows from the pretension to the title and the elaborate lifestyle acquired at the Villa Medici and carried forward to the furnishing and entertaining at the hillside Grand Chalet. The gesture is one of putting off or keeping at bay. It is a familiar signal in the arts; even Modernists and Postmodernists who might cavil at the word *elitist* are nonetheless among the guilty parties. Art tends to create its circles, clubs, cliques, and aristocratic codes. The dense prose of artists and theorists barely tuned from dissertation gibberish cuts off all but the converted from the discourse upon which much of contemporary art rests. High Minimalism, to take one example, aggressively staked out an almost puritanically extreme preciosity and reveled in the uproar it created among those who "didn't get it." (By creeping in the back way through design and architecture, Minimalism eventually opened a door to a wider following and now verges on popularity). The velvet-rope mentality of galleries and auction houses and the silence of museums have only recently broken down to become more democratic. The "serious" music scene is similarly resistant to mass media, and concerts of new music are often almost embarrassingly low in attendance: pockets of family, fellow students, and ideologically like-minded supporters applauding vigorously the work of their favorite and sitting glumly through the pieces by rivals.

The elitism of Balthus was practiced by him and belies his appeal to know-it-all adolescents or would-be psychologists. His paintings are tests. The questions they pose are similar in tone to the inquisition of Wilde's Lady Bracknell in *The Importance of Being Earnest*, sounding out our fitness for merely being in the presence of the paintings. And surely you know Monsieur Poussin's *Et in Arcadia Ego*? "Who was your father? He was evidently a man of some wealth. Was he born in what the Radical papers call the purple of commerce, or did he rise from the ranks of the aristocracy?" Have you read much Rilke? The viewer who fields these basic questions correctly has the experience to be admitted to the levels of meaning that are among the privileges available to those that more recent educational theorists have deemed the "culturally literate" and many call elitist. Balthus coded his paintings and then stubbornly refused to explicitly annotate them for the most persistent critics, acting just like the typical Lady Bracknell who assumes the right sort will simply know what to say or not to say in her company.

Artists who show their work, no matter how arcane or elitist, are implicitly willing to assume a public role. Those who take on major government appointments, such as the French Academy in Rome, have Federico Fellini write the essays for exhibition catalogs, or allow fashion and shelter magazines to do shoots at their homes (the largest chalet in all Switzerland) are obviously comfortable with the celebrity status that is also a part of being an aristocrat. One of the last long interviews with Balthus was conducted by David Bowie for the British magazine *Modern Painters*. Over the years the artist allowed more about his background and views on aesthetics to be published; earlier, he was famously uncooperative with desperate museum authorities begging for the merest touch of cooperation and information for the catalogs and publicity materials. With the help of the recent biography, the inevitable personal references have been spelled out more clearly than ever before, including a chain of significant allusions to his mother and his own childhood, not just in the elegiac vision of *The Mountain* but in *The Guitar Lesson* or the sadistic image of the mother that he wound up rejecting and ignoring, thanks mainly (according to Weber) to his discomfort about her Jewish heritage. The deeply erotic woman often on display in the paintings is also his mother, as are many of the young girls. Weber writes: "As for the other group of women Balthus has painted repeatedly—the victims and dreamers, in their twenties, seemingly overcome by their emotions—these are stand-ins for his mother. I see them as Baladine herself, but also as the Baladine whom Balthus resembled and with whom he identified."[16]

As important as it is to be alert to the play of self-portraiture and maternal images in the work, it is also vital to link this reading with the other, one might say 'higher' lore drawn from art history, philosophy, poetry, and music that informs Balthus's work. The bridge between the two sides of interpretation is Rilke. Despite the fact that his genuine father was an art historian and decent painter, Balthus chose Rilke, not surprisingly, for his own genealogical claims to the status of Modern artist and aristocrat. It was a splendid choice. Rilke pretended to aristocratic origins (nonexistent) and performed on paper best when ensconced in palaces and castles (the Castle of Duino and the thirteenth-century chateau at Muzol with Balthus's mother are the best-known examples of this, if one considers the splendid elegies Rilke wrote there in 1922), generally under the patronage of countesses and baronesses. He claimed to be an aristocrat from Carinthia and designed a coat of arms, in true Yeatsian style, playing his multinational background to the hilt as a German-speaking Czech with a French mother, especially when he lived in Switzerland.

The connection between Balthus and Rilke was deep in fact, and the parallels between these two immensely talented, multilingual, emotionally ravenous, and consummately Modern artists go even deeper. If there could be official fictive texts to accompany the haunting scenes of adolescence that Balthus painted, they might well be extricated from Rilke. In *The Notebooks of Malte Laurids Brigge* he offers a description of the great hall in which Court Brahe, the uncle of the little boy who is narrating, offers dinner each night. The forbidding, muscular castle figures in the novel as a character, similar to the mansion of Giuseppe di Lampedusa's great novel, *The Leopard*. In an atmosphere reminiscent of Axel's castle or the brooding, shadowy chambers of Hofmannsthal's dramas, Rilke draws upon dim memories of his own Uncle Jaroslav and cousin Egon in Prague to create a bizarre ensemble. The nobleman and uncle conducts alchemical experiments and dissects the corpses of prisoners in a region of the house unknown to all. A beautiful cousin with a bad case of what in our time we could call chronic fatigue, Miss Mathilde Brahe, corresponds with a spiritualist she calls Baron Nolde, while the little boy lives in awe of his grandfather, called variously Excellency, Marshall, General, and Count, and his mother, the countess. Some of the mystery is suggested by a brief description of the dining hall where these extraordinary characters gather each evening for two hours of misery: "The lofty, and, as I suspect, vaulted chamber was stronger than everything else. With its darkening height, with its never quite clarified corners, it sucked all images out of one without giving one any definite substitute for them. One sat there as if dissolved; entirely without will, without consciousness, without desire, without defense. One was like a vacant spot."[17]

The disturbing vacancy of the children in Balthus's paintings offers an echo of this powerful passage from Rilke. One relatively small and unknown painting now in private hands offers a potent lesson in Balthus's approach. He painted *Jeune Fille à sa Toilette* in 1948, lavishing particularly dense passages of paint upon the young girl's face and delicately modeled body. The gaze is frontal—she is the younger sister to those stern women in Picasso's *Les Desmoiselles d'Avignon*, the most intimidating portrait of women ever rendered. The girl's right eye is cast in shadow and blurred with a harmonious blend of gray and pink, also suggesting the asymmetries of Picasso. That medley of blue and brown and the patterning of the background, however, belong to the school of Vuillard, as does the elderly figure (a grandmother perhaps?) in profile in the next room. The child is small but strong and, typical of Balthus, sexually ambiguous. He has troubled over the degree to which he wants her to have breasts, for instance, much more than over the painting of the arms, one of which is quite sketchy. The muscular strength that Balthus favored even in his young girls is there in the stiff arms and the plump thighs, one of which is lifted toward the viewer. A big hand grips the chair back, not unlike the strong hand he gave himself in the self-portrait as King of the Cats. Where even a small, disturbingly austere painting such as this succeeds most, however, is in that nebulous area that André Malraux once called the poetry of painting, magic in the brush that brings surfaces and colors alive. Against the bronze patination we are not surprised to find in a Balthus is the vibrant red and yellow of a canister on the table. Most dashing, however, are the passages in white—the towel or turban on the child's head and a towel draped by the older figure, whose white hair is answered in the white of the tablecloth as well. These are the moments when Balthus as painter was able to stand up to comparison with the giants of the age, including Picasso and Braque. The power of the girl's stare, confident and defiant, is pure autobiography.

One of Weber's prime sources for the biography is, improbably enough, Claus von Bulow, himself an alleged fake aristocrat as well as alleged murderer. He knew Balthus quite well through the aristocratic circle of the Countess de Noialles, and he said that the pleasure that Balthus took in the young women was more that of an observer, a "fantasist," than of an active participant, making Balthus more like Warhol than Picasso. Strangely enough, Bulow and Balthus share a common propensity to maintain the world at a calm distance. "At the crisis moment in my life, I was criticized for not showing emotion. Well, you can't help your physiognomy. I look like a stand-in for Curt Jurgens as a U-boat captain. Balthus looks like Chopin. And his girls are calculated images of his own profile. Happiness is very distracting," Bulow says, offering one of the oddest and yet most accurate moments in recent art criticism.[18]

Balthus never lived down the accusations of erotic perversity that unfairly color the reception of his painting. As with Swinburne's poetry after the most libelous attacks or Wilde's poetry once the more fanatical proponents of gay rights had turned his every word into an anthem, the rhetorical overwhelms the lyrical. Yet so much is left over, and arguably that is the enduring part. Davenport suggests as much in his reflections upon the way Balthus's son Stanislaus has come to the painter's defense:

> In the Wittgenstein convergence where *Ethik und Aesthetik sind Eins* we can locate a subsistent morality far more cogent for Balthus than Stanislas Klossowski de Rola's "higher realm" of archetypes. Centuries before Plato beauty was a kind of good, and the appreciation of it a pleasure. Beauty has also traditionally been an outward sign of the soul's beauty. Balthus integrates this ancient tradition with Darwinian naturalism (beauty as sexual attraction). Darwin suspected that there was always "something left over" after sexual attractiveness has done its work, and that this something was what we call beauty, and that it may have given rise to art. The grace of line in a Lascaux horse is not the horse, but something that has been abstracted from it.[19]

To draw an ethical conclusion from the "perverse" painting of Balthus seems a touch of Surrealism indeed, but these connections—Wittgenstein, Plato, Darwin, the artists of Lascaux—make eminent sense. Balthus held a place for beauty in its oldest, most timeless sense. The Modern function, as defined by Darwin, is covered, as is the Classical, with Plato as delegate and the so-called primitive. As a principle worth defending, the essential beauty Balthus incorporated in every painting is not just another anachronism. It lies at the core of the achievement of each figure in this study. Sand and her circle demanded it in the salons of Paris; Leighton fought for it in the Royal Academy, as did Hofmannsthal in the opera houses of Austria; Puvis and Degas made it glow; Lautrec and Bacon could never shake it from their compositions; Russell saw it in the night sky and Wittgenstein in the well-crafted sentence or object. Balthus, compatible if not contemporary with all of them, comprehended the values they embodied. He painted them for all time.

Epilogue

THE MASKED BALL

The odd case of Balthus, who died just as this book went to press, suggests that being either an artist or an aristocrat entails role playing. He constructed an aristocratic identity obliquely connected to his aesthetic style and stance. Others deny their nobility in deference to the artist they prefer to be. This indulgence in performance art reminds us of the dandy, a principal in the story of Modernism whose persona is an interpretation of the role of the aristocrat. He is the swing figure between the ranks of the aristocrats and the artists, the fin-de-siècle pivot between high society and the demimonde. Arguably, the artists in this study are more than just dandies (although the outward impression made by Chopin, Delacroix, Hofmannsthal, Leighton, and Balthus would seem well suited to the part). For one thing, they are too productive to match the qualification that a dandy must be idle and ineffectual. Moreover, they are too genuinely noble; their acquaintance with the original code upon which dandyism is based is available to them for exposing "wannabe" nobility (as Sand does in her novels).

Thanks in large part to Baudelaire, the character of the isolated, intellectual aristocrat would undergo an aesthetic metamorphosis to become the *flaneur*, wandering the boulevards and arcades of Paris dressed as a young lord. He ushered the alienated artist from the wilderness of the tormented *fauve* (William Blake, Ludwig von Beethoven, Vincent van Gogh, Paul Gauguin) to the civil if subversive urbanity of the the likes of James Abbott McNeill Whistler, Marcel Proust, and James Joyce. Defiant, different, but dignified, these latter-day versions of the courtly Rubens advanced Modern art into the sophistication of the twentieth century, in part by bridging the divide to private patronage that made artists less dependent upon church or state. At his best, the dandy also managed to secure the heroic place of the artist in the ironic aftermath to Romanticism.

Many notable historians have given the dandy his due since the self-reflexive contemporary accounts of Baudelaire defined him. He was powerfully examined in dreamlike terms (with Hofmannsthal playing an important role as a forger) by Walter Benjamin.[1] Isolated from the urban crowd, the dandy watches life through opera glasses and recollects the lost beauties of the past. Arnold Hauser, whose forgotten four-volume study, *The Social History of Art*, is an indispensable prelude to this topic, described the dandy in this way: "He unites within himself all the gentlemanly virtues that are still possible today, he is a match for every situation and is never astonished at anything, he never becomes vulgar and always preserves the cool smile of the stoic. Dandyism is the last revelation of heroism in an age of decadence, a sunset, a last radiant beam of human pride. . . . This 'inward superiority' of a figure who is purposeless or useless, unmotivated, has no agenda and is essentially hedonistic, a man of the moment, makes him the type of the Modernist."[2] Susan Sontag brings the type up to the present, uses him as a model for the detachment of the elite in her "Notes on 'Camp'" (which she calls "the modern dandyism").[3]

While the male side of this equation is well known, an extraordinary chapter in art history offers the female side of the dandy. The buzz in Paris in the fall of 1999 and in New York a year later surrounded an exhibition at the Musée d'Orsay culled from a massive collection of nearly five hundred photographs of the Countess de Castiglione taken by Pierre-Louis Pierson, a Parisian photographer at the court of Napoleon III. Notorious in their time because the countess bared her legs and put on enormously seductive airs, even when costumed in a nun's habit, they were collected by Pierre Apraxine, the leading curator of photographs in our own age, who bought them for the Gilman Paper Company. Hinting at performance art as well as the photographic work of such Contemporary stars as Cindy Sherman, they appealed at once to Postmodern critics for what Pierson called their neurotic "look of contact with reality." The story behind them is delightfully quirky. The countess's father was the Marquis Oldoini, a diplomat from La Spezia whose maternal grandfather had been a lawyer to the Bonaparte family in Italy. She was married at seventeen to a rich young widower, the Count Verasis de Castiglione, and arrived in Paris in 1856, sent there by Camillo Cavour, her cousin and a minister in the court of Victor Emannuel II of Sardinia and Piedmont, to become the mistress of Napoleon III, to keep him interested in the unification of Italy after the Crimean War during the Paris peace talks in April of that year. That was also when she began to pose for the photographs, initially shown only to friends and other lovers. Instantly famous, she appeared onstage in tableaux vivants (to her credit, for the benefit of charities) and was particularly renowned for the beauty of her feet and ankles, which she frequently showed off at the salons of the Rothschilds, among others. Her feet were compared to the perfection of Greek sculpture.

One of the most celebrated encounters of her career was with Frederick, Lord Leighton, a virtuoso renowned for his rendering of feet, who later remarked that she was not just the most beautiful woman he'd ever met but also the most vain. She became in her time an iconic presence through photographs and popular prints. Resurrected by the Paris exhibition of the photographs, she was compared not only to Sherman but to Nan Goldin. Art historians have been captivated by the photographs' prophetic quality in bringing together art and celebrity. As one reviewer wrote in *Artforum*, "To use a medium usually viewed as an authoritative record of reality in the service of the imagination—that is a very contemporary notion. And of course, there is the idea of using the self-portrait as a vehicle for an imaginary self. You can go in many directions with that: Cindy Sherman, Yasumasa Morimura. In the case of the countess, though, the only thing she ever impersonates is her idea of herself. Impersonating is the right word here. One feels, looking at hundreds of images of her, that behind the façade of impassive beauty there is turmoil, panic, despair—a very modern condition."[4]

The meaning of the pose changes with the artist. The countess projects noblesse oblige, one stance associated with the aristocracy. Another is the distancing gesture meant to keep the world at bay. An aristocrat in disguise, like a twentieth-century dandy in drag, deliberately hides his or her "quality" in an active effort to enjoy real contact with real people, building the experiential capital needed to enliven the art. This type of dissembling is the essence of Degas, Lautrec, and Bacon, slumming in the demimonde in search of an exciting string of experiences that stimulated them while adding to their visual repertoire a broad range of faces, bodies, and tawdry interiors. The works that arise from these undercover encounters soar beyond essays in class consciousness or anecdotes from the other side. As one historian has noted vis-à-vis Lautrec, by subordinating his own emotions to the "inner urgency" of his subjects he attained that sort of universality that is inherently democratic: "The ultimate way in which his aristocracy of spirit showed itself was in his assumption that he could absorb any expression of individuality, however violent, into the larger individuality of his art."[5] Lautrec was not alone in turning his comprehensive powers of insinuation into material for art. Sand, internationally notorious for her manly costume, could play the titled lady or be one of the boys, taking her cue from the situation and relying upon instincts sharpened as a young girl struggling in Paris with her distinctly unaristocratic mother or on manners polished in the courtly splendor of Nohant. Wittgenstein affected the humility of the foot soldier or village schoolmaster, but glimmers of his imperial upbringing would shine through.

There are two memorable Shakespearean antecedents to these aristocrats in disguise. Prince Hal enjoys being among the denizens of the Boar's Head tavern, where he "mingled his royalty with capering fools," in the words of his father. His first-act speech in *I Henry IV*, the aria of the second scene, reveals to the audience that he is more than aware of the situation and its ironies, but will emerge true to his station in the real test, the confrontation with Hotspur that is the culmination of the play. His return will be redemption of a debt incurred by birth and therefore "never promised." As he vows:

> I know you all, and will awhile uphold
> The unyok'd humor of your idleness:
> Yet herein will I imitate the sun,
> Who doth permit the base contagious clouds
> To smother up his beauty from the world,
> That when he please again to be himself,
> Being wanted, he may be more wonder'd at,
> By breaking through the foul and ugly mists
> Of vapors that did seem to strangle him.
> If all the year were playing holidays,
> To sport would be as tedious as to work;
> But when they seldom come, they wish'd for come,
> And nothing pleaseth but rare accidents.
> So when this loose behavior I throw off,
> And pay the debt I never promised,
> By how much better than my word I am
> By so much shall I falsify men's hopes;
> My reformation, glittering o'er my fault
> Shall show more goodly and attract more eyes
> Than that which hath no foil to set it off.
> I'll so offend to make offence a skill,
> Redeeming time when men think least I will.[6]

This also suggests the power mingled with creativity of Hamlet, who can command Horatio and Marcellas to swear to keep his secret because he is their prince. His ruse is madness and familiarity, assumed to attain his ends. Explaining his plan to Horatio he says, "Here, as before, never, so help your mercy, / How strange or odd so e'er I bear myself, / As I perchance hereafter shall think meet / To put an antick disposition on"

(1.5.169–72). Hamlet holds a special place in the history of Modern art and thought. As the epitome of the thinking, distressed, or ambiguous hero, he has charmed the pens of Freud, Mallarmé, Eliot, Valéry, and so many others. His progeny include Huysman's Des Esseintes, Hofmannsthal's imprisoned prince, and Villier de l'Isle Adam's Count Axel von Auersperg, whose castle hung with ancestral portraits of rhinegraves, chatelaines, and higher barons ironically was a birthplace of Modern aestheticism for Yeats and Edmund Wilson.

A crucial link in the literary tradition of later incarnations of Hamlet is the high-born original of the foil to Bloom, Stephen Daedalus. He expands upon the psychological complexity and paralysis that have qualified Hamlet as the first great Modern hero. His finely aristocratic nature, far from being a barrier, only enhances his role as the prophet of a revolutionary new way of thinking: aesthetically and intellectually rich, emotionally open, he commits regicide (attacks the old order) while holding desperately to tradition and the past (his "fault" is his too firm grasp of the memory of his mother and his sense of propriety). Both Hamlet and Hal are of interest here, not just as stage royals with Modern qualities but as types of the artist, whose function is to create dramas, as putative, junior playwrights who, like Shakespeare, had parts to play. Hamlet takes pride in his ability to deliver a text ("a prologue to my brains") that has its intended effect. The practice was previously beneath him: "I once did hold it, as our statists do, / A baseness to write fair and labor'd much / How to forget that learning, but, sir, now / It did me yeoman's service" (5.2.32–35). This magnificently anticipates not only the careers of Swinburne, Hofmannsthal, Russell, and Wittgenstein but the truth of Hauser's observation, "The relationship between the feudal lord and the scribe has not changed much in the course of the centuries—even though sons of the lords have become scribes themselves."[7]

This whole study has been full of Hamlets and Hals. Some are as tormented or guilt-ridden as the originals (Bacon and Russell), finding in art a means of redemption. Others, such as Hofmannsthal and Puvis de Chavannes, bear the magnificent pride of Hamlet or Hal too often lost in performance. For them, Modern art is a secret, even subversive, signal of the tradition passed under the semblance of the new to the next generation. If that is accomplished, then either way—whether one is or is not a noble in the eyes of society—one is always an artist.

Notes

Introduction (pages 1–31)

1. Robert Storr, *Modern Art Despite Modernism* (New York: Museum of Modern Art, 2000), p. 28.

2. Bernhard Giesen, "Cosmopolitans, Patriots, Jacobins, and Romantics," *Daedalus* 127 (Summer 1998): 224.

3. Hermann Broch, *Hugo von Hofmannsthal and His Time: The European Imagination, 1860–1920*, trans. Michael P. Steinberg (Chicago: University of Chicago Press, 1984), pp. 73–74.

4. Renato Poggioli, *The Theory of the Avant-Garde* (Cambridge, Mass.: Harvard University Press, 1968), p. 39.

5. Ibid., p. 52.

6. Peter Burger, *Theory of the Avant-Garde*, trans. Michael Shaw (Minneapolis: University of Minnesota Press, 1984), p. 10.

7. Ibid., p. 27.

8. Wallace Stevens, *The Necessary Angel* (New York: Vintage, 1951), pp. 35–36.

9. Villiers de L'Isle Adam, *Axel*, trans. Marilyn Gaddis Rose (Dublin: Dolmen Press, 1970), p. 48. Yeats's favorite line in the play was "Our existence is already full, and its cup runneth over. As for living? Our servants will do that for us" (p. 170).

10. David Thomson, *New York Times*, February 20, 2000.

11. As Hermann Broch observes in his study *Hugo von Hofmannsthal and His Time*, "The fact that the Rothschilds, Wertheimsteins, Sinas, Eskeles, Arnheims, with whom now the Hofmannsthals were also to associate, were socially, or at least halfway socially, accepted by the old aristocracy was based not so much on economic motives as on their Judaism, that is, on their membership in an exotic lineage which in them had dispatched its princes to the capital with the claim to equal status with the nobility. This is how they felt themselves, and this was the ambition of these banker barons, an ambition dedicated to the creation of a Jewish-feudalistic noble class, insane as such, even more insane in its fulfillment, nevertheless one of the few social realities grounded purely in romanticism and in this case supported above all by the penchant for the international, for the foreign, for the exceptional, to which the Viennese nobility of the time fell prey" (p. 84).

12. T. J. Clark, *Farewell to an Idea: Episodes from a History of Modernism* (New Haven, Conn.: Yale University Press, 1999), p. 7.

13. Ibid., p. 130.

14. Ibid., p. 160.

15. Ibid., p. 299.

16. Ibid., p. 300.

17. Ibid., p. 389.

18. Ibid., p. 302.

19. Robert Storr, *Modern Art despite Modernism*, p. 29.

20. Jean Baudrillard, *Seduction*, trans. Brian Singer (New York: St. Martin's, 1990), p. 1.

21. Thomas Ades, *Powder Her Face* (London: Faber Music), pp. 104–13.

22. Joan M. Lukach, *Hilla Rebay: In Search of the Spirit in Art* (New York: G. Braziller, 1983).

23. Lynn Garatola, ed. *The Ballets Russes and Its World* (New Haven: Yale University Press, 1999), pp. 68–69.

24. Richard Taruskin, *New York Times*, October 25, 1998.

25. Interview, *New York Times*, May 9, 1999.

26. Deborah L. Silverman, *Art Nouveau in Fin-de-Siècle France: Politics, Psychology, and Style* (Berkeley: University of California Press, 1989), p. 20.

27. Ibid., p. 51.

28. Lawrence Rainey, *Institutions of Modernism: Literary Elites and Public Culture* (New Haven, Conn.: Yale University Press, 1998).

29. Cleanth Brooks, *Modern Poetry and the Tradition* (Chapel Hill: University of North Carolina Press, 1939), p. 69.

30. Hermann Broch, *Hugo von Hofmannsthal and His Time*, p. 105–6.

1. *Genius over Genes (pages 32–64)*

1. Sand crossed the line of discretion in the eyes of Chopin's supporters when she used the fastidious and moody composer as the model for the character of Prince Karol de Roswald in the novel *Lucrezia Horiani* (1846). Sand's friend, some say lover, and Liszt's paramour, Marie D'Agoult, another aristocrat, copied this maneuver under the pseudonym Daniel Stern when she wrote a thinly veiled attack on Liszt in the novel *Nelida*. In her memoirs and elsewhere, Sand vehemently denied that Chopin was the basis for the character. From *The Story of My Life*: "I have traced in Prince Karol the character of a man determined in his nature, exclusive in his sentiments, exclusive in his exigencies. Chopin was not such a man. . . . He was modest in principle, gentle by habit, but he was imperious by instinct and full of a legitimate pride, which was not unconscious of itself."

2. Samuel Edwards, *George Sand: A Biography of the First Modern, Liberated Woman* (New York: David McKay, 1972), p. 213.

3. George Sand, *Story of My Life*, p. 82.

4. Ibid.

5. Ibid., p. 85.

6. Ibid.

7. Ibid., p. 90.
8. Ibid., p. 518.
9. Ibid., pp. 687–688.
10. Ibid., p. 77.
11. Germaine Bree, introduction to George Sand, *Story of My Life*, p. 95.
12. George Sand, *Story of My Life*, pp. 885–86.
13. George Sand, *Marianne*, trans. Sian Miles (New York: Carroll & Graf, 1987), p. 97.
14. Susan Sontag, "Notes on 'Camp,'" in *Against Interpretation* (New York: Farrar, Strauss, 1978), p. 288.
15. George Sand, *Horace*, trans. Zack Rogow (San Francisco: Mercury House, 1995), p. 147.
16. Eugène Delacroix, *The Journal of Eugène Delacroix*, ed. Hubert Wellington, trans. Lucy Norton (London: Phaidon Press, 1980), pp. 333–34.
17. One can't help admiring Delacroix's taste in music. The only one of Domenico Cimarosa's (1749–1801) operas ever heard after his time is *Il Matrimonio Segreto*, a hit in 1792 when it was first presented in Vienna when Cimarosa was kapellmeister, the successor to Antonio Salieri. On opening night the emperor, Leopold II, called for an encore of the entire work after the supper. When Cimarosa returned to his native Naples upon the emperor's death in 1792, he became kapellmeister to the king and teacher of the princesses; and *Il Matrimonio Segreto* dominated the operatic stage, performed fifty-seven times in a row. A comedy of near-Mozartean precision, Cimarosa's masterpiece has a lightness and balance that deserve to be heard in major opera houses today. Cimarosa was imprisoned and condemned to death by the French when they conquered Naples in 1799, but Ferdinand commuted the sentence. The composer attempted to return to St. Petersburg, where, as in Paris and London, he had enjoyed some of his earliest successes, but he died en route, in Venice, in 1801.
18. Delacroix, *Journal*, p. 117.
19. Ibid., p. 159.
20. Ibid., pp. 182–83.
21. Ibid., p. 211.
22. Terry Eagleton, *Scholars and Rebels in Nineteenth-Century Ireland* (Oxford: Blackwell, 1999), p. 29.
23. Delacroix, *Journal*, p. 226.
24. *Eugène Delacroix: The Late Work* (Philadelphia: Philadelphia Museum of Art, 1998), p. 150.
25. Delacroix, *Journal*, p. 227.
26. Lee Johnson, "The Late Work: Continuity and Variation," in *Delacroix: The Late Work* (Philadelphia: Philadelphia Museum of Art, 1999), p. 33.
27. Delacroix, *Journal*, p. 209.
28. Cited in T. J. Clark, *Farewell to an Idea*, p. 423. Clark appends this comment: "By this time the identification of Cézanne with his hero was more or less complete. Painting Delacroix's apotheosis was thus painting his own, which maybe was why it never could be done directly."
29. *Eugène Delacroix: The Late Work*, p. 129.

30. Ibid., p. 130.
31. Alfred Brendel, *Music Sounded Out* (New York: W. W. Norton, 1990), p. 162.
32. Ibid., p. 184.
33. Ibid., p. 162.
34. Ibid., p. 158.
35. Lawrence Kramer, *Music as Cultural Practice, 1800–1900* (Berkeley: University of California Press, 1990), pp. 89–90.
36. Charles Rosen, *The Romantic Generation* (Cambridge, Mass.: Harvard University Press, 1995), p. 474.
37. Kramer, *Music as Cultural Practice*, p. 111.
38. Ibid., p. 112.
39. Adam Zamoyski, *Chopin* (New York: Doubleday, 1979), p. 241.
40. Tad Szulc, *Chopin in Paris* (New York: Scribner, 1998), p. 91.
41. Ibid., p. 95.
42. Zamoyski, *Chopin*, p. 52.
43. Ibid., p. 16.
44. Szulc, *Chopin in Paris*, p. 271.
45. The opening sentence of a recent biography of Sir Osbert Sitwell captures this dialectic of genealogy and artistic ambition perfectly: "Francis Osbert Sacheverell Sitwell was a man whose pride in his aristocratic ancestry coexisted uneasily with his conviction that the artist was the sole truly superior being." Philip Ziegler, *Osbert Sitwell* (New York: Knopf, 2000), p. 3.
46. George Sand, *Story of My Life*, p. 1084.
47. Ibid., p. 1092.
48. Rosen, *Romantic Generation*, p. 285.
49. Ibid., p. 360.
50. Ibid., p. 86.
51. Ibid., p. 237.
52. Ibid., p. 380.
53. Ibid., p. 383.
54. Szulc, *Chopin in Paris*, p. 23.
55. Ibid., p. 241.
56. Rosen, *The Romantic Generation*, p. 395.

2. *Painters of Privilege (pages 65–90)*

1. Aimee Brown Price, *Pierre Puvis de Chavannes* (New York: Rizzoli, 1999), p. 49.
2. T. J. Clark, *Farewell to an Idea* (New Haven, Conn.: Yale University Press, 1999), p. 83.
3. Elizabeth Gilmore Holt, ed., *The Art of All Nations: 1850–1873* (New York: Anchor, 1981), p. 248.
4. Gary Tinterow and Henri Loyrette, *The Origins of Impressionism* (New York: Metropolitan Museum of Art, 1994), p. 42.
5. Price, *Pierre Puvis de Chavannes*, p. 61.

6. Holt, *Art of All Nations*, p. 187.
7. Price, *Pierre Puvis de Chavannes*, p. 47.
8. Ibid., p. 46.
9. Ibid., p. 47.
10. *The Musée d'Orsay, Paris* (New York: Abrams, 1986), p. 41.
11. John Milner, *The Studios of Paris: The Capital of Art in the Late Nineteenth Century* (New Haven, Conn.: Yale University Press, 1988), p. 141.
12. Ibid., p. 190.
13. Clark, *Farewell to an Idea*, p. 84.
14. John Rewald, *Studies in Impressionism* (New York: Abrams, 1985), pp. 28–29.
15. Jean Sutherland Boggs, *Degas* (New York: Metropolitan Museum of Art, 1988), p. 23.
16. Ibid., p. 24.
17. Ibid., p. 25.
18. John Rewald, *Studies in Impressionism*, p. 50.
19. Boggs, *Degas*, p. 23.
20. John Ashbery, *Reported Sightings* (New York: Knopf, 1983), p. 131.
21. Julia Frey, *Toulouse-Lautrec: A Biography* (New York: Knopf, 1998), p. 6.
22. Ibid., p. 394.
23. Ibid., pp. 144–145.
24. Ibid., p. 270.
25. Ibid., p. 338.
26. Ibid., p. 340.
27. Ibid., p. 430.
28. Ibid., p. 463.
29. Ashbery, *Reported Sightings*, p. 132.

3. *A Knight at the Opera (pages 91–123)*

1. According to biographer Brian McGuiness, "Ludwig gave little sign at any period of interest in contemporary literature. Hofmannsthal was a distant family connection and his idea of a return to the Baroque as a refuge from the decline of culture in his own day had some attraction. At any rate, Ludwig liked to quote his saying, 'One has to behave decently / Some day, somehow, somewhere, it will pay off.'" From *Wittgenstein: A Life* (Berkeley: University of California Press, 1988), p. 37. Strauss also had his Wittgenstein connection as one of the composers who was commissioned by Paul Wittgenstein, Ludwig's brother, who had been wounded in World War I, to write a piece that could be played by left hand alone. It had its debut at a private recital in London, with Strauss himself accompanying.
2. Michael Hamburger, introduction to Hugo von Hofmannsthal, *Selected Plays and Libretti* (New York: Pantheon, 1963), p. xxxiii.
3. Harry Kessler, *Berlin Lights: The Diaries of Count Harry Kessler (1918–1937)* (New York: Grove, 2000).
4. Hermann Broch, *Hugo Von Hofmannsthal and His Time* (Chicago: University of Chicago Press, 1984), p. 89.

5. Ibid., pp. 91–92.

6. Carl Schorske, *Fin-de-Siècle Vienna: Politics and Culture* (New York: Knopf, 1980), pp. 15–16.

7. Ibid., p. 7.

8. Ibid., pp. 313–19.

9. Hugo von Hofmannsthal, *Selected Prose* (New York: Pantheon, 1952), p. 247.

10. Schorske, *Fin-de-Siècle Vienna*, p. 22.

11. E. R. Curtius, *European Literature and the Latin Middle Ages*, trans. W. R. Trask (Princeton, N.J.: Princeton University Press, 1953), pp. 395–97.

12. Hofmannsthal, *Selected Prose*, p. 131.

13. Ibid.

14. Carl E. Schorske, *Thinking with History: Explorations in the Passage to Modernism* (Princeton, N.J.: Princeton University Press, 1998), p. 136.

15. Hofmannsthal, *Selected Prose*, pp. 140–41.

16. David H. Miles, *Hofmannsthal's Novel* Andreas*: Memory and Self* (Princeton, N.J.: Princeton University Press, 1972), p. 48.

17. Broch, *Hugo von Hofmannsthal and His Time*, p. 182.

18. Hofmannsthal, *Selected Prose*, pp. 147–48.

19. Ibid., p. 261.

20. Ibid., pp. 261–62.

21. Broch, *Hugo von Hofmannsthal and his Time*, pp. 115–16.

22. Hugo von Hofmannsthal, *Selected Plays and Libretti*, ed. Michael Hamburger (New York: Pantheon, 1963), pp. liii–liv.

23. Schorske, *Thinking with History*, pp. 138–40.

24. Hofmannsthal, *Selected Plays and Libretti*, p. 190.

25. Ibid., p. 194.

26. Ibid., p. 195.

27. Ibid., p. 325.

28. Ibid., p. 371.

29. Hofmannsthal, *Selected Prose*, p. 57.

30. Ibid., p. 77.

31. Ibid., p. 108.

32. Ibid., p. 114.

33. Ibid., p. 367.

34. Hofmannsthal, *Selected Plays and Libretti*, p. 820.

35. Ibid., p. 746.

36. Ibid., p. 673.

37. Ibid., p. 687.

38. Ibid., p. 731.

39. Ibid., p. 818.

40. Ibid., p. 822.

41. Miles, *Hofmannsthal's Novel* Andreas, p 76.

42. *A Working Friendship: The Correspondence between Richard Strauss and Hugo von Hofmannsthal*, trans. Hans Hammelman and Ewald Osers, with an introduction by Edward Sackville-West (New York: Random House, 1961), p. 60.

43. Ibid., p. xx.
44. Ibid., p. 30.
45. Ibid., p. 30.
46. Ibid., p. 58.
47. Verlyn Klinkenberg, "What the Marschallin Makes of Time," *New York Times*, 23 January 2000.
48. Derrick Puffett, "'Las Er die Musick, wo sie ist,' Pitch Specificity in Strauss," in Bryan Gilliam, *Richard Strauss and His World* (Princeton, N.J.: Princeton University Press, 1992), p. 156.
49. Ibid., p. 173.
50. Alfred Kalisch, introduction to Alfred Newman, *Richard Strauss* (New York: Norton, 1958), p. xvi.
51. Julius Korngold, profile in the *Neues Wiener Tagblatt*, in Bryan Gilliam, *Richard Strauss and His World* (Princeton, N.J.: Princeton University Press, 1992), p. 343.
52. Alfred Newman, *Richard Strauss* (New York: Norton, 1958), p. 136.
53. Theodor Adorno, "Richard Strauss at 60," in Bryan Gilliam, *Richard Strauss and His World* (Princeton, N.J.: Princeton University Press, 1992), pp. 185–86.
54. Ibid., pp. 409–10.
55. E. M. Cioran, *All Gall Is Divided*, trans. Richard Howard (New York: Arcade Publishing, 1999), p. 118.

4. *Members of the Club (pages 124–153)*

1. The Nazarenes, also called the "Early Christians," included Johann Friedrich Overbeck (1789–1864) and Peter von Cornelius (1783–1867) and were based in Germany.
2. Tim Barringer and Elizabeth Prettejohn, eds., *Frederick Leighton: Antiquity, Renaissance, Modernity* (New Haven, Conn.: Yale University Press, 1999).
3. Roger Shattuck, *The Innocent Eye: On Modern Literature and the Arts* (New York: Washington Square Press, 1986).
4. Edmond Gosse, *The Life of Algernon Charles Swinburne* (New York: Macmillan, 1917), p. 277.
5. Cecil Y. Lang, ed. *The Letters of Algernon Swinburne*, vol. 6 (New Haven, Conn.: Yale University Press, 1962), p. 180.
6. Cited in Barringer and Prettejohn, *Frederick Leighton*, p. 236.
7. Barringer and Prettejohn, *Frederick Leighton*, p. xxx.
8. A. C. Swinburne, *The Poems of Algernon Charles Swinburne* (New York: Harper and Brothers, 1904), 3:79.
9. Edmund Wilson, introduction to *The Novels of Algernon Charles Swinburne* (New York: Farrar, Strauss, 1962), p. xi.
10. Cited in Edmund Gosse, *The Life of Algernon Charles Swinburne* (New York: Macmillan, 1917), p. 151.
11. Max Nordau, *Degeneration* (New York: D. Appleton & Co., 1895), p. 58.
12. Camille Paglia, *Sexual Personae: Art and Decadence from Nefertiti to Emily Dickinson* (New Haven, Conn.: Yale University Press, 1990), p. 460.

13. Ibid., p. 460–61.

14. Ibid., p. 475.

15. Ibid., p. 461.

16. Georges Lafourcade, *Swinburne: A Literary Biography* (London: G. Bell & Sons, 1932), p. xi.

17. See particularly William E. Buckler, *The Victorian Imagination* (New York: New York University Press, 1977); Jerome J. McGann, *Swinburne: An Experiment in Criticism* (Chicago: University of Chicago Press, 1972); Carol Christ, *Victorian and Modern Poetics* (Princeton, N.J.: Princeton University Press, 1984); Linda Dowling, *Language and Decadence in the Victorian Fin-de-Siècle* (Princeton, N.J.: Princeton University Press, 1986). Dowling focuses on Swinburne's consummate mastery of Greek and Latin, one of the advantages of his upper-class education, and its role in his creation of an autonomous language: "Literary Decadence as it was to emerge form the Victorian linguistic crisis was no attempt to oppose in direct terms the spectre of disintegration or collapse, but rather was an attempt to save something from the wreck by turning to literary advantage what had otherwise appeared only as one of the incidentally bleak implications of the new linguistic science: the idea that written language, the literary tongue of the great English writers, was simply another dead language in relation to living speech" (p. xv).

18. Leslie Brisman, "Swinburne's Semiotics," *Georgia Review* 31 (fall 1977): 578–97; and Nicholas Tredell, "Tristram of Lyonesse: Dangerous Voyage," *Victorian Poetry* 20 (summer 1982): 97–112. As Tredell writes, "It undermines the explicitness which would censor metaphor and metonymy and restores us to the zone in which eros and high rhetoric interact" (p. 157).

19. Swinburne, *Poems of Algernon Swinburne*, 4:144.

20. George Steiner, *Extraterritorial: Papers on Literature and the Language Revolution* (New York: Athenaeum, 1971), pp. 163–64.

21. Susan Sontag, *Styles of Radical Will* (New York: Farrar, Straus & Giroux, 1969), p. 6.

22. Clyde K. Hyder, ed. *Swinburne Replies* (Syracuse, N.Y.: Syracuse University Press, 1966), pp. 23–24.

23. Swinburne, *Poems of Algernon Charles Swinburne*, 3:21.

24. T. S. Eliot, *The Complete Poems and Plays* (New York: Harcourt, Brace & World, 1971), p. 118.

25. C. K. Hyder, ed., *Swinburne: The Critical Heritage* (New York: Barnes & Noble, 1970), p. 124.

26. Albert Thibaudet, *La Poesie de Stephane Mallarmé* (Paris: Nouvelle Revue Française, 1912), p. 393.

27. Cecil Y. Lang, ed., *The Swinburne Letters: Volume I* (New Haven, Conn.: Yale University Press, 1950), p. 131.

28. Swinburne, *Poems of Algernon Charles Swinburne*, 3:161.

29. Henri Mondor, ed., *Correspondance de Stephane Mallarmé* (Paris: Gallimard, 1959–1985), 6:236.

30. Richard Ellmann, *James Joyce* (New York: Oxford University Press, 1983), p. 101.

31. T. S. Eliot, *Selected Essays* (New York: Harcourt, Brace, 1932), p. 285.

32. Ezra Pound, *Literary Essays* (New York: New Directions, 1968), pp. 292–94.

33. Ezra Pound, *The Collected Early Poems of Ezra Pound*, ed. Michael John King (New York: New Directions, 1976), pp. 40–41.

34. Ibid., p. 261.

35. Pound, *The Cantos* (New York: New Directions, 1950), p. 522.

36. Ibid., p. 523.

37. Swinburne, *Poems of Algernon Charles Swinburne*, p. 273.

5. Peer Review (pages 154–186)

1. Bertrand Russell, *The Autobiography of Bertrand Russell: Vol. I. 1872–1914* (Boston: Little, Brown, 1961), pp. 316–17.

2. George Santayana, *Persons and Places*, ed. William G. Holzberger and Herman J. Saatkamp Jr. (Cambridge, Mass.: MIT Press, 1987), p. 441.

3. Russell, *Autobiography*, 1:82.

4. Ibid., 1:87.

5. Ibid., 1:250.

6. Ibid., 1:36.

7. Bertrand Russell, *The Basic Writings of Bertrand Russell*, ed. Robert E. Egner and Lester E. Denonn (New York: Touchstone, 1961), p. 341.

8. Bertrand Russell, *My Philosophical Development* (London: George Allen and Unwin, 1959), p. 41.

9. Russell, *Autobiography*, 1:36.

10. Ibid., 1:82.

11. Ibid., 1:2.

12. Ibid., 1:20.

13. Nicholas Griffin, ed., *The Selected Letters of Bertrand Russell: Vol. I. The Private Years (1884–1914)* (Boston: Houghton Mifflin, 1992), p. 284.

14. A. J. Ayer, *Russell and Moore: The Analytical Heritage* (Cambridge, Mass.: Harvard University Press, 1971), p. 11.

15. Russell, *Basic Writings*, p. 138.

16. Ibid., p. 383.

17. Ibid., p. 371.

18. Ibid., p. 175.

19. Ibid., p. 173.

20. Ibid., pp. 613–14.

21. Ibid., p. 182.

22. Ibid., p. 183

23. Ibid.

24. Bertrand Russell and Patricia Russell, eds., *The Amberley Papers* (New York: Simon and Schuster, 1937), 1:146.

25. Ibid., 1:341.

26. Ibid., 2:31.

27. Ibid., 2:383.

28. Andrew Brink, *Bertrand Russell: The Psychobiography of a Moralist* (Atlantic Highlands, N.J.: Humanities Press International, 1989), p. 36.

29. Russell, *Autobiography*, 1:94–95.

30. Brink, *Bertrand Russell: The Psychobiography of a Moralist*, p. 161.

31. Russell, *Autobiography*, 1:299. Russell's note to this letter reads, "I have worn the watch and chain ever since 1949."

32. Ibid., 1:250.

33. Russell, *Basic Writings*, p. 567.

34. Russell, *Autobiography*, 1:238.

35. Russell, *Basic Writings*, p. 191.

36. Ibid., p. 213.

37. Griffin, *Selected Letters*, p. 398.

38. Brian McGuiness, *Wittgenstein: A Life* (Berkeley: University of California Press, 1988), p. 18.

39. Ray Monk, *Wittgenstein: The Duty of Genius* (New York: Free Press, 1990), p. 237.

40. Russell, *Basic Writings*, p. 45.

41. McGuiness, *Wittgenstein: A Life*, p. 24.

42. Ibid., p. 167.

43. Ibid., p. 156.

44. Griffin, *Selected Letters*, p. 418.

45. Monk, *Wittgenstein: The Duty of Genius*, p. 110.

46. McGuiness, *Wittgenstein: A Life*, p. 245.

47. Ibid., p. 269.

48. Ibid., p. 279.

49. Raymond Monk, *Bertrand Russell: The Spirit of Solitude* (New York: Random House, 1996), p. 280.

50. Griffin, *Selected Letters*, p. 459.

51. Russell, *My Philosophical Development*, p. 118.

52. Bertrand Russell, *The Problems of Philosophy* (London: Oxford University Press, 1912), p. 1.

53. William R. Everdell, *The First Moderns: Profiles in the Origins of Twentieth-Century Thought* (Chicago: University of Chicago Press, 1997), p. 192.

54. McGuiness, *Wittgenstein: A Life*, p. 156.

55. Monk, *Wittgenstein: The Duty of Genius*, p. 533.

56. Ludwig Wittgenstein, *Tractatus Logico-Philosophicus*, trans. D. F. Pears and B. F. McGuinness (New York: Routledge, 1961), p. 1.

57. Monk, *Wittgenstein: The Duty of Genius*, p. 190.

58. Ibid., p. 141.

59. *The Complete Essays of Montaigne*, trans. Donald Frame (Stanford, California: Stanford University Press, 1965), p. v.

60. Ludwig Wittgenstein, *Lectures and Conversations on Aesthetics, Psychology and Religious Belief*, ed. Cyril Barrett (Berkeley: University of California Press, 1966), p. 8

61. Ibid., p. 9.

62. Ludwig Wittgenstein, *Culture and Value*, trans. Peter Winch (Chicago: University of Chicago Press, 1980), p. 60e.

63. Maurice Blanchot, *The Gaze of Orpheus*, trans. Lydia Davis (Barrytown, N.Y.: Station Hill Press, 1982), p. 130.

64. Ibid.

65. Ibid.

6. *The Irish Ascendant (pages 187–201)*

1. John Stallworthy, "An Irish Window: Remaking W. B. Yeats," *Encounters*, August 1974, p. 59.

2. Michael Peppiatt, *Francis Bacon: The Anatomy of an Enigma* (New York: Farrar, Straus, 1998), p. 68.

3. Robert Storr, *Modern Art despite Modernism* (New York: Museum of Modern Art, 2000), p. 77.

4. Ibid.

5. Francis Bacon, interview by Hugh Davies, 1973, in Hugh Davies and Sally Yard, *Bacon* (New York: Abbeville, 1991).

6. Peppiatt, *Francis Bacon*, p. 15.

7. Ibid.

8. David Farson, *The Gilded Gutter: A Life of Francis Bacon* (New York: Pantheon, 1993), p. 16.

9. Peppiatt, *Francis Bacon*, p. 150.

10. *Francis Bacon: A Retrospective*, essays by Dennis Farr, Michael Peppiatt, Sally Yard (New York: Abrams, 1999), p. 86.

11. Peppiatt, *Francis Bacon*, p. 55.

12. Ibid.

7. *King of the Cats (pages 202–221)*

1. Guy Davenport, *A Balthus Notebook* (New York: Ecco, 1989), p. 30.

2. Ibid.

3. Ibid., p. 60.

4. Nicholas Fox Weber, *Balthus: A Biography* (New York: Knopf, 1999), p. 428.

5. Nicholas Fox Weber, "The Balthus Enigma," *New Yorker*, 6 September 1999, p. 37.

6. Weber, *Balthus*, p. 536.

7. Davenport, *Balthus Notebook*, p. 76.

8. Weber, *Balthus*, p. 119.

9. Cited in Weber, *Balthus*, p. 264.

10. Weber, *Balthus*, pp. 267–68.

11. Michel Foucault, "The Prose of Actaeon," foreword to *The Baphomet* by Pierre Klossowski, trans. Sophie Hawkes and Stephen Sartarelli (New York: Marsilio Publishers, 1992), pp. xxiv–xxv.

12. Robert Storr, *Modern Art despite Modernism* (New York: Museum of Modern Art, 2000), p. 50.

13. Davenport, *Balthus Notebook*, p. 67.
14. Storr, *Modern Art despite Modernism*, p. 51.
15. Weber, *Balthus*, p. 499.
16. Ibid., p. 182.
17. Rainer Maria Rilke, *The Notebooks of Malte Laurids Brigge*, trans. M. D. Herter Norton (New York: Norton, 1964), p. 31.
18. Weber, *Balthus*, p. 447.
19. Davenport, *Balthus Notebook*, p. 61.

Epilogue (pages 222–226)

1. Walter Benjamin, *Illuminations*, trans. Harry Zohn (New York: Schocken, 1969), *Selected Writings* (Cambridge: Harvard University Press, 1999), and *The Arcades Project*, trans. Howard Eiland and Kevin McLaughlin (Cambridge, Mass.: Harvard University Press, 1999).
2. Arnold Hauser, *The Social History of Art* (New York: Knopf, 1952), 2:757.
3. Susan Sontag, "Notes on 'Camp,'" in *Against Interpretation* (New York: Farrar, Strauss, 1978), p. 288.
4. Carol Squiers, "Noble Cast," *Artforum*, September 1999, p. 184.
5. Edward Lucie Smith, *Toulouse-Lautrec* (London: Phaidon, 1983), p. 23.
6. William Shakespeare, *I Henry IV*, 1.2.218–241.
7. Hauser, *Social History of Art*, p. 862.

Bibliography

Alphon, Ernst van. *Francis Bacon and the Loss of Self*. Cambridge, Mass.: Harvard University Press, 1993.

Archimbaud, Michel. *Francis Bacon: Entretiens avec Michel Archimbaud*. Paris: Jean-Claude Lattes, 1992.

Ashbery, John. *Reported Sightings*. New York: Knopf, 1989.

Atwood, William G. *The Parisian Worlds of Frédéric Chopin*. New Haven, Conn.: Yale University Press, 1999.

Ayer, A. J. *Bertrand Russell*. New York: Viking, 1972.

———. *Russell and Moore: The Analytical Heritage*. Cambridge, Mass.: Harvard University Press, 1971.

Baker, G. P., and P. M. S. Hacker. *An Analytical Commentary on Wittgenstein's Philosophical Investigations*. Vol. I. Chicago: University of Chicago Press, 1980.

Barringer, Tim, and Elizabeth Prettejohn, eds. *Frederic Leighton: Antiquity, Renaissance, Modernity*. New Haven, Conn.: Yale University Press, 1995.

Beller, Steven. *Vienna and the Jews, 1867–1938: A Cultural History*. New York: Cambridge University Press, 1989.

Borges, Jorge Luis. *Everything and Nothing*. New York: New Directions, 1999.

Bowie, David. "The Last Legendary Painter," *Modern Painters*, autumn 1994.

Boyden, Matthew. *Richard Strauss*. Boston: Northeastern University Press, 1999).

Brendel, Alfred. *Music Sounded Out*. New York: Farrar, Straus and Giroux, 1990.

———. *Musical Thoughts and Afterthoughts*. Princeton, N.J.: Princeton University Press, 1976.

Brink, Andrew. *Bertrand Russell: The Psychobiography of a Moralist*. Atlantic Highlands, N.J.: Humanities Press International, 1989.

Broch, Hermann. *Hugo von Hofmannsthal and His Time: The European Imagination, 1860–1920*. Translated by Michael P. Steinberg. Chicago: University of Chicago Press, 1984.

Buckler, William E. *The Victorian Imagination: Essays in Aesthetic Exploration*. New York: New York University Press, 1980.

Burger, Peter. *Theory of the Avant-Garde*. Translated by Michael Shaw. Minneapolis: University of Minnesota Press, 1984.

Carandente, Giovanni. *Balthus: Drawings and Watercolors*. Translated by James Mitchell. London: Thames and Hudson, 1983.

Cioran, E. M. *All Gall Is Divided.* Translated by Richard Howard. New York: Arcade, 1999.

Clark, T. J. *Farewell to an Idea.* New Haven, Conn.: Yale University Press, 1999.

Dalley, Jan. *Diana Mosley.* New York: Knopf, 2000.

Davenport, Guy. *A Balthus Notebook.* New York: Ecco Press, 1989.

Davies, Hugh, and Sally Yard. *Bacon.* New York: Abbeville, 1986.

Delacroix, Eugène. *The Journals of Eugène Delacroix.* Edited by Hubert Wellington, translated by Lucy Norton. London: Phaidon, 1995.

Deleuze, Gilles. *Francis Bacon: Logique de la sensation.* Paris: Editions de la Difference, 1981.

Denvir, Bernard. *Post Impressionism.* London: Thames and Hudson, 1992.

Die Reihe. *Anton Webern.* Edited by Herbert Eimert and Karlheinz Stockhausen. Bryn Mawr, Pa.: Theodore Presser, 1958.

Edwards, Samuel. *George Sand: A Biography of the First Modern, Liberated Woman.* New York: David McKay, 1972.

Eliot, T. S. *Selected Essays.* New York: Harcourt Brace, 1932.

Eugène Delacroix: Paintings, Drawings, and Prints from North American Collections. New York: Metropolitan Museum of Art, 1991.

Everdell, William R. *The First Moderns: Profiles in the Origins of Twentieth-Century Thought.* Chicago: University of Chicago Press, 1997.

Farson, David. *The Gilded Gutter: A Life of Francis Bacon.* New York: Pantheon, 1993.

Foucart, Jacques, ed. *La génese des peintures murales de Puvis de Chavannes.* Amiens: C.N.D.P., 1976.

Francis Bacon: A Retrospective. Essays by Dennis Farr, Michael Peppiatt, Sally Yard. New York: Abrams, 1999.

Gale, Matthew. *Francis Bacon: Working on Paper.* London: Tate Gallery, 1999.

Garafola, Lynn, and Nancy Van Norman Baer, eds. *The Ballets Russes and Its World.* New Haven, Conn.: Yale University Press, 1999.

Gilliam, Bryan. *Richard Strauss and His World.* Princeton, N.J.: Princeton University Press, 1992.

Gowing, Lawrence, and Sam Hunter. *Francis Bacon.* Washington, D.C.: Hirschhorn Museum and Thames and Hudson, 1989.

Graham-Dixon, Andrew. *The Paper Museum.* New York: Knopf, 1997.

Griffin, Nocholas. *The Selected Letters of Bertrand Russell.* Vol. I: *The Private Years.* (1884–1914). Boston: Houghton Mifflin, 1992.

Hammelman, Hanns, and Ewald Osers, trans. *A Working Friendship: The Correspondence between Richard Strauss and Hugo von Hofmannsthal.* With an introduction by Edward Sackville-West. New York: Random House, 1961.

Hannoosh, Michele. *Painting and the Journal of Eugène Delacroix.* Princeton, N.J.: Princeton University Press, 1995.

Hobhouse, Janet. *The Bride Stripped Bare.* London: Jonathan Cape, 1988.

Hofmannsthal, Hugo von. *Selected Plays and Libretti.* Edited by Michael Hamburger. New York: Pantheon, 1963.

Huysmans, J. K. *Against the Grain.* With an introduction by Havelock Ellis. New York: Dover, 1969.

———. *L'Art Moderne*. Paris: Nizet, 1883.

Kennedy, Michael. *Richard Strauss: Man, Musician, Enigma*. New York: Cambridge University Press, 1999.

Klossowski, Pierre. *The Baphomet*. Translated by Sophie Hawkes and Stephen Satarelli. New York: Marsilio, 1992.

Kolneder, Walter. *Anton Webern: An Introduction to His Works*. Translated by Humphrey Searle. Berkeley: University of California Press, 1968.

Kramer, Lawrence. *Music as Cultural Practice*. Berkeley: University of California Press, 1993.

Krauss, Rosalind E. *The Originality of the Avant-Garde and Other Modernist Myths*. Cambridge, Mass.: MIT Press, 1985.

Lafourcade, Georges. *Swinburne: A Literary Biography*. London: G. Bell and Sons, 1932.

Lampedusa, Giuseppe Tomai di. *The Leopard*. Translated by Archibald Colquhoun. New York: Pantheon, 1960.

———. *Two Stories and a Memory*. Translated by Archibald Colquhoun. New York: Pantheon, 1962.

———. *The Siren and Selected Writings*. Translated by Archibald Colquhoun, David Gilmour, and Guido Waldman. London: Harvill Press, 1995.

Leymarie, Jean. *Balthus*. Geneva: Skira Editions, 1978.

———. *Balthus*. New York: Rizzoli, 1979.

Lightbrown, Ronald. *Piero della Francesca*. New York: Abbeville, 1992.

Liszt, Franz. *An Artist's Journey*. Translated by Charles Saltoni. Chicago: University of Chicago Press, 1989.

Lord, James. "Balthus: The Strange Case of the Count de Rola." *New Criterion* 2 (December 1983): pp. 9–25.

———. *Giacometti: A Biography*. New York: Farrar, Straus and Giroux, 1985.

Merrill, James. *Braving the Elements*, New York: Atheneum, 1972.

———. *The Country of a Thousand Years of Peace*. Rev. ed. New York: Atheneum, 1970.

Miles, David H. *Hofmannsthal's Novel* Andreas: *Memory and Self*. Princeton, N.J.: Princeton University Press, 1972.

Monk, Ray. *Bertrand Russell: The Spirit of Solitude*. London: Jonathan Cape, 1996.

———. *Ludwig Wittgenstein: The Duty of Genius*. New York: Free Press, 1990.

Monk, Ray, and Anthony Palmer. *Bertrand Russell and the Origins of Analytical Philosophy*. Bristol: Thoemmes Press, 1996.

O'Hara, Daniel T. *Tragic Knowledge: Yeat's Autobiography and Hermeneutics*. New York: Columbia University Press, 1981.

Opienski, Henryk, ed. *Chopin's Letters*. New York: Dover, 1988.

Pears, David F. *Bertrand Russell and the British Tradition in Philosophy*. New York Random House, 1967.

Peppiatt, Michael. *Francis Bacon: Anatomy of an Enigma*. New York: Farrar, Straus and Giroux, 1998.

Price, Aimee Brown. *Pierre Puvis de Chavannes*. New York: Rizzoli, 1994.

Puvis de Chavannes. Paris: Editions des Musées Nationaux, 1976.

Rainey, Lawrence. *Institutions of Modernism: Literary Elites and Public Culture.* New Haven, Conn.: Yale University Press, 1998.

Rewald, Sabine. *Balthus*. New York: Metropolitan Museum of Art, 1984.

Rimbaud, Arthur. *A Season in Hell/The Illuminations*. Translated by Enid Rhodes Peschel. New York: Oxford University Press, 1973.

Rosen, Charles. *The Romantic Generation.* Cambridge, Mass.: Harvard University Press, 1995.

———. *Romantic Poets, Critics, and Other Madmen.* Cambridge, Mass.: Harvard University Press, 1998.

Russell, Bertand. *The Autobiography of Bertrand Russell.* Vol. I: *1872–1914.* Boston: Little, Brown, 1961.

———. *Basic Writings of Bertrand Russell.* New York: Touchstone, 1961.

———. *My Philosophical Development*. London: George Allen and Unwin, 1959.

———. *Portraits from Memory and Other Essays*. New York: Simon and Schuster, 1951.

Russell, Bertrand, and Patricia Russell, eds. *The Amberley Papers: Bertrand Russell's Family Background*. New York: Simon and Schuster, 1937.

Russell, John. *Francis Bacon*. New York: Thames and Hudson, 1993.

Ryerson, Scott D., and Michael Orlando Yaccarino. *Infinite Variety: The Life and Legend of the Marchesa Casati*. New York: Viridian, 2000.

Sand, George. *The Story of My Life*. Edited by Telma Jurgran. Albany: State University of New York Press, 1991.

Schimmel, Herbert D., ed. *The Letters of Henri de Toulouse-Lautrec*. New York: Oxford University Press, 1991.

Schorske, Carl E. *Fin-de-Siècle Vienna: Politics and Culture*. New York: Knopf, 1980.

———. *Thinking with History: Explorations in the Passage to Modernism.* Princeton, N.J.: Princeton University Press, 1998.

Searle, Humphrey. *The Music of Liszt*. New York: Dover, 1966.

Sheridan, Alan. *André Gide: A Life in the Present.* Cambridge, Mass.: Harvard University Press, 1999.

Sitwell, Sacheverell. *Liszt*. New York: Dover, 1967.

Soby, James Thrall. *Balthus*. New York: Museum of Modern Art, 1956.

Steiner, George. *Errata: An Examined Life*. New Haven, Conn.: Yale University Press, 1998.

Stravinsky, Igor. *An Autobiography*. New York: Norton, 1998.

Sylvester, David. *Interviews with Francis Bacon*. New York: Pantheon, 1995.

Szulc, Tad. *Chopin in Paris: The Life and Times of the Romantic Composer*. New York: Scribner, 1998.

Tinterow, Gary, Michael Pantazzi, and Vincent Pomarede. *Corot*. New York: Metropolitan Museum of Art, 1996.

Villiers de l'Isle Adam, Auguste. *Axel*. Translated by Marilyn Gaddis Rose. Dublin: Dolmen Press, 1970.

———. *Axel*. Translated by June Guicharnaud. Englewood Cliffs, N.J.: Prentice-Hall, 1970.

Watson, Derek. *Liszt*. New York: Schirmer, 1989.

Wattenmaker, Richard J. *Puvis de Chavannes and the Modern Tradition.* Toronto: Art Gallery of Ontario, 1975.

Weber, Nicholas Fox. *Balthus: A Biography.* New York: Knopf, 1999.

Wilhelm, Kurt. *Richard Strauss: An Intimate Portrait.* Translated by Mary Whittall. New York: Thames and Hudson, 2000.

Wittgenstein, Ludwig. *Lectures and Conversations on Aesthetics, Psychology, and Religious Belief.* Edited by Cyril Barrett. Berkeley: University of California Press, 1966.

———. *Philosophical Investigations.* Translated by G. E. M. Anscombe. New York: Macmillan, 1953.

Yeats, William Butler. *Memoirs: Autobiogaphy, First Draft and Journal.* Edited by Denis Donoghue. New York: Macmillan, 1972.

Zamoyski, Adam. *Chopin.* New York: Doubleday, 1979.

Zweig, Stefan. *The World of Yesterday.* Edited by H. Zohn. Lincoln: University of Nebraska Press, 1964.

Index

A Fine Disregard (Varnedoe), 2
A la Recherche du Temps Perdus (Proust), 13
A Rebours (Huysmans), 11–12
Abakanowicz, Magdalena, 21
Abdy, Lady Iya, 210
Abstract Expressionism, 2, 15–16, 30, 52, 64, 87, 123
Académie Julian, 85
Adam, Robert, x
Adam, Villiers de L'Isle, 11–12, 42, 92, 103, 136, 226
Adams, Henry, 5, 29, 130, 136
Ades, Thomas, 21, 24, 121
Adorno, Theodor W., 16, 119, 121–122
Agoult, Countess Marie d', 58, 61, 228n
Ahna, Pauline de, 93
Aitshicon, George, 132
Alden, Eric, 199–200
Alexander III, 29
Alt, Rudolf von, 174
Amberley Papers, The (Russell), 37, 166–167
American Journal of Human Genetics, 22
anachronism (art or aristocracy as), 8, 71, 106–107, 204–205
Andre, Carl, 17, 213
André Derain (Balthus), 204, color plate
Andreas (Hofmannsthal), 103–105
Andreou, George, 23
Années de pélerinage (Liszt), 56
Apostles, 158
Apraxine, Pierre, 223
Argyll, Duke and Duchess of, 24
Ariadne auf Naxos (Strauss and Hofmannsthal), 6, 92, 118–119
Ariosto, Ludovico, 106
Aristotle, 162
Arman, 20
Arp, Jean (Hans), 208
Art Brut, 14
Art Institute of Chicago, 203
Art Nouveau, 29
Artaud, Antonin, 210, 212
Artforum, 224
Ashbery, John, 62, 82, 88, 141, 153
Aspen Festival, 24–25
At Home with the Marquis de Sade (Gray), 23
Atget, Eugene, 145
Auden, W. H., 115
Augustus II, 37
avant-garde, 7–9
Axel (Adam), 11–12, 104
Ayer, A. J., 160–161, 181

Bach, Johann Sebastian, 28, 56, 58, 59, 62, 63, 106, 165
Bacon, Francis, x, 3, 7, 8, 13, 18, 19, 21, 22, 48, 51, 74, 76, 81, 82, 83, 88, 92, 96, 119, 125, 131, 139, 147, 161, 178, 187–201, 207, 208, 213, 221, 224, 226
Bacon, Francis, Viscount of St. Albans, x, 18, 21, 98, 193
Bacon, Ianthe, 193
Balanchine, George, 28
Balla, Giacomo, 197
Ballets Russes de Monte Carlo, 27–28
Balthus, x, 1, 5, 7, 8, 11, 13, 21, 24, 46, 48, 65, 71, 72, 81, 91, 97, 106, 119, 127, 139, 159, 160, 161,

164, 180, 190, 192, 193, 202–221, 222
Balthus, Stanislaus, 221
Balzac, Honoré de, 36, 59, 85, 150
Banville, Théodore de, 148
Barbizon School, 124
Barr, Alfred, 3
Barrés, Maurice, 87
Barthes, Roland, 23
Bartlett, Bo, 212
Bartok, Bela, 28, 57, 58
Basquiat, Jean-Michel, 27, 200
Basket of Flowers Overturned in a Park (Delacroix), 53, color plate
Bataille, Georges, 23, 211
Baudelaire, Charles, 8, 12, 13, 57, 71, 136, 138, 147, 149, 212, 222, 223
Baudrillard, Jean, 24
Bazille, Frédéric, 69
Beardsley, Aubrey, 130
Beaton, Cecil, 199
Beckett, Samuel, 72, 97, 122, 189
Beckford, William, 23–24, 103
Beethoven, Ludwig von, 19, 22, 24, 54–56, 58, 96, 122, 174, 190, 205, 222
Belgiojoso-Trivalziao, Princess Cristian di, 59
Belleli, Baron, 22
Belleli Family, The (Degas), 78–81
Bellini, Vicenzo, 36, 62
Bellow, Saul, 214
Benjamin, Walter, 223
Bergson, Henri, 161
Berkeley, George, 160
Berlin Philharmonic, 93
Berlin University, 176
Berlioz, Hector, 36, 56, 59
Bernard, Emile, 52, 87
Berry, Duchesse de, 45
Berryman, John, 205
Bertolucci, Bernardo, 18
Besnard, Paul Albert, 87
Betjeman, John, 137
Birley, Maxime, 203
Birley, Sir Oswald, 203
Blake, William, 11, 146–147, 149, 222
Blanchot, Maurice, 185–186
Bloom, Harold, 21, 97, 111, 126, 191
Bloomsbury, 124, 132, 158, 169, 177
Boetie, Etienne de, 183
Boggs, Jean Sutherland, 78
Boldini, Giovanni, 12
Boni, Comte de Castellane, 13
Bonnard, Pierre, 3, 76, 79, 204, 211, 216
Boole, Thomas, 163
Borges, Jorge Luis, 12
Borgia family, 25
Borodin, Alexandr, 55
Boston Public Library, 65–66
Boston University, 21
Boticelli, Sandro, 124
Boucher, Francois, 53, 214
Bouders, Jean Pierre Louis, 43
Boulez, Pierre, 17
Bowie, David, 218
Bradley, Bill, 158
Brahms, Johannes, 2, 6, 71, 94, 119, 174
Brancovan, Princesse de, 13
Brancusi, Constantin, 7
Braque, Georges, 2–3, 20, 208–209, 211, 216, 220
Bree, Germaine, 40
Brendel, Alfred, 54–55, 57
Breton, André, 211
Bride of Abydos, The (Delacroix), 51
Brideshead Revisited (Waugh), 24, 160
Brisman, Leslie, 140
British Broadcasting Corporation (BBC), 22
British Museum, 132
Britten, Benjamin, 13, 24
Broch, Hermann, 5, 30, 94, 97, 99, 102, 108
Bronzino, Agnolo Torri, 79
Brooklyn Academy of Music, 24
Brooklyn Museum, 4, 212
Brooks, Cleanth, 30
Brown, Tina, 35
Browning, Robert, 32–33, 137, 139, 149
Bruckner, Anton, 122
Buchanan, Robert, 142
Buckler, William, 140
Buffon, George-Louis Leclerc, Comte de, 38
Bulow, Claus von, 220

Buñuel, Luis, 12
Burge, William, 132
Burger, Peter, 9
Burke's Peerage, 5, 113, 164
Burne-Jones, Edward, 126, 137, 167
Burton, Richard, 132
Busoni, Feruccio Benvenuto, 58, 119
Byron, George Gordon, Lord, 17 23–24, 41, 50, 51, 56, 131, 137, 140, 193, 206

Cage, John, 17, 141–142
Caillebotte, Gustave, 69, 78
Calder, Alexander, 206
Calderon de la Barca, Pedro, 103
Calvino, Italo, 97
Cambridge University, 18, 154, 156, 158, 160, 164, 167, 175, 177, 182, 184
Camus, Albert, 211
canon formation, 1
Cantacuzene, Princess Marie, 69
Cantos, The (Pound), 13, 20, 152
Caravaggio, Michelangelo Merisi, 34, 212, 214
Carlyle, Thomas, 37, 141, 167
Carnap, Rudolf, 160, 181
Carnegie Hall, 54
Carter, Elliott, 62, 205
Cassatt, Mary, 29, 67
Castiglione, Count Verasis de, x, 223–224
Castle Howard, 160
Castro, Eugene de, 149
Catalani, Angelica, 60
Catherine the Great, 25
Cavell, Stanley, 185
Cavour, Camillo, 223
Cavour, Count, 68
Centre Pompidou, Paris, 210
Cézanne, Paul, 2, 15, 52, 199, 204, 214
Chamberlain, John, 20
Chamberlain, Sir Austen, 200
Chandos, Philip Lord, 98
Chapman, Dinos and Jake, 212
Chardin, Jean-Baptiste Simeon, 211
Charles, Prince of Wales, 25, 131
Charles I, 136
Charles II, 157
Charles IX, 183
Charles X, 37
Cheltenham International Festival, 24
Chereau, Patrice, 109
Cherubini, Luigi, 55
Childhood of St. Genevieve, The (Puvis), 67, color plate
Chinnay, Princesse de, 13
Chomsky, Noam, 161
Chopin, Frédéric, 1, 5, 7, 13, 22, 32–64, 121, 122, 129, 134, 146, 149, 161, 178, 202, 215, 220, 222
Christ, Carol, 140
Church, Edwin, 129, 133
Churchill, Lord Randolph, 169
Churchill, Winston, 2, 169, 171
Cigar Aficionado, 35
Cimabue, Cenni de Pepi, 124, 191
Cimarosa, Domenico, 46, 229n
Cincinnatus, 158
Cioran, E. M., 123
City College of New York, 23
Clark, Lord Kenneth, 3
Clark, T. J., 14–16, 64, 67, 75, 82
Classicism, 10, 26, 28, 66, 75, 91, 135, 185, 213, 214, 216
Clemente, Francesco, 26, 205
Coleridge, Samuel Taylor, 9, 137, 177
Colet, Louise, 186
Collinson, James, 127
Comédie Française, 32
Conceptualism, 25
Concerning the Spiritual in Art (Kandinsky), 25
Connelly, Lucy Martin, 170
Conrad, Joseph, 150
Constable, John, 76, 198
contingency, 14, 76, 82
Coole Park, 187
Copland, Aaron, 117
Coquiot, Gustave, 89
Corigliano, John, 21, 109, 110, 121
Cornwall, Barry, 135
Corot, Camille, 36, 48–50, 79, 128, 214
Courbet, Gustave, 15, 204, 214, 216
Craft, Robert, 177
Crane, Hart, 136, 141, 147

Crane, Walter, 132
Crutchfield, Will, 10
Cubism, 2, 13, 20, 129, 169, 213, 215
Cui, César, 56
Curtius, E. R., 98
Custine, Marquis de, 63
Cuvelier, Adelbert, 48
Czartoryinski, Prince Adam, 59
Czerny, Carl, 57

D'Agoult, Countess Marie, 33, 35
dandy, 16, 23, 42, 217, 222–223
Dante, 56, 151
Darnton, Robert, 24
Darwin, Charles, 180, 221
Daumier, Henri, 80, 66, 89
Davenport, Guy, 203, 204, 209, 211, 221
David, Gerard, 211
De Chirico, Giorgio, 3, 106, 213
De Gas, Auguste-Hyacinthe, 22, 77
De Gas, René, 77, 80
De Gaulle, General Charles, 214
De Heem, Jan Davidz., 53
De Kooning, Willem, 2, 29
De La Tour, 211
Deakin, John, 192
Death in Venice (Mann), 105
Death of a Salesman (Miller), 13, 79
Death of Sardanapalus, The (Delacroix), 51
Debussy, Claude, 57, 62, 148
decadence, 22–23, 138
Decamp, Alexandre, 49
Deconstruction, 23, 96, 146
Degas, Edgar, 11, 13, 19, 22, 48, 65–90, 133, 203, 221, 224
Degeneration (Nordau), 22, 138
Delacroix, Charles, 43
Delacroix, Charles-Henry, 44
Delacroix, Eugène, x, 1, 5, 10, 11, 13, 15, 17, 19, 32–64, 66, 70, 97, 128, 134, 180, 204, 205, 214, 216, 222
Delacroix, Henri, 44
Delacroix, Henriette, 43
Delaroche, Paul, 49
Delaunay, Robert, 208
Deleuze, Gilles, 21
Denis, Maurice, 67, 72
Derain, André, 3, 204, 211, 213–214, color plate
Desavary, Charles, 48
Descartes, René, 162
Detroit Institute for the Arts, 209
Dewey, John, 172
Diaghilev, Sergei, 27
Diana, Princess of Wales, 18
Difficult Man, The (Hofmannsthal), 105, 107–109
Dinesen, Isaak (Baroness Blixen), 12
Discreet Charm of the Bourgeoisie (Buñuel), 12
Dobson, Frank, 184
Donnelly, Lucy, 156, 160
Dorval, Marie, 36
Dostoevsky, Fyodr Mikhailovich, 179
Douglas, Lord Alfred Bruce, 12
Dowling, Linda, 140
Dowson, Ernest, 130, 137
Dubuffet, Jean, 14, 126
Duccio di Buoninsegna, 209
Duchamp, Marcel, 20, 87
Dudevant, Baron Casimir, 37
Dujardin, Baron, 85
Dujardin, Edouard, 87
Dumas, père et fils, 36
Durand-Ruel, 78, 85
Dürer, Albrecht, 47
Dutilleux, Constant, 48
Dvorak, Antonin, 14, 58

Eagleton, Terry, 48
Ecole des Beaux-Arts, 44
Education of Henry Adams, The (Adams), 136, 163
Edward II, 136
Edward VII, 5
Einstein, Albert, 29, 117, 163, 169
Eisenstein, Sergei, 192
elegance, 46–47
Elektra (Strauss and Hofmannsthal), 92, 111
Elgar, Sir Edward, 131
Eliot, T. S., 7, 10, 13, 16, 20, 21, 29, 101, 106, 130, 136, 146, 147, 150, 175, 187, 209, 226
Elizabeth I, 18

Elle et Lui (Sand), 36
Elliott, Frances Anna Maria, 158
Ellmann, Richard, 149–150
Elsner, Jozef, 60
Emerson, Ralph Waldo, 158
Engelmann, Paul, 175
Englishman at the Moulin Rouge, The (Lautrec), 66, 84–86, 204, color plate
Esperandrexu, Henri, 76
Esterhazy, 55–56
Eton College, 2, 6, 135, 136, 164, 193
Etty, William, 194
Euripedes, 141
European Literature and the Latin Middle Ages (Curtius), 98
Exposition Universelle, 50, 52

Factory, The, 200
Falaise, Comte Alain de La, 203
Falaise, Loulou de La, 203
Falkland, Lord, 146
Falmouth, Lord, 59
Fantin-Latour, Henri, 147
Farewell to an Idea (Clark), 14, 67
Farson, David, 194–195
Fauvism, 52, 54, 66
Fellini, Federico, 218
Feodorova, Empress Maria, 59
Field, John, 60
Finnegans Wake (Joyce), 99, 140
Fischer-Dieskau, Dietrich, 54
Fischl, Eric, 21, 212, 213
Fitz-James, Duc de, 45
Flaming June (Leighton), 19, 132
Flaubert, Gustave, 8,16, 33, 41, 46, 71, 142, 148, 149, 185–186, 212
Flavin, Dan, 26
Fleming, Renée, 116
Fontana, Lucio, 20
Ford, Ford Madox, 152
Forget, Josephine de, 53
Foucault, Michel, 21, 23, 211
Four Last Songs (Strauss), 122
Four Quartets (Eliot), 146, 150
Fox, Judy, 212
Fragonard, Jean-Honoré, 53, 214
France, Anatole, 148
Franz Joseph I, 5
Frege, Gottlieb, 163, 183
French Academy in Rome, 206, 214–216
Freud, Lucian, 21, 213
Freud, Sigmund, 15, 91–92, 226
Frey, Julia, 84
Frick Collection, New York, 45
Fried, Michael, 15, 17
Fry, Roger, 155
Fuentes, Carlos, 33
Fuseli, Henry, 211

Gaddi, Taddeo, 127
Gainsborough, Duchess of, 59
Garcia-Marquez, Gabriel, 12
Gauguin, Paul, 2, 53, 67, 72, 87, 222
Gautier, Théophile, 53, 70–71, 135, 147, 148
Gazzoli, Benozzo, 127
Gehry, Frank, 20
genealogy, x, 21–22
gens de robe, 4
George, 35
Germ, The, 129
Gérome, Jean Louis, 74
Ghosts of Versailles, The (Corigliano), 91
Giacometti, Alberto, 7, 14, 204, 206, 208, 215, 216
Giaour, The (Delacroix), 50
Gide, André, 139, 211
Giesen, Bernhard, 4
Gilbert and George, 19
Gilbert, Alfred, 132
Gilman Paper Company, 223
Giotto, 124, 126, 209
Giuliani, Rudolph, 4
Glackens, Edward, 76
Gladstone, William Ewart, 131
Glass, Phillip, 17, 106, 109
Glinka, Mikhail Ivanovich, 56
Gödel, Kurt, 181
Goethe, Johann Wolfgang von, 107
Gogh, Vincent van, 2, 13, 15, 51, 53, 67, 100–101, 191, 222
Goldin, Nan, 224
Goldsworthy, Andy, 205
Goncourt, Edmund and Jules de, 29, 36, 148
Gore-Booth, Eva, 190

Gosse, Edmund, 131
Gottlieb, Adolph, 87
Gounod, Charles, 45, 56, 60
Gowrie, Earl "Gray," 195
Graffman, Gary, 63
Graham, Martha, 125
Grand-Duke Karl Alexander, 58
Grandguillaume, Leandre, 49
Gray, Francine du Plessix, 23
Great Gatsby, The (Harbison), 21
Greco, El, 200
Greenberg, Clement, 15, 213
Gregory, Major, 188
Grey, Lord, 158
Grieg, Edvard, 117
Gryzmala, Count Wojciech, 45, 61
Guattari, Felix, 21
Guerin, Pierre-Narcisse, 44
Guggenheim Museum, 25–26, 89
Guggenheim, Solomon, 25
Guthrie, Mrs. James (Ellinor Stirling), 134

Halley, Peter, 54
Hamburger, Michael, 92, 103
Hamlet (Shakespeare), 103, 225–226, color plate
Handel, George Frederick, 60
Hansel, Mareile, 175
Hanslick, Eduard, 120
Harbison, John, 21, 109, 119
Hardy, Thomas, 139
Haring, Keith, 27
Harley, Lady Charlotte, 193–194
Hartford Atheneum, 27
Harvard University, 27
Hatch, Edwin, 137
Hauser, Arnold, 223, 226
Haussmann, Baron, 50
Havel, Václav, 33
Hawking, Stephen, 107, 163
Haydn, Joseph, 22, 55, 205
Heaney, Seamus, 189
Hegel, G. W. F., 141, 162
Heidegger, Martin, 142
Heine, Heinrich, 36, 59
Henri V, Comte de Chambord, 83
Henry III, 183
Henry of Navarre, 183
Hensher, Philip, 24
high and low, 13–14, 58, 218–219
Hirst, Damien, 125, 131
Hitler, Adolf, 176, 196
Hoffmann, Josef, 174
Hofmann, Hans, 177
Hofmannsthal, Hugo von, x, 3, 5, 6, 7, 11, 12, 13, 15, 17, 18, 19, 20, 21, 22, 24, 30, 39, 44, 46, 48, 50, 67, 72, 74, 81, 86, 91–123, 131, 159, 160, 172, 173, 179, 186, 200, 214, 219, 221, 222, 223, 226
Hogarth, William, 115
Holbein, Hans, 79
Holmes, Augusta, 148
Homer, 150
Hopkins, Gerard Manley, 136, 147
Horace (Sand), 42
House of Lords, x, 4, 18
Houssonville, Countess d', 45, 203
Hubert-Robert, 214
Huc, Arthur, 89
Hughes, Robert, 20
Hugo, Victor, 36, 42, 56, 59, 135, 145, 147, 148, 149
Hulme, T. E., 129
Hume, David, 160
Hummel, Johann Nepomuk, 55, 60
Hunt, Holman, 127, 132
Husserl, Edmund, 181
Huxley, Aldous Leonard, 139
Huysmans, J. K., 11, 103, 149, 226
Huysum, Jan van, 53
Hwang, David Henry, 106
Hyde, Henry, 190

Impressionism, 52, 66, 68, 75, 133
Ingram, J. H., 147
Ingres, Jean Auguste Dominique, 26–27, 45, 68, 79, 203, 216
Intermezzo (Strauss and Hofmannsthal), 112
Isabey, Jean-Baptiste, 68
Ives, Charles, 9, 29

James I, 169
James II, 157

James, Henry, 29, 109, 133
James, William, 29
Janin, Jules, 42
Janis, Byron, 63
Jederman (Hofmannsthal), x, 101–102
Jeune Algerienne couchée sur la Gazon (Corot), 50
Jeune Fille à sa Toilette (Balthus), 220, color plate
Jewish Wedding in Morocco, The (Delacroix), 45
Joachim, Joseph, 94
John, Augustus, 155
Johns, Jasper, 75, 185, 217
Johnson, Lionel, 130, 137
Johnson, Philip, 17, 20
Johnson, Samuel, 177
Jonson, Ben, 62
Jowett, Benjamin, 6, 177
Joyce, James, 13, 29, 62, 99, 105, 139, 150, 189, 212, 222, 226
Judd, Donald, 2, 17, 213
Jung, Carl Gustav, 177

Kafka, Franz, 211
Kalisch, Alfred, 120
Kandinsky, Wassily, 2, 3, 25, 73, 152, 191
Katz, Alex, 67, 212–213
Keats, John, 64, 205
Kelley, Mike, 213
Kelly, Ellsworth, 17, 75
Kessler, Count, 93
Keynes, John Maynard, 166, 169, 177
Kiefer, Anselm, 205
Kierkegaard, Soren, 99, 211
King Jean at the Battle of Poitiers (Delacroix), 45
King of the Cats (Balthus), 217
Kittens (Leighton), 134, color plate
Klimt, Gustav, x, 91–92, 101, 174
Kline, Franz, 123
Klinger, Max, 174
Klinkenberg, Verlyn, 116
Klossowska, Balladine, 202, 216, 218
Klossowski, Erich, 202, 206
Klossowski, Pierre, 206, 211
Kokoschka, Oskar, 178
Konigsmarch, Aurore von, 38
Konstanty, Archduke, 59
Koolhaas, Rem, 20
Koons, Jeff, 212–213
Korngold, Julius, 120
Korngold, Wolfgang, 120
Kramer, Lawrence, 56, 58, 174
Kraus, Karl, 103
Kripke, Saul, 181
Kurtag, Gyorgy, 57

L'Echo de Paris, 88
La Dépeche de Toulouse, 89
La Goulue, 66, 85
La Révue independente, 85
La Révue Wagnerienne, 85
Lacan, Jacques, 177
Laclos, Choderlos de, 24
Lacy, Peter, 199
Lacynska, Countess, 58
Lady Macbeth of Mtensk (Shostakovich), 27
Lafenestre, Georges, 73
Lafourcade, George, 139
Lagerfeld, Karl, 203
Lamartine, Alphonse de, 32, 36
Lamb, Henry, 155
Lampedusa, Giuseppe di, 11, 219
Lanckoronsky, Count, 30
Landor, Walter Savage, 147, 152, 177
Lane, Hugh, 190
Laurent, Yves Saint, 203
Lawrence, D. H., 12, 139, 155
Le Corbusier (Charles-Edouard Jeanneret), 175
Le Courier Français, 34
Le Figaro, 33
Le Monde, 204
Leger, Fernand, 3, 213, 217
Legros, Alphonse, 147
Leibniz, Franz, 163
Leighton House, 132–133
Leighton, Frederick, Lord, x, 7, 19, 21, 46, 63, 66, 69, 124–153, 167, 193, 194, 209, 222, 224
Leiris, Michel, 211
Lelia Mourning over Stenio's Body (Delacroix), 34

Lenz, Wilhelm von, 60
Leopard, The (Lampedusa), 11
Leopold II, 229n
Lepelletier, Edmond, 88
Leroux, Pierre, 59
Les Femmes d'Algier (Delacroix), 50
"Letter of Lord Chandos," 21, 96, 98–100, 103
Levine, James, 117
Levi-Strauss, Claude, 185–186
LeWitt, Sol, 74
Liaisons Dangereuses (Laclos), 24, 110
Liberty Leading the People (Delacroix), 44
Lichnowsky, Princess, 110
Lichtenstein, Roy, 213
Ligeti, Gyorgy, 57
Lisle, Leconte de, 139, 148–149
Liszt, Adam, 55–56
Liszt, Franz, 1, 5, 6, 7, 10, 17, 19, 21, 22, 24, 32–64, 94, 96, 119, 121, 129, 146, 161, 215
Llosa, Mario Vargas, 33
Locke, John, 160
Lolita (Nabokov), 212
Loos, Adolf, 178
Louis XVIII, 37
Louis XV, 29, 39, 83
Louvre, Le, 32, 53
Lowell, Robert, 9, 29, 205
Loyrette, Henri, 80
Lucrezia Horiani (Sand), 34
Ludwig, King, 25
Lyotard, Jean Francois, 185
Lyrical Ballads (Wordsworth and Coleridge), 9

Mach, Ernst, 99
Madonna, 23
Maeterlinck, Maurice, 92, 103, 149
Mailer, Norman, 23, 214
Maillot, Jean-Christophe, 28
Malevich, Kasimir, 25
Mallarmé, Stéphane, 9, 12, 16, 67, 71, 75, 97, 99, 136, 141, 142, 147–150, 226
Malraux, André, 11, 206, 207, 214, 220
Man Without Qualities, The (Musil), 105
Manet, Edouard, x, 42, 66, 69, 71, 134, 148, 199
Mangold, Robert, 75
Mann, Thomas, 105
Mantegna, Andrea, 124
Mapplethorpe, Robert, 4, 26–27, 212
Marden, Brice, 17, 197
Marechal de Saxe, 35, 37–38
Marianne (Sand), 41, 44
Markiewicz, Con, 190
Marlborough Gallery, 193
Marseilles, Gateway to the Orient (Puvis), 76, color plate
Martins, Peter, 28
Marvell, Andrew, 141
Marx, Karl, 48
Marxism, 1, 48
Massacre at Chios (Delacroix), 51
Masur, Kurt, 33
Matisse, Henri, 3, 53, 67, 73, 75, 76, 206
Matthews, Elkin, 152–153
Matthews, William, 153
Maupassant, Guy de, 148–149
Mauprat (Sand), 37
Mayer and Pierson, 68
Mazzini, Giuseppi, 137
McGann, Jerome, 140
McGuiness, Brian, 178
"Meditations in Time of Civil War" (Yeats), 188–190
Mendelssohn, Felix, 36, 122, 135, 205
Mendes, Catulle, 148
Meredith, George, 130, 139, 146
Merrill, James, 9, 29, 62, 141, 153, 205
Messiaen, Olivier, 109
Metropolitan Museum of Art, New York, 3, 207
Metropolitan Opera House, New York, 21, 117
Michelangelo, Buonarotti, 47, 56
Mies Van der Rohe, Ludwig, 17, 20
Miles, David, 99
Mill, John Stuart, 158, 159, 160, 167, 171
Millais, John Everett, 127, 130, 194
Miller, Arthur, 13, 79
Millet, Jean-François, 47, 73

Milnes, Monckton (Lord Houghton), 136, 147
Milton and his Daughters (Delacroix), 45
Milton, John, 41, 45
Minimalism, 2, 13, 17, 25, 49, 50, 109, 175, 180, 213, 217
Miró, Joan, 206, 208, 213–214
Mitchell, Charles, 194
Modern Art Despite Modernism, 3, 204, 213
Molière (Jean-Baptiste Poquelin), 6, 92, 118
Mondrian, Piet, ix, 2, 3, 25, 53, 211
Monet, Claude, 15, 68, 70, 71
Monk, Ray, 175, 182
Monnoyer, Jean-Baptiste, 53
Montaigne, Michel de, 183, 214
Montebello, Phillippe de, 3–4
Montesquiou, Comte Robert de, 12, 25
Montherlant, Henry de, 209
Moody, Ken, 26
Moore, G. E., 168, 171
Moore, George, 149, 190
Morandi, Giorgio, 213
Moray, Duc de, 45
Moreas, Adolphe, 85
Moreau, Gustave, 12, 67, 69
Morimura, Yasumasa, 224
Morley, John, 142, 149
Morrell, Lady Ottoline, 155–157, 160, 161, 163, 172–174, 178
Morrell, Phillip, 155
Morris, Marshall, Faulkner and Company, 130
Morris, Robert, 17, 213
Morris, William, 87, 124, 126, 130, 137, 138
Moscheles, Ignaz, 57
Moses und Aron (Schoenberg), 103
Mosley, Diana, 196
Moulin de la Galette (Toulouse-Lautrec), 88
Moulin Rouge, 85
Mountain, The (Balthus), 209, 214, 218
Mozart, Wolfgang Amadeus, 6, 19, 22, 34, 45, 46, 50, 59, 61, 62, 110–112, 114
Munich Opera, 93
Murasaki, Lady, 12
Murder of the Bishop of Liege, The (Delacroix), 45
Musée Calvet, 49
Musée d'Orsay, 22, 73, 223
Musée de Douanier, 48
Musée de Metz, 49
Musée du Luxembourg, 50, 72
Museum of Fine Arts, Boston, 76
Museum of Modern Art, New York (MOMA), 2–3, 14, 191, 200, 211
Music as Cultural Practice (Kramer), 56
Musil, Robert, 105
Musset, Alfred de, 35, 40, 46
Musson, Marie-Celestine, 77
Muybridge, Eadweard, 192, 195

Nabis, The, 66
Nabokov, Vladimir, 212
Napoleon III, 36, 45
Natanson, Thadée and Misia, 86–87
National Gallery, London, 3
National Gallery, Washington, 89
Nauman, Bruce, 213
Nazarenes, The, 124
Neel, Alice, 213
Negative Dialectics (Adorno), 16
Neue Freie Presse, 176
Neumann, John von, 181
Neurath, Otto, 181
New Criticism, 16, 30
New York Academy, 21
New York City Ballet, 28
New York Times, The, 23, 26, 116
Newman, Alfred, 119
Newman, Barnett, 177
Nietzsche, Friedrich, 21, 85, 89, 105
Nijinsky, 27, 148
Noailles, Countess de, 13, 27, 203, 220
Nobel Prize, 164, 170–171, 190
noblesse d'epée, 4
noblesse de robe, 4
Nordau, Max, 22, 138
Norman, Jessye, 122
Notebooks of Malte Laurids Brigge (Rilke), 219

"Notes on 'Camp'" (Sontag), 42
Novalis (Friedrich Leopold von Hardenberg), 141

Occam's Razor, 175
Oeben, Jean-Francois, 43
Ofili, Chris, 4
Olana, 133
Oldoini, Marques, 223
Ono, Yoko, 30
Orleans, Duc d', 45, 49
Out of Africa (Dinesen), 12
Oxford Ancestors, 22
Oxford University, 126, 130, 135, 137, 138, 149, 177

Pac, Count, 58
Paganini, Niccolò, 19, 55–56, 59, 60
Paglia, Camille, 138–139
Paik, Nam June, 19
Palmerston, Lord, 68
Panthéon, Paris, 67, 73
Pantonality, 20
Panza, Count Giuseppe di Buomo, 25
Parak, Franz, 179
Paris Opera, 66
Pärt, Arvo, 109, 125
Pascal, Blaise, 141
Pater, Walter, 97, 132, 133, 137
Peano, Giuseppe, 163
Pei, I. M., 32
Peirce, C. S., 163
Peladin, Sar Merodach Josephein, 85
Peppiatt, Michael, 191, 193, 199
Pergolesi, Giovanni Battista, 38
Perthuis, Comte de, 59
Peter Grimes (Britten), 13
Petrarch, 56
Philadelphia Museum, 52
Phillips, Duncan, 76, 82
Piaget, Jean, 9, 96
Picasso, Pablo, 2–3, 7, 14, 20, 67, 72, 75, 79, 88–90, 106, 125, 150, 168, 200, 204, 206, 208, 209, 211, 215, 220
Piero Della Francesca, 209
Pierrot Lunaire (Schoenberg), 10
Pierson, Pierre-Louis, 223–224
Pinsent, David, 183
Plato, 32, 221
Plummer, Christopher, 18
Poe, Edgar Allan, 140, 147, 148
Poems and Ballads (Swinburne), 137, 142
Poggioli, Renato, 8–10
Pollexfen, Major George, 187
Pollock, Jackson, 2, 5, 25–16, 24, 29, 123
Poniatowski, King Stanislaw August, 206
Poor Fisherman (Puvis), 67, 72–73
Pope, Alexander, 62
Positivism, 13, 15, 181
Postmodernism, 21, 91, 140, 181, 205, 217, 223
Potocka, Countess Delfina, 13, 33, 59
Poulenc, Francis, 12, 30
Pound, Ezra, 7, 13, 20, 29, 50, 71, 130, 136, 150–153
Poussin, Nicolas, 53, 209, 211, 218
Powder Her Face (Ades), 24
power, 4, 168, 218
Prendergast, Maurice, 67, 76
Pre-Raphaelite Brotherhood, 7–8, 11, 46, 65, 124–131, 134, 137–138, 142–146, 194
Price, Aimee Brown, 67
Princeton University, 24
Principia Mathematica (Russell), 164, 173
Prokofiev, Sergei, 28
Proust, Marcel, 12, 13, 139, 140, 163, 181, 222
Pu Yi, Emperor, 18
public art, 15–17, 44, 71, 97, 161, 214, 218
Puccini, Giacomo, 116, 119, 214
Puffett, Derrick, 119–120
Pushkin, Alexander Sergeyevich, 148
Puvis de Chavannes, Pierre, x, 11, 12, 15, 17, 46, 49, 65–90, 97, 125, 160, 205, 209, 214, 221, 226
Pynchon, Thomas, 214

Quills, 23
Quine, W. V. O., 181

Radziwill, Prince, 60
Rainer, Prince, 27
Rainey, Lawrence, 29
Rake's Progress, The (Stravinsky), 91
Raphael (Raffaello Sanzio), 33, 49, 56, 125, 209
Rauschenberg, Robert, 16
Read, Herbert, 15
Rebay, Baroness Hilla von, 25–26
Redon, Odilon, 52, 69
Reinhardt, Joseph, 211
Reinhardt, Max, x, 5, 102
Rembrandt, Harmensz Van Rijn, 50
Renoir, Pierre Auguste, 68, 88, 89
République des letters, La, 147–149
Rewald, John, 77, 81
Reynolds, Sir Joshua, 127
Rhees, Rush, 184
Rilke, Rainer Maria, 99, 202, 204, 211, 218, 219–220
Rimbaud, Arthur, 46, 147
Rivera, Diego, 75
Robaut, Alfred, 49
Robbins, Jerome, 148
Rochefort, Duc de, 77
Rochefoucauld, Comte Antoine de, 84
Rochester, Earl of, 24
Rockefeller family, 25
Rodin, Auguste, 174, 216
Romanticism, 1, 9, 15, 42–43, 51, 56, 140, 147, 160, 191, 223
Rorty, Richard, 161
Rosen, Charles, 54, 57, 62, 63
Rosenberg, John, 140
Rosenkavalier, Der (Strauss and Hofmannsthal), 3, 6, 21, 91, 92, 93, 95, 103, 104, 110–118
Rossetti, Dante Gabriel, 127, 130, 131, 138
Rossetti, William Michael, 127, 132
Rossini, Gioacchino Antonio, 36, 60, 114
Rothenstein, John, 197
Rothko, Mark, 54, 71, 76
Rothschild, Baroness Charlotte de, 59
Rothschild family, 36
Rousseau, Henri, 126
Rousseau, Jean-Jacques, 38
Royal Academy of Art, 20, 126, 127, 129, 130, 131, 134
Rubens, Peter Paul, 19, 32, 40, 49, 52, 74, 214, 222
Rubenstein, Artur, 94
Ruskin, John, 10, 20, 125, 126, 128–129, 133, 141, 161
Russell, Bertrand, Earl of Bedford, ix, 6, 12, 15, 17, 18, 19, 20 21, 22, 37, 39, 48, 49, 97, 110, 137, 154–186, 214, 221, 226
Russell, Frank, 159
Russell, Lord John, 5, 18, 156–157, 159, 170
Russell, Lord William, 157
Rye House Plot, 157
Ryle, Gilbert, 181
Ryman, Robert, 17, 142

Saatchi, Charles, 25
Sackville-West, Vita, 111
Sacred Grove, The (Puvis), 68
Sade, Marquis de, 11, 23–24, 138, 211
Sainte-Beuve, Charles-Augustin, 36, 59
Saint-Saens, Camille, 56
Salzburg Festival, 101–102
Sand, George, 1, 5, 6, 17, 19, 20, 21, 32–64, 97, 158, 166, 167, 177, 188, 221, 222, 224
Sandeau, Jules, 42
Sanderson, Thomas, 167
Santayana, George, 156
Sargent, John Singer, 26, 29, 199
Satie, Erik, 12
Saussure, Ferdinand de, 96
Sayn-Wittgenstein, Princess, 35, 56, 58
Schaeffer, Neil, 23
Scheffer, Ary, 49
Schiele, Egon, 91, 101
Schlegel, Friedrich von, 62
Schloss Leopoldskron, x, 5, 102
Schnitzler, Arthur, 92
Schoenberg, Arnold, 7, 10, 11, 13, 20, 29, 54, 57, 71, 103–104, 109, 119, 142, 183
Schopenhauer, Arthur, 142, 183
Schorske, Carl, 94, 97, 103
Schubert, Franz, 56, 175

Schumann, Clara, 94
Schumann, Robert, 36, 122
Schwitters, Kurt, 20
Scribe, Eugène, 85
Secret Marriage, The (Cimarosa), 46
Segantini, Giovanni, 174
Sellars, Peter, 109
Sensation, 3–4, 125, 212
Serra, Richard, 26
Serrano, Andres, 87
Sessions, Roger, 62
Seurat, Georges, 2, 15, 67, 68, 217
Sevigny, Madame de, 12
Sexual Personae (Paglia), 138–139
Shakespeare, William, 27, 101, 141, 150, 165, 193, 205, 225–226
Shattuck, Roger, 127
Shaw, Bernard, 57
Shawe-Taylor, 190
Shelley, Percy Bysshe, 2, 52, 129, 140, 146, 162
Sherman, Cindy, 223, 224
Shikibu, Lady Murasaki, 12
Shock of the New, The (Hughes), 20
Shostakovich, Dmitri, 27
Sickert, Walter, 133, 136
Sidney, Sir Philip, 205
Signac, Paul, 68
Silverman, Deborah L., 29
Simon and Schuster, 23
Site d'Italie (Corot), 49
Sitwell, Sir Osbert, 230n
Sitwell, Sir Sacheverell, 56
Skarbek, Countess Ludwicka, 58
Smith, Kiki, 213
Smith, Matthew, 197–198
Smithson, Robert, 205
Smythies, Yorick, 184
Social History of Art, The (Hauser), 223
Society of Apostles, 177
Socrates, 177
Sonntag, Henrietta, 60
Sontag, Susan, 42, 141–142, 189, 223
Sound of Music, The, 18
Soutine, Chaim, 5
Spenser, Sir Edmund, 205
Spinoza, Benedict, 160
Spiro, Abraham Beer, 207
St. Denis, Ruth, 125
Stael, Madame de, 36
Stalin, Joseph, 27
Stanley, Kate, 158, 167
Steiner, George, 141
Stella, Frank, 74
Stenio (Sand), 34
Stephens, F. G., 127
Sternberg, Josef von, 12
Stevens, Wallace, 9–10, 29, 136, 147, 191
Stirling Jane, x, 59, 134
Stirling, Ellinor (Mrs. James Guthrie), 134
Stirling, James, 134
Stonborough, Margaret (née Wittgenstein), x, 175
Storr, Robert, 3, 8, 23, 112, 191, 210, 211–213
Story of My Life, The (Sand), 37–41, 166
Strachey, Lytton, 169
Strauss, Franz, 92
Strauss, Johann, 92
Strauss, Richard, 6, 13, 21, 50, 57, 91–123, 173, 179
Stravinsky, Igor, 14, 20, 27–28, 46, 115, 177
Street, The (Balthus), 208–209, 211, 213
Stroheim, Erich von, 12
Structuralism, 23
style moderne, 29
Styron, William, 214
Sultan, Donald, 205
Suprematism, 25
Surrealism, 2, 107, 204, 208, 211, 213
Swinburne, Algernon Charles, 2, 5, 6, 7, 10, 13, 16, 17, 18, 19, 20, 21, 22, 23, 24, 48, 49, 50, 61–62, 71, 72, 83, 91, 99, 124–153, 159, 177, 186, 221, 226
Swinburne, Lord John, 136
Swinburne, Lady Jane Henrietta, 136
Sykes, Brian, 22
Symbolism, 12, 75, 85, 135, 147
Symonds, John Addington, 137
Synge, John Millington, 190
Szulc, Tad, 63

Tale of Genji (Murasaki), 12
Talleyrand, 35, 45
Taruskin, Richard, 28
Tate Gallery, 197
Taylor, James, 184
Te Kanawa, Dame Kiri, 116
Tennyson, Alfred, Lord, 131, 139
Theory of the Avant-Garde (Burger), 9
Thibaudet, Albert, 148
Thiers, Adolphe, 45
Thomas, Helen, 169
Thomson, David, 12
Thurber, James, 153
Thurn und Taxis, Prince and Princess, 26–27, 109
Tiepolo, Giovanni Battista, 74
Time magazine, 208
Times (of London), 7, 128, 177, 199
Tintoretto, Jacopo Robusti, 40
Titian (Tiziano Vecellio), 24, 39–40, 49
Tosca (Puccini), 215
Toulouse-Lautrec, Adele, 83 and color plate
Toulouse-Lautrec, Henri de, 5, 11, 17, 19, 20, 21, 63–90, 97, 126, 131, 139, 147, 195, 199, 204, 221, 224
Tower, The (Hofmannsthal), 12, 92,103–105, 200
Tractatus Logico-Philosophicus (Wittgenstein), 1, 166, 179, 182
Trakl, Georg, 178
Transcendental Etudes (Liszt), 56
Tredell, Nicholas, 140
Tristram of Lyonesse (Swinburne), 140
Trollope, Anthony, 149
Troubezkoy, Prince, 13
Turgenev, Ivan, 148
Turner, Joseph Mallord William, 10, 76, 198
Twombly, Cy, 63, 71
Tyszkiewicz, Count, 45

Ulysses (Joyce), 212
Updike, John, 214
Utrillo, Miquel, 89

Valadon, Suzanne, 89
Valery, Paul, 146, 226
Van Dyck, Sir Anthony, 79–80
Van Gogh Museum, Amsterdam, 67
Varnedoe, Kirk, 2, 3
Vathek (Beckford), 23, 103
Vatican, 56
Vaudemont, Princess, 59
Velazquez, Diego de, 192, 214
Vens, Joao de, 149
Verdi, Giusseppe, 114, 119, 214
Verlaine, Paul, 85, 147, 149
Verninac, Raymond de, 44
Viardot, Pauline, 45
Victor Emannuel II, 223
Victoria, Queen, 59, 131, 159, 167, 194
Vigny, Alfred de, 32, 36
Villa Medici, 206, 214–216
Villot, Frederic, 45
Vlaminck, Maurice de, 3
Vollard, Ambrose, 89
Voltaire, 38
Von Bulow, Hans, 93
Von Bulow, Claus, 220
Vuillard, Edouard, 220

Wagner, Richard, 10, 25, 36, 54, 56, 57, 89, 93, 110, 112, 119, 120, 147, 148, 176
Walter, Bruno, 174
Warhol, Andy, 14, 19, 26, 47, 67, 81, 85–88, 200–203, 220
Warrener, Sir William Thomas, 84–86 and color plate
Warsaw Conservatory, 60
Waste Land, The (Eliot), 13, 16, 20, 106
Water Mill, 215
Watteville, Rose Alice Antoinette de, 203
Watts-Dunton, Theodore, 18, 150
Waugh, Evelyn, 24, 160
Webber, Sir Andrew Lloyd, 125
Weber, Carl Maria von, 59
Weber, Max, 76
Weber, Nicholas Fox, 206, 207, 210, 216, 218, 220–221
Webern, Anton von, 7, 11, 13, 15, 22, 57, 117, 205
Weill, Berthe, 89

Weill, Kurt, 119
Weininger, Otto, 183
Whistler, James Abbott McNeill, 12, 128, 130, 132, 134, 141, 146, 149, 196, 222
Whitehead, Alfred North, 163, 168, 173–174
Whitehead, Evelyn, 173
Whitman, Walt, 11, 146–147
Wilczek, Count, 30
Wilde, Oscar, 12, 89, 128, 130, 132, 137, 149, 189, 218, 221
Wilhelm I, 5
Wilmarth, Christopher, 27
Wilson, Edmund, 136, 226
Wilson, Robert, 14, 215
Wilson, Woodrow, 200
Winfrey, Oprah, 35
Wittgenstein, Gretl. *See* Margaret Stonborough
Wittgenstein, Karl, 174
Wittgenstein, Ludwig, x, 5, 6, 13, 16, 18, 20, 72, 75, 99, 110, 137, 139, 154–186, 203, 221, 225, 226
Wittgenstein, Paul, 176, 231n
wittgensteinisch, 174–175
Wodzinski, Count, 59
Women in Love (Lawrence), 12
Woolf, Virginia, 7
Woolner, Thomas, 127
Wordsworth, William, 9, 136, 137, 188
Wright, Frank Lloyd, 25

Xenakis, Iannis, 17

Yard, Sally, 199
Yeats, William Butler, 7, 11, 14, 17, 44, 66, 70, 97, 130, 131, 136, 137, 145, 146, 147, 150, 152, 155, 159, 187–201, 208, 219, 226

Zola, Emile, 33, 139, 149